Library of
Davidson College

ESSAYS IN
LAW AND POLITICS

Kennikat Press
National University Publications
Multi-disciplinary Studies in the Law

General Editor
Rudolph J. Gerber
Arizona State University

ESSAYS IN LAW AND POLITICS

FRANCIS DUNHAM WORMUTH

edited by
Dalmas H. Nelson
and
Richard L. Sklar

National University Publications
KENNIKAT PRESS // 1978
Port Washington, N.Y. // London

Copyright © 1978 by Kennikat Press Corp. All rights reserved. No part of this publication may be reproduced, stored in a retrieval system, or transmitted, in any form or by any means, electronic, mechanical, photocopying, recording, or otherwise, without the prior written permission of the publisher.

Manufactured in the United States of America

Published by
Kennikat Press Corp.
Port Washington, N.Y./London

Library of Congress Cataloging in Publication Data

Wormuth, Francis Dunham, 1909-
   Essays in law and politics.

   (Multi-disciplinary studies in law) (National university publications)
   "Works by Francis D. Wormuth": p.
   Includes bibliographical references and index.
     1. Law and politics—Addresses, essays, lectures.
2. Jurisprudence—Addresses, essays, lectures.
3. Political science—Addresses, essays, lectures.
I. Nelson, Dalmas H. II. Sklar, Richard L.
III. Title.
K487.P65W67   340   78-5057
ISBN 0-8046-9211-4

To the Memory of
HORACE M. KALLEN
Champion of Liberty

CONTENTS

Preface   vii

PART ONE: LAW

1. The Dilemma of Jurisprudence   5
2. Aristotle on Law   14
3. Astraea and Diké: *Ius Naturale* in Roman Law   27
4. Return to the Middle Ages   37
5. Administrative Control of Science   52
6. Learned Legerdemain: A Grave but Implausible Hand   63
7. Legislative Disqualifications as Bills of Attainder   79
8. The Impact of Economic Legislation upon the Supreme Court   93
9. Haddock v. Civil Service Commission   114
10. Presidential Wars: The Convenience of "Precedent"   118

PART TWO: POLITICS

11. Matched-Dependent Behavioralism: The Cargo Cult in Political Science   129
12. The Walgreen Political Science   163
13. Macropolitics: Aggression in Group Theory   170
14. A Typology of Revolution and Ideology   177

15.	The Presidency as an Ideal Type	200
16.	The International Power Elite (Coauthor: Hobert P. Sturm)	215
17.	The Domino Theory	220
18.	The Politics of Bedlam	223
	Notes	235
	Works by Francis D. Wormuth	264
	Index	268

PREFACE

Francis Dunham Wormuth, Distinguished Professor of Political Science at the University of Utah, is known for his *The Royal Prerogative, 1603-1649* (1939), his justly celebrated work *The Origins of Modern Constitutionalism* (1949), *Private Enterprise and Public Policy* (in collaboration, 1954), *The Vietnam War: The President versus the Constitution* (1968), other books, and articles and reviews. In this volume we have assembled many of Professor Wormuth's essays, widely scattered in time (1941 to 1976) and place of publication. None of the pieces gathered here appears in his books, except for one essay which has been extensively revised. Two of the others were originally published in shorter form but are presented here in their entirety. Of the remaining essays a few were published in journals not likely to be available in American libraries.

As is true of the books, these essays bring to bear a profundity of analytical scholarship in a remarkably distinctive conjunction of fields: law, history, political theory, and American politics. They are addressed to issues of continuing significance, most especially concerning human freedom and human survival. Professor Wormuth's political thinking deserves to be comprehended as a whole. Although presenting his voluminous works in their entirety is of course far beyond the reach of this project, this collection of selected essays involves a large proportion of the topics that have drawn his attention over the years. This book consequently affords the reader access to much of his thought.

In an era characterized by frequent prolixity and opacity in scholarly expression, and when one of the greatest needs of young political scientists is the development of writing skills, Professor Wormuth's essays stand as instructive models of conciseness, clarity, and penetration of the subject matter, wrought with disciplined craftsmanship of a high order.

The essays in Part One, "Law," illuminate classic human struggles with the idea of law and the great difficulties inherent in that concept; the combination in law of normative and predictive elements, of obligational and of behavioral elements; the conflict of particularized needs and general principles; law as reflector of noble aspirations and of base motives; law as handmaiden of tyranny and human exploitation, and as positive instrument for regulation of society for the common good. In particular there is supplied a criticism of the historiography of the natural law tradition and an account of the abuses to which this has led. The whole set of essays is pervaded by a passion for intellectual, spiritual, and political freedom; for equitable justice and truth; for constitutionalism as a restraint upon governmental negligence and governmental abuse of power; for morality as a critic of authority and law; for the ideals of the Reformation, of the American and French revolutions, of the Declaration of Independence, and of the Declaration of the Rights of Man.

The essays in Part Two, "Politics," display a mode of thought that exemplifies intellectual independence and philosophical skepticism. Professor Wormuth's theory of political behavior is rigorously individualistic: collective behavior should be analyzed into its component parts of individual attitudes, interests, and motivations; individual behavior is the result of emotional and irrational urges as well as of rational calculations. Political behavior can and should be studied scientifically with tools of analysis that rely upon affective and subjective methods (such as Weber's method of *Verstehen*) as well as those that involve formal modeling. Given the central position of subjectivist methods in political science, the values and attitudes of political scientists themselves will determine the nature and extent of their discoveries. At bottom, we should know, political science is built upon a foundation of moral sentiments.

As editors, we have had the limited tasks of conceiving the project, obtaining Professor Wormuth's consent to it, selecting the essays to be included, working out the order of their presentation, choosing a publisher, obtaining permission to reprint from the various original publishers, standardizing the form of the end notes, developing the bibliography—including the tracking down of numerous book reviews—physically preparing the manuscript, proofreading galley sheets, and making an index.

The editors are two of numerous students whom Professor Wormuth has directed into the profession of political science, and for them the compilation of this volume has been an act of filial piety as well as of enjoyment.

The most difficult part of the editorial task was obtaining the permission of the author to go ahead with the collection. We are very grateful for what ultimately became his full albeit skeptical cooperation.

We are also indebted to the officers of Kennikat Press for their very helpful guidance; to the political science department of the University of Utah for financing the typing of the manuscript; to the department's chairman, Professor L. Kent Kimball, for his encouragement; to the department's administrative assistant, Mrs. Jessie V. Diamond, and Mrs. Stephanie Dastrup and Mrs. Kass Moffat, secretaries, for various kinds of aid; to a superb typist, Mrs. Debra Harrison; to Hobert P. Sturm for permission to republish an essay of which he was coauthor; to the Work Study Program of the University of Utah, and to James R. Thomas, whose valuable assistance to the project was made possible by that program; to the secretarial staff of the Department of Political Science, California State University, Northridge, for helping in the early stages of the project; and to the various publishers, identified on the first page of each chapter, whose consent to reprinting enabled us to have this collection produced.

Dalmas H. Nelson
Richard L. Sklar

ESSAYS IN
LAW AND POLITICS

ABOUT THE AUTHOR

Francis Wormuth has been recognized for many years as a brilliant and learned constitutional scholar and political scientist. He is, perhaps, best known for his celebrated work *The Origins of Modern Constitutionalism.* Among his other books and monographs, *The Vietnam War: The President versus the Constitution* (1968) has been widely noted, and together with subsequent writings on the war powers establish him as an author whose views have to be reckoned with by serious commentators, scholars, and statesmen.

Dalmas H. Nelson is Professor of Political Science at the University of Utah. *Richard H. Sklar* is Professor of Political Science at the University of California, Los Angeles. They share the belief that Professor Wormuth's work over the years constitutes a cumulative effort that should be comprehended as a whole.

PART ONE

LAW

1

THE DILEMMA OF JURISPRUDENCE

Law, we are accustomed to say, comprises two elements. It is a body of obligatory rules of conduct, but it differs from other obligatory rules, such as moral precepts or the rules of a game, in that it is enforced by the state. On the one hand, law exists as a conceptual system of normative rules; on the other, it dwells as well in the realm of brute fact, where it is something that is "done" or enforced by the state. But here surely is a snake swallowing its own tail, for the state which concretizes law on the level of actuality is itself a creature of the realm of ideality: the state is meaningless except as a legal concept.

What is needed is a treatment of law which will equate the actual practice of government with the conceptual system of rules that are obligatory, not merely upon citizens, but upon government as well. There seem to be good a priori reasons for believing that this cannot be done, and for believing, furthermore, that no definition of law in terms of either of the elements alone will be satisfactory.

The American writers loosely grouped as "realistic" have made a thoroughgoing effort to solve the problem by omitting the normative element. With individual variations, these authors have argued that law is simply the behavior of the judge. Since the judge is a man, the law which he makes is a by-product of his personal existence, secreted, perhaps, as a result of a bad breakfast, as a pearl is secreted by an oyster. It is meaningless to talk of law as obligatory, or law as rule. Law is occurrence, on the simple level of fact, and it is not to be discussed in terms of

---

Reprinted from *American Political Science Review* 35 (1941): 44–52. Used by permission of the American Political Science Association.

obligation or validity, ideas which are the product of folklore or father-fixation.

This position involves two distinct affirmations. The first is the contention that law is nothing more than the behavior of judges; the second, the assertion that all judicial behavior is law. Neither is tenable. Let us examine the proposition that law can be reduced to the behavior of judges. The objection arises that the very use of the term "judge" implies the normative scheme which the realists deny, for what marks off the judge from other men except that he occupies a preappointed place in a legal scheme? But it may be said that the judge is defined not by law but by function: one discovers who is a judge just as one discovers who is a milkman, by observation. This is the point of view of "social anthropology," popularized by Thurman Arnold. For its purposes this view is adequate and admirable; but these differ from the purpose of jurisprudence. The purpose of jurisprudence is to localize law, to identify law as we identify the milkman. But Arnold's point of view gives us no help here. For law cannot include all of the judge's behavior. It cannot be the judge's behavior in the capacity of father, or gambler, or Mason: it is his behavior in the capacity of judge. There is at the core of this identifiable man a Platonic essence, the essence of the judge. His judicial character consists in his correspondence to an abstract category external to him. This category of judge is not the behavior of the judge, but an independent legal norm.

But it may be denied that the judge possesses an abstract character of judgeness. It may be said that law is merely an identifiable part of the behavior of an identifiable man: it is that part which occurs at given hours of the day in courtroom or in chambers. But here again the need for discrimination arises: we must eliminate the process of respiration, and the witty asides to counsel, and the other nonjudicial activities which occur simultaneously with the "judicial process." In short, in order to discover law in the behavior of the judge we must know what it is before we begin our inquiry. Law is only a part of the behavior of the judge; and the judge is a man who undertakes behavior of this order. His character as judge, then, is derived from the fact that he practices law; and we have here a legal rather than an anthropological norm for the identification of judges. This is a conclusion we might have anticipated from the beginning, for a functional category, as Socrates demonstrated to Thrasymachus, is a normative category.

It seems necessary, then, to reject the first realist contention, that all law is judicial behavior. This involves also a rejection of the second position, the statement that all judicial behavior is law. The very nature of a functional classification is to constrain behavior within limits, and it is certainly possible for a judge to exceed the limits of judicial office. To call such excessive behavior law is once more to spill law outside the judicial capacity of the judge, and to make it useless as a term of discrimination. This can be demonstrated on the practical level. If law is equated to occurrence, not merely is every occurrence legal, but no occurrence, at least none produced by the judge, is illegal. But law needs illegality as God needs the devil—a proof, perhaps, of its normative character. Take the mythical case of the justice of the peace who mistook his powers and hanged a man. This, according to the realists, is lawful, for it is the conduct of the judge. Now let us suppose that a superior court hangs the justice of the peace for murder, as would happen according to a properly appointed normative scheme. This also is lawful, for it is likewise the conduct of a court. A view of law which introduces such absurdities into a situation so well understood by ordinary men is surely to be suspected.

It is clear that in the realist scheme the word "illegal" can have no meaning, and in fact it cannot occur except as a mouthing on the part of the judge. This makes the duties of police officers altogether too easy. There is no need for them to strive for law enforcement, for the actions of supposed criminals are legal; or at any rate they become illegal only when the judge, provoked perhaps by the dyspepsia characteristic of magistrates, denounces them as such. A record of one hundred percent legality cannot be improved; why hale persons before the police court?

The realists have not taken up this position without provocation. Apparently the decisive factor impelling them to their conclusions has been observation of the judicial process. No candid observer will deny the allegation of Jerome Frank that a very considerable part of judicial business is determined on some other basis than the application of settled rules to the facts. The law is altogether too fluid and too episodic to be regarded as a regular balancing of the scales. By calling attention to the uncertainty attending the judicial process, the realists have done a great public service.

The feature of obligation rather than the alleged certainty of a normative system of law has been the cause for objection by other writers. Justice Holmes evolved a settled philosophy, echoed also in casual phrases by Justice Cardozo, which attempted to retain the element of certainty and predictability in law, but to banish the idea of obligation. "What I mean by law," said Holmes, "is nothing more or less than the prediction of what a court will do." And Cardozo: "A principle or rule of conduct so established as to justify a prediction with reasonable certainty that it will be enforced by the courts if its authority is challenged ... is a rule of law."

Apparently the purpose here is to evade the troublesome concept of obligation by defining law not simply in terms of human conduct, but in terms of the predictable aspects of human conduct rather than the personal caprice which is law to the realists. Law is to be assimilated to judicial behavior, but only to the regularities of judicial behavior. This raises the same problem that vexes the realists. If law is predictable behavior, predictable behavior is law. When law abandons its character of obligation and sinks to the level of motivation, it becomes indistinguishable from other motives whose effects are predictable.

There are circumstances under which a prediction as to the outcome of a case can be made with reasonable certainty, and yet we would shrink from applying the name of law to the process. If a judge accepts a bribe, for example, his decision is predictable. It may be law, but is it law by virtue of its predictability? During the "Popish Plot" prosecutions before Judge Scroggs, the charges to the jury were eminently predictable: were they therefore law? The prediction Holmes and Cardozo have in mind is not prediction in terms of uniformity, on the level of invariable behavior, but in terms of conformity—conformity to a set of rules which exist behind the judge, and in some sense are obligatory upon him.

This becomes clear if we analyze their statements. The rule must be so well established that prediction is justified. Perhaps this means that the rule is law if the prediction is a reasonable one, even though it is not vindicated by actual application by the judge. In this case clearly the rule exists apart from the judge, and it is meaningful to stigmatize the judge's conduct as a departure from law. Law, then, has a normative element. Or perhaps the prediction is "justified" only if the court actually applies the rule and makes the prediction come true. Here we have two choices. Either we regard the rule as being merely motivation in the judge, to be treated as on all fours with other motivation, which, as we have seen, extends the name "law" to all predictable influences; or else we hold it apart from the judge, and regard his action in applying the rule as some sort of tribute to the rule which justifies the earlier prediction that he would follow it. The first alternative plunges us into the chaos of the realists; the second is a normative conception of law.

The realists, then, have boggled at the definition of law as rule, because it is evident that in many cases the actual behavior of courts does not consist in the application of rules. Holmes has retained the conception of law as rule, but has attempted to oust the obligatory element. But this attempt is bound to be unsuccessful, for the very nature of a rule is to be normative, and to deprive it of its normative character in favor of predictability is to destroy its identity and sink it in the great mass of predictable motivation. With regard to both attempts to equate law to human behavior, it can be said that law disappears in the process. Certainly human behavior exists, and it is possible to say that "what I mean by law" is all judicial behavior, or predictable judicial behavior. It is possible to say that law is what the judge or the government does. But this is a lifting of oneself by one's bootstraps, for the word "judge" and the word "government" imply a normative scheme of law. Further, it is to deprive law of any meaning apart from what actually occurs, and even the realists, even Holmes, believe in the utility of a definition of law as a criticism of what exists, a normative definition. The attempt to equate law to actuality lops the ideal head from the feet of clay, and leaves a truncated thing which merely is, but is not "law."

On the other hand, treatments of law have been multiplied which define law as a normative, conceptual system of rules without attaching the requirement that these rules be "done" on the level of fact. This is a dangerous game. The creation of ideal realms of fantasy is in some quarters called schizophrenia, and it may be only a question of time before the "heaven of concepts" of jurisprudence which Ihering denounced, and the kingdom of pure money-metal, the gold standard of economics, are added to the roster of delusive retreats from reality. At any rate, it is clear that a normative scheme which has no connection with reality has little claim to be the law of jurisprudence. A definition of law which would permit the Spanish and Mexican and American legal systems to coexist in Texas would possess little utility. The test by which law is to be distinguished from other systems of rules is the critical requirement that it actually be enforced, or done, by government. But a definition of law in terms purely of its normative character cannot meet this requirement. According to the champions of the phonograph theory, the law, that "brooding omnipresence in the skies," is valid, whether or not it is successfully applied by the courts. A rule does not lose its normative character by virtue of being violated; it is only descriptive rules which must mirror the facts. So a judicial decision which does not truly recite, in phonograph fashion, the provisions of the immutable code in the skies simply is not law. A wrong decision is not law. This introduces a cleft too wide to be bridged. What good is a system of jurisprudence which remains in the skies, and is not given effect by the courts? What is the standing of judicial decisions which depart from the ideal code, and are illegal? For practical purposes, one must assume that the courts, like the archbishop of Canterbury, are not infallible, yet never err. But courts do reverse themselves, and either the earlier or the later rule must be wrong. We must be still more generous to the courts, and must say, with the New Jersey Court of Errors and Appeals, that the present holding is always the right one: "What a court declares to be the law always was the law, notwithstanding earlier decisions to the contrary." Still, at other dates the courts have been in error, and it may prove to be true at some future date that what the courts are at present doing is not law.

The phonograph theory can stand as the representative of all schemes which establish a normative code apart from and behind the government. A constitution which is the will of a popular sovereign mandatory upon a government is the same kind of thing. All systems of rules of this sort purport to be instruments of censorship of governmental action; yet they are actually at the mercy of government, for, as we have seen, it is meaningless to call a rule which is flouted by government a rule of law. The framers of the United States Constitution required that "every order, resolution, or vote to which the concurrence of the Senate and the House of Representatives may be necessary (except on a question of adjournment) shall be presented to the President of the United States, and before the same shall take effect, shall be approved by him," and declared, further, that "the Congress, whenever two-thirds of both Houses shall deem it necessary, shall propose amendments to this Constitution." Clearly the sovereign authority in the United States has decreed that the president shall have a voice in the proposal of amendments. Only one of the twenty-one amendments was approved by the president. In case of a conflict of this sort between the ideal code and settled governmental practice, which is actually law? He would be a bold soul who declared that the amendments were not part of our constitutional law. We gloss over such affronts to the fundamental law by calling them interpretations, but clearly "repeal" or "usurpation" would be a better term. No question of popular ratification of the usurpation can arise, for by its very terms the Constitution can be changed only by the amending process. Nor is prescription a possible argument, for *Nullum tempus occurrit regi* is a maxim as sound in American law as in English.

If the standing of the ideal code as law is dependent upon its recognition and enforcement by government, it is clear that the action between law and government is reciprocal. Government derives its standing as government from law, and governmental actions in violation of law are illegal; but law derives its standing from government, and rules not given effect by government lose their legal validity.

It may be worthwhile to examine the formulas which purport to rationalize this situation. Such formulas must of necessity accept both of the aspects of law with which we began. It is necessary to argue that law exists apart from and behind the judge, confers upon him his legal status, and supplies him with rules which are obligatory upon him; but it is necessary likewise that the judge obey and practice these rules, or they cease to be law. To meet our needs, law must constrict the facts like a vise, and yet must yield to the facts like a glove. Simple observation raises serious doubts as to whether there exists a law which meets these tests. Reflection raises doubts as to whether such duality can be meaningful. But let us examine the positions taken in jurisprudence.

The rules must be obligatory upon the judge; they cannot be reduced, as Holmes's definition would reduce them, to mere motivation. That would give us a psychology rather than a jurisprudence. This quality of obligation evidently lies at the heart of the mystery of law. What is the character of legal obligation? It cannot be moral obligation, for we have already rejected this by including as an element of law the requirement that courts actually enforce the rules. Moral obligation cannot stoop to this necessity. We are back at our old dilemma. Solutions of two sorts are offered, in terms of law and in terms of fact. It is argued that the obligation exists and is meaningful only within a postulated jural scheme, and the modesty of this position is thought to disarm criticism. Or, alternatively, it is argued that the obligation of law is a compulsion of the will which actually exists on the practical level.

To ascribe the obligation of law to its legal character involves us either in a circle or in a tautology. The system of rules is law, because it is obligatory, and it is obligatory because it is law. All attempts to explain the obligation of law in terms of law are attempts to make law self-obligatory. So Jellinek refers law back to a legal sovereign who is a mere abstraction from the rules of law. Kelsen remarks that the nature of law is to be obligatory. But is it possible to confine the discussion of law and its obligation to this rarefied level? An obligatory rule should not cease to be obligatory because it is disobeyed by the courts; and yet this is the fate of a rule of law. Nor is it any solution to pretend that the courts never disobey the rules of law. For one thing, all the evidence is against this assumption. Furthermore, this leaves unresolved the question of the source of the obligation: if law is simultaneously the invariable practice of the courts and a set of obligatory rules, it is by no means clear that the second characteristic does not derive from the first. If the second exists only in the presence of the first, there is surely some sort of dependence, and the attempt to make law self-obligatory is unsuccessful.

John Austin chose the other road and undertook to ground his scheme in fact. As a matter of solemn fact, there is in every political society an uncommanded superior who receives habitual obedience from the citizenry. The commands of this sovereign superior are known as law; they exist in point of fact, and they receive habitual obedience from the courts. The rules exist; they coerce the judges; and they can meaningfully be referred to a human source. Many potent objections have been urged to this scheme: one will suffice here. That is the argument that there is in no society a sovereign capable of enforcing complete subordination to his will. The reply of Austinians is that the sovereign has jural omnicompetence though not factual omnicompetence. The sovereign then possesses authority in fact in the fields in which he can safely issue commands, and possesses legal authority in other fields in which he possesses in fact no power. But in these other fields clearly some person or persons, nominally subject, possess in fact the power of commanding obedience to their will. The sovereign's conduct in refraining from legislating is testimony to their power. Could it be argued that they are in fact sovereign in these fields, and that in other fields in which they hold no veto power they possess nevertheless jural omnicompetence? This gives us an embarrassing plurality of sovereigns and of legal systems.

Of course, there is in the modern world, though not in the medieval world, an easy means for distinguishing Austin's sovereign from these spurious ones. Government is a recognizable institution if not a definable one. But does it become a "legal" institution merely because it is identifiable? Not if the test of legality is the power of enforcing submission to its will, and this is the test that Austin offers us. The wills which do succeed in effectuating their purposes are multitudinous, and by this practical test they can fairly compete with the governmental will for the name of sovereign. What Austin does is to attach the name "law" to a set of everyday practices in which there does occur with a fair degree of regularity the subordination of will to official command, and then to expand this practical sovereignty, whose power to bind was originally defined as a matter of fact, into a "jural" sovereignty whose authority is not a description of an actual coercion of wills but a purely postulated right to command not dependent upon any sort of obedience. This sovereign is not measurably different from Jellinek's; and this law is still an unmanageable combination of the ideal and the actual.

The question may be stated thus: Can government be defined in terms of law if law must be defined in terms of fact, when the fact is governmental action? Can law be defined in terms of governmental action, if governmental action is measured in terms of law? Is it meaningful to validate law in terms of government, and at the same time to validate government in terms of law? It is submitted that the idea of law necessarily includes both the concept of obligation and the concept of actual practice, and that these two ideas, the world being what it is, cannot be included in the same term. In point of fact, of course, we recognize the stress between these two elements. We recognize that rules of law exert some sort of compulsion upon judges, and that judges exercise a very real power of life and death over rules of law. A practical definition perhaps would read as follows: Law is not a body of obligatory rules, but approximates a body of obligatory rules, which are not completely enforced, but are approximately enforced, by government. It is a denizen of two worlds, which lives in neither, and does not live in both at once. It is a conception peculiar to man, the rule-making animal, a product, perhaps, of the evolutionary development of a gregarious creature. Surely the impossible idea does serve a purpose: it would be difficult to picture a human society which could afford not to make this useful confusion.

2

ARISTOTLE ON LAW

"The rule of law, it is argued, is preferable to that of any individual."[1] This sentence of Aristotle's has had an extraordinary history. Harrington in his *Oceana* by the phrase "the empire of laws and not of men" described the impartiality which he fancied would result from bicameralism. John Adams detached "the government of laws and not of men" from bicameralism and in the Massachusetts Declaration of Rights in 1780 made it a consequence of the separation of legislative, executive, and judicial powers. Roscoe Pound has identified the rule of law with judicial review of legislation;[2] the Supreme Court has made it the ground for judicial review of administrative action;[3] in 1937 the Senate Judiciary Committee reported that the President's bill to enlarge the Supreme Court, although constitutional, violated the rule of law;[4] to Walter Lippmann[5] and Frederick Hayek[6] the rule of law means an economy which lacks central direction. The trial of the German leaders at Nuremberg by a law made ex parte, ex post facto, and ad hoc has been hailed as a vindication of the rule of law.

Aside from these specific applications, the phrase "the rule of law" is widely used as a rhetorical expression. Law becomes the highest of all values, or the indispensable medium in which values are set. Liberty, equality, and justice are somehow subsumed under the rubric "law." In this usage law is a flexible term; it can mean either of two diametrically opposite things. It can stand for the idea of an austere and inflexible

---

Reprinted from Milton R. Konvitz and Arthur E. Murphy, eds., *Essays in Political Theory Presented to George H. Sabine* (Cornell University Press, 1948), pp. 45-61. Used by permission of Cornell University Press.

code, not to be mitigated by administrative discretion or other purposeful adaptation. There is no pretext here that law is other than positive law, yet by its invariability it somehow borrows the impressiveness of cosmic justice. On the other hand, the expression "the rule of law" is sometimes used in denouncing governmental actions which are indisputably legal in terms of positive law; here the appeal is to a higher law which overrides mere human fiat.

Both of these senses of the term are thought to have originated in Aristotle.[7] He did indeed write the sentence quoted above; and he also spoke of a natural justice superior to human laws. Yet he could hardly have believed both in the inflexible application of positive law, to the disregard of meliorative considerations, and in a superior morality which nullified positive law. The argument of this essay is that he believed in neither—or, rather, in the former not much, in the latter not at all.

Aristotle's views on law are not easily discovered. The relevant material is not confined to one branch of his system. Fortunately, it is not in all cases necessary to describe the theoretical framework in which significant ideas are embedded. Even so, the approach must be slow, and the path leads through many of his works.

Politics deals with human action, and rests therefore on psychological considerations. "There are," said Aristotle in his treatise on psychology,[8] "two powers in the soul which appear to be moving forces—desire and reason, if one classifies imagination as a kind of reason." Voluntary action always involves desire *(orexis)*; reason *(nous)* alone cannot originate activity. Moral action consists in the guidance of desire by reason. Moral choice is desire penetrated by reason *(orexis dianoëtike)* or reason prompted by desire *(nous orektikos)*.[9]

There are three qualities of the *psyche:* faculty, passion, and habit. Since virtue is neither of the first two, it must be a habit.[10] Accordingly, moral virtue is acquired through habituation. One becomes virtuous through doing virtuous acts.[11] But such a habit is not enough to solve the problem of choice. An intellectual virtue—practical wisdom, or *phronesis*—must also be present. "Virtue makes us aim at the right mark, and practical wisdom makes us take the right means."[12] The intellectual virtue of *phronesis* is therefore indispensable to all the moral virtues.[13]

Now, the area of action and choice is the area of the variable and contingent, as opposed to the realm of scientific thought, which deals with the necessary and immutable.[14] Consequently ethics and politics—the latter embraces the former—must be content with rough and imprecise rules, which cannot solve particular cases with any exactness. At this point Aristotle has recourse to Plato's favorite examples of the physician and the pilot, who deal with the unique by their peculiar skills and not by general rules.[15] The man possessed of the moral skill suitable to the solution of particular cases is the *phronimos*,[16] for he has practical wisdom. Since practical wisdom deals with action, it involves particulars as well as universals. The *phronimos* has a grasp of both. The particulars are more important, and an empiric who has had experience with particulars but lacks knowledge of universals is a better guide than one who knows the universals only.[17]

Phronesis when applied to the affairs of the state is political wisdom.[18] It is the virtue of the ruler.[19] The controlling part of political wisdom is legislation. The *Ethics* is primarily directed to the legislator. According to Aristotle, the end of life is happiness; the happy man is virtuous; and virtues are habits inculcated by laws. A primary function of laws, indeed, is to educate the young in the habits of virtue.[20] It is true that laws are also needed to prevent injustice,[21] for most people respond to punishment rather than to persuasion.[22]

Since the laws achieve their effect through habit, they should not lightly be changed. "For the law has no power to command obedience except that of habit, which can only be given by time, so that a readiness to change from old to new laws enfeebles the power of the law."[23] This is the only deterrent Aristotle finds to change. Politics should advance as the arts do.[24] The ancient customs and laws were "exceedingly simple and barbarous,"[25] and Aristotle has a very low opinion of contemporary laws. The cities reputed to be the best governed do not have constitutions framed with a regard to the best end;[26] and every city has failed in the elementary requirement of adapting its laws to the spirit of its constitution.[27] In most cities "the laws may be said generally to be in a chaotic state," and "if they aim at anything, they aim at the maintenance of power: thus in Lacedaemon and Crete the system of education and the greater part of the laws are framed with a view to war."[28]

In addition to the question of the relation of the laws to the ruled, there is the question of the relation of laws to the ruler. Plato in his *Statesman* had asked whether it is better to be governed by the discretion of an absolute ruler or by the laws, and in the *Laws* had definitely concluded in favor of laws. He assumed, of course, that the laws would be good laws—the very laws, in fact, that he was laying down. In his discussion of the comparative virtues of monarchy and law in book 3 of the *Politics*, Aristotle also assumes that the laws are good. But he does not come out with a complete endorsement of the rule of law.

His discussion takes the form of a canvass of the arguments on each side. The fifteenth chapter offers Plato's major argument in favor of monarchy, that "laws speak only in general terms, and cannot provide for circumstances; and that for any science to abide by written rules is absurd."

To this Aristotle offers the current reply, also from Plato,[29] that the king is likely to be influenced by passion, whereas the law is impersonal. The rejoinder is made that discretion is needed in particular cases, to deal with what Plato in the *Statesman* called "the endless irregular movements of human things," which cannot adequately be anticipated in general laws. Aristotle disposes of the whole problem by proposing that the best man, he who possesses the statesman's art, establish general laws, but leave it open to determine by discretion particular cases to which the law is not well suited. The power of discretionary decision should be vested in a considerable number, rather than in the one wise man, for their aggregate wisdom will outweigh his, and they are less corruptible and less likely to be influenced by passion.

Turning now to the topic of law, Aristotle observes that the argument for equality, and a constitution in which the citizens govern and are governed in turn, is in a sense an argument for law, "for an order of succession implies law." And then he reverts to Plato's argument for law in the *Laws,* which Aristotle renders in the oft-quoted phrase, "The law is reason *(nous)* unaffected by desire *(orexis)*." Now, this is perfectly good Platonic psychology, for to Plato reason was indeed a moral faculty which dominated but was unaffected by desire.[30] It is the point of view Aristotle attacked as Socratic: "Socrates, then, thought the virtues were rules or right principles (for he thought they were, all of them, forms of scientific knowledge), while we think they *involve* a rational principle."[31] For Aristotle moral action was reason penetrated by desire, and law was the handmaid of morality: it existed in order to habituate men to virtue. Law must therefore share the appetitive and purposive element which is found in virtue itself. This is suggested in the only definition of law, unfortunately a casual one, that Aristotle has left us. In the *Ethics* he recognizes two features of law: it has coercive power, and it is a rule resulting from "a sort of *phronesis* and *nous.*"[32] Since *phronesis* is linked to virtue,[33] this definition imports desire into law. The language of the *Politics* must be taken as a paraphrase of Plato rather than an encomium by Aristotle. This is made clear when Aristotle concludes his weighing of rival arguments: "These are the principal arguments concerning monarchy. But may not all this be true in some cases and not in others?" And Aristotle goes on to say that laws are suited to some peoples and polities, and not to others.

Aristotle's argument in favor of law and against discretionary decision is stated more fully in the *Rhetoric* than in the *Politics.* There he gives three reasons for confining the jury to the application of preestablished rules of law rather than permitting them to decide cases as they arise. First, one or a few legislators will possess better judgment than the jurymen called upon to decide particular cases. Moreover, legislation is the result of long deliberation, whereas judgments in suits are decided on the spur of the moment.[34]

But what is most important of all is that the judgment of the legislator does not apply to a particular case, but is universal and applies to the future, whereas the member of the public assembly and the dicast have to decide present and definite issues, and in their case love, hate, or personal interest is often involved, so that they are no longer capable of discerning the truth adequately, their judgment being obscured by their own pleasure or pain.

The upshot is that Aristotle found two advantages in laws in relation to the ruled: they trained some citizens in virtue; and they restrained the others from evil. Leaving aside the makeweight arguments—the superiority of the legislator to the jurymen, and the like—there is one virtue in law in relation to the ruler or the dicast: it corrects the bias which pleasure or pain may introduce into his uncontrolled judgment in a case in which he is interested. This reminds one of the advice in the *Ethics:* "Since to hit the mean is hard in the extreme, we must as a second-best, as people say, take the least of the evils" by "drawing well away from error, as people do in straightening sticks."[35] It would be best to find the solution uniquely suited to the situation by *phronesis,* but the fact that the case is individual raises the possibility of interest on the part of the ruler. He should therefore lean backward into general law, which although inaccurate is also dispassionate. This is all that the rule of law meant to Aristotle.

It was clear enough to Aristotle that rules of law were inaccurate tools for the solution of problems. The whole area of conduct was one of contingency, in which reasoning was only probable, and general rules fitted roughly a majority of the cases. Only the *phronimos,* making a particular decision, could hit the center of the target in a particular case. This appears, indeed, to have been the usual Greek view of human affairs in the fourth century. The true physician, says Plato, will cure a man by his proper skill, which is superior to written rules, and will even compel his patient for his own good against the written rules;[36] and the only objection Aristotle raises to this proposal is that the physician may be in league with the patient's enemies.[37] Isocrates, urging Philip of Macedon to lead the Greeks against the Persian king, said that he had singled out Philip "because I saw that all the other men of high repute were living under the control of polities and laws, with no power to do anything save what was prescribed"; Philip, on the other hand, had "untrammeled freedom" to consider all Hellas his fatherland.[38] It has been complained that Aristotle's *Ethics* is deficient in casuistry. Aristotle himself makes a point of the difficulty of prescribing formulas.[39] Circumstances alter cases; unique problems demand unique solutions.

It follows that legal justice is likely to fall short of complete justice. This is recognized in the *Ethics,* where Aristotle passes from the consideration of law to equity.[40] The law speaks generally, but about some subjects it is not possible to make a general statement which will be correct. Equity is a correction of legal justice where the law errs because of its generality. Equity says what the legislator himself would have said "if he had known." It is therefore better than legal justice, although not better than absolute justice.[41]

In fact this is the reason why all things are not determined by law, viz. that about some things it is impossible to lay down a law, so that a decree is needed. For when the thing is indefinite the rule also is indefinite, like the leaden rule used in making the lesbian moulding; the rule adapts itself to the shape of the stone and is not rigid, and so too the decree is adapted to the facts.[42]

The reference to a decree needs explanation. There was at Athens a yearly scrutiny of the laws by a large jury of *Nomothetai,* which after hearing argument enacted new laws and repealed old. Decrees were a subordinate form of legislation passed by the citizenry assembled in the *Ecclesia.* One of the laws forbade the adoption of any legislation dealing with an individual, except in the extraordinary procedure of ostracism. Laws were thought of as necessarily general, as Aristotle testifies.[43] He defined decrees, on the other hand, as dealing only with particulars, and considered it a reproach to democracies that they resorted to government by decree.[44] But in the passage quoted above he concedes that decrees may be needed in order to introduce equity into the law.

Aristotle proposed two other corrections of law by equity. The generality of legislation makes exact definition impossible, and a literal application of the law may work injustice; here it is better to follow the intention of the legislator than the written law.[45] Moreover, arbitration should be preferred to the law courts, for the arbitrator looks to equity.[46]

Aristotle's views on the relation of law to justice are clear enough in the discussion of equity, but they are clouded by his importation of three other ideas from common speech: the unwritten law, universal law, and natural justice. These ideas should be carefully held apart, but Aristotle himself does not do so.

The expression *agraphoi nomoi,* unwritten laws, had a variety of uses. On one occasion Aristotle assimilated equity to the idea of unwritten law.[47] But what might be called the technical use of the term treats the unwritten laws as divine commands which enjoy an authority superior to human laws. Sophocles in *Oedipus the King*[48] speaks of

> those laws ordained on high,
> Whose birthplace is the bright ethereal sky.
> No mortal birth they own,
> Olympus their progenitor alone.

The same poet's Antigone defies human law in the name of[49]

> The immutable unwritten laws of Heaven.
> They were not born today nor yesterday;
> They die not; and none knoweth whence they sprang.

The speech *Against Andocides*,[50] wrongly attributed to Lysias, speaks of "the unwritten laws... whose very author is unknown." These and similar expressions refer, as Grace Macurdy has shown,[51] to religious customs inherited from the past and attributed to the gods. They were largely limited to the duty of piety to gods and parents, the incest taboo, and the requirement of burial of the dead.

The idea of the unwritten laws was broadened out in Xenophon's *Memorabilia*[52] to something like a *jus gentium*, for there they are said to be uniformly observed in every country. They are still derived from the gods. The *Rhetorica ad Alexandrum*[53] speaks of an "unwritten and universal law" practiced by the whole or the greater part of mankind. Here there is no reference to the gods. Euripides considered the rules of morality to be universal: "In foreign land, as here, shame is but shame."[54] Aristotle in the *Rhetoric* speaks of a universal law, *koinos nomos*, unwritten and everywhere recognized, which he contrasts with particular or written law.[55] He then asserts that universal law exists by nature, for there is a common idea of natural right and wrong among men, even when there is no communication or agreement among them. As examples to be cited by the rhetorician who is obliged to appeal from the established laws to this higher law, he offers Antigone's defiance of Creon, Empedocles' "universal precept" against taking life, and Alcidamas' declaration that nature condemns slavery.[56] Probably these examples are to be considered merely as weapons of the rhetorician, and not the opinion of Aristotle, for he certainly thought that some men are slaves by nature; and it is hard to believe that he supposed burial customs to be invariable.[57] He makes his purpose clear enough:[58]

For it is evident that, if the written law is contrary to our case, we must have recourse to the general law and equity, as more in accordance with justice; and we must argue that, when the dicast takes an oath to decide to the best of his judgment, he means that he will not abide rigorously by the written laws; that equity is constant and never changes, even as the general law, which is based on nature, whereas the written laws often vary (this is why Antigone in Sophocles justifies herself for having buried Polynices contrary to the law of Creon, but not contrary to the unwritten law)....

And he goes on to offer arguments to be used when the written law favors the disputant: that the dicast's oath is not intended to emancipate him from the law; that universal law, like absolute good, is not adapted to the peculiar needs of the community; that one might as well not have laws if one does not use them; that disobedience to the laws does a permanent harm which outweighs any immediate gain; that the most approved laws forbid one to try to be wiser than the laws.[59]

Still, it is true that Aristotle in the *Rhetoric* does seem to recognize a *koinos nomos* which exists by nature. And the *Nicomachean Ethics*[60] declares that there is a natural justice which has the same force everywhere and does not depend upon opinion, in contrast to legal justice, which specifies among things originally indifferent.

This is an astonishing evolution. The *agraphos nomos* had as its background the ancestral customs and ritualistic practices of the Greeks. It was a provincial idea, the creed of conservatives like Sophocles.[61] The idea of *physis* or nature as a standard, on the other hand, had been used by the sophists and "physical investigators," as Plato called them, to discredit *nomos,* local usage and custom. But the unwritten law passed into a universal law which was a kind of *jus gentium,* and ended, in the hands of Aristotle, as a sort of *jus naturale*—although Aristotle usually speaks of natural justice rather than natural law.

The idea of a natural justice superior to *nomos* is quite at variance with the method of the *Nicomachean Ethics,* which Stewart has accurately said undertakes to form common opinions into a system.[62] Marshall thought, "It is remarkable that Aristotle, who has traced quite correctly the genesis of moral conduct, should have been carried away by the fiction of a natural justice."[63] But at a superficial view, natural virtue and justice seem quite in harmony with one aspect of Aristotle's system, its teleology. If there is a function for which men exist,[64] if even the lower animals seek some good,[65] one would expect these to be called natural. So, by what may be a metaphorical use of the word *physis*,[66] Aristotle says that man is by nature political,[67] and that slavery, the family, the village, and the state are natural institutions.[68]

Some passages in Aristotle's discussion of *physis* are compatible with the idea of natural virtue. In speaking of the nature of a thing, we mean its entelechy, its completed realization.[69] Indeed, by "nature" we mean the goal or purpose for which everything exists.[70] Popular morality did not hesitate to declare virtue to be natural. Euripides thought that right action, which seeks the mean, is in accordance with *physis;* wrong action is a violation of *physis*.[71] And not only popular morality: the *Eudemian Ethics* says that by nature the good is an object of wish, and it is a contravention of nature when one wishes evil;[72] a wicked man is contrary to nature.[73] It is not clear how these expressions are to be taken, for the *Eudemian Ethics* also recognizes that full-fledged virtue, the exercise of *phronesis,* is not natural;[74] but if the author did not intend to assimilate virtue to *physis,* his language is extremely incautious.

In any case, nothing is clearer than that the idea of natural virtue is inconsistent with the Aristotelian system. Aristotle expressly excluded the subject of ethics from the domain of *physis*. The *Physics*[75] recognizes as natural those things which have a principle of change or rest within themselves. Such are material forms, animate and inanimate. A change resulting from this innate principle of movement is natural; that produced by an outside agent is not natural. When the body "naturally" achieves health, this is the work of nature; a physician who cures himself achieves the result by art rather than nature, for it is not by the intrinsic principle of his being that he recovers. Art, and intelligence generally, lie outside the domain of nature.

The *Parts of Animals*[76] declares that it is the business of the science of nature to study the *psyche,* but only that part of it which man has in common with the other animals, the irrational part. If the intellect were included, all studies would be swallowed up in natural science, since when intellect was introduced all the objects of cognition would also be introduced. Moreover, it is evident that it is the irrational rather than the rational part of the *psyche* that is responsible for growth and movement, which are the preoccupation of natural science.

The *Metaphysics,*[77] like the *Physics,* limits natural science to the area of theoretical knowledge, to the exclusion of the arts and of practical studies—such as ethics. Moreover, it says that natural science is concerned exclusively with material substances, and with the psyche only to the extent that it is dependent upon matter. Marcel de Corte finds here a suggestion that intelligence, being incorporeal, is reserved for metaphysics.[78]

Another passage in the *Metaphysics*[79] has a bearing on the question. Discussing potencies, Aristotle points out that nonrational potencies behave always in the same way, and produce the same effects; and this, we know from the *Physics,* is the hallmark of nature. Rational potencies, on the other hand, produce effects which depend upon the will or desire of the actor. The *Nicomachean Ethics* recognizes four "efficient causes" of motion: nature, necessity, chance, and "reason and everything that depends upon man."[80] This does not mean that man cannot be a natural cause—he is, for example, the efficient and natural cause of his offspring[81]—but insofar as he acts through reason and choice he is a cause outside nature.

It appears, then, that nature does not reach up to the rational element in the *psyche* of man. The practical studies—politics and ethics—and the productive studies—Aristotle has left us in this field only the *Poetics,* unless the *Rhetoric* be considered also to belong here—must develop their own principles. This the *Nicomachean Ethics* undertakes to do. Virtue is not natural, but acquired. If virtue were natural, it would be inevitable; all men would have been born good or bad. But we acquire good or bad characters by the activities in which we engage. "Neither by nature, then, nor contrary to nature do the virtues arise in us; rather we are adapted by nature to receive them, and are made perfect by habit."[82] It is true that Aristotle speaks of "natural virtues,"[83] but what he seems to have in mind chiefly is that courage which is a passion rather than a virtue.[84] In the *Politics* he says that citizens should be by nature intelligent and courageous; i.e., they should be Hellenes.[85] To these natural capacities must be added habit and rational principle.[86]

Aristotle's explicit teachings on nature and ethics make it necessary to reexamine the passages in which he speaks of a universal law and a natural justice. It has always been assumed that these were intended to establish a Thomistic jurisprudence with natural law at its apex.[87] But two considerations make the passages in the *Rhetoric* of doubtful value as evidence of Aristotle's opinions. To begin with, the book is intended to teach rhetoricians to plead cases; and Aristotle in fact offers arguments on both sides of the question. The discussion seems quite in the spirit of that in the *Sophistic Elenchi,*[88] where Aristotle says that the contrast between *physis* and *nomos* is a sophistical device for involving one's opponent in a paradox. We are not obliged to believe that the *Rhetoric* is doing anything more than reporting the stock phrases of current oratory; and indeed the huddling together of unwritten law, universal law, natural justice, and equity is unlike the careful analysis Aristotle bestows on ideas he takes seriously. Furthermore, we know that Aristotle was willing to accept popular premises which he considered imprecise if they led to conclusions he endorsed; the *Nicomachean Ethics,* for example, adopts for convenience the popular twofold analysis of the psyche, although it differs from that in the *De Anima.* Now, the unwritten, universal, and natural laws are used in the *Rhetoric* to introduce equity, an idea which Aristotle did take seriously—and one which he subjects to careful analysis. It is not safe to build a jurisprudence on the basis of a few sentences in the *Rhetoric*.

The difficulties offered by the *Nicomachean Ethics* appear to be terminological rather than substantial. Book 5, chapter 7, where the account of "natural justice" occurs,[89] is concerned with political justice, which it divides into natural and legal. Political justice has been declared in the preceding chapter to exist by and under positive law, so we cannot really be confronted here by a conflict between *physis* and *nomos*. Nor does chapter 7 suggest such a conflict. It deals with the area of the morally indifferent. Some things are intrinsically right and wrong; others require legal specification, as the amount of a prisoner's ransom and the size of measures in markets. Aristotle's natural justice is the division of law dealing with what we call *mala in se;* his legal justice is our *mala prohibita*. This distinction between the two kinds of wrong is found in every legal system; and it is found, as with Aristotle, within the system. *Malum in se* is *malum* at positive law; it is true that it was prohibited because of moral opinions, but its status as law does not raise a question of natural law or of the invalidity of positive law. *Malum prohibitum* exists, as Aristotle says, where it is necessary to specify, because of expediency, among things originally indifferent. Aristotle's choice of terms was unfortunate, although not much more so than ours. Evidently he adopted the nomenclature of *physis* and *nomos* because the sophists had already made it familiar to his audience. Perhaps his division of positive law into natural and legal justice is the strongest evidence that he had no conception of a natural law which annuls positive law. He believed that laws were good or bad, but he never denied the name of law to bad laws.

To Aristotle virtue and justice were not natural, nor yet merely conventional. Ethics comes from *ethos* or habit; one becomes virtuous by habituation, which it is the function of laws to establish. But there are bad habits as well as good,[90] and bad laws as well as good.[91] There is a standard by which habits and laws are to be judged. Good habits implant this standard. The process of becoming virtuous seems not to be intellectual, and yet not unintellectual. Aristotle draws a parallel between the method of science and the method of ethics. Science proceeds by induction from particulars to universals, and then reasons downward from universals to particulars by the logical syllogism.[92] Morality has its universals also, but these are achieved by habituation rather than by induction; from the universals one proceeds to action by the practical syllogism, which it is the task of *phronesis* to apply.[93] Undoubtedly Aristotle believes that there are universals in ethics, but they seem less at home there than in the scientific studies. A happier term is his *orthos logos*. In a man with the proper natural endowments, good habits establish an *orthos logos*. This supplies a rule, or is a rule, for conduct; more than that, it seems to be a sort of mental character or disposition or personality.

The *orthos logos* of Aristotle has been variously translated—right reason, right plan, right thought, right rule, right disposition, ratio.[94] The meaning is probably somewhat fluid. Plato had used the expression without fixed meaning.[95] It was in common use in the Academy.[96] With Aristotle not merely is *logos* right, but *orexis* is sometimes *orthe*.[97] But with all reservations, the *orthos logos* of Aristotle appears to represent a moral set which results from good habituation, and stands at an apex corresponding to the position of the universals in scientific thought. It supplies the point of departure, the end to be accomplished; *phronesis* discovers the means to the end, although it must be confessed that Aristotle runs this intellectual virtue over to some degree into the moral area, and confuses it with *orthos logos*.[98]

The Aristotelian *orthos logos* calls to mind at once the *orthos logos* and *recta ratio* of the Stoics. But the *orthos logos* of the earlier Stoics was not concerned with ethics at all; it was a concept in the field of epistemology.[99] The right reason of late Stoicism was an undifferentiated reason applied in the field of ethics; the Aristotelian *orthos logos*, on the other hand, is not an intellectual operation, although it has indefinite intellectual overtones.

This is a sufficiently unsatisfactory way to establish an ethics; but it is Aristotle's. He believed, as we have seen, in an intrinsic right and wrong. But he believed also in adaptation to purpose. This does not get him into any difficulties in the *Ethics*. Fixed ethical standards are not inconsistent with particularized applications in variable circumstances. But in the *Politics* the standards also become relative.

There is such a thing as the perfect state.[100] But there is also a state best suited to the particular circumstances,[101] and here the form of the perfect state would be inappropriate—in fact, bad. There is a form best suited to states in general.[102] And these demand different qualities in their citizens. In the perfect state the good man is the good citizen.[103] In other states the bad man may be a good citizen.[104] The virtue of the citizen is relative to the constitution.[105] It is no longer possible to say, as Aristotle says in the *Ethics*, that the interests and ends of the individual and the state are the same.[106]

The laws, too, must be suited to the constitution.[107] If we remember the role of laws in forming character, it appears that all virtue is being sacrificed to expedience. To a degree this can be explained. Aristotle is describing how to maintain one of the three legitimate forms of government, and presumably the best the situation will permit, although they are all perversions in comparison with the perfect state.[108] But this is carrying the idea of the second-best pretty far. It means accepting a second-best virtue. Every state will have its own ethics, and virtue will become conventional after all.

This illustrates a strong bias in Aristotle's thought. He was convinced of the uniqueness of situations, and the appropriateness of unique solutions. As we have seen law prove inadequate because of its generality, so virtue itself fails to meet the demands of the variable. It is this bias that deserves emphasis in a study of Aristotle's conception of law. His attitude toward law was thoroughly pragmatic. Law was a means to an end, and not always the best means to that end. This is generally true of the pre-Hellenistic Greeks. Jowett has said that to the Greeks law was "a sacred name" and "the highest object of reverence."[109] If this were so, they would not deserve the respect they have received.

3

ASTRAEA AND DIKÉ:
IUS NATURALE IN ROMAN LAW

Apparently the mythologies of the early civilizations had a common origin. Certainly they had a common structure. The names and the genealogies differ, but there are always two series of gods. In the days of the elder gods, man lived at ease on the bounties of nature. There were no laws, no government, no hardship, no evil. But the elder gods—the chief of these in Greek mythology is Cronus—are always overthrown by a new generation whose leader—with the Greeks, Zeus—institutes government, laws, metes and bounds—the present social order.

Two distinct ideas of justice emerged from this mythology. Using the Greek designations, we may call them Astraea, the Justice of Cronus, and Diké, the Justice of Zeus. Secondary literature largely ignores the Justice of Cronus; it assimilates this to the Stoic conception of the Justice of Zeus. The latter is regarded as a single integrated justice, the law of nature, which controlled both physical phenomena and human affairs. At the human level, it is said, the law of nature informed civil law. It simultaneously shaped positive law and supplied a measure of the validity of that law. So A. J. Carlyle says of Gaius: "Natural reason is the guide and director of all civil legislation; this natural reason is itself the source of the *jus gentium,* and therefore controls both the general law of mankind and the particular law of any one state."[1]

The thesis of this essay is that the *ius naturale* of Roman law is the Astraea of Cronus, the vanished justice of a primitive age. The Nature of the Stoics was not a jurisprudence; it was a personal ethics. Civil law was

---

Reprinted from Morris D. Forkosch, ed., *Essays in Legal History in Honor of Felix Frankfurter* (The Bobbs-Merrill Company, Inc., 1966), pp. 585-99. Used by permission of The Bobbs-Merrill Company, Inc. All rights reserved.

neither natural nor Natural. This is not to say that the civil law was devoted to no values. It contented itself with the Epicurean value of utility, and made no claim to the values of the universe.[2]

The version of the ancient mythology which served as the source of classical thought originated in two works attributed to a Greek poet of the eighth century B.C., the *Theogony* and the *Works and Days* of Hesiod. The *Theogony* appears to be a ritual hymn for the invocation of Zeus; for this purpose it identifies him by detailing his ancestry.[3] Chief of the elder gods was Cronus; he was overthrown by his son Zeus. Zeus married bright Themis (Law), who bore him the Horae (Hours), Eunomia (Order), Diké (Justice), and blooming Eirene (Peace) and the Moerae (Fates).[4]

The *Works and Days* supplies the human history; this is divided into four or five stages. In the reign of Cronus the deathless gods made a Golden Race which lived in ease and peace "with hearts free from sorrow and remote from toil and grief." They died and became "pure daimons"; Zeus and his fellows replaced them with the Silver Race, markedly inferior, and these Zeus soon "hid away" because of their impiety. Then Zeus made a Bronze Race, strong, violent, and cruel; they destroyed each other. The fourth race is evidently an interpolation in an older chronology; it is the Race of Heroes, included in order to take account of Homer. The fifth race is the contemporary Race of Iron, which lives a life of toil, violence, war, and evil. The goddesses of righteousness, Aidos and Nemesis, will soon withdraw from the earth. In the version of Hesiod's myth which became popular in the ancient world, the *Phaenomena* of Aratus, these goddesses coalesce into Astraea, the goddess of justice. She presided among men in the Golden Age; she was present but seldom appeared in the Silver Age. But when the Bronze Race appeared "then Justice hated the race of those men and flew to Heaven," where she became the star Virgo.[5]

The social morals of this narrative are clear. The Golden and Silver ages are those of happiness and virtue; they take their names from the precious metals, and by their order register an inevitable decline in the human race. The Bronze and Iron ages represent the advance of technology; this means violence and injustice, culminating in the total withdrawal of Astraea from this earth. This is the central theme of ancient thought.

Aratus was translated into Latin by Cicero, by Caesar Germanicus, and by Festus Avienus; but Cicero himself did not subscribe to this scheme.[6] The most influential expression of moral primitivism is of course that of Ovid.[7] The first age was golden; men practiced faith and righteousness without law or judge. But then Saturn was sent to shadowy Tartarus, and Jove ruled. With noxious iron and more noxious gold came division of the land, war, and the most terrible crimes. Piety lay vanquished and the virgin Astraea left the earth.

The Golden Age of common property, lawlessness, and virtue became a convention of Roman literature. Virgil's Fourth Eclogue, describing the return of the virgin Astraea and of the Golden Age, came in the middle ages to be taken as a prediction of Christianity.[8] Although primitivism is more congenial to Cynicism than to Stoicism, Seneca accepted the whole outlook.[9] The first men lived simple, harmless lives, enjoying nature in common; but avarice and luxury brought in property and vice. Seneca saves his Stoicism by insisting that the first age was one of innocence rather than virtue. Only the wise man can achieve true virtue. One infers that the innocent man follows the Justice of Cronus, the wise man that of Zeus.

The idea of the Golden Age was also deeply rooted in popular culture. During the Greek Cronia and the Roman Saturnalia—Saturn was the Roman Cronus—no public business or legal business could be undertaken, no criminals might be punished, slaves were treated as free. The festival was a time of relaxation of conventional restraints, a recapturing of the Golden Age.

Hebraic-Christian literature borrowed this historical scheme from pagan sources. Philo Judaeus converted the Old Testament into allegory. Accordingly, the Fall of Adam ceases to be an historic event. Nature prescribes a simple life, but luxury has introduced indulgence, selfishness, and toil. Nevertheless, virtue is still possible; it is the virtue of the wise man.[10] The argument is structurally identical with Seneca's; there is the same inconsistency between a primitive virtue—that of Cronus—and a celestial present ideal—the Stoic version of the Justice of Zeus.

The first Christian author to reproduce with fidelity the pagan historical outlook is Lactantius.[11] By adopting the theory of Euhemerus he makes the Golden Age a historical event, the reign of a real king Saturn in Latium, when God was worshiped. But Jove, the son of Saturn, deposed Saturn and introduced polytheism, boundary lines between fields, and vice. God permitted this to occur in order to afford a choice between good and evil. "God, as a most indulgent parent, when the last days drew near, sent His messenger to bring back that ancient age and the justice which had been put to flight."

The idea of the Golden Age denigrates the Justice of Zeus. But the same authors erect Diké into an absolute value. The Stoic was able to attain complete virtue in the present world by conforming to Nature; the Christian, by paying to God his due. This virtue, however, was a personal attribute of the individual; it was not a conceivable quality of contemporary human society. Indeed, its whole significance was its rejection of existing society, for existing society had rejected Nature and God.

It is familiar that in the fifth century B.C. the Greek sophists contrasted Nature *(physis)* with positive law and convention *(nomos)*.[12] Nature was universal, permanent, and valid; *nomos* was local, transitory, and artificial. Indeed, *nomos* was false. Hippias said: "All of you who are here present I reckon to be kinsmen and friends and fellow-citizens, by nature and not by law; for by nature like is akin to like, whereas law is the tyrant of mankind, and often compels us to do many things which are against nature."[13] Euripides wrote that Nature is the fatherland of every man.[14] When asked his citizenship, Diogenes replied, "I am cosmopolitan."[15]

This outlook caused an expansion of the meaning of *nomos*. The unwritten laws, *agraphoi nomoi,* were originally ancestral customs, "which the Eumolpidae follow in their exposition";[16] this is the meaning of Sophocles, Xenophon, and Plato.[17] But in his *Rhetoric*[18] Aristotle describes the current notion of a universal law, *koinos nomos,* unwritten and everywhere recognized, which exists by nature. The *Eudemian Ethics* says that the natural is that which accompanies everyone as soon as he is born, or comes to him by development.[19] By this test the pursuit of the good is natural; of the bad, unnatural.[20] The *Rhetorica ad Alexandrum*[21] speaks of an "unwritten and universal law" practiced by the whole or the greater part of mankind.

According to the author of the *Rhetorica ad Alexandrum,* the universal law distinguishes honorable actions from base ones. He contrasts this ethical idea with law in the usual sense, "the common agreement of the state, enjoining in writing how men are to act in various matters." With the Stoics the universe becomes a *polis,* and the universal law has a lawgiver, Zeus. According to Zeno, there is a "law common to all things, that is to say, the right reason which pervades all things, and is identical with this Zeus, lord and ruler of all that is."[22] Law, however, is an uncommon term with Stoic authors. More often the standard of right judgment is *physis* or Nature.

But nature is a complex idea. Aristotle had pointed out: "Of things constituted by nature some are ungenerated, imperishable, and eternal, while others are subject to generation and decay. The former are excellent beyond compare and divine...."[23] The Stoics conceived of the universe as four concentric spheres: earth, water, air, and fire. Generation and decay occur in the moist part; the outer ring is divine and eternal. Earthly history is one of degeneration, with periodic renewals by fire; only the stars, which are the gods, are pure and unchanging. Man has two natures. His soul is a bit of the divine fire; his body and his life belong to the perishable. His human nature, insofar as it is rational, participates in the divine Nature; he is virtuous when he conforms to Nature, but not when he follows nature.

Three things belong to man: soul, body, and things external; only the soul has value.[24] In the Dream of Scipio, with which Cicero concludes the *Republic,* the shade of Africanus points to the beauty of the distant orbs; he calls the body a prison, and life a duty to be endured.[25] For Epictetus man is "a little soul bearing up a corpse."[26] Marcus Aurelius wrote: "Such as bathing appears to thee—oil, sweat, dirt, filthy water, all things disgusting—so is every part of life and everything."[27]

A rigorous prosecution of this outlook would lead to the asceticism and withdrawal from society that some of the Cynics practiced; but the Stoics agreed that man was formed for social life.[28] Marcus Aurelius suggests that this is an aspect of his animal nature.[29] The ethics of Nature seems to be nothing but integrity and apathy. The wise man will cast away from him his property, his children, wife, and brothers.[30] He suffers no harm, though he is flogged, imprisoned, or beheaded.[31] Whatever happens, he is free.[32] This is according to Nature; but man has also a mundane nature. He shares with the animals the natural instinct of self-preservation; he has natural desires.[33] It is natural to mourn the death of a child, although Nature gives no justification.[34] Stoic authors were not successful in relating the ethics of Nature to the concerns of nature.[35]

In reporting Stoic argument Cicero frequently uses expressions like *ius naturale* and *lex naturae.* The terms *ius* and *lex* have usually been read in a legal sense; in particular, a passage in book 3 of the *Republic*,[36] preserved by Lactantius,[37] is interpreted as standing for the proposition that "no state can ever enact any binding law in derogation of this law of nature."[38]

The passage reads: "Indeed true law is right reason in agreement with nature, diffused among all, constant and eternal, which calls to duty by commanding, deters from wrongdoing by forbidding." But this true law—Cicero calls it a "celestial law"[39]—is ethical rather than legal. "We cannot be relieved of this law by Senate or people; we need no other expounder or interpreter of it [than ourselves; i.e., our rational conscience]; there will not be one law of Rome, another of Athens, now one thing, now another, but one eternal and immutable law will bind together all peoples for all time." The sanction of this law is that the wrongdoer renounces his nature as a man. Clearly Cicero is not speaking of positive law. Indeed, in the *Laws* he contrasts the two systems: "We ought to seek the law of nature in ourselves *(per nos);* the law of the Roman people we should seek in precedents and traditions."[40]

The writings of other Stoics make it clear that Nature is an ethical ideal quite unconnected with any positive legal order. In language reminiscent of Cicero, Epictetus says that the man who departs from Nature becomes a wolf, or a snake, or a wasp, instead of a human being.[41] Seneca said that man was a member of two commonwealths, and perhaps the better course is to live in retirement, meditating upon virtue, God, and the world.[42] Marcus Aurelius paraphrased Cicero: there is a law common to all, and therefore the universe is as it were a state.[43] What that state is he tells us: "There is one who says 'Dear city of Cecrops'; and wilt not thou say 'Dear city of Zeus'?"[44] Dio Chrysostom said that there has never been a city of mortal men that was wholly good, nor can such a city arise in the future.[45] In human cities men do not follow the valid laws of Zeus but tablets and statute books and slabs of stone inscribed with fruitless symbols.[46] The only true city is that of the gods, into which men by virtue of reason enter, like boys in human society, citizens by birth but not comprehending the tasks of citizens or the law.[47]

The Emperor Julian distinguished Nature from nature. Diogenes had rightly refused to acquire Athenian citizenship; he regarded himself as a citizen of the cosmos and associated himself with the gods who govern the entire universe rather with any local system.[48] It is at the local level that one finds diverse natures: the Celts and the Germans are fierce; the Greeks and Romans are more humane. Men's laws reflect their natures: constitutional and humane laws have been established by those who have a humane disposition, savage and inhuman laws by those of that temper. A lawgiver cannot change nature.[49]

From the standpoint of Nature, positive law and all human institutions can be called shams. In the heavens, says Cicero, there is no chance, no hazard, no error, no frustration, but absolute order, truth, reason, and constancy. Whatever is deceitful and spurious and full of error belongs to the region below the moon and to the surface of the earth.[50] Cicero tells the story of Aulus Albinus, who said in jest that philosophically speaking he was not a real praetor because he was not wise, nor was Rome a city or a body politic.[51] It is in this sense that Cicero says that the wise man may call all things his own, not by the civil law but by the common law of Nature, which forbids that anything belong to anyone who does not know how to use it.[52] And when Cicero says that the many ruinous, the many fatal laws which are adopted by the nations do not qualify for the name "law," he is not denying that these are positive laws; when he says that a state with such laws is not to be held a state, he is not denying that such a state is a positive legal order.[53]

On the other hand, when Cicero praises the state founded on law he is talking about civil law and not natural law.[54] A *res publica* is a collection of the multitude associated in agreement to law and mutual participation in utility.⁵⁵ Law is the bond of civil society; a state is a partnership in law.⁵⁶ At no point is this called natural law. It is *civilis ratio*,⁵⁷ and not *naturalis ratio*, that teaches about politics. Scipio, who presents the Stoic argument in the *Republic*, says that when there is no such bond, no agreement to law, no partnership in law—when a tyrant rules—there is, logically speaking, no *res publica*, no affair of the people.⁵⁸ This, however, does not mean that there is no *civitas*. Plato and Aristotle had said that states governed by law were—in the main—superior to those without; but the latter were still states. And Scipio also accepts the classification of good and bad states.⁵⁹

Cicero was popular with Christian authors, and the Stoic outlook passed into Christianity. The only true city, says St. Augustine, is the City of God.⁶⁰ The ambiguity of Stoic teachings on nature is mirrored in St. Augustine's treatment of the Worldly City, which is sometimes morally indifferent, sometimes evil. Most representative of his thought is the proposition that the Worldly City may perform a useful role by easing the weary pilgrimage of Christians through this life.⁶¹ To admit utility as a value is inconsistent with his single-valued ethics; but this inconsistency is also found in Stoicism.

The *ius naturale* of Cicero is the *Natura* of other Stoic authors, a personal code and not a jurisprudence. As we shall see from an examination of the texts, the *ius naturale* of *Justinian's Institutes* is the Justice of Cronus, a historical condition which antedated positive law. First, however, it is necessary to introduce another term, the law of the nations, *ius gentium*.

The first surviving references to this term occur in Cicero, but he attributes it to the ancestors of his generation.⁶² He seems to mean a law generally practiced, in contrast to the *ius civile* peculiar to a single city. Some two hundred years later Gaius wrote: "All peoples who are governed by laws and customs use in part their own law, in part the common law of all men.... What natural reason *(naturalis ratio)* has established among all men is observed by all everywhere and is called the *ius gentium*."⁶³ Natural reason is that excellent faculty which Sir Edward Coke attributed to James I; civil reason *(civilis ratio)* is Coke's "artificial reason" of the law.⁶⁴ With Gaius natural reason is the method of *ius gentium;* civil reason is that of *ius civile*. The authority of the Senate cannot overcome natural reason, but its commands are nevertheless binding. So the Senate cannot make that a usufruct which is not so by natural reason; but it can make it a quasi-usufruct, and can apply the same rules.⁶⁵

A number of institutions and practices of Roman law were attributed to the *ius gentium*. In the main these seem to be, not an importation from without, but an extension of concepts and relationships from within the civil law. The creation of rights at *ius civile* required the use of the appropriate ritual, and only a Roman citizen might employ it. A new informal method of accomplishing the legal result—as *traditio*—was introduced; this produced the legal consequence not by the form and artifice of the civil law, not by *civilis ratio*, but by *naturalis ratio*.

Infrequently Gaius uses the expression *ius naturale*. At one point he says that *traditio* operates by *naturalis ratio;* at another, by *ius gentium;* at another, by *ius naturale*.[66] He really means *naturalis ratio*. He also speaks of natural rights, *iura naturalia*, which cannot be abolished by *civilis ratio;* but all he is saying is that, at existing law, rights derived from blood relationship—a "natural" relationship—are not lost by the legal fiction *(civilis ratio)* of adoption in another family.[67] A. J. Carlyle has correctly observed that Gaius has no conception of *ius naturale* as a body of law.[68]

Of course, every legal order deals with and of necessity mirrors a natural world. Gaius assumes that he is characterizing this world with the *iura naturalia* of blood relationship, with *naturalis ratio*, and with *naturalis aequitas*,[69] all of them conceptions within Roman law. Ulpian too uses *ius naturale* to characterize certain basic problems which nature poses to every legal order: "*Ius naturale* is what nature has taught all animals"—mating and the procreation and rearing of the young.[70]

But Ulpian also uses "natural law" in another sense. By *ius naturale* all men were born free, and servitude was unknown; but subsequently by the *ius gentium* slavery was introduced.[71] All men are known by one natural name, but the *ius gentium* has brought in the law of status: free men, slaves, and freedmen.[72]

Ulpian may have been anticipated by his contemporary Florentinus, who is also quoted in the *Digest:* "Slavery is an institution of the *ius gentium*, by which one is subjected to the mastery of another contrary to nature."[73] Tryphoninus treats the idea so casually it must have been commonplace: "Liberty is a function of *ius naturale* and slavery was introduced by the *ius gentium*."[74]

By the beginning of the third century, *ius naturale* had been identified with the freedom of the Golden Age; the introduction of *ius gentium* was an historic event which ended primitive liberty. Toward the end of the century Hermogenianus explicitly translated Hesiod into Roman law: "By this *ius gentium* were introduced wars, separate nations, kingdoms, lordships, the division of the soil, buildings, commerce, bargain and sale, rents, and pledges, except for those relationships which were introduced by *ius civile*."[75] Thus *ius gentium* occasioned the departure of *ius naturale*, of Astraea, from the earth.

Justinian's Institutes embodies legal opinion at the beginning of the sixth century. Echoing Ulpian, the *Institutes* divides private law into the precepts of nature, those of nations, and the civil law.[76] It repeats Ulpian's characterization of *ius naturale* as that which nature has taught all animals.[77] It then borrows from Gaius on *ius gentium* and *ius civile*.[78] But the *Institutes* asserts that *ius gentium* has superseded *ius naturale*. By *ius naturale* from the beginning all men were born free; but wars arose, and captivities and servitude, contrary to natural law.[79] The *ius gentium* also introduced almost all commercial relationships.[80] Thus, *ius gentium* is a generic term embracing all the local systems of civil law.

But not everything has been reduced to lordship. Air and running water and the sea, and consequently the shores of the sea, are common to all by natural law,[81] which is the older law; *ius civile* began when cities were founded and magistracies created and laws written.[82] Wild beasts and birds and fish have no owner and belong to the captor by *ius gentium* and *naturalis ratio*.[83] Similarly, islands emerging from the sea belong to the occupier.[84] Hens and geese are not *res nullius*, but by the *ius gentium* they belong to one who takes them from the enemy.[85]

Thus, *ius gentium* was the foundation of private property, whether the thing was withdrawn from the community of property which existed at *ius naturale* by the *naturalis ratio* of occupation or was taken from another by war, which was itself introduced by *ius gentium*. Long before the term *ius gentium* was used, Roman civil law recognized that violence was the foundation of many property rights. What a man had captured from the enemy was thought to be in the highest degree his own, says Gaius, and therefore the lance entered into civil process as the symbol of just dominion. So in centumviral trials a lance was set up; and in the early action of *sacramentum* the rival claimants struck the disputed object with wands and laid claim in these words: "I have established my right by the imposition of my lance."[86]

The identification of *ius naturale* with the Justice of Cronus is a consistent theme in *Justinian's Institutes*. But the words *natura* and *ius naturale* also had a broader and less definite meaning. Occasionally *ius gentium* is identified with *ius naturale*.[87] Cognates are said to be related by *ius naturale*—that is, by blood.[88] And Justinian follows Gaius in saying that the *civilis ratio* of adoption does not abolish the natural rights of cognation.[89] The praetor, moved by natural equity, has given *bonorum possessio* to emancipated children who cannot inherit at *ius civile*.[90] Theft is forbidden by *lex naturalis*.[91] These usages should not obscure the clear historical teaching of *Justinian's Institutes:* there was a prelegal condition of *ius naturale;* but this was ended by the introduction of *ius gentium*, an historical event associated with war, slavery, and legal relationships. The civil laws of various cities are special cases of *ius gentium*.

The Justice of Cronus is a familiar idea in the middle ages. No doubt Virgil, Ovid, and *Justinian's Institutes* would have been adequate vehicles of transmission. But, as it happened, there was a more direct channel. In the *Recognitions of Clement* there is a forged account—our version dates from the fourth century—of a debate between Pope Clement I, St. Peter, and the father of Clement, a pagan. In the course of the debate the father argues—he says from Plato—that all property should be held in common. The Pseudo-Isidore, compiled in the ninth century, borrowed from the *Recognitions of Clement*, but transposed the roles. Now Pope Clement describes the Golden Age, and assimilates it to the communism practiced by the Jerusalem congregation in the Acts of the Apostles. Gratian's *Decretum* adopts this conflation, and thus introduces the Justice of Cronus into canon law.[92] Drawing upon Gratian, William of Occam restored the ancient theme to the central position in political philosophy. As the leader, however, of the nominalist revolution of the fourteenth century, he brought the argument to a new level of sophistication. The universe is no longer symbolized by the endless regularity of the stars; it is directed by the arbitrary will of God, and, in a subsidiary way, by the arbitrary will of men. Natural law was created and is sustained by the will of God. William recognizes three kinds of natural law, which he designates by number. The first he calls absolute; it corresponds to Stoic ethics. The second is the Justice of Cronus: it is the state of innocence that prevailed before and after the Fall, when all was held in common. The third is contemporary and is directed at the problem of violence. It is a subjective natural right much more than an objective natural law; it might be called legal capacity. It resembles Locke's executive power in the state of nature, and includes Locke's principle of freedom of contract. Man by arbitrary will shapes his legal relations, as God shapes the entire universe by will. By human will property, law, and institutions were introduced; this action or series of actions is *ius gentium*, which therefore hangs on *ius naturale tertio modo*.[93] This *ius gentium* is in effect a social contract, and thus differs from the *ius gentium* of *Justinian's Institutes*. But it resembles the latter in being a historic event which founded *ius civile*. Later theory follows William. The state of nature of Hobbes, Locke, and Rousseau is the *ius naturale* of Roman law; their "civil society" is *ius civile*.

4

RETURN TO THE MIDDLE AGES

During the First World War it was usual for the Allies to represent their cause as that of democracy, which was defined as the free and spontaneous movement of the human spirit, unfettered by logic. Germany, on the other hand, stood for machine-like regularity and cold, calculating rationality. Henri Bergson and Gustav LeBon grew quite eloquent on this theme. During the Second War the roles were reversed. This time Germany was the country of blind instinct and wild emotional surges, moving in a kind of somnambulism and thinking with its blood. The West stood for reason and logic, for an ordered view of life in conformity with permanent rational values. In defiance of all respectable historiography, the United Nations were made the heirs of the cool and tranquil culture of Rome, with Christian universalism added, whereas Germany represented the survival of the frenetic barbarism of the Nordic pagans. Even the boundary line was supplied: it was the Wall, or *Limes*, in southern Germany, which marked the farthest outpost of permanent Roman settlement. Now that the Third War is in the offing, the boundary line has been changed, but the protagonists remain much the same. The *Limes* has moved to the Elbe, a shift which makes naturalized democrats of the Germans, who a short time ago were regarded as the mortal foes of democracy. On the west bank of the Elbe today stands Christian democracy, a sort of Joan of Arc, the champion of reason and natural law, while atheistic Bolshevism, foe of this two-millennial culture, glowers from the east bank. The reader can document this picture from his daily paper.

Reprinted from *Western Political Quarterly* 2 (1949): 193–207. Copyrighted by the University of Utah and reprinted by permission.

There is nothing new or out of the way about this. The Incas, before conquering an adjoining people, used always to spread the story that their enemies were cannibals and deserved what they were about to get. What the Incas said may or may not have been true, but it is certain that the current representation of the East-West dispute is false. The idea of a unified Christendom with a common heritage was always a myth, and the myth itself was shattered at the Reformation. Democracy, again, is the product of the spiritual individualism and the secular rationalism which replaced the theocratic conception of a law of nature of the middle ages, and is altogether inconsistent with that conception. Ten years ago no one would have had the face to talk the kind of history that is now current.

Truth may have a local and short-range inutility; it may be positively detrimental for particular purposes. But it has a long-range utility, and falsehood too has long-range implications and effects.

Eduard C. Lindeman thus explained the provocation for the Conference on the Scientific Spirit and Democratic Faith held in New York in 1943:[1]

World War II had, as might have been expected, opened many doors leading to reaction and to claims of authority. Indeed, a new authoritarian movement, almost a coalition although not consciously organized, had arisen in our midst. Strange voices using masked words were heard throughout the land, voices demanding a new authority in education, in morals, in government. These voices used the familiar words of the democratic tradition but the ideas were not of that tradition. They asked for allegiance to fixed principles, inflexible rules of morality, and unquestioning acceptance of a supernatural interpretation of human experience. On the one hand they asked for absolutes and on the other they seemed to demand something as experimental and as relative as freedom. Was this inconsistency representative of an inner contradiction, or was this merely a propaganda device used for the purpose of beguiling the unwary? The words certainly had an American flavor but the ideas behind the words stemmed directly from that Central European philosophy of absolutism which ultimately gave birth to the historical monstrosity known to us as fascism.

These voices came from divergent sources. There were, first of all, the elite, intellectuals with fine educational backgrounds in the humanities, in law, in philosophy and in aesthetics. These new authoritarians were almost excessively articulate but they were also situated in positions of great power and influence, especially in the sphere of education. Far below this group, measured in terms of intelligence, stood the religious fundamentalists who, as in the last war, found themselves again in ascendancy. Next, but certainly near the top of the list so far as influence goes, came certain mass-circulation publications; the editors of some of these were, no doubt, acting upon conviction but others had joined the reaction because they believed this trend to be inevitable and hence profitable. Certainly, many of their contributors revealed this form of opportunism. The so-called "essentialists" in education (How easily good words are ruined through propaganda use, words such as "fundamental" and "essential"!) were also beginning to filter into the new combination of reactionary movements, and finally, a few men and women of wealth, fearful of the future and embittered against all progressive tendencies, were discovering solace among those whose faces were turned towards the past.

This reaction is not new, nor was it occasioned merely by the events of the past decade. It is a newly emerging phase of the protest against the French Revolution, and all that underlay the French Revolution, which began with Edmund Burke. Burke declared that the French had rejected "the religion and the law by which they were in a great political communion with the Christian world."[2] He mourned that "the age of chivalry is gone: that of sophisters, economists, and calculators has succeeded; and the glory of Europe is extinguished forever."[3] The French had abandoned "the ancient principles and models of the old common law of Europe";[4] they had "destroyed all the balances and counterpoises which serve to fix the state, and to give it a steady direction; and which furnish sure correctives to any violent spirit which may prevail in any of the orders. These balances existed in their oldest constitution, and in the constitution of this country; and in the constitutions of all the countries of Europe. These they rashly destroyed, and then they melted down the whole into one incongruous, ill-connected mass."[5] In short, the French Revolution destroyed the formal structure of medieval pluralism and denied the authority of king and church. It introduced liberty, equality, and democracy.

The French Revolution made a decisive and spectacular break with the middle ages. But it only completed a work which had begun centuries earlier. The middle ages had produced an authoritarian and, within limits, a theocratic society. Man's political and economic life was fixed for him at birth; his opinions, political and religious, were likewise prescribed, and heresy incurred the fate of the Albigenses. The Renaissance marked a revival of free thought, and the Reformation largely blasted the authority of the clergy. Secularism emerged as the dominant intellectual attitude of the seventeenth and eighteenth centuries, and modern science resulted. In economic life the closed economy of the feudal manor and the monopolistic guild gave way, everywhere west of the Rhine, to the competitive economy which produced the free man and the free market. The French Revolution merely swept away the last vestiges of the middle ages. It proclaimed the freedom—spiritual, political, and economic—of the individual man.

In the course of the nineteenth century, authoritarian orders crumbled or tottered everywhere in Europe. It was observed that those nations where monarchy and clericalism retained command were backward in economic life, in science, and in education. It was assumed that individualism and secularism were inevitably the heirs of this dying culture; no one supposed that it could produce another child. Yet in recent years we have seen the reassertion of the theocratic and authoritarian ideal of the Middle Ages in Spain; we have seen a convulsive reaction against modernism in Italy, Germany, and Austria; we see today, in continental Europe, the emergence of powerful political parties, the so-called Christian Democratic parties, dedicated to a return to the middle ages and supported by the largest single Christian church and by the enormous financial resources of the United States. Looking back, it is possible to discern the historical roots of this movement, and to realize that the very advances of individualism pushed up a towering wave of reaction.

If we were to seek out the one common element in the progressive developments in thought since the middle ages, we would find it in the denial of institutional authority. With the collapse of institutional authority, beliefs which could not maintain themselves by the appeal to reason likewise failed.

The denial of authority was of course nothing new. The middle ages had had Marsiglio and William of Occam. But it did not suit a powerful political movement to make use of their ideas. The Holy Roman Empire, which because of its feud with the papacy sheltered freethinkers like Marsiglio, was a dying institution. But when Luther, resisting bitterly, was forced by Ecke to make the appeal to the individual conscience, the ambitious German princes found his doctrines useful. Although Luther was obliged to deny human authority in matters of conscience, he retained an organized church and put it at the service of the princes, who were thus enabled to loot and use the church in the name of their own divinity. Calvinism too was authoritarian: it took up a position in the Protestant world parallel to that of the Roman church in the Catholic, and insisted upon a theocratic society dominated by Protestant clericalism. When we remember who burned Bruno, we must not forget who burned Servetus. But the left-wing Protestant faiths—Brownists, Congregationalists, Baptists, Quakers, Unitarians—insisted upon freedom of religious belief. This brought them into collision with the state also, and the solvent of the anti-authoritarian spirit dissolved the traditional claims of political as well as religious orthodoxy. The English Civil Wars of the seventeenth century introduced the social compact doctrine, which prepared the way for democracy.

Other traditional values crumbled before the onslaught of free thought.

Descartes in his *Discourse on Method* began by rejecting all opinions save that of his own existence. It is true that he soon restored the world, and Divinity as well; but free thought did not always bear such fruit. Supernaturalism was the first but not the only casualty. Its adjunct, the doctrine of natural law, yielded to utilitarian ethics, which itself proved a quicksand. Positivism emerged from the work of Hume and Kant as the modern world-view. Man is the measure of all things; and he himself is certified by no Sealer of Weights and Measures. He recognizes no authority, and he possesses none.

All this was disturbing enough to the emotionally insecure and the intellectually timid, but it was not what provoked the nineteenth- and twentieth-century reaction. What dismayed Edmund Burke was the dissolution of the hierarchical society of inequality and privilege by the legislation of the French Revolution. An authority on the Revolution has said:[6]

The drive of the French Revolution was to disengage the individual from the *état* in every sense. It was to prevent every form of determination of individual life by any *état;* it abolished the "estates" of the realm, it repudiated the very notion of "status," it undertook to break up "stations in life" as lawfully influential things. It held that all men were of the same *état* (in the sense of condition, status, or station), and that there was only one *état* to which men owed any loyalty or obedience, or from which they obtained any benefit—this *état* is what we call the state. . . . The Revolution thus exalted the individual and the state together, and with individualism went what has been recognized as the totalitarian tendency of the Revolution. But the Revolutionary doctrine of the state is not really totalitarian, for even from the sovereign state the individual is, so to speak, disengaged; he remains free, a voluntary, rational, and eagerly participating member, one who helps to make the state, not one to be made by it—in short, a citizen.

The reaction came earliest in Germany. Fichte formulated his *Closed Commercial State* in which the hierarchical conception of society is restored. Society is to be functionally organized into fixed estates which rise rank on rank to a summative value, the state. Hegel also in his *Philosophy of Right* assigns to civil society a pluralistic and corporative organization; fulfilling and transcending the divisions of civil society is the integral value, the state. Here already is the intellectual framework of fascism.

But without economic developments of an entirely unanticipated character, ideas of this sort would have remained what they long appeared to be, marginal speculations of no real importance for politics. The assumption of the French Revolution was that the principle of freedom would solve all economic problems (to freedom Condorcet added insurance). The competitive economy released by the Revolution did lead to a great increase in material production; it led also to severe trade crises and to the establishment of two new and inescapable *états*, that of the great employer and that of the proletarian employee. Eventually these institutionalized themselves in the form of trade associations and cartels on the one side, trade unions and socialist parties on the other. The vision of the Revolution was gone.

This was not the worst of it. Despite the prediction of Marx, the dynamics of revolution lay in neither of these classes. The struggle of capital and labor merely supplied the setting in which other classes, those disinherited by the Revolution and its consequences, were able to assert themselves. Three important social groups suffered serious dislocation in the nineteenth century. The aristocracy and its appendage, the professional military class, resented their displacement, and looked back to a society characterized by order, stability, discipline. The clergy lost its lands, its prestige, its monopoly over birth, marriage, death, and education. The petty bourgeois—the small manufacturers, artisans, and tradesmen—who in central Europe survived into the late nineteenth century as a substantial part of the economy, were deprived of their livelihood by the advance of capitalism in manufacture, transportation, and distribution.[7] In varying combinations these groups formed the revolutionary classes of the twentieth-century reaction. In all cases, however, they received some measure of assistance from wealthy financiers and industrialists who were willing to abandon a laisser-faire economy for a closed economy which they could dominate. In Italy fascism was created by the lower middle class with the assistance of great capital and mercenaries paid from the funds of industrialists. In Germany National Socialism was chiefly the expression of a distressed lower middle class; it found allies among the feudal landlords of Ostelbe, the professional soldiers, and the Ruhr industrialists. In Austria the clergy, the petty bourgeoisie, and the peasantry cooperated in the institution of fascism. In Spain the feudal landowners, their political arm the generals, and the higher clergy were the chief agents in the fascist movement.

The social form which all these groups demanded was what we have come to call the corporative state. Their various ambitions coincided, for they all desired a hierarchical society based upon what Mussolini called "the irremediable, fruitful and beneficent inequality of men," a frozen order which would arrest change and would guarantee to each class the gratification of its traditional demands. This meant a rejection of the French Revolution and a return to the closed economy and the authoritarian society of the middle ages.

The immediate reaction to the French Revolution was literary, as in the monistic authoritarianism of Maistre and the pluralistic monism of Fichte and Hegel. The literary tradition continued in the work of Gierke and the formulation of pluralism. But the problem became real on the economic level, and it was as a practical solution of economic ills that corporativism emerged into prominence. Dr. Ralph Bowen[8] has traced the development of corporativist doctrine: the chief names are von Baader, Marlo, Gerlach, Ketteler, and Hitze. Bishop Ketteler deplored the fact that "the old Christian corporations have been dissolved."[9] "This pulverization method, this chemical solution of humanity into individuals, into grains of dust equal in value, into particles which a puff of wind may scatter in all directions—this method is as false as are the suppositions on which it rests."[10] He would substitute for individualism "the principle of association," "a natural law of humanity," which was to be found in the German spirit more than in any other. In 1870 the Catholic Center Party, in part through the influence of Ketteler, dedicated itself to "the preservation and strengthening of a powerful middle class in town and country," and in 1873 it endorsed the demand for "the corporative reconstruction of society," but it soon abandoned corporativism.[11]

Pope Leo XIII's encyclical letter *Rerum Novarum* (1891)[12] is usually said to have made corporativism official Catholic doctrine. It does deplore the destruction of the "ancient workingmen's guilds" and praises the principle of association, but what it chiefly recommends is Catholic trade unions. The *Quadragesimo Anno* (1931)[13] of Pius XI is more explicitly corporativist, but this document too is concerned with the lot of the proletariat. The history of corporativist political parties shows that the appeal of the doctrine does not lie in this quarter. Not the industrial workers but the small independent proprietors longed for a restoration of the guild system.

German corporativism was thrust most vigorously into politics by a Lutheran pastor, Adolf Stoecker, court chaplain to Wilhelm I. In 1878 Stoecker founded the Christian Social Workers party for the purpose of winning back the proletariat to king and church. He soon discovered that only the petty bourgeoisie offered a receptive audience for reactionary sentiment, so he dropped the word "Workers" from his party title and thereafter devoted himself to the teaching of anti-Semitism and corporativism. This is the first conjunction of these two ideas, which are natural allies. The myth of a Jewish conspiracy is the means by which a depressed middle class explains its predicament; corporativism promises the restoration of the status of the class in a closed hierarchical economy. Stoecker lost control of the movement to the "radical anti-Semites," who in 1924 joined forces with Hitler.[14]

The second Christian Social party was that founded by Karl Lueger in Vienna. Capitalizing on the economic distress of the petty bourgeoisie, giving expression to its very genuine hostility to capitalism, and assuaging its self-esteem by offering the scapegoat Jew as explanation of its plight, Lueger succeeded in founding a party which dominated Vienna until the full extension of the franchise to all classes after the First World War. Austrian corporativism, however, owes more to Vogelsang than to Lueger. After the war these strains were brought together. The Christian Social party, anti-Semitic and corporativist, guided by the cunning brain of Monsignor Seipel, emerged as the dominant factor in Austrian politics. In 1934 the Christian Socialists overthrew the republic and instituted the Dollfuss-Schuschnigg dictatorship, with an explicitly theocratic constitution and a corporativist legal order. This achievement has caused Dollfuss to be called "the one man whose memory deserves to be enshrined wherever serious thought is given to the Restoration of the Christian Social Order" and "the most inspiring of modern statesmen."[15] It seems unfair to take this seriously, and to charge the corporativist philosophy with responsibility for the despotism, cruelty, and dishonesty of Austrian fascism;[16] nevertheless, we must record the fact that the supporters of corporativism have never repudiated this outstanding application of their theory.

The German National Socialist program of 1920 promised "the creation of corporative and professional chambers," and after the seizure of power in 1933 the economic life of the country was organized into *Staende.* Mussolini's state took the formal shape of corporativism, and Pius XI found in the fascist "special syndical and corporative organization" certain advantages: "peaceful collaboration of the classes, repression of socialist organization and efforts, the moderating influence of a special magistracy," although he found also "an excessively bureaucratic and political character."[17] The Portuguese dictatorship is corporativist in philosophy, and the Spanish dictatorship has made representations of the same sort. French corporativism has been much weaker,[18] but Marshal Pétain undertook the introduction of a "corporative order" in 1940.[19]

Since the Second World War the Christian Democratic parties have adopted corporativist doctrine.[20] The Christian Social party of Austria and the Center party of Germany have changed their names to suit the times. They continue to be confessional parties, although in Germany many Protestants who have been denied normal political expression through the suppression of explicitly antidemocratic parties have found the Christian Democratic party the most congenial of those remaining.[21] In Italy the Popular party, which was founded in 1919 by Don Luigi Sturzo to carry out the mandate of *Rerum Novarum,* has come to power under the name of the Christian Democratic party. Its surprising strength is due in part to the support it has attracted from the monarchist and fascist right.[22] In France the *Mouvement Républicain Populaire* is the analogue; and similar parties exist in four other European countries. These parties include members from all social levels, but of course their appeal is strongest in those circles where traditionalism and authoritarianism constitute the native outlook on life. Their program is the hopeless dream of a return to the middle ages. At present their professed political orientation is democratic, but this is in considerable measure opportunist. Gabriel Almond quotes the report of an observer from a British Catholic journal, the *Tablet*, in 1948: "'Even today most Christian Democrats to whom I have talked have only a conditional belief in the democratic process; they frankly face the possibility that the most honest election might menace the Common Good.'"[23] This does not mean that Christian Democrats consciously desire the restoration of fascism. There is humane sympathy as well as class ambition in corporativism. They have doubtless learned what Pius XI is reported to have learned: "Late, too late in my life, have I discovered that the dangers for religion are not only on one side, but also on the opposite side."[24] But in the light of history it seems possible to say that fascism is the unintended fulfillment of corporativism; only fascist methods can reap the harvest sown by the corporativists.

The nostalgia for a stable hierarchical society which finds its politico-economic expression in corporativism leads on the philosophical level to a revival of the medieval philosophy of natural law. The two ideas are closely related. Although corporativism is equipped with a theory of sovereignty, it makes at least a formal profession of pluralism by incorporating the individual in groups which are supposed to fulfill his being. Pluralism implies as its setting a sustaining natural law. So the literature of corporativism and pluralism is also in considerable measure the literature of natural law.[25]

Undoubtedly the current vogue of natural law owes much to the events of recent years. An eminent Calvinist theologian, Emil Brunner, understandably frightened by the recent war, concluded that natural law had been "the Western conception of justice for two thousand years. Its disintegration set in with the Age of Reason."[26] "The totalitarian state is simply and solely legal positivism in political practice, the abrogation in actual fact of the classical and Christian idea of a 'divine law of nature.'"[27] He therefore proposed a return to the middle ages, including the adoption of the corporative principle.[28] The spectacle of a Calvinist attempting to come to terms with St. Thomas Aquinas is not without its entertaining side, and one should recognize Brunner's fidelity to his creed by admitting that he does not altogether succeed in the endeavor.

In fact, natural law is very largely a Catholic property, and the most conspicuous champion of natural law today is a Catholic layman, Jacques Maritain.[29]

The idea of natural law has been used for two radically different purposes. As an offshoot of Cynicism, it was originally a challenge to and a repudiation of all human authority. In the hands of St. Thomas, however, it was made the justification for authority. The divine and rational plan which organized the universe established all institutions and gave to the hierarchical society of the middle ages the sanction of God's endorsement. Natural law ceased to operate as a repudiation of institutional jurisdiction; instead, it was employed to confer jurisdiction. The state was inferior to the church, but it had a moral claim to obedience.[30]

Thus the profound meaning to assigning this relative value to the end of the state is not a depreciation of the moral nature and value of the state. On the contrary, this insertion of the end of the state into the supereminent moral order gives to the state a moral dignity as a servant to the eternal, transcendental end of man.

In this usage, natural law is authoritarian. Its function is to provide a moral justification for the exercise of political power. Hans Kelsen has recognized this:[31]

The philosophy of state and law of this so-called "idealistic" dualism unfolds itself in complete parallel to its philosophy of nature. It is far removed from the assumption that justice resides only beyond positive law; it regards the political order of positive law as a system of perfectly valid "ought" norms and by no means as the mere expression of naked force.... Positive law must accordingly be regarded, if not as perfect, yet as the best possible approximate reproduction of natural law, and any positive law must be admitted to have the innate tendency to resemble the original image.... Within the system of idealistic dualism there is the obvious tendency to legitimize the positive law of the State as just, as that which is humanly possible, and to heighten, or even to render absolute, its claim to validity by regarding it as an emanation of divine natural law.

The social function of natural law is therefore conservative.

This is widely denied. In the revision of history which has recently become popular, democracy is identified not with the libertarian principles of the Reformation and the French Revolution but with the teachings of the Jesuit writers of the late sixteenth century: Bellarmine, Mariana, and Suarez.[32] Certainly these authors did advocate resistance to the state, and even tyrannicide. But it is a mistake to consider their views as for that reason anti-authoritarian. They taught resistance in the name of divine and natural law, and the custodian of this law was the church. Above secular authority they placed clerical authority, as in Bellarmine's "indirect" power of the pope. An authoritative writer puts it thus: "To the Church belongs the power to judge the sins of the political power and to proclaim what is morally right or wrong in politics upon the basis of natural law or positive divine law."[33]

A similar situation has existed in American constitutional law. It is a commonplace that American judges in invalidating state and national laws have often relied upon natural law assumptions. Nevertheless, it is not always accurate to call this practice, as Professor Corwin does in his recent book, "liberty against government."[34] The judges are government; the "liberty" which they have protected has as its substantive content simply the laws which they have laid down by virtue of a jurisdiction conferred upon them by a "higher law." In the Bertrand Russell case Justice McGeehan ruled that a court of equity has inherent power to protect youth from teachings which conflict with "the law of nature and of Nature's God."[35] Here natural law is used in one of its congenial roles—to suppress freedom of thought. The very idea of liberty emerged in the modern world as a consequence of the abandonment of natural law;[36] to speak of natural law as a protector of liberty is a travesty.

In sharp contrast with natural law as the apology and instrument of constituted authority is the doctrine of natural rights. The natural rights philosophy arose in the seventeenth century as an expression of individualism. It did not undertake to confer jurisdiction or to sanctify law; its purpose was to challenge government. It set up "the idea of the just and natural order which is confronted with positive law and the real state to expose them in their essential nothingness."[37] Implicit in this contrast is legal positivism. Talk about the indebtedness of Locke to the "judicious Hooker" has obscured the fact pointed out by one acute student, that at bottom both Locke and Rousseau "meant by government as such the same as Hobbes and Bentham meant."[38] At the political level the doctrine of natural rights recognizes the distinction between fact and value by which Hume later overthrew the natural law philosophy. There is a kinship not only temperamental but methodological between the rationalism and anticlericalism of the seventeenth century and the skepticism of the eighteenth. What links them is reliance upon private judgment, which destroys the institutional monopoly of righteousness and rightness taught by natural law.

Contemporary writers on natural law find it convenient to lay claim to Thomas Jefferson[39] and indeed to everyone who recognizes any other than a subjective sanction of ethics. This ignores the fact that one can believe, as John Austin believed, in a "divine law" without confusing it with positive law.[40] This sort of argument is also specious in another respect, for nothing is clearer than that the intuitionalist ethics of Locke and Jefferson is completely at variance with the natural law philosophy.[41]

The state which rests upon natural law has the duty of implementing it. Jurisdiction based upon truth implies persecution. St. Thomas said that "heretics not only may be excommunicated but also may justly be put to death."[42] The papal *Syllabus of Errors* of 1864 condemned the proposition that "every man is free to embrace and profess the religion he is led by the only light of his reason to find as being the true one," and declared "subject to anathema" the teaching that Protestants must necessarily "enjoy the public exercise of their own worship" in Catholic countries.[43] Monsignor John A. Ryan, the leading American corporativist,[44] put it thus:[45]

> But Pope Leo goes further. He declares that the State must not only "have a care for religion," but recognize the *true* religion. This means the form of religion professed by the Catholic Church. It is a thoroughly logical position. If the State is under moral compulsion to profess and promote religion, it is obviously obliged to profess and promote only the religion that is true; for no individual, no group of individuals, no society, no State is justified in supporting error or in according to error the same recognition as to truth.
>
> Those who deny this principle may practically all be included within three classes: First, those who hold that truth will by its own power speedily overcome error, and that the State should consequently assume an attitude of impartiality toward both; second, those who assume that all forms of religion are equally good and true; third, those who hold that it is impossible to know which is the true one. The first theory is contradicted and refuted by the persistence of a hundred errors side by side with truth for centuries. In the long run and with sufficient enlightenment, truth will be sufficiently mighty to prevail by its own force and momentum, but its victory can be greatly hastened by judicious assistance from the State and, indeed, from every other kind of organized social power. The successful opposition of the Church to the Protestant Reformation in those countries where the Church had the sympathy and assistance of the State, is but one of a vast number of historical illustrations. Against the theory that all forms of religion are equally sound, it is sufficient to cite the principle of contradiction; two contradictory principles cannot be true, any more than yes can be identified with no. Finally, it is not impossible to know which religion is the right one, inasmuch as the Church of Christ comes before men with credentials sufficient to convince all those who will deliberately examine the evidence with a will to believe.

The same argument justifies suppression of free speech. The *Syllabus* declared that "the full power given to all of overtly and publicly manifesting their opinions and their ideas, of all kinds whatever, conduce to corrupt the morals and minds of the people and to the propagation of the pest of indifferentism." We have the testimony of Justice Holmes: "Persecution for the expression of opinions seem to me perfectly logical. If you have no doubt of your premises or your power and wish a certain result with all your heart you naturally express your wishes in law and sweep away all opposition."[46]

But persecution reflects uncertainty even more than certitude. It would not occur to legislators to pass laws for the suppression of those who deny the existence of the sun and the moon. It is only the absolute truths which are incapable of demonstration that need to be vindicated by the public power.[47] The doctrine of natural law, by clothing received opinion with intellectual respectability, undertakes to justify the suppression of competing ideas. By and large, this is the purpose of all jurisprudences which confuse what Bentham distinguished as descriptive and censorial jurisprudence, and attempt to assign a necessary substantive content to law. German National Socialist jurisprudence, the law of "blood and soil," was, as its historical origins show, generically the same thing as natural law. It is curious to find it so often said that legal positivism opens the door to the totalitarian state.[48] Legal positivism denies moral authority to the state; it asserts that law as such has no moral sanction, and thus preserves morality as an independent critic of law. Natural law, on the other hand, sanctifies authority and forecloses criticism. This is precisely what we mean by "totalitarian."

The reactionary movement which finds its expression in corporativism and natural law has a firm basis in the European social structure. It is true that there were "two Germanies," but they were not Latin and pagan Germanies. There were two Germanies as there are two Frances:[49] the one, the child of the Revolution, standing for intellectual and political freedom; the other, traditionalist, authoritarian, clerical, looking to a restoration of the Old Regime.

This basis for reaction does not exist in the United States. There is no formal aristocracy, and our clergy have neither the power nor the ambition of the European. There is no memory of a guild economy to draw the lower middle class to corporativism. Indeed, the experiment with corporativism under the NRA aroused enthusiasm only in big business, which is of course the natural beneficiary of the corporativist principle.[50] Nevertheless, the reaction of which Professor Lindeman wrote[51] has grown measurably in recent years. Of literary symptoms the most prominent is the vogue of natural law. Undoubtedly the chief cause of this development is fear. In the face of a dissolving world, the myth of a natural order gives comfort to those who have the capacity for self-delusion. The profound social convulsions of the twentieth century can be regarded as mere temporary suspensions of cosmic orderliness, to be redressed by the punishment of the small group of wilful and sinful conspirators who have interrupted the natural harmony of the world. This appears to be the explanation of the Nuremberg trials, which vindicated "the rule of law" in the very teeth of positive law. Likewise the North Atlantic Pact wistfully recites that its purpose is to insure "the rule of law."[52] This reading of a world which is palpably in a state of revolutionary change suggests the Freudian retreat to the womb; it is no fit tool of social analysis, but it appears to be the point of departure for our statesmen.

The same fear manifests itself elsewhere—in suspicion and suppression of unorthodox opinions, and punitive action toward the unorthodox; in the adoption of fascist standards of loyalty; in the attempt to insulate America against every form of novelty and change. The same cause seems to be responsible for the abandonment by the United States since March of 1947 of all serious attempts to solve international problems through the United Nations, a retreat officially attributed to vaguely identified provocations which, when one considers that the peace of the world is at stake, must be regarded as inadequate justifications for such an action. Certainly we live in a dangerous world. The times are

> As full of peril and adventurous spirit
> As to o'er-walk a current roaring loud
> On the unsteadfast footing of a spear.

Armaments and military alliances are a recoil from the roaring current; but there is no escaping the future. Perforce, the political elements in continental Europe with which we conclude alliances are the reactionary social classes. This is an alliance not so much against Russia as against Time; it is our own future we dread. But our inward apprehensions have been externalized upon Russia, and this has momentous political consequences. A distinguished political scientist has advanced this analysis and has predicted the outcome: "The world will be riven in two camps, hostile, watchful and ready to spring. Both will be totalitarian, both committed to violence."[53]

Does this mean that America has come full circle? The Declaration of Independence made more than a political rupture. It set up the ideals of liberty and equality against authority and hierarchy. The New World was made independent of the Old World and the Old Regime. But isolation could not continue, and the North Atlantic Pact is not merely a recognition of interdependence but a Declaration of Dependence, dependence upon the survivals of feudalism. We stand on the threshold of that return to the middle ages which the Germans essayed. It led them to Dachau and to Belsen; it led them also to Stalingrad.

5

ADMINISTRATIVE CONTROL OF SCIENCE

The current involvement of government in science and technology has produced or threatens to produce not dangers but certain injury of very great magnitude. Aboveground tests of atomic weapons, underground tests, and nuclear power plants have caused poisoning and pollution from radioactivity and will cause more. Nuclear power plants will produce thermal pollution destructive of property and recreation values and aquatic life. The supersonic transports which are to be developed with federal funds will cause what is called noise pollution on a nationwide scale. The national government has repeatedly tested such poisons as nerve gas in the open air; it is sheer accident that only the 6,400 Skull Valley sheep have thus far been killed. It has paid out large sums to breed new diseases and has sometimes released diseases experimentally, as in the seeding of part of the Dugway base with anthrax and the release of infected animals at Dugway. Recently the Defense Department reluctantly admitted that it had released tularemia in Alaska; this action was followed by a belt of cases southeastward across Canada and seventy cases, the first in history, in Vermont in 1968. The Interior Department licensed the extraction of oil off Santa Barbara under circumstances that made it likely that what did occur would occur: the destruction of property, of bird life, of sea lions, seals, and fish.

Other harms are inflicted by private action. In some cases the federal

---

Originally published in a shorter version, "Government and Science," *The Center Magazine* 3 (Mar., 1970): 41–46. Reprinted with permission from The Center for the Study of Democratic Institutions, Santa Barbara, Calif.

government supervises the activity; in others Congress has ignored evils of steadily increasing magnitude. The interstate marketing of drugs has long been supervised; it will be suggested below that the procedures could be improved. According to the 1968 report to Congress of the General Accounting Office, enforcement of federal laws for the control of pesticides already on the books has been lax. Although DDT may be brought under control before it altogether destroys the streams and oceans, air and water pollution from a variety of other sources will cause irreversible damage to the atmosphere and the waters unless they are arrested.

It is not simply a matter of the death of a fraction of the human population. The ecological damage is cumulative and will destroy the very conditions of life.

It is impossible to halt the technological revolution. It is imperative to control it. Controlling it requires that experiments which threaten to produce harm be evaluated in advance, and prohibited if there is reasonable ground to apprehend harm. It requires that the distribution and employment of harmful products of technology, and the use of harmful processes, be forbidden.

Recently the President renounced chemical and biological warfare, and presumably some hazardous experiments will be discontinued. But CBW is only one source of concern. In other fields experimentation continues without effective disinterested supervision or evaluation. Congress cannot perform these tasks. It cannot master the detail relevant to the authorization of experiments; only in the case of total success or total disaster can it evaluate an experiment after the fact.

Legislative regulation is a very primitive device. In the past, in establishing intimate control of activities which Congress desired to permit but to regulate, Congress has found it necessary to create administrative agencies and to delegate to them rule-making power, the authority to supervise and inspect, and an adjudicative power for the evaluation of some actions. It would be an advantage if this scheme could be adapted to the control of science. There is greater readiness to accept a proposal to deal with new problems if familiar tools are employed, and rightly so. These familiar forms have an established place within the legal order, whereas the relation of new techniques to the rest of the legal order would be in doubt. Moreover, we know what kinds of behavior to expect from established institutions, and can take account of these in extending the administrative structure.

But some aspects, at any rate, of our present system of administrative law have other virtues besides familiarity. In particular, any rectification or extension of the administrative structure should observe the prudential considerations which have found partial expression in the rule against the delegation of legislative power and the requirement that government observe due process of law.

Congress may authorize an administrative agency to make rules applying a general policy prescribed by Congress, but it must specify the purpose and the means and set boundaries to administrative discretion. Otherwise there is an unconstitutional delegation of legislative power. This formula is imprecise and is easily manipulated, and for this reason some students of administrative law consider that it serves no useful purpose. But in fact it expresses a fundamental political principle. With all its faults, Congress is dependent upon and to some degree responsive to the citizenry. It embodies a variety of interests, concerns, and points of view. On the other hand, an administrative agency, as we shall see, tends to espouse rather narrow and exclusive interests. Decisions on fundamental policy should be made after the broadest review of the problems our institutions can afford. In some cases Congress does perform this function.

But we must take account of the fact that in the field of science Congress does not, and in the nature of things cannot, perform this function adequately. A single appropriation supports a large variety of activities and experiments; these cannot even be known at the time the act is passed, nor could they be evaluated in the time available. But comprehensive evaluation cannot be supplied by a group of specialists chosen for technical proficiency. The proposals of these specialists should be subjected to the scrutiny of other interests and other values. This is not to say that the scientific interests ought necessarily to yield to these other interests. It does mean that the choice should be made deliberately after all relevant considerations have been canvassed.

It would be a step in this direction to remove the power of decision from the operating agencies, as will be proposed later. But this is not enough. The due process clause requires that certain determinations of administrative agencies be taken by an adversary procedure in which those whose interests are threatened have a right to a hearing at which they may present countervailing arguments. The adversary procedure was imported into administrative practice from judicial practice, and therefore has been thought appropriate only in quasi-judicial actions. This idea is reinforced by the popular prejudice which assimilates legislative action to will whereas the judiciary stands for reason or judgment. But, as Michael Oakeshott says, "Wherever there is volition there is judgment." If the adversary method, the method of dialectic, is useful in adjudication, it must be useful also in legislation. And indeed this is generally recognized. Before legislating Congress ordinarily holds hearings, and at least undertakes to give the impression that it solicits conflicting views as an aid to judgment. In 1935, in *Panama Refining Company* v. *Ryan,* 293 U.S. 338, the Supreme Court said that the due process clause requires that executive rule-making be preceded by findings of fact. The Court has somewhat withdrawn from this position, but in the Administrative Procedure Act of 1946 Congress required notice before most administrative actions, whether rule-making or adjudication, which affect conventional private interests. If administrative decisions on matters of purely private import, such as licensing, require the assistance of the adversary method, surely this method is indispensable in arriving at sound judgments on the fateful questions raised by modern science and technology.

If these considerations—the desirability of the evaluation of a proposal from many points of view and, as a means to this end, the use of adversary procedure—are to be given full scope, our administrative agencies need to be reorganized. In the typical case, all aspects of the regulation of an industry or a topic—rule-making, adjudication, licensing, dispensing, inspection—are entrusted to a single agency. This pattern came into existence by historical accident, but a rationale has been invented for it. It is said that effective regulation requires expertise. If a single agency deals with all facets of a problem, it acquires much more information than if it dealt with only one. The performance of each of its diverse functions helps to equip it to perform the others.

During the second administration of Franklin D. Roosevelt, the American Bar Association mounted a sustained attack against the practice of uniting in a single agency the function of investigating and initiating complaints with that of adjudicating. It was argued that an agency which performed both functions was simultaneously prosecutor and judge; what it decided in a judicial capacity would therefore have been prejudged. The reply offered by defenders of the existing system was that the commissioners who sat as judges took no part in the preparation of the prosecution. Yet it was true that on many occasions the commission itself initiated the cases it later decided. The ABA abandoned its campaign upon the death of the New Deal. Nevertheless, the possibility of abuse is apparent. When the attorney general instructed his hearing board that an alien should be deported, and the board duly confirmed this judgment, the Supreme Court held that the attorney general had unlawfully influenced the judgment of his subordinates. See United States ex rel. *Accardi* v. *Shaughnessy,* 347 U.S. 260 (1954).

The ABA objection applied only to agencies which made decisions as to the illegal conduct or culpability of individuals or corporations. But the device of the independent commission is exposed to other objections, on broader grounds. A commission which is tailored to a particular industry and which possesses wide regulatory authority over the industry is likely to be converted from a policeman to a protector. In part, this is a natural consequence of continual intimate association. In part, no doubt, it results from a feeling on the part of the agency of responsibility for the industry; since its decisions spell health or decline for the industry, it feels obliged to maintain it in good health. The indulgence and favoritism shown by the Interstate Commerce Commission for the railroads are well known. It has discriminated against pipelines and water carriers in order to benefit the railroads. This identification of the regulator with the regulated is much less likely to occur with a commission which has the assignment of prohibiting a given practice throughout the business world, such as the Federal Trade Commission, which has attempted to enforce the antitrust laws through much of its history. When the FTC was given a particularized assignment comparable to that of ICC, the supervision of Webb-Pomerene associations, it behaved, according to some observers, with great partiality toward these associations.

The Food and Drug Administration has had a checkered history. For a long time it had a very friendly relationship with the pharmaceutical industry, which it regulates; in recent years it has been more strict and has evoked loud protests from the industry. But the principal federal agencies which have to do with science are not regulatory: they are themselves engaged in operations, like the Atomic Energy Commission and the Defense Department, or in subsidizing the activities of others, as are the National Institutes of Health. These are charged with the active prosecution of specified lines of endeavor against a wider background of public policy. To a much greater degree than is the case with the ICC, the immediate and narrower concern blots out the larger and more remote. This is strikingly illustrated in the history of the Atomic Energy Commission. It is infatuated with atomic energy. It has no responsibility for delivery systems, but only for producing explosives. It has produced enough of these to destroy the world many times over, but continues tests—it contemplates no end to these—to refine the bomb. It grants licenses to construct nuclear power plants without considering the possibility of thermal pollution; in fact, it denies that this is a relevant consideration. It is so anxious to find new uses for atomic energy that it is carrying on a series of explosions to release natural gas, although each such explosion appears to violate two provisions of the Atomic Energy Act. 42 U.S.C. 2121(a) authorized explosions as research "in the military application of atomic energy"; no provision of the act appears to authorize explosions for nonmilitary purposes, although research which employs atomic by-products may be licensed by AEC. And Section 2122 forbids the interstate transportation of explosive devices, with certain exceptions which do not include nonmilitary use.

There are several reasons for the gruesome enthusiasm of AEC. Almost inevitably one's occupation comes to seem meritorious. Indeed, a man's work is built into his personality. Not only does he consider it to be as much justified as his own existence: it becomes the justification for his existence. Moreover, the career aspirations of everyone in the enterprise hang on the continuance or the extension of the enterprise. In public administration this produces not only Parkinson's law but the well-known institutional imperialism of administrative agencies. In the case of scientific experimentation, there are the further interests of scientific curiosity and scientific reputation, which represent themselves to the scientists as an absolute called "truth." It is an article of faith that the pursuit of truth cannot do harm; in the face of rapidly accumulating evidence to the contrary, it is still supposed by scientists and laymen that every advance of scientific knowledge must contribute, in the language of Francis Bacon, to "the relief of man's estate." Science is the Jehovah or the Moloch of our society.

In the case of agencies created to carry out operations of a highly specialized sort, such as the AEC, there is another danger so probable as almost to amount to a certainty. The personnel of the agency will be chosen because of their competence in this narrow branch of science. Such competence is indispensable. But this means that they will have not only an official and institutional but a personal commitment, the result of a lifetime of specialization, to the extension of this single probing finger of science. In all probability, the price they have paid for competence in nuclear science is unfamiliarity with other branches of science, such as genetics and ecology, which are highly relevant to the activities of the agency. If by chance the nuclear scientist is aware that the findings of these sciences raise doubt as to the wisdom of a particular experiment, nevertheless his personal involvement in nuclear science is likely to cause him to attach greater weight to the chance of extending knowledge of the atom than to the chance of adverse consequences. The division of opinion between nuclear scientists and geneticists on not only the propriety of projected tests but the consequences of past ones illustrates the bias that a discipline gives to its practitioners. To entrust the decision of questions which involve not only the behavior of the atom but the continuance of life on earth to nuclear scientists is like taking as one's sole medical advisor a surgeon who has no other tool than the knife.

It may well be that the heads of operating agencies—the secretary of defense or the commissioners of the AEC—are not themselves scientists. In this case, they will not personally experience the fanatical devotion to a single area of inquiry that characterizes the scientific specialist—Edward Teller, for example. But this does not improve the situation; it may well make it worse. The nonprofessional head has an institutional commitment to the work of his agency. He is entirely dependent for advice on the specialists on his staff, and is entirely unable to evaluate their advice. The specialists, however, do not have the authority to decide and therefore have a lessened feeling of responsibility. They are likely to fall into a partisan posture in dealing with their superiors; they envisage their role as one of advocacy rather than judgment. Consequently the agency may undertake rash action which the specialists themselves would not have endorsed if they bore official responsibility for the decision.

When those engaged in experimentation are the sole judge of the question whether experiments should be undertaken, adverse considerations are likely to receive short shrift. During the 1950s AEC regularly assured us that its open air tests could cause no physical injury. But in the April, 1969, *Bulletin of the Atomic Scientists* Dr. Ernest J. Sternglass offered statistical evidence—the only kind the case admits of, and as conclusive as evidence of that kind can be—that these tests caused 375,000 infant deaths between 1951 and 1966 and are still producing 34,000 deaths a year. His findings seem to be confirmed by the inadequacy of the criticisms offered by partisans of AEC in the October and December issues of the *Bulletin*.

The power to make rules should not be entrusted to those who are to be governed by those rules, especially when the latter have personal and professional interests in laxity. In order to justify projected tests, AEC revised its level of tolerance of radioactivity upward. The power to fix levels of tolerance should be assigned to an independent agency staffed by experts who are in no way involved in the operation of AEC. If this agency had no other function than to supervise AEC, it might well develop a paternal concern for AEC like that of ICC for the railroads. But if it is given the task of supervising a number of operating agencies, if it is patterned after FTC rather than ICC, this is less likely to occur. Let us therefore postulate a large administrative agency like the French Council of State, staffed by scientific generalists who are supported by specialists in all fields. This should be given jurisdiction over a number of operating agencies; let us call it the Public Science Council.

The Public Science Council should have power to make rules for the AEC and the other operating agencies which it supervises. It should authorize particular tests or activities before they are undertaken. Both rule-making and the licensing of tests should occur only after a hearing in which adversary procedure is employed.

The successful evaluation of competing considerations, which is common to rule-making and to the authorization of individual experiments, can occur only if all the arguments pro and con are presented in their most persuasive form to the Public Science Council. The AEC or other operating agency is qualified to present the favorable case; there should be an agency whose official duty is to offer countervailing arguments to those of AEC. A comparable function is performed in Indiana by a public counsel who argues for rate reductions before the Public Service Commission. This adversary agency might be called the Public Safety Council; the staff should contain scientists capable of evaluating the projects of operating agencies and should be particularly strong in biology and environmental science. To this end it should have cordial relations with university departments in the fields of conservation and ecology and should administer whatever grants-in-aid are given in these fields.

However, it is not likely that all the interests which should be heard will be represented in the Public Safety Council. The residents in an area which may suffer local injury from an atomic explosion or the testing of gases or diseases should be allowed to present their case. Conservation groups may wish to offer arguments which are not merely scientific. There should be generous provision for intervention in hearings by volunteer groups.

Like AEC, the Defense Department conducts experiments; the present level of its biological and chemical experiments is obscure. Its tests should be administered under general rules established by the Public Science Council and, unless there is compelling reason for secrecy, should be subject to challenge by the Public Safety Council. Since the justification offered for developing chemical and biological weapons was to prevent other countries from employing them, there seems to have been no occasion for secrecy. The possession of these weapons could not serve as a deterrent unless potential foes knew that they existed.

Hearings before the Public Science Council should be conducted under the general rules of administrative law. Congress should enact a general standard to govern both rule-making and the authorization of particular experiments. This would require that the council make findings of fact on two questions: the case for the proposed agency action, taking into account the probability of success, the utility of the probable result, and the need for the action, considering here not only the need for the anticipated result but the availability of alternative and preferable routes to this result; and the case against the proposed agency action, taking into account the probability of substantial injury to private interests and to public interests in health, the physical environment, conservation, and aesthetics. The agency action should be approved only if the Public Science Council finds that there is reasonable ground for undertaking the experiment on the affirmative side and no reasonable ground for believing in the probability of harm on the negative side.

A substantial body of opinion opposes judicial review of administrative decisions on the theory that these are founded in administrative expertness and the courts, lacking this skill, ought not to upset them. But it was argued above that decisions ought not to be made solely in terms of professional competence; a wide array of values should be brought into play. In this respect, at least, the American system of administrative law is superior to the European. The specialized administrative courts in Europe habitually administer narrow bodies of law. Their values are shaped by the law they administer, the law of the administrative process. With us the ordinary courts administer the whole range of jurisprudence. In reviewing the decisions of administrative agencies, they bring to bear not only the values of the administrative process but the values of other branches of the law: those of constitutional law, the law of property, and the law of civil rights, for example. In reviewing scientific decisions one would expect the courts to give weight to the values of individualism, which usually receive short shrift at the hands of scientists. Administrative decisions should not be made solely with reference to scientific values, however scrupulously administered. They should be reviewed in the context of the whole legal order. It therefore seems desirable that the decisions of the Public Science Council be reviewed by the Court of Appeals for the District of Columbia. They should be reversed for error of law, or if there is not substantial evidence, on the basis of the whole record, that the proposed action will meet the affirmative standards specified above, or if there is substantial evidence, on the basis of the whole record, that the proposed action will work one of the harms specified above. The Supreme Court should review by certiorari.

In passing, we should recognize that in particular cases other forms of judicial review may also be available. Where the doctrine of constitutional fact applies, there is a right to trial de novo in the district court. There may also be cases in which the members of an operating agency may be personally suable in an injunction proceeding or a tort action.

The considerations that apply to the supervision of governmental operations, such as those of AEC and the Defense Department, apply equally to the supervision of private action. The FDA licenses new drugs for distribution. The testing of these drugs is carried out by the manufacturers, who have a strong financial interest in launching new drugs. FDA licenses drugs on the basis of the manufacturers' reports without confirmatory tests of its own. The Public Safety Council should carry out independent tests and should present its evidence at a hearing. Who should conduct the hearing? Under the last two commissioners FDA has attempted to police the drug industry and has incurred its ill will. But at an earlier date it had the cordial relation to the industry this administrative structure invites. Probably the task of approving new drugs should be transferred to the Public Science Council. The Public Science Council should also enact general rules concerning testing and eligibility for licensing.

A further reason for transferring the power of decision from a specialized agency to the Public Science Council is that the latter would be less vulnerable to the importunities, the badgering, and the political attacks that have been leveled against such regulatory bodies as the Bureau of Standards and the FDA. We know of cases in which these tactics on the part of industry have been unsuccessful; but one supposes that there are unreported cases in which they have been successful.

An enormous amount of scientific research is supported by the federal government. The appropriation is made to a governmental agency without meaningful specification of the object for which it is to be spent; the agency—one of the National Institutes of Health, for example—then distributes the money to universities or other contractors for research projects. Sometimes the research project is initiated by the governmental agency; in other cases, as with many contracts of the NIH, the projects are proposed by individuals and grants are awarded in the manner of prizes to the best research projects. The abandon with which the money has been spent is incredible. Between 1940 and 1967 the annual appropriation for science increased from $100 million to $17 billion. This occurred, as Michael D. Reagan pointed out in the April, 1968, *Bulletin of the Atomic Scientists,* entirely without the establishment of priorities even on the part of the scientific sponsors of research; it occurred by the simple aggregation of requests. The physicist Charles Schwartz has said that when he was with the Institute of Defense Analyses "The house rule was that any weapon that cost less than 10 percent of the GNP was worth working on." A university esteems a member of its faculty in proportion to the magnitude of the grants he wins: accordingly, the expensiveness of a project, rather than its intrinsic merit, is likely to determine the professor's choice of a research problem. It appears to be the case, as one might expect, that the contracting agency, the dispenser of benefits, takes a benevolent interest in its proteges and applies no harsh standard of evaluation. In addition, since it awarded the contract, it has a selfish interest in concealing its errors of judgment. The Defense Department has gone to the length of discharging an auditor who answered the questions of a congressional committee concerning cost overruns.

It would be desirable that Congress scrutinize the purposes and topics for which it appropriates money for research, but this is utopian. Except where military secrecy precludes this, every contract for research which a federal agency purposes to grant should be submitted to a panel of the

Public Science Council. In the case of animal experimentation, the intervention of animal protection associations should be actively solicited, and rules to insure humane treatment of laboratory animals should be imposed upon every experimenter. In addition, it would be well to emulate the British practice and require every experimenter upon animals to be licensed. The licensing should be administered by the Public Science Council.

In the award of contracts and in licensing, the public interest should be protected by the appearance in opposition of the Public Safety Council.

There remains the function of evaluation. At present the General Accounting Office evaluates some of the activities of executive agencies for financial misconduct; some are exempted from its authority, and it is inadequately staffed to audit all the activities that fall within its jurisdiction. It has the power to refuse settlement; and it reports its findings to Congress, where they are usually ignored. The General Accounting Office should be enormously enlarged by the addition of members competent to evaluate all the scientific and technological adventures of the national government. It should duplicate the skills of the Public Science Council and the Public Safety Council. This is not wasteful: if there is any area in which checks and balances are needed, it is in controlling the ills that spill from Pandora's box. The General Accounting Office should report to Congress the success or failure of experiments. To finance this supervision, five percent of every appropriation for research should go to the General Accounting Office.

These administrative considerations arise in connection with federal activities already undertaken. There remain vast areas which should be brought under administrative control. The distribution of insecticides should be subjected to the scrutiny of the Public Science Council. Water and air pollution still go largely uncontrolled. The Public Safety Council should be given the task originally assigned to the National Resources Committee, which more than thirty years ago issued a warning against water pollution, of preparing studies which inform the public of these dangers.

6

LEARNED LEGERDEMAIN:
A GRAVE BUT IMPLAUSIBLE HAND

John Peter Altgeld, in his pardon of the Haymarket anarchists, observed: "No matter what the defendants were charged with, they were entitled to a fair trial, and no greater danger could possibly threaten our institutions than to have the courts of justice run wild or give way to public clamor...."[1] The verdict of historians has vindicated Governor Altgeld. Probably Justice Jackson is the only living man who believes that Spies and his codefendants were guilty of the Haymarket bombing.[2]

The prosecution in the Haymarket case was on the theory of criminal conspiracy. This is not the only point of resemblance to the conviction of eleven Communist leaders in the *Dennis* case.[3] In both cases the conviction was for speech; in both cases the speech was punished because of a conjectural relation to a criminal act. The logic of the Haymarket case is superior in one respect. The action charged in that case actually occurred, and it was indeed the action called for in the speech. The defendants had advocated violent resistance to the police; and violent resistance—by some unknown person—occurred. In the *Dennis* case, however, there was no action, but only a "danger" of an action; and the danger did not flow from the speech. The defendants were indicted for conspiring to advocate revolution; they were convicted, apparently, because they were thought to have a propensity to commit sabotage. This disjunction between the speech that was punished and the facts that supposedly justified the punishment makes the *Dennis* case unique in jurisprudence.

Reprinted from *Western Political Quarterly* 6 (1953): 543–58. Reprinted by permission of the University of Utah, copyright holder.

Apparently it was only with reluctance that the government brought its prosecution for speech. It kept the case before the grand jury for more than a year, evidently in the hope of getting an indictment for violation of one of the numerous nonspeech offenses of a political character in the federal Criminal Code.[4] It was unable to persuade the grand jury that the defendants were agents of a foreign power,[5] or that they had carried on political activity on behalf of a foreign power,[6] or that they had incited to rebellion[7] or committed seditious conspiracy,[8] sabotage,[9] or espionage,[10] or that they had conspired to commit any offense whatever against the United States.[11] But it did obtain an indictment for conspiring to advocate revolution in violation of the Smith Act.[12]

The indictment charged the defendants with organizing the Communist party, an organization for the advocacy of the overthrow of the government of the United States by force and violence; with organizing classes for the study of certain books, which were said to teach the duty and necessity of such overthrow; and with being members of the party.[13] It will be observed that the defendants were not charged with advocacy, but only with conspiracy to advocate. The indictment does recite, however, that the Communist party was in 1948 engaged in advocacy. What is the character of this advocacy? In earlier prosecutions for advocacy or incitement—in the *Schenck, Debs, Frohwerk, Gitlow,* and *Musser* cases, for example—it had been possible to adduce the defendants' words against them. Not so in the *Dennis* case. Here the evidence lies in the endorsement by the Communist party in its constitution of "Marxism-Leninism" and in the fact that the defendants conspired to organize classes for the study of a number of writings, chiefly four books—the *Communist Manifesto,* Lenin's *State and Revolution,* Stalin's *Foundations of Leninism,* and *The History of the Communist Party of the Soviet Union*—the contents of which were supposed to add up to a coherent and systematic creed called Marxism-Leninism. Incidentally, it is noteworthy that both the prosecution and the defendants, although they differed as to its content, insisted that there was a single integrated body of doctrine called Marxism-Leninism, a proposition which no competent political theorist could endorse. The voluminous writings of Marx, produced over a long period in the face of varying political and economic circumstances, contained the potentialities of revisionism, of Bolshevism, and of Trotskyism, to name only a few of the legitimate offspring of Marxism.[14] One of the most vital aspects of the thought of Lenin, the idea of the conspiratorial party, has its ancestry in Blanqui and Bakunin, and not in Marx. If the Czechoslovakian coup can be taken as evidence of Stalinism, Stalinism is not Leninism, for this action rejects the theory of the "dual state" which constitutes virtually the whole content of Lenin's *State and Revolution.*[15] It is well known to all serious students that the term "Marxism-Leninism" is as devoid of specific doctrinal content as the term "Christianity."

The prosecution, however, was obliged to insist that there was in fact a concrete doctrine called Marxism-Leninism, which emerged inevitably from the miscellaneous books in question, and was as explicit in its call to revolution as the Declaration of Independence. And the defendants were as firmly convinced that there was a doctrine by that name, just as a Nestorian is convinced that there is a single Christian faith, and that Nestorian. It is, however, a pity that the defendants were not permitted to describe the content of Marxism-Leninism as they understood it.[16] It is quite possible that if the eleven defendants had been permitted to testify there might have emerged eleven different versions of Marxism-Leninism. Certainly if Earl Browder had been put on the stand the jury would have heard a convinced account of Marxism-Leninism which did not agree with the indictment.

The meaning of Marxism-Leninism was supplied by excerpts dealing with revolution from the books in question,[17] and by the testimony of witnesses. Chief of the witnesses was Mr. Louis Budenz, whose impact upon constitutional law by now begins to rival John Marshall's.[18] Mr. Budenz, formerly an editor of the *Daily Worker,* spoke as an expert on Marxism-Leninism. The explicit disavowal of revolution in the Communist party platform, he said, did not represent what the party really advocated; the true advocacy was the endorsement in the same platform of Marxism-Leninism, a term which, he said, was secretly understood necessarily to embrace revolution. A considerable number of other witnesses testified that individual Communists had spoken favorably of violence, and supplied a good deal of blood-and-thunder anecdote of doubtful relevancy which did, however, impress the jury.[19] The jury concluded that the teaching of Marxism-Leninism was advocacy of revolution.

This advocacy, however, differed from that for which men have been punished in the past. Gitlow, for example, advocated an event which could be brought to pass by his readers, if he could but persuade them. Marxism-Leninism, in the view of the evidence taken by the courts, contemplates revolution at some indefinite future date, after changes have transpired which are beyond the control of the readers. The prosecution conceded that its case rested upon the assumption that the revolution in question might occur one hundred or five hundred years later.[20] A more exact description of the defendants' fault, therefore, would be, not conspiring to teach and advocate the duty and necessity of revolution, but conspiring to teach the duty and necessity of advocating revolution at some future date. Our legislators neglected to make this fault punishable; but the courts by a graceful elision remedied the defeat, and we need not dwell on it.[21]

In the Court of Appeals Chief Judge Learned Hand summarized the evidence on Marxism-Leninism thus:[22]

> There was abundant evidence, if believed, to show that they were all engaged in an extensive concentrated action to teach what indeed they do not disavow—the doctrines of Marxism-Leninism. These doctrines were set forth in many pamphlets put in evidence at the trial, the upshot of which is—indeed an honest jury could scarcely have found otherwise—that capitalism inescapably rests upon, and must perpetuate, the oppression of those who do not own the means of production; that to it in time there must and will succeed a "classless" society, which will finally make unnecessary most of the paraphernalia of government; but that there must be an intermediate and transitional period of the "dictatorship of the proletariat," which can be established only by the violent overthrow of any existing government, if that be capitalistic. No entrenched bourgeoisie, having everything to lose and nothing to gain by the abolition of capitalism, by which alone it can continue to enjoy its privileged position, will ever permit itself to be superseded by the means which it may have itself provided for constitutional change: e.g., by the ballot. No matter how solemnly it may profess its readiness to abide by the result, and no matter how honestly and literally the accredited processes of amendment may in fact be followed, it is absurd to expect that a bourgeoisie will yield; and indeed to rely upon such a possibility is to range oneself among the enemies of Marxist-Leninist principles. Therefore the transition period involves the use of "force and violence," temporary it is true, but inescapable; and, although it is impossible to predict when a propitious occasion will arise, one certainly will arise: as, for example, by financial crisis or other internal division. When the time comes the proletariat will find it necessary to establish its "dictatorship" by violence.
>
> The defendants protest against this interpretation of their teaching and advocacy. They say that the use of "force and violence" is no part of their program, except as it may become necessary after the proletariat has succeeded in securing power by constitutional processes. Thereafter, being itself the lawful government, it will of course resist any attempt of the ousted bourgeoisie to regain its position; it will meet force with force as all governments may, and must.... It is unnecessary to quote in detail the many passages in the pamphlets and books, published and disseminated by the defendants, which flatly contradict their declarations that they mean to confine the use of "force or violence" to the protection of political power, once lawfully obtained.

This is the whole extent of the advocacy for which the defendants were convicted. They were found to have taught that the succession of socialism to capitalism was historically inevitable and morally desirable; that the change would and could be accomplished only by force, because no ruling class voluntarily surrenders power; that some future occasion—"financial crisis or other internal division"[23]—would offer the opportunity for revolution; and that as yet unknown members of the conspiracy which the defendants had organized should then incite the proletariat to revolution. This is highly abstract teaching. It does not urge anyone to do anything substantively illegal at the present time; and the exhortation which it contemplates is to occur after events in the indefinite future which it is beyond the power of the conspirators to produce.

Obviously the reconciliation of a statute punishing such teaching with the First Amendment offered difficulties. In order to uphold a statute curtailing speech, it is necessary to show, at the minimum, some relation between the speech, which by itself is immune from regulation, and other conduct which Congress has a right to prohibit. Such a relation may draw the speech out from under the protection of the First Amendment. The problem is, of course, how close the relationship must be. It is familiar that Justice Holmes in the *Schenck* case[24] laid down the rule that the words must be used in such circumstances as to create "a clear and present danger of the substantive evils that Congress has the right to prevent." After a series of decisions in the fourth and fifth decades of the present century, it was universally assumed that the clear and present danger test was controlling law.[25] In the trial court Judge Medina withheld the question of the closeness of the relation of the speech to the prohibited conduct from the jury,[26] and charged them as a matter of law that the teaching, if it existed, raised "sufficient danger of a substantive evil that the Congress has a right to prevent to justify the application of the statute under the First Amendment of the Constitution." The substantive evil is attempted revolution.[27]

Judge Medina was not obliged to write an opinion explaining what "sufficient danger" meant. That task fell to Chief Judge Learned Hand in the court of appeals. Judge Hand's opinion requires careful analysis.

Judge Hand used what might be called a Y-shaped argument. The two branches of the Y purport to rest on a common stem, but upon inspection this proves not to be true. The first branch of the Y follows a line of argument that at first glance seems to be independent of the second branch; but closer scrutiny shows a dependence of the first on the second. In the end the whole case rests on the second branch of the Y, which is itself independent both of the stem and of the first branch.

The stem of the Y is the proposition which Judge Hand declares to emerge from the record, that the defendants in conspiring to teach Marxism-Leninism had conspired to teach the duty and necessity of revolution upon some "propitious occasion" in the future. The first branch of the Y inquires whether the punishment of such advocacy is precluded by the clear and present danger test, which has traditionally been taken to require that there be imminent danger from the speech. Judge Hand concludes that there is no constitutional requirement of imminency. For the clear and present danger test he substitutes a "grave and probable" danger test; speech which raises a grave and probable danger may be punished even though the danger is remote in time. There is a lengthy examination of precedents, but the significant doctrinal formulation is that which follows.[28]

> The phrase, "clear and present danger," has come to be used as a shorthand statement of those among such mixed or compounded utterances which the Amendment does not protect. Yet it is not a *vade mecum;* indeed, from its very words it could not be. It is a way to describe a penumbra of occasions, even the outskirts of which are undefinable, but within which, as is so often the case, the courts must find their way as they can. In each case they must ask whether the gravity of the "evil," discounted by its improbability, justified such invasion of free speech as is necessary to avoid the danger. We have purposely substituted "improbability" for "remoteness," because that must be the right interpretation. Given the same probability, it would be wholly irrational to condone future evils which we should prevent if they were immediate; that could be reconciled only by an indifference to those who come after us. It is only because a substantial intervening period between the utterance and its realization may check its effect and change its importance, that its immediacy is important, and that, as we have said, was the rationale of the concurrence in *Whitney* v. *California,* supra. We can never forecast with certainty; all prophecy is a guess, but the reliability of a guess decreases with the length of the future which it seeks to penetrate.

Judge Hand's next task is to establish a danger grave, probable, and remote in time. It would indeed be interesting—and instructive to professional historians—to see the judge show a probable though remote danger as a consequence of the utterances of these defendants. If he were to do that, the case would be the typical free speech case. One might consider it doctrinally sound or doctrinally unsound, but at least it would be intelligible.[29] But when the judge comes to prove the existence of a danger, he defines it in terms of imminency, and concludes: "We hold that it is a danger clear and present." It is a danger clear and present because the Communist party is a seditious conspiracy. This proposition as to the nature of the Communist party constitutes the second branch of the Y. It is itself independent both of the stem of the argument and of the first branch; but the first branch rests completely for the establishment of a danger upon the second branch. The passage from the one line of argument to the other is the feat of legerdemain upon which the *Dennis* case rests, both in Judge Hand's opinion in the Court of Appeals and in the Chief Justice's opinion in the Supreme Court.

Since the argument on seditious conspiracy is decisive of the case, it should be reproduced at some length:[30]

> The American Communist Party, of which the defendants are the controlling spirits, is a highly articulated, well contrived, far spread organization, numbering thousands of adherents, rigidly and ruthlessly disciplined, many of whom are infused with a passionate Utopian faith that is to redeem mankind.... The violent capture of all existing government is one article of the creed of that faith, which abjures the possibility of success by lawful means....
>
> We need not say that even so thoroughly planned and so extensive a confederacy would be a "present danger" at all times and in all circumstances; the question is how imminent: that is, how probable of execution—it was in the summer of 1948, when the indictment was found. We must not close our eyes to our position in the world at that time. By far the most powerful of all the European nations had been a convert to Communism for over thirty years; its leaders were the most devoted and potent proponents of the faith; no such movement in Europe of East to West had arisen since Islam. Moreover in most of West Europe there were important political Communist factions, always agitating to increase their power; and the defendants were acting in close concert with the movement....
>
> ... Any border fray, any diplomatic incident, any difference in construction of the *modus vivendi*—such as the Berlin blockade we have just mentioned—might prove a spark in the tinderbox, and lead to war. We do not understand how one could ask for a more probable danger, unless we wait till the very eve of hostilities.... We hold that it is a danger clear and present.

This is a flat statement that the defendants have organized and command a seditious conspiracy, a conspiracy to revolt, which is a very different thing from a conspiracy to teach the duty and necessity of revolution. Judge Hand does not tell us where he gets his evidence of seditious conspiracy. His summary of the record is found in the stem of the Y; it deals solely with the propositions that the defendants conspired to teach Marxism-Leninism and that Marxism-Leninism teaches the desirability of revolution on some propitious occasion in the indefinite future. There is no word of sedition or of assistance to the Soviet Union. We are finally in a position to assess the word "probable." The advocacy of Marxism-Leninism raises a probable—i.e., imminent—danger because the defendants are "probably" guilty of seditious conspiracy.

It was no mere oversight that Judge Hand failed to point to evidence of seditious conspiracy in the record. The case was not tried on that theory, and it appears that the record was altogether barren of such evidence. In the Supreme Court Justice Douglas summarized the sixteen-thousand-page record thus:[31]

> If this were a case where those who claimed protection under the First Amendment were teaching the techniques of sabotage, the assassination of the President, the filching of documents from public files, the planting of bombs, the art of street warfare, and the like, I would have no doubts.... This case was argued [by the prosecution on appeal] as if those were the facts. The argument [of counsel] imported much seditious conduct into the record.... *But the fact is that no such evidence was introduced at the trial....* So far as the present record is concerned, what petitioners did was to organize people to teach and themselves teach the Marxist-Leninist doctrine contained chiefly in four books.... [Italics supplied.]

This characterization of the record is not disputed by any of the seven opinions in the Court of Appeals and the Supreme Court.

Summarizing the whole process, it seems fair to say that Judge Hand established a danger resulting from the defendants' conspiracy to advocate Marxism-Leninism by imputing to them guilt of seditious conspiracy. The danger remote in time which is threatened by the defendants' teaching of Marxism-Leninism is an imminent danger resulting from the defendants' seditious conspiracy. The first branch of the Y depends upon the second; it depends upon the existence of a seditious conspiracy. On the other hand, the second branch of the Y—guilt of seditious conspiracy—does not depend upon or derive any support from either the stem of the Y, which deals with the abstract doctrine of Marxism-Leninism and contains no reference to seditious conspiracy or the Soviet Union, or from the first branch, which follows out the theoretical—and, as we have seen, empty—problem of the punishment of the teaching of abstract doctrine which threatens temporally remote consequences.

In effect, we have two revolutions. The first, the Marxist-Leninist, which is remote in time, is the one that is punished. The second, the pro-Soviet revolution imminent of execution, is that which is dreaded. The first is punished because the second is dangerous. It really appears that the fact that revolutionary words are comprised in Marxist-Leninist teaching is accidental. The danger to which these words give rise is remote and would not sustain a conviction. But the danger raised by the seditious conspiracy is transferred to the revolutionary words incidental to Marxism-Leninism in order to punish the teaching of Marxism-Leninism.

If the defendants were guilty of seditious conspiracy, they might have been punished for this offense under the appropriate statute.[32] They might also be punished under the Smith Act, since seditious conspiracy would necessarily involve advocacy of the revolution contemplated by the conspiracy. But the revolution contemplated by the alleged seditious conspiracy is not the indefinite and temporally remote revolution of the Marxist-Leninist doctrine proved at the trial, which constitutes the stem of the Y. It is not a doctrine but a plot imminent of execution. If the defendants were to be convicted for having made such a plot, evidence of the plot should have been introduced, and this evidence should have gone to the jury. Neither of these requirements was met.

Judge Hand may have felt that he made amends for these omissions in another way. Seditious conspiracy is not a speech offense, and it has never been suggested that there need be any danger, clear and present or remote and improbable, of execution of the conspiracy before it is punishable. But Judge Hand does require that there be danger—in fact, imminent danger—of the execution of the seditious conspiracy as a condition of punishing the defendants for advocating Marxism-Leninism. This seems to indicate that he does not really believe in his seditious conspiracy; that he views the case as a speech case rather than a seditious conspiracy. But of course the seditious conspiracy is necessary to supply the danger that makes the speech offense punishable. Judge Hand does not really balance the scale by omitting the requirement of proof of the seditious conspiracy on the one hand and adding a totally unnecessary requirement of danger from the conspiracy on the other.

Judge Hand's explicit formulation of the argument is as we have described. It straddles the ground between a treatment of the case as a speech case and a treatment of it as a nonspeech offense, seditious conspiracy. It may, however, appear to the reader that he was not forced to this position in order to sustain a conviction. Two alternative lines of argument may appear to have some plausibility.

First of all, it might be thought that the conspiracy to advocate Marxism-Leninism raised a probable danger without a pro-Soviet seditious conspiracy. According to Judge Hand's formulation of Marxism-Leninism, war might be considered a "propitious occasion" for revolution; and war was imminent in 1948 when the indictment was found. It is immaterial that there is no evidence that the defendants advocated sedition in the event of war with the Soviet Union. The doctrine does not distinguish between wars; any war will do. What is wrong with this is the assumption that facts can be equated to abstract doctrine. It is simply not plausible to regard any war at all as the "propitious occasion" for revolution. It is notorious that there was no Communist revolution during World War II. Of course not, it will be replied; during that war the United States and the Soviet Union were allies. But during a war between the United States and the Soviet Union, Communists would engage in sedition, for the Communist party is an agency of the Soviet Union. The adoption of this position concedes that it is not possible to support the conviction on the theory that advocacy of Marxism-Leninism by itself raises a probable danger; there must be added a pro-Soviet seditious conspiracy, which is entirely distinct from the conspiracy to advocate Marxism-Leninism. This is obviously true. It is possible to entertain all the Marxist-Leninist views which Judge Hand finds to have been proved at the trial and also to believe that the Soviet Union is a counterrevolutionary force that must be crushed. Presumably this was the case with the first defendants convicted under the Smith Act, a group of Trotskyists; their Marxism-Leninism taught them that the Soviet Union was the great enemy of Marxism-Leninism.[33] On the other hand, it is possible to sympathize with the Soviet Union to such an extent that one would support it in war without entertaining the views described as Marxism-Leninism. This, we are told, is the case with most Russian citizens. There is a fatal disjunction between the teaching that was proved—Marxism-Leninism—and the facts necessary to support conviction—guilt of seditious conspiracy. We are back in the position of Judge Hand. The danger flowing from the speech arises from an imputed but unproved guilt of a nonspeech offense.

The second possible line of argument runs like this. The defendants have taught an abstract doctrine called Marxism-Leninism which by itself would not raise a danger. The defendants are not shown to have formed a pro-Soviet seditious conspiracy. But the defendants are warmly sympathetic to the Soviet Union, and will probably commit sedition or other crimes. By their teaching of Marxism-Leninism they have achieved influence over their pupils, so that they will probably be able to induce the pupils to commit sedition too. This theory is of particular interest because it is relied upon by Justice Frankfurter in his concurring opinion in the Supreme Court. He agrees that the defendants have not been shown to have committed seditious conspiracy: "Mr. Justice Douglas quite properly points out that the conspiracy before us is not a conspiracy to overthrow the Government"; "There are no reliable data tracing acts of sabotage or espionage directly to these defendants"; and "There appears to be little reliable evidence demonstrating directly that the Communist party in this country has recruited persons willing to engage in espionage or other unlawful activity on behalf of the Soviet Union." The jury made no findings about the character of the Communist party beyond its advocacy of revolution. But the Court may take judicial notice of other facts. These facts are that: (1) "The Communist doctrines which these defendants have conspired to advocate are in the ascendancy in powerful nations which cannot be acquitted of unfriendliness to the institutions of this country"; (2) "In 1947, it has been reliably reported, at least 60,000 members were enrolled in the Party"; (3) "A Canadian

Royal Commission appointed in 1946 to investigate espionage reported that 'the Communist movement was the principal base within which the espionage network was recruited'"; (4) The English spy Dr. Klaus Fuchs was a Communist; (5) "Evidence supports the conclusion that members of the Party seek and occupy positions of importance in political and labor organizations"; and (6) "Former Senator Robert M. La Follette, Jr., has reported his experience with infiltration of Communist sympathizers into congressional committee staffs" in *Collier's*. These facts "would amply justify a legislature in concluding that recruitment of additional members of the Party would create a substantial danger to national security."[34]

Establishing the facts that make defendants guilty of felony is a new function for judicial notice; and one may doubt that facts of this order, however established, are adequate for the task. But at least this line of argument escapes one difficulty that confronts Judge Hand. If one does not assume seditious conspiracy, it is no longer embarrassing that there is no seditious conspiracy in the record. Of course, the "probability" of the danger is considerably less impressive than when one proceeds on the theory of seditious conspiracy; but Justice Frankfurter is willing to dispense with probability. Nevertheless, the heart of the difficulty remains. Structurally this argument parallels Judge Hand's. This too is a Y-shaped argument. We have in the one branch the advocacy of Marxist-Leninist doctrine; in the other branch, not a pro-Soviet seditious conspiracy but an evil propensity toward pro-Soviet crimes. The advocacy is not punished because it raises a danger of a Marxist-Leninist revolution for the overthrow of capitalism in the indefinite future. The danger relied upon is immediate and is of a different order; it is a danger of pro-Soviet activities. There appears to be no close causal link between the speech that is punished and the evil character that justifies the punishment. The speech enters the argument only because it is supposed to be a means by which the defendants sour the dispositions of their pupils. The case is only in a casual way a speech case. The speech becomes a convenient peg on which to hang an indictment the substance of which is supplied by the defendants' malignancy.

Like the argument of Judge Hand, this argument lies halfway between the theory of a speech offense and the theory of a nonspeech offense. In all the previous speech cases, the speech when uttered initiated a chain of events which passed out of the control of the speaker. This chain of events might be subjected to a clear and present danger test, or the Court might, as in the *Gitlow* case,[35] be satisfied with a "dangerous tendency"; but the danger, whatever it was, flowed solely and irrevocably from the speech. Here, however, the speech raises no danger without the threat of subsequent culpable conduct quite different from that called for in the speech. Two elements are needed to create the defendants' guilt: the speech which advocates the overthrow of capitalism, and the bad character that raises the probability of miscellaneous pro-Soviet activities. This goes beyond the *Gitlow* case. Gitlow was held accountable for the recommendations he made in his speech, on the theory that others might follow those recommendations. Dennis is held accountable for actions he never recommended at all, on the theory that he and his associates are a bad lot and there is a danger that they will commit those actions.

It is clear that the defendants could not have been punished solely on the ground that they had evil dispositions and would probably commit crimes in the future. It has been held to be compatible with due process of law to carry out a temporary preventive detention on the ground of suspected bad character of the persons detained,[36] but it cannot be made a crime, punishable by imprisonment for a stated term of years, to have a bad character or an evil state of mind. The common law requirement that there be an overt act in addition to an evil intent is regarded as an element of due process in the field of criminal law. The law of conspiracy is no exception to the rule, for the formation of a conspiracy constitutes the requisite overt act. In the *Dennis* case there is, to be sure, a conspiracy; but it is a conspiracy to advocate Marxism-Leninism, not a conspiracy to commit sedition. The conspiracy to advocate Marxism-Leninism is accompanied by the evil intent of advocating Marxism-Leninism; but the imputed evil intent of committing sedition is not accompanied by any conspiracy to commit sedition. There is no overt act appropriate to the alleged evil disposition which will make the evil disposition punishable under the due process clause. The due process clause forbids Congress to make it a crime not to be considered trustworthy.

Judge Hand avoided these profitless blind alleys. He affirmed the convictions for the advocacy of Marxism-Leninism on the theory that the defendants were guilty of seditious conspiracy. This procedure simplifies the task of prosecutors enormously. If you have a defendant who is "probably" guilty of violating a nonspeech statute but have not the evidence to convict under that statute, indict under a speech statute, and the court will convict under the speech statute. The question of guilt under the nonspeech statute need not even go to the jury, as it did not here. The court will take judicial notice of probable guilt of the nonspeech offense in order to support conviction under the speech statute. There need be no relation between the speech and the substantive offense; the speech need not be in itself punishable.

The decision written by Chief Justice Vinson for four judges in the

Supreme Court is a kind of blurred copy of Judge Hand's opinion. Like Judge Hand, the Chief Justice rejects the requirement of imminency in the clear and present danger test. That requirement had been intended for isolated agitation such as that of Gitlow.[37] But a lesser degree of danger will suffice in the case of a conspiracy, because a conspiracy raises a greater danger than individual advocacy! That lesser degree of danger is defined by the grave and probable danger test of Judge Hand. How is probability established? As with Judge Hand, by the assumption that the defendants are not only guilty of the speech offense for which they were convicted but also of the nonspeech offense of seditious conspiracy.

The formation by petitioners of such a highly organized conspiracy, with rigidly disciplined members subject to call when the leaders, these petitioners, felt that the time had come for action, coupled with the inflammable nature of world conditions, similar uprisings in other countries, and the touch-and-go nature of our relations with countries with whom petitioners were in the very least ideologically attuned, convince us that their convictions were justified on this score.

If these are the facts, there is of course no need to prove any kind of danger; the First Amendment does not protect seditious conspiracy. But evidently a danger is required, and probability here as with Judge Hand is defined in terms of imminency. But, as with Judge Hand, the danger does not flow from the defendants' advocacy. Their fault is not the advocacy of an abstract doctrine called Marxism-Leninism; it is imputed guilt of seditious conspiracy. The Chief Justice goes on to make this clear: "And this analysis disposes of the contention that a conspiracy to advocate, as distinguished from the advocacy itself, cannot be constitutionally restrained. It is the existence of the conspiracy which creates the danger."

The danger created by a conspiracy to advocate, "as distinguished from the advocacy itself," is the danger of advocacy. The danger created by a seditious conspiracy is the danger of sedition. Clearly, it is of the latter that the Chief Justice is speaking. This opinion creates a middle ground between the law of free speech and the law of seditious conspiracy. Where no conspiracy to commit a substantive crime has been made, a conviction cannot be had under the conspiracy statute. Advocacy of the substantive crime can be punished only after an appraisal of the likelihood that the advocacy will be influential. But *conspiracy to advocate* may be punished without meeting the requirements either of the law of free speech or of the law of seditious conspiracy. This is done by effecting a confusion between conspiracy to advocate and seditious conspiracy.

Justice Frankfurter rejected the clear and present danger test, and admitted that the grave and probable danger test was disingenuous. He would himself apply what has sometimes been called the "rational basis" test. It is not for the Court to reverse a legislative decision unless it is clearly erroneous. And "there is ample justification for a legislative judgment that the conspiracy now before us is a substantial threat to national order and security." Probably he does not actually mean that Congress in passing the Smith Act in 1940 arrived at "a legislative judgment" concerning "the conspiracy now before us"—a conspiracy which, according to the indictment, came into existence in 1945. But if he means "conspiracies of the order of the conspiracy now before us," we are left with another problem. For Congress did not define the order of conspiracies it wished to punish. The language of the act is so broad that it applies, as Judge Hand remarked, to "a half crazy zealot on a soap box, calling for an immediate march on Washington."[38] However, in the separability clause Congress instructed the courts to determine the coverage of the act: "If any provision of this Act, or the application thereof to any person or circumstances, is held invalid, the remainder of the Act, and the application of such provision to other persons or circumstances, shall not be affected thereby." This provision, which Judge Hand and the Supreme Court held not to be void for indefiniteness, makes it clear that there was no legislative judgment on any particular order of conspiracies; it might, indeed, be called a delegation of legislative power to the courts.[39] This time Justice Frankfurter's habitual deference to legislative judgment is misplaced.

As we have already seen, Justice Frankfurter's argument then proceeds to establish a danger resulting from the conspiracy to advocate in the same way as Judge Hand. The conspiracy to advocate a Marxist-Leninist revolution for the overthrow of capitalism may be punished because the defendants and their pupils are persons of bad character, and persons of bad character are dangerous.

Justice Jackson gives a new interpretation to the clear and present danger test. "The test applies and has meaning where a conviction is sought to be based on a speech or writing which does not directly or explicitly advocate a crime but to which such tendency is sought to be attributed by construction or by implication from external circumstances." He insists that "even an individual cannot claim that the Constitution protects him in advocating or teaching overthrow of government by force and violence." Moreover, it is possible to punish a conspiracy to advocate, even where the advocacy has not occurred. "The Constitution does not make conspiracy a civil right." Since "conspiracy" is merely a denigratory term for "association," this means that there is no civil right of association.[40]

Justice Jackson did put his finger on an essential feature of the case. "What really is under review here is a conviction of conspiracy, after a trial for conspiracy, on an indictment charging conspiracy, brought under a statute outlawing conspiracy. With due respect to my colleagues, they seem to me to discuss anything under the sun except the law of conspiracy." Certainly the heart of the case lies in the fact that the charge was under a conspiracy statute. The strategy of the Court was to fudge over the difference between a conspiracy to advocate revolution and a seditious conspiracy. This is what really distinguishes the *Dennis* case from the *Gitlow* case. Gitlow was not convicted under a conspiracy statute. His individual advocacy could not be converted into a seditious conspiracy. In the *Dennis* case a conspiracy to advocate could be run over into a seditious conspiracy.

As Mr. John Raeburn Green, in his petition for rehearing on behalf of the defendant Gates, asked:[41]

> May it not fairly be said, from a review of all this, that the real crime for which these petitioners have been convicted and the conviction affirmed, lay in their subservience to and readiness to obey the order of Soviet Russia, our enemy in the "cold war"? Is not this really quite a different thing from punishing them for what the indictment charged, conspiring to teach and advocate the doctrines of the Marxist-Leninist books?

The upshot of the whole matter is, of course, that ten defendants went to jail for five years, and one for three, and that the Department of Justice is free to proceed with its announced plan of prosecuting twelve thousand other political offenders. However, as Justice Jackson said, "Communism will not go to jail with these Communists. No decision by this Court can forestall revolution whenever the existing government fails to command the respect and loyalty of the people and sufficient distress and discontent is allowed to grow up among the masses." This does not mean that the decision was politically insignificant. Mr. Justice Frankfurter described the political consequences of his own decision thus:

> It is a commonplace that there may be a grain of truth in the most uncouth doctrine, however false and repellent the balance may be. Suppressing advocates of overthrow inevitably will silence critics who do not advocate overthrow but fear that their criticism may be so construed. No matter how clear we may be that the defendants now before us are preparing to overthrow our Government at the propitious moment, it is self-delusion to think that we can punish them for their advocacy without adding to the risks run by loyal citizens who honestly believe in some of

the reforms these defendants advance. It is a sobering fact that in sustaining the convictions before us we can hardly escape restriction on the interchange of ideas.

The legal consequences are more difficult to predict. The fact that the result of the *Dennis* case can be achieved only under a conspiracy statute is not a serious limitation, since the mere hiring of a hall or the publication of a pamphlet may constitute a conspiracy.[42] The appropriate technique of repression now seems to be to pass statutes forbidding conspiracies to speak words of one sort or another, rather than to forbid the speech itself. How far will the Court permit Congress to go? Justice Douglas, dissenting, observed that we have entered "territory dangerous to the liberties of every citizen." Justice Black concluded that the majority position "waters down the First Amendment so that it amounts to little more than an admonition to Congress. The Amendment as so construed is not likely to protect any but those 'safe' or orthodox views which rarely need its protection." But perhaps the dissenting justices were merely ingenuous. Chief Judge Hand had already warned us: "I often wonder whether we do not rest our hopes too much upon constitutions, upon laws and upon courts. These are false hopes; believe me, these are false hopes."[43]

7

LEGISLATIVE DISQUALIFICATIONS AS BILLS OF ATTAINDER

The separation of powers was first introduced into political discussion during the English Civil Wars of the seventeenth century by the political party known as Levellers.[1] The object was to insure that persons be judged by general and prospective rules. If the legislative authority should decide a particular case, it might be tempted through partiality or prejudice to improvise a special rule for the situation. So the separation of powers was intended to achieve that impartiality in government which Aristotle called "the rule of law."

The doctrine of checks and balances was also introduced into political discussion during the Civil Wars, and with the Stuart Restoration in 1660 it became the official description of the English constitution.[2] King, Lords, and Commons were in a condition of equilibrium. "Like three distinct powers in mechanics, they jointly impel the machine of government in a direction different from what either, acting by itself, would have done; but at the same time in a direction partaking of each, and formed out of all; a direction which constitutes the true line of the liberty and happiness of the community."[3] By the time Blackstone wrote these words, the tripartite division of legislative power had already yielded to what we call today the cabinet system.

The separation of powers was an idea about law; checks and balances was an idea about legislation. The proposition that men should be judged by general and prospective rules implies nothing about the composition

---

Reprinted from *Vanderbilt Law Review* 4 (1951): 603–19. Used by permission of *Vanderbilt Law Review*.

of political forces in the legislature. It does imply a division of function between the framing of rules on the one hand and the administration of rules on the other.

Most of the early American constitutions explicitly endorsed the separation of powers—those adopted by Virginia, Maryland, and North Carolina in 1776, by Georgia in 1777, by Massachusetts in 1780, and by New Hampshire in 1784. The principle was incorporated in the distribution of powers in the new federal Constitution as well as in all state constitutions adopted subsequently. Yet of the early state constitutions J. Allen Smith has said truly: "The English system of checks and balances was discarded for the more democratic one under which all the important powers of government were vested in the legislature."[4]

Checks and balances, however, reappeared with a new object. Thomas Jefferson protested against the Virginia constitution that it left the executive and judiciary dependent upon the legislature. "If therefore the legislature assumes executive and judiciary powers, no opposition is likely to be made; nor, if made, can it be effectual: because in that case they may put their proceedings into the form of an act of assembly, which will render them obligatory on the other branches."[5] To prevent this, he believed that "the powers of government should be so divided and balanced among several bodies of magistracy, as that no one could transcend their legal limits, without being effectually checked and restrained by the others."[6] The same reasoning underlies some of the debates in the Constitutional Convention and the argument for checks and balances in the *Federalist*, where, indeed, Madison quotes Jefferson as an authority.[7] The federal Constitution incorporated both the separation of powers and checks and balances; and this plan prevailed in the revision of state constitutions thereafter.

So the separation of powers was invented in order to insure generality and prospectivity in law. Checks and balances was originally a political doctrine, but with Jefferson it became a device to protect the separation of powers. It has never lost its political flavor; instead, it has imparted that flavor to the separation of powers, so that today both ideas are commonly thought to rest on the proposition that the division of power is a salutary political principle. This proposition has fallen on hard times, with the consequence that both the separation of powers and checks and balances are in considerable disrepute among political scientists.

Nevertheless, it is true that the most characteristic mechanical features of our Constitution were not addressed to the problem of power but to an idea about law. Their purpose was further implemented by the prohibitions on bills of attainder and ex post facto laws, by the contract clause in the federal Constitution, and by the prohibitions on special legislation in state constitutions. This idea about law is one of the most striking features in the Anglo-American constitutional tradition. The passages in which John Locke,[8] Blackstone,[9] and Daniel Webster[10] endorsed it are well known. Webster's definition—"By the law of the land is most clearly intended the general law; a law, which hears before it condemns; which proceeds upon inquiry, and renders judgment only after trial"—epitomizes a whole epoch of constitutional law.[11]

The most familiar example of the evils of joining legislative with judicial power is the bill of attainder. Protest first arose against the use of this device in 1641.[12] It was with difficulty that the last bill of attainder in English history, that of Sir John Fenwick in 1696, was pushed through Parliament. In America bills of attainder were passed in colonial days and during the Confederation, but informed opinion disapproved of the practice, and it was apparently without debate that the framers of the federal Constitution forbade both the national government and the states to pass bills of attainder.

At the time of the adoption of the Constitution, the term "bill of attainder" had been given no precise legal definition. Only with the constitutional prohibitions on action of this sort did definition become necessary. There was, to be sure, a body of practice to which the term referred and which supplied guidance. Justice Story described the practice thus:[13]

> Bills of attainder, as they are technically called, are such special acts of the legislature as inflict capital punishments upon persons supposed to be guilty of high offenses, such as treason and felony, without any conviction in the ordinary court of judicial proceedings. If an act inflicts a milder degree of punishment than death, it is called a bill of pains and penalties.... In such cases, the legislature assumes judicial magistracy, pronouncing on the guilt of the party without any of the common forms and guards of trial, and satisfying itself with proofs, when such proofs are within its reach, whether they are conformable to the rules of evidence or not. In short, in all such cases, the legislature exercises the highest power of sovereignty, and what may be properly deemed an irresponsible despotic discretion, being governed solely by what it deems political necessity or expediency, and too often under the influence of unreasonable fears or unfounded suspicions.

Bills of pains and penalties commonly imposed civil disabilities, such as ineligibility for public office. It is in this area that controversy has arisen. Clearly it is appropriate for the legislature to establish qualifications for officeholders and for the practitioners of a wide variety of professions and callings. Clearly it is inappropriate for the legislature to assume judicial magistracy, determining fault without trial, and by legislative act to exclude the persons thus condemned from office or a designated vocation. The problem is to distinguish these two situations.

Two tests have been advanced, one by Justice Field and the other by Justice Frankfurter. It is not certain that Justice Field considered his test to be exhaustive; Justice Frankfurter believed his to be so. It appears that each correctly identified a particular use of the bill of attainder; but there are situations which are explained by neither test. The bill of attainder clause, like the ex post facto clause, can be violated in more than one way.

In *Cummings* v. *Missouri*[14] Justice Field held that a provision in the Missouri constitution of 1865 which forbade persons to hold office or to follow certain callings unless they took an elaborate oath disclaiming participation in or sympathy with the rebellion was a bill of attainder. He relied heavily but not exclusively upon the assertion that many of the disclaimers required by the oath were irrelevant to many of the activities in question. This made them penalties rather than qualifications. In *Pierce* v. *Carskadon*[15] in 1872 a West Virginia statute which conditioned access to the courts upon the taking of an oath that the applicant had not participated in the rebellion was held to be a bill of attainder. Here the disability clearly had no relevance to the privilege. Probably no one will quarrel with the holdings in these cases.[16]

On the other hand, relevant disqualifications have also been held to be penalties. In Ex parte *Garland*,[17] a companion case to *Cummings* v. *Missouri,* a federal statute which required attorneys to take an oath disavowing any part in the rebellion as a condition of admission to practice in the federal courts was declared to be a bill of attainder. It could not honestly be said that this requirement was irrelevant to the practice of law. Justice Field, who wrote the opinion, made no such claim, although he purported to rely on *Cummings* v. *Missouri.*[18] And in *United States* v. *Lovett*[19] a provision of a congressional appropriation act which barred three named individuals from public employment as subversive was held to be a bill of attainder, although subversiveness is clearly a valid disqualification for public employment.[20]

In his concurring opinion in the *Lovett* case, Justice Frankfurter undertook to shift the problem. He argued that the disqualification of the three was not a bill of attainder because Congress had failed to announce that it was punishing a past offense. The bills of attainder with which the framers were familiar had always nakedly declared their purpose; consequently no congressional act is a bill of attainder if Congress does not state a prohibited purpose. This viewpoint was rejected by the majority in the *Lovett* case, but it apparently contributed to the holding in *American Communications Association* v. *Douds,*[21] where Chief Justice Vinson upheld section 9(h) of the Labor Management Relations Act of 1947, the Taft-Hartley Act,[22] which denied the facilities of the National Labor Relations Board to unions whose officers did not file affidavits disavowing membership in the Communist party. The Chief Justice attempted to distinguish the *Cummings, Garland,* and *Lovett* cases:[23]

> Those cases and this also, according to the argument, involve the proscription of certain occupations to a group classified according to belief and loyalty. But there is a decisive distinction: in the previous decisions the individuals involved were in fact being punished for *past* actions; whereas in this case they are subject to possible loss of position only because there is substantial ground for the congressional judgment that their beliefs and loyalties will be transformed into *future* conduct. Of course, the history of the past conduct is the foundation for the judgment as to what the future conduct is likely to be; but that does not alter the conclusion that sec. 9(h) is intended to prevent future action rather than to punish past action.

This of course flies in the teeth of the *Garland* and *Lovett* cases, in both of which the alleged fault which gave rise to the disqualification was highly pertinent to future conduct. If there is a difference in the legislative intent, the Court can have discovered it only by intuition. But the premise as well as the application seems to be unsound. It means that a completely capricious measure must escape condemnation as a bill of attainder because it is grounded on no offense whatever. If the legislature is forbidden to punish a man for cause, surely it is forbidden to punish a man without cause. It has also been suggested that under some circumstances a measure penalizing a future act or omission may be a bill of attainder.[24]

Justice Frankfurter justified his truncation of the bill of attainder clause by saying, "There are other provisions in the Constitution, specific and comprehensive, effectively designed to assure the liberties of our citizens."[25] Presumably he refers to the Bill of Rights and the due process clause of the Fourteenth Amendment; but these were not in existence when the Constitution was drafted. If Mr. Justice Frankfurter is right, the state legislatures, from 1789 to 1868, were in no way restrained by the federal Constitution from putting a man to death by vote, provided that his life had been so blameless that he escaped all reproach for past conduct. Probably the framers of the Constitution did not intend that.

Justice Field was right in saying that the imposition of a disability on a principle of discrimination which is irrelevant to the proscribed activity discloses a penal intent. Justice Frankfurter was right in saying that a measure avowedly intended to penalize past conduct discloses a penal intent. But these are not the only ways in which legislatures are capable of giving effect to penal intents, nor are they the only cases in which courts have uncovered such intent. *United States* v. *Lovett* presents a third type of case; Ex parte *Garland* presents a fourth. Both these cases involve what Freund called "censorial" judgment of individuals.[26] In the *Lovett* case the individuals were measured against a general standard; in *Garland* the standard was defined in terms of the individuals.

"In such cases, the legislature assumes judicial magistracy, pronouncing on the guilt of the party without any of the common forms...of trial...."[27] The bill of attainder clause forbade a process as well as an outcome. In many cases the outcome would not be a penalty without the use of the prohibited process. Administrative discharge of subversive employees is not a penalty, but legislative discharge is penal. By appropriate judicial proceedings an attorney may be disbarred, and this is not penal, although direct legislative proscription, as in Ex parte *Garland*, is penal. It appears that there are certain results which the legislature is forbidden to achieve directly; the legislative decision is a bill of attainder.

There is nothing objectionable about the legislative establishment of appropriate qualifications for an office or vocation. In establishing qualifications the legislature spells out the affirmative qualities which are implied in the activity to which admission is restricted.[28] These qualifications do not exclude any designated person or class of persons; all are eligible to acquire the qualifications. The establishment of disabilities is another matter. Here the legislature does not confine itself to reciting the requisite virtues which serve as qualifications; it specifies a characteristic which it declares to constitute a disqualification. Even here, however, the legislative action is not necessarily censorial or penal. When the legislature declares that persons suffering from communicable disease shall not be teachers, or that epileptics shall not drive automobiles, it is not passing judgment on those excluded. Another example is afforded by the statutes which impose disabilities upon persons occupying a given position or status because admitting them to the activity in question would expose them to a temptation to which many people would succumb. Public servants have been excluded by law from business transactions related to their official positions,[29] and from political activities;[30] railroads are forbidden by the commodities clause to haul the products of their own mines or factories;[31] certain shippers are forbidden to act as freight forwarders;[32] elaborate restrictions hedge in officers and employees of banks[33] and investment companies,[34] the directors of other concerns,[35] trustees under trust indentures,[36] and some other persons who act in a fiduciary capacity. Although these disqualifications are established in terms of anticipated fault of character, there has been no legislative judgment of the particular persons. The legislature relies upon common knowledge, that temptation leads in some cases to misconduct. Its judgment is in terms of general psychology. It is discharging the proper legislative function of establishing general rules of conduct, not the judicial function of appraising the faults of individuals.

We have a very different situation when the legislature inquires into the character of the persons disqualified.[37] Here the disqualification results from a legislative judgment that the proscribed persons possess a characteristic not found in people in general. It rests, not upon general psychology, but upon evidence. It is a determination, judicial in nature, of culpability or blameworthiness. It is usual to assess such states of mind in awarding penalties—criminal penalties, civil penalties, exemplary damages. Blackstone said that crime involved a "vicious will."[38] In *Bailey* v. *Drexel Furniture Company*[39] Chief Justice Taft found the child-labor tax a penalty rather than a tax because its incidence depended on a state of mind: "Scienter is associated with penalties not with taxes."[40] And in *United States* v. *Lovett* it was held that when Congress determined that certain named individuals were "subversive" and were unfit for public employment this was a bill of attainder.

There are, of course, cases in which character is evaluated in administrative and judicial proceedings and the outcome is not a penalty—in licensing and in awarding the custody of children, for example. In such proceedings the issue ordinarily cannot be raised by the tribunal which judges (although in revocation of licenses it may be); the test applied has already been established by a general law; the hearing observes appropriate procedural safeguards. In legislative disqualification, on the other hand, the legislature takes the initiative in raising the question; it enacts the standard which it applies; and it proceeds, as Story pointed out, "without any of the common forms ... of trial, and satisfying itself with proofs, when such proofs are within its reach, whether they are conformable to the rules of evidence or not."[41] Acting in this manner discloses a penal intent.

So viewed, the bill of attainder clause is a more specific implementation of the separation of powers. It represents the view universally held at the time of the framing of the Constitution: "It is the peculiar province of the legislature to prescribe general rules for the government of society; the application of those rules to individuals in society would seem to be the duty of other departments."[42]

This problem has arisen rather seldom, because legislatures have seldom had the impertinence to attempt to appraise character. In upholding the Ohio law for the licensing of dealers in securities, Justice McKenna remarked: "It is certainly apparent that if the conditions are within the power of the State to impose, they can only be ascertained by an executive officer. Reputation and character are quite tangible attributes, but there can be no legislative definition of them that can automatically attach to or identify individuals possessing them, and necessarily the aid of some executive agency must be invoked."[43] And in *Bratton* v. *Chandler*[44] the Court at least thought it possible that the due process clause requires that an applicant for a license as real estate broker or salesman be given a hearing and an opportunity to meet adverse evidence. It construed a Tennessee statute to authorize these, on the ground that any other interpretation would raise grave constitutional doubts.

If we assume that the bill of attainder clause forbids the legislature to inquire into character and to impose a disability as a result of its findings, *Hawker* v. *New York*[45] must be considered. In that case the Court upheld a New York statute which forbade persons who had previously been convicted of felony to practice medicine.[46]

> But if a state may require good character as a condition of the practice of medicine, it may rightfully determine what shall be the evidences of that character. We do not mean to say that it has an arbitrary power in the matter, or that it can make a conclusive test of that which has no relation to character, but it may take whatever, according to the experience of mankind, reasonably tends to prove the fact and make it a test.... Whatever is ordinarily connected with bad character, or indicative of it, may be prescribed by the legislature as conclusive evidence thereof. It is not the province of the courts to say that other tests would be more satisfactory, or that the naming of other qualifications would be more conducive to the desired result. These are questions for the legislature to determine.
>
> It is not open to doubt that the commission of crime, the violation of the penal laws of a State, has some relation to the question of character. It is not, as a rule, the good people who commit crime. When the legislature declares that whoever has violated the criminal laws of the State shall be deemed lacking in good moral character it is not laying down an arbitrary or fanciful rule—one having no relation to the subject-matter, but is only appealing to a well recognized fact of human experience; and if it may make a violation of criminal law a test of bad character, what more conclusive evidence of the fact of such violation can there be than a conviction duly had in one of the courts of the State? The conviction is, as between the State and the defendant, an adjudication of the fact. So if the legislature enacts that one who has been convicted of crime shall no longer engage in the practice of medicine, it is simply applying the doctrine of *res judicata* and invoking the conclusive adjudication of the fact that the man has violated the criminal law, and is presumptively, therefore, a man of such bad character as to render it unsafe to trust the lives and health of citizens to his care.

The difference between this and the *Lovett* case is readily apparent. Here, as in establishing disqualifications for persons of given status because of the temptation offered by the conjunction of the status and the proscribed activity, the legislature acts upon a "well recognized fact of human experience." It does not take evidence or inquire into the character of individuals; in fact, the individuals involved are unknown at the time the act is passed. This seems to be a legislative rather than a judicial act.

In conformity with *Hawker* v. *New York* it has been held that conviction of felony may be made a disqualification for public office.[47] Other statutes have carried the policy further. New York has also disqualified dentists and veterinarians who have been convicted of felony.[48] The secretary of the treasury is instructed not to license any person to deal in liquor who has been convicted of felony within the past five years, or of a misdemeanor under any federal law relating to liquor within three years.[49] The Investment Company Act bars those convicted of crimes in securities transactions from any connection with investment companies.[50] Persons adjudged guilty of violating the antitrust laws by monopolizing or attempting to monopolize radio communication are not eligible for licenses to construct or operate radio stations.[51] The Packers and Stockyards Act appears to be unique in that it requires no judicial proceeding; the secretary of agriculture is authorized to refuse a license to deal in poultry if he finds that the applicant has engaged in any of the practices forbidden by the act within two years prior to his application.[52]

All these statutes rest on the argument of *Hawker* v. *New York*. There is in each case a notorious connection between the disqualification and the activity barred. No legislative investigation of character occurs; the disability is testified to by "the experience of mankind."

But this was true also of the disqualification in Ex parte *Garland*. It cannot be argued that the disqualification in the *Garland* case was irrelevant to the activity in question. As Justice Miller pointed out in his dissent: "Fidelity to the government ... [is] among the most essential qualifications which should be required in a lawyer."[53] So it has been held that admission to the bar may be conditioned not only on loyalty but on willingness to bear arms.[54] Past acts of disloyalty are certainly evidence, as notorious as a judicial conviction of felony, of unfitness. Nor is there any difference in the reliability of the findings of fact. Inability to take the oath establishes the fact as surely as a judicial conviction would have done. Where, then, is the difference between the *Garland* and *Hawker* cases?

The difference is this. In the *Hawker* case, as we have seen, the legislature did not identify the persons disqualified. These were determined by an impersonal process outside the control of the legislature. In the *Garland* case the statute must be treated as though it enumerated all the persons affected and by name excluded them from the practice of law. Garland's position was exactly as though the statute read: "A. H. Garland, having served in the legislature of the Confederacy, is forbidden to practice law in any federal court." The device of the oath made it possible to pass a John Doe bill of attainder covering thousands and to put upon the individuals proscribed the duty, under pain of prosecution for perjury, of filling in their own names in the blanks. As Justice Frankfurter said of the *Garland* and *Cummings* cases: "That the persons legislatively punished were not named was a mere detail of identification. Congress and the Missouri legislature, respectively, had provided the most effective method for insuring identification."[55]

Certainly it is proper for the legislature to establish a general requirement of loyalty for attorneys. What is improper is for the legislature to disqualify specified individuals. The statute in Ex parte *Garland* both created and applied a disqualification. It is irrelevant that those proscribed actually came within the disqualification. It could not be otherwise, since the disqualification was tailored to the exact dimensions of the proscribed group. Congress acted simultaneously as legislature and judge. This is forbidden by the bill of attainder clause.

There is one point of difference between the *Garland* and *Lovett* cases. In *Garland* those disqualified were undoubtedly justly accused of the fault, for the fault was defined in terms of them, and they in terms of the fault. In the *Lovett* case there is only a legislative finding, which on the merits appears to deserve no respect, that those accused were justly accused of a fault which others were capable of sharing. But in both cases the legislature undertook to impose a disqualification for fault of character; in both cases this was held to be a bill of attainder, for the reason that Congress is forbidden to make these judgments about individuals.

In three of the five cases involving exculpatory oaths disclaiming a designated fault of character—in *Cummings* v. *Missouri,* Ex parte *Garland,* and *Pierce* v. *Carskadon*—the Supreme Court has held the requirement to be a bill of attainder. In the fourth, *Davis* v. *Beason,*[56] in which the Court upheld a territorial statute imposing a test oath for the disfranchising of Mormons, the attainder question was not discussed. In *American Communications Association* v. *Douds*[57] the exaction of a disclaimer of membership in the Communist party was upheld. The Court merely remarked that the imposition of oaths is a common and necessary practice. This is certainly true. The requirement of an oath that the applicant possesses the necessary affirmative qualifications for an office or activity is not a legislative determination of fault. The requirement of an oath that one lacks a disqualification not turning on blameworthiness—a disclaimer of epilepsy by an applicant for a driver's license, for example—is not a legislative judgment of fault of character. But the requirement of an exculpatory oath is the legislative identification of persons upon whom the legislature has passed a blanket judgment of fault of character; it is an instrument in a bill of attainder.

To summarize, it is proper for the legislature to establish relevant disqualifications for an office or occupation so long as these are not grounded on a legislative determination of fault or culpability in the persons disqualified; but a legislative disqualification so grounded is a bill of attainder. So the *Lovett* case stands for the proposition that the legislature may not apply a valid standard of disqualification to individuals and itself determine their blameworthiness. According to Ex parte *Garland*, the legislature may not enact a blanket disqualification of a group of individuals who are identified by the possession of a common characteristic, even when that characteristic would be a proper disqualification in an administrative or judicial adjudication of character. It is, however, proper for the legislature to disqualify a class of persons, not in terms of its own appraisal of their fault but in the light of "the experience of mankind," when the members of the class are ascertained by some other organ of the government than the legislature—in *Hawker v. New York*, by the judiciary through a conviction of felony.

As we have seen, the *American Communications Association* case conflicts with both the *Lovett* and *Garland* cases. It requires extended discussion. The majority opinion was written by Chief Justice Vinson and was subscribed to by Justices Burton and Reed. Justices Frankfurter and Jackson concurred in upholding the non-Communist affidavit. The Court applied to the legislative decision the substantial evidence rule, which is appropriate in reviewing the actions of administrative tribunals.[58]

Substantial amounts of evidence were presented to various committees of Congress, including the committees immediately concerned with labor legislation, that Communist leaders of labor unions had in the past and would continue in the future to subordinate legitimate trade union objectives to obstructive strikes when dictated by Party leaders, often in support of the policies of a foreign government.... At the committee hearings, the incident most fully developed was a strike at the Milwaukee plant of the Allis-Chalmers Manufacturing Company in 1941, when that plant was producing vital materials for the national defense program.... Congress heard testimony that the strike had been called solely in obedience to Party orders for the purpose of starting the "snowballing of strikes" in defense plants.

Under this decision, ex parte testimony from interested witnesses, consisting largely of hearsay, is enough to justify Congress in determining that designated persons possess a special character which warrants their exclusion from any activity under federal control. In his dissent Justice Black said: "Under today's opinion Congress could validly bar all members of these [minority] parties from officership in unions or industrial corporations; the only showing required would be testimony that some members in such positions had, by attempts to further their party's purposes, unjustifiably fostered industrial strife which hampered interstate commerce."[59] This is not far-fetched. It may be said also that if persons should testify before congressional committees as to the validity of the *Protocols of the Elders of Zion,* this would, under the majority opinion, constitute substantial evidence on the basis of which Congress might legitimately exclude all Jews from positions in national banking associations. The Court was at pains to point out that "accidents of birth and ancestry under some circumstances justify an inference concerning future conduct...."[60] To come closer to the question in hand, what is to prevent Congress from passing an act forbidding a union to be represented before the National Labor Relations Board by John L. Lewis? He has frequently interrupted interstate commerce, and "substantial evidence" of discreditable motives, if that be necessary, would be forthcoming from the appropriate sources.

The Chief Justice's opinion deals summarily with the attainder issue. He disposes of the *Cummings, Garland,* and *Lovett* cases by saying that in those cases individuals were being punished for past actions; here the statute is grounded on apprehension over future conduct, although "the history of the past conduct is the foundation for the judgment as to what the future conduct is likely to be."[61] It would be hard to think of better evidence of disloyalty or a more ominous augury for future conduct than Garland's past career. It also seems odd to concede that Lovett, Watson, and Dodd had been subversive because the House of Representatives had accumulated "substantial evidence" to that effect, and yet to say that the House was moved by the desire to punish past conduct rather than to guard against future harm in barring them from public employment.

But it cannot be said that the Chief Justice's opinion rests entirely on this distinction. He converts the disqualification into a qualification by pointing out that the act proscribes only present membership in the Communist party. "Here the intention is to forestall future dangerous acts; there is no one who may not, by a voluntary alteration of the loyalties which impel him to action, become eligible to sign the affidavit."[62] This statement does not seem to be a fair report of the facts.

The non-Communist affidavit is not an affidavit of loyalty or an avowal of any principles which impel to action. It is merely a disclaimer of membership in an organization. Members of the organization have been proscribed by Congress because Congress has formed an adverse judgment on their character; nor are they allowed any opportunity to profess or demonstrate the loyalty or the virtuous principles which the Court seems to believe are implied in the non-Communist affidavit. This is clearly enough a disqualification. To be sure, the statute allows them to escape the disqualification by resigning from the organization; but this does not involve an abjuration of political strikes or the affirmative profession of any new loyalty. Assuming that a man is wedded to political strikes, coercion such as this will merely deepen his attachment. The escape from disqualification afforded by the statute does not convert the disqualification into a qualification; rather, it exhibits the statute as what it is—a measure which attaches a legislative penalty to membership in an organization, and serves no other purpose whatever.

Justice Frankfurter concurred, saying that "the judgment of Congress that trade unions which are guided by officers who are committed by ties of membership to the Communist Party must forego the advantages of the Labor Management Relations Act is reasonably related to the accomplishment of the purposes which Congress constitutionally had a right to pursue."[63] But the provision of the oath which required disavowal of belief in the overthrow of the government by illegal or unconstitutional methods appeared to him too vague to meet the requirements of due process.

Justice Jackson found his own reasons for concurring in the majority decision. "If the statute before us required labor union officers to forswear membership in the Republican Party, the Democratic Party, or the Socialist Party, I suppose all agree it would be unconstitutional. But why, if it is valid as to the Communist Party?"[64] Justice Jackson found: "From information before its several Committees and from facts of general knowledge, Congress could rationally conclude that, behind its political facade, the Communist Party is a conspiratorial and revolutionary junta, organized to reach ends and to use methods which are incompatible with our constitutional system."[65] A footnote refers the reader to literature which "the Congress *may or could have considered*"[66] in arriving at the conclusion endorsed by Justice Jackson. The least trammeled of our justices, he is not disturbed by the fact that Congress failed to reach this conclusion. In the *Herzog* case counsel for the NLRB, in defending the oath, conceded:[67]

I agree there is a wide gap there and Congress did not find—I might as well make it clear now—it did not find and it did not purport to find, and it is our position that it did not need to and could not properly have found, that the Communist party advocates the doctrine of the violent overthrow of the Government by force or other unconstitutional means. That is just no part of this case.

After a lengthy argument resting chiefly on his own views on political science, Justice Jackson asserts that Congress, by virtue of its rational conclusions about the nature of members of the Communist party, might properly protect interstate commerce from Communists. But he proceeds to argue with equal vehemence against the remainder of the oath, which requires a disclaimer of revolutionary opinions. It is proper to exclude from the ranks of union officials Communists who are willing to swear allegiance to the United States and to disavow a belief in "the overthrow of the United States Government by force or by any illegal or unconstitutional methods," but not to bar those who cannot swear such allegiance or disclaim such belief. It is a little hard to justify this. Justice Jackson finds the difference in the presence of an overt act, affiliation, in the case of Communists, and the absence of an overt act in the case of revolutionaries. The non-Communist oath is an inquiry into action, whereas the oath as to opinion unassociated with an overt act is "thought control." This objection raises some doubt as to the propriety of exacting an oath of allegiance from public officials and members of the armed forces.

Justices Douglas, Clark, and Minton took no part in the decision. In *Osman* v. *Douds*,[68] however, a case involving the same issues, Justice Minton, who had already upheld the oath in its entirety on the Court of Appeals,[69] concurred in the Chief Justice's opinion. Justice Douglas concurred with Justices Frankfurter and Jackson in declaring the oath as to opinion void, and since he considered the statute not to be severable he did not pass on the requirement of the non-Communist affidavit. Justice Black dissented in both cases; in the *American Communications Association* case he wrote a brief but eloquent opinion in which he denounced the requirement of an affidavit as to membership or opinion as a bill of attainder and a violation of the First Amendment. This was unavailing. The attitude of the majority of the Court was aptly stated by Justice Jackson. The Court must act, he said, "in the light of present-day actualities, not nostalgic idealizations valid for a simpler age."[70] The nostalgic idealization at stake in the *American Communications* case was that stated by James Madison: "The accumulation of all powers, legislative, executive, and judiciary, in the same hands, whether of one, a few, or many, and whether hereditary, self-appointed, or elective, may justly be pronounced the very definition of tyranny."[71]

8

THE IMPACT OF ECONOMIC LEGISLATION UPON THE SUPREME COURT

Analytically we can distinguish two questions which must be confronted by the courts in a constitutional system which practices judicial review. The first is the purely legal question of the meaning or content of terms employed in the fundamental law: What is commerce, a legislature, a bill of attainder? Ordinarily this question is settled by a definition, formula, or rule which attaches legal consequences to a generalized set of facts. A comforting illusion of certainty pervades this realm of pure doctrine. The second question is in a sense factual. It may be in part evidentiary, but this is not the most significant aspect of the problem. In the most abstract form, it is a question of causal efficacy: Will a given statute produce the factual results prescribed or proscribed by a formal doctrine? But measuring the factual relation of cause to consequence involves the application of legal standards of proximity, so that the question becomes a legal one. And the definition of standards of proximity exerts a tension on the content of the doctrinal formulation: our two questions are only analytically distinct.

The Supreme Court has employed a variety of techniques for coping with these problems.[1] During the whole of the nineteenth century, the principal reliance was the practice of converting factual questions into purely legal ones by introducing a formula which would immediately subsume the undisputed facts under a legal rubric. So the boundaries of the commerce power were fixed by definition; its counterpart the state

---

Reprinted from *Journal of Public Law* 6 (1957): 296-318. Reprinted by permission of the *Emory Law Journal* (formerly *Journal of Public Law*) of the Emory University School of Law.

police power was similarly defined, and then was ringed in with other formulae, the "original package" doctrine and the like. The privileges and immunities clause of Article IV responded to the same treatment. But as early as *McCulloch* v. *Maryland*[2] it was necessary to inquire into the factual appropriateness of the means chosen to a legitimate end; the question arose again with the issuance of treasury notes during the Civil War.[3] The due process and equal protection clauses obviously raised factual issues.

But this was not soon recognized. Counsel persisted in presenting cases in terms of legal dogmas, with little or no effort to establish the facts which might determine constitutional issues. The Supreme Court supplied the want in various ways. If the "necessary operation" of the statute was unconstitutional, this disposed of the matter.[4] Otherwise the presumption of constitutionality justified upholding the statute without inquiry into fact. But sometimes the Court took judicial notice of facts which validated or invalidated the statute.

The fatal fascination of precedent tended to convert such holdings, however established, into legal doctrines independent of fact. So the category of "business affected with a public interest" automatically validated some statutes and invalidated others. The doctrine of freedom of contract reversed the presumption of constitutionality in its area. It was primarily to combat the conclusiveness of such dogmas that Louis D. Brandeis introduced the Brandeis brief; the purpose was to restore the presumption of constitutionality by adducing facts which showed the inapplicability of the dogma.

Even in the nineteenth century evidence against a statute was sometimes offered at a trial. The practice came slowly into popularity in the twentieth century, and the Supreme Court considered evidence when it was available. Between 1924 and 1938 the Court several times sent cases back for trial when the facts which determined constitutionality were not established. This practice might have displaced other expedients and supplied a partial solution to the problem of establishing constitutional facts, but the promise was never fulfilled. For twenty years there had been complaint at the invalidation of economic legislation passed or challenged under the commerce clause, the due process clause, and the equal protection clause. This was an attack upon dogmatic jurisprudence; unfortunately, the alternatives to dogma offered by the critics were those devices which were loose enough to sustain the legislation in question without serious inquiry—the presumption of constitutionality, judicial notice, the Brandeis brief. The fatal pliability of these tools, which unfitted them for any intellectual purpose, went unnoticed.

As is well known, the Court made a moral capitulation to its critics in 1937. This was not merely a surrender to political pressures but an act of contrition. Dogmas which led to the invalidation of statutes—and even some others—were renounced. Those techniques for coping with factual questions which brought more or less automatic validation—necessarily the techniques which were least exact and searching—were indiscriminately exalted. While it could not be said that the trial of facts was abandoned, it receded in popularity.

This uncritical repentance amounted to an abdication of judicial review of economic legislation. The new law in this field exerted an inevitable gravitational pull upon all other topics in constitutional law, and led there also to a leveling of rule and structure and the triumph of the looser techniques for establishing fact. In the 1920s and 1930s there was complaint at the impact of the Supreme Court on economic legislation: we are suffering now from the impact of this legislation upon the Court. A brief review of the alternative expedients employed for the purpose of establishing facts will clarify the problem and show the unsatisfactory state of the law today; perhaps it will also afford a basis for affirmative conclusions on the subject.

James Bradley Thayer called judicial review "the American doctrine of constitutional law."[5] This was a "substantive principle" which was accompanied by a "rule of administration."[6] This rule of administration taught that a court "can only disregard the Act when those who have the right to make laws have not merely made a mistake, but have made a very clear one—so clear that it is not open to rational question."[7]

As early as 1796 Justice Chase said that if there were a power of judicial review he would exercise it only "in a very clear case";[8] in 1798 Justice Iredell said that the power should be used only "in a clear and urgent case."[9] In 1800 Justice Paterson said that there must be "a clear and unequivocal breach of the Constitution, not a doubtful and argumentative implication."[10] In 1819 Chief Justice Marshall said: "It is but a decent respect due to the wisdom, the integrity, and the patriotism of the legislative body by which any law is passed, to presume in favor of its validity, until its violation of the Constitution is proved beyond all reasonable doubt."[11] Thereafter the rule of administration was rendered as a presumption of constitutionality.

Apparently Thayer would have confined federal use of the presumption to cases in which federal statutes were challenged, and would not have given state statutes the benefit of a presumption when challenged under the federal Constitution.[12] Willoughby argued that state legislatures should also enjoy the benefit of the presumption, except where state action was alleged to collide with "the power of Congress" under the commerce clause, the bankruptcy clause, or some other delegated power.[13] This fits the language of the cases in the twentieth century fairly well.

The formulations of the earlier cases, and of Thayer and Willoughby, attach a presumption of constitutionality to legislative decisions on questions of law as well as of fact. As late as 1953 Justice Jackson took the same position.[14] But there seems to be no case in which Congress was actually given the benefit of a presumption that its definition of the commerce power was legally correct, or a state legislature was allowed latitude in determining that one or another purpose was a proper objective under the police power. The very idea of a legal order precludes an indeterminate area of tolerance about legal terms which purport to define or limit legislative power, so that the terms relax their boundaries to accommodate new assertions of power. It is one thing to say that a legal term may have different meanings in different factual settings, and quite a different one to say that it may have a variable meaning in a single setting. Where the question is one of pure law, the idea of two defensible answers is intolerable. A presumption of constitutionality may describe a subjective state of indecision on the part of the judge, but it can hardly describe the condition of the law.

Thayer attempts to deal with this problem by rejecting the proposition that "there is but one right and permissible way of construing the constitution."[15] "In the class of cases which we have been considering, *the ultimate question is not what is the true meaning of the constitution, but whether legislation is sustainable or not.*"[16] Italics will not take the place of logic. The legislation is not sustainable unless it is in conformity with the Constitution. If we assume that the presumption enlarges the constitutional power of the legislature, the problem is then to establish the boundaries of this enlarged power; the question is "What is the true meaning of the Constitution" thus diluted. This question of (enlarged) constitutional power is an intellectual question to be solved by inquiry and not by a second presumption. Nor has the presumption actually played any part in determining questions of pure law. Justice Holmes, who was as vigorous a champion of the presumption as we have had, never indulged a legislature in a presumption of constitutionality when the question was purely legal. He would not permit a legislature, on whatever plausible pretext, to exercise police power when the appropriate legal instrument was eminent domain.[17]

It is in the area of fact that the presumption has played a part. In this area, indeed, it has played several parts. In its most general form it has defined the conditions which a statute must meet when it is challenged on constitutional grounds. The statute will be sustained if there are reasonable grounds in fact for the legislative decision.

But who determines reasonableness? The most readily intelligible test assigns this function to the Court. But ordinarily the Court shifts it to other shoulders. So it says that if a substantial body of opinion supports the legislative decision, if the subject seems fairly debatable, the Court will not attempt to resolve the issue but will uphold the statute. Accordingly, it has held that the state may require persons to be vaccinated because some medical opinion upholds the practice, even though other medical opinion opposes it;[18] the state may forbid the sale of boric acid as a food preservative in reliance on scientific opinion, although other scientific opinion pronounces the substance harmless.[19] Congress may limit the amount of alcohol a physician may prescribe for a patient, although the physician himself believes that a larger quantity is called for and some medical opinion supports him.[20]

Thayer formulated the presumption in terms of an abstract reasonable man. This was not such a man as we actually see in legislatures— "untaught it may be, indocile, thoughtless, reckless, incompetent."[21] The presumption of constitutionality is "that reasonable doubt which lingers in the mind of a competent and duly instructed person who has carefully applied his faculties to the question. The rationally permissible opinion of which we have been talking is the opinion reasonably allowable to such a person as this."[22] Holmes was much less definite. He sometimes spoke of opinions which a reasonable man reasonably might hold;[23] on other occasions he seems to employ as a touchstone the "otherwise reasonable" man—if the opinion is one which might conceivably be entertained by a man reasonable on other topics, it will validate the statute, however irrational the particular opinion may be.[24] Nor are the standards of "otherwise reasonableness" exacting: apparently the untaught, indocile, reckless, and incompetent legislator automatically meets them. So in 1910 Holmes held for a unanimous Court that a San Francisco ordinance forbidding the burial of bodies within the city limits did not violate due process.[25] The Laurel Hill Cemetery asked the Court to take judicial notice of expert opinion to the effect that no possible health hazard was involved, but Holmes declared that "if every member of this bench clearly agreed that burying grounds were centers of safety, and thought the board of supervisors and the supreme court of California wholly wrong, it would not dispose of the case. Opinion still may be divided, and if, on the hypothesis that the danger is real, the ordinance would be valid, we should not overthrow it because of our adherence to the other belief." Nevertheless, in his First Amendment dissents[26] Holmes showed no deference to legislative judgment.

Another line of cases identifies the reasonable man with local authorities.[27] So in eminent domain cases it is said that what constitutes a public use depends upon local conditions, of which the state legislature and the state court are the best judges. A decision of the state court upholding an exercise of eminent domain will be reversed only when it is "clearly wrong," and none has ever been found to be so.[28] When zoning laws limiting the height of buildings[29] or fixing building lines[30] have been upheld by the state court, the Supreme Court has affirmed on the ground of the superior topographical knowledge of the local authorities. Deference to local knowledge has been extended to topics not obviously peculiar to a locality. There seems to be nothing local about the considerations involved in determining the validity of a milk ordinance[31] or an ordinance against cemeteries,[32] but here too the Court expressed unwillingness to substitute its judgment for that of the better-informed local authority. The Court has assumed that the Pennsylvania legislature had access to facts which showed that aliens constituted a peculiar threat to wild game in Pennsylvania,[33] and that the Cincinnati City Council knew that "aliens in Cincinnati are not as well qualified as citizens" to conduct public billiard and pool rooms.[34]

Another means of sampling the opinion of reasonable men is to count statutes. The Court has sometimes adverted to the widespread adoption of statutes on a topic as evidence of a need and therefore of the validity of the statute.[35] This approach implies that there might be doubt as to the validity of the first statute, but the passage of the tenth statute would remove the doubt. The same kind of thinking has given rise to the counting of judges from various jurisdictions who have passed on the same problem or similar problems. The palm of superior rationality is awarded to the majority if they uphold the legislation; oddly enough, no one has attempted to compile such informal majorities against a statute, although of course marshaling adverse judicial decisions is an old practice. In recent years, however, there has been less occasion to reinforce the decision of the legislature which passed the statute from other sources; the judgment of the legislature itself becomes the standard of reasonableness.

Of course, it must be understood that the Court is not obliged to employ any of these tests. If the state court has upheld the state legislature and the Court nevertheless wishes to strike the statute down, it says something like this: "When a party appeals to this court for the protection of rights secured to him by the Federal Constitution, . . . upon these matters this court cannot, in the proper performance of its duty, yield its judgment to that of the state court."[36] In the field of railroad and utility rate-fixing, no presumption of validity attaches to rates fixed by the legislature or an administrative agency, although the administrative agency now enjoys a measure of allowable discretion in valuation.[37]

Establishing the validity of legislation by reference to the opinions of others is as irrational as it would be to establish its invalidity by the same means. If this were an appropriate test, Gallup would be a greater judge than Marshall. Yet this is what the presumption of constitutionality has led to. It means shifting the responsibility of decision onto others who are not officially charged with the duty, nor in most cases equipped to discharge it. It seems especially odd that when state action is alleged to violate the federal Constitution the very action complained of should be taken as virtually conclusive evidence of its own validity; but this is the consequence of adopting state action as the standard of rationality. If local judgment is controlling, was Justice McReynolds wrong in his dissent in *Moore* v. *Dempsey*[38] when he argued that a conviction obtained by mob violence was due process because the district judge, "acquainted with local conditions," had so held?

The presumption of constitutionality is a standard of reasonableness; in addition, it is a rule of evidence. It puts upon the party challenging the statute the burden of offering proof.[39] There are exceptions. A statute may be void on its face.[40] Or its "necessary operation" may demonstrate its unconstitutionality.[41] Or judicial notice may supply evidence invalidating the statute; in this case there is no need to offer factual proof of invalidity.

And in special cases there may be a presumption of unconstitutionality. It appears that legal dogmas have sometimes attained so absolute a character as to render presumptively invalid any statute which collided with them, and thus to shift the burden of proof. During the ascendancy of freedom of contract, it was necessary for the party relying on a statute abridging this right to show exceptional circumstances which justified the restraint.[42] During the life of the "preferred position" test, a statute restricting a First Amendment freedom was "infected with presumptive invalidity."[43] It has been held that when a state tax is levied on vehicles operating in interstate commerce, "the tax cannot be sustained unless it appears affirmatively, in some way, that it is levied only as compensation for the use of highways or to defray the expense of regulating motor traffic."[44] Similarly, it has been held that when a state charges a fee for the supervision of public utilities, and combines the administration of this function with other functions, it must affirmatively show the reasonableness of the fee.[45] In the law of free speech the doctrine of previous restraint has invalidated a statute by its sole force, despite some evidence of reasonableness.[46]

Perhaps one further generalization can be ventured. When the presumption of constitutionality obtains, a statute will be sustained over a challenge if a tenable view of the facts supports its validity; the Court will not attempt to evaluate either this or a competing view.[47] But in areas where the presumption of unconstitutionality prevails, it appears that the party supporting the statute must affirmatively demonstrate that his view of the facts is the correct one.[48] It is not enough to show that many people hold it, or that it has some plausibility. This is a much more rigorous standard of proof.

In many cases it does not seem improper to put on the person challenging the statute the burden of going forward. But in other branches of the law special considerations have been found to justify exceptions to the general rules as to burden of proof, and this may be true also in constitutional law. How would an alien set about proving that aliens did not menace wildlife more than citizens, or that they were as responsible licensees of poolrooms as citizens? Here is an apt case for a doctrine which will shift the burden of proof; and there are no doubt others.

Questions of fact enter into constitutional law at either or both of two levels. Borrowing from Kenneth C. Davis, we may call them legislative facts and adjudicative facts.[49] In constitutional law legislative facts will be theories of causal efficacy which purport to link undisputed facts to a constitutionally legitimate result and thereby justify the statute, or, conversely, undertake to show that the statute leads to an illegitimate result. Disputes about legislative facts are disputes about scientific or social processes rather than about the immediate posture of the litigants. Adjudicative facts are the disputed basic facts which concern the litigants; e.g., what is the value of the physical properties of a public utility? At least until recently the presumption of constitutionality has operated in a somewhat different way at these two levels of fact. To understand its impact we must consider them separately.

Whether vaccination[50] or boric acid[51] is harmful, whether any patient of any physician needs more than a pint of whiskey every ten days[52] —these are questions of legislative fact on which the Court has sustained the statute without attempting to arrive at the truth, relying on a substantial body of scientific opinion as evidence and rejecting the adverse opinion. A question of legislative fact may also be a question of social or economic causation. Here the Court dips into social science to determine whether any theory of social or economic processes will attribute the desired result to the statute. In *Rast* v. *Van Deman*[53] the Court thought it a tenable hypothesis that if trading stamps are given with a purchase, "by an appeal to cupidity, they lure to improvidence." In *Gitlow* v. *New York*[54] the Court indulged the New York legislature in the theory that revolutions are caused by literature, which "may kindle a fire that, smouldering for a time, may burst into a sweeping and destructive conflagration." If a tenable hypothesis can be found which supports the statute, it is conclusive.[55] It is therefore not error to exclude evidence of legislative facts attacking the validity of the statute, for such evidence is irrelevant.[56] In 1938 Justice Stone said:[57]

By their very nature such inquiries, where the legislative judgment is drawn in question, must be restricted to the issue whether any state of facts either known or which could reasonably be assumed affords support for it. Here the demurrer challenges the validity of the statute on its face and it is evident from all the considerations presented to Congress, and those of which we must take judicial notice, that the question is at least debatable whether commerce in filled milk should be left unregulated, or in some measure restricted, or wholly prohibited. As that decision was for Congress, neither the finding of a court arrived at by weighing the evidence, nor the verdict of a jury can be substituted for it.

This rule has forced the Court to desperate measures. Since the presumption renders the statute invulnerable, the Court must, in order to invalidate a statute which it considers absurd, destroy the presumption. It has done this by denying that any conceivable theory would support the proposition that used shoddy might menace health;[58] by insisting that there was absolutely no evidence of the reasonableness of the shrinkage allowance of the Nebraska bread-weight law;[59] by asserting that the ownership of shares in a corporation operating a drugstore had no conceivable relation to public health.[60] These decisions all drew strong protests from Justices Brandeis and Holmes, who were able to come up with some sort of validating theory each time; but it is doubtful that anything valuable was lost when any of these statutes was struck down. It would be more decent, however, if the Court were able to weigh the competing arguments, rather than being forced by the law of presumption to deny the existence of one of them, and even to take liberties with the record.

Of course, where the presumption of unconstitutionality prevails, the burden is on the party sustaining the statute to offer proof—and genuine proof rather than a hypothesis. In one other area, that of the commerce clause, the Court did not supply legislative facts by presumption until after the constitutional revolution of 1937. It could not be said that a presumption of unconstitutionality obtained here, but the Court scrutinized all federal legislation on its merits[61] until the Filled Milk Act was upheld, in part on the basis of the presumption, in 1938.[62] It appears that state legislation challenged under the commerce clause still lacks the shelter of the presumption so far as reasonableness goes, although it has been said that the burden of proof is on the party challenging the statute.[63]

The question is a difficult one. Some problems of legislative fact could be settled on their merits rather than by presumption. The Court has not hesitated to weigh the most intricate factual problems of the effects of state legislation on state interests, on the one hand, and on interstate commerce on the other.[64] There are other questions which no one can solve, and the courts ought not to try. But they do in fact purport to solve them through the device of the presumption. They adopt the opinion of some more or less respectable group, or the findings of government agencies. Opposing opinion, however respectable, is disregarded. In the end, therefore, the decision follows automatically from the enactment of legislation; the validity of the legislative decision is vouched for by the existence of the pressure group which manipulated the legislature. Not a legal rule but a folk saying describes this practice: "The longest pole knocks down the perisimmon." It is merely a hoax to call the application of such a test an intellectual process.

In the nineteenth century the Court dealt with equally uncharted areas by discriminating between types of problems and erecting legal doctrines. This procedure might bring order here; but today the presumption is triumphant and dogma is in discredit.

The legitimacy of the legislative objective is a question of law; the appropriateness of the means is a question of legislative fact. But the whole program will collapse if it restricts a constitutionally protected right and there is not a state of affairs which justifies the restriction. Congress may have the power to cope with a housing shortage in Washington, D.C.; rent control may be an appropriate means; but if there is in fact no housing shortage the restriction is invalid.[65] The existence or nonexistence of the shortage is a question of adjudicative fact. Of course, the problem of adjudicative facts takes as many different forms as there are constitutional rights, but it always involves disputes as to evidential matters of a tolerably familiar sort.

The existence of the adjudicative facts implied in a statute is presumed. This version of the presumption was introduced in *Munn* v. *Illinois*[66] in 1877 when Chief Justice Waite said: "For our purposes we must assume that, if a state of facts could exist that would justify such legislation, it actually did exist when the statute now under consideration was passed." This formulation has been repeated in both due process[67] and equal protection[68] cases. When it is used, the Court ordinarily recites the facts which it supposes to exist. But in *O'Gorman & Young* v. *Hartford Ins. Co.*[69] Justice Brandeis hardly troubled to imagine a justificatory set of facts: "It does not appear upon the face of the statute, or from any facts of which the court must take judicial notice, that in New Jersey evils did not exist in the business of fire insurance for which this statutory provision was an appropriate remedy." Therefore the existence of validating facts was presumed. This has become a common approach in recent years.

Unless the law has been changed by recent decisions, the presumption of the existence of adjudicative facts, unlike the presumption attached to prima facie legislative facts, is not conclusive. The party challenging the statute may introduce countervailing evidence. The question then arises as to whether the presumption survives in the face of adverse proof.[70] In 1934, in *Borden's Farm Products Co.* v. *Baldwin*,[71] Chief Justice Hughes spoke of the challenger's "burden of establishing that the classification is without rational basis."[72] But he also said that "where the legislative action is suitably challenged, and a rational basis for it is predicated upon the particular economic facts of a given trade or industry, which are outside the sphere of judicial notice, these facts are properly the subject of evidence and of findings."[73] When a question of fact has been reduced to proof, the evidence should supply an answer; there seems to be no further room for a presumption. In the case of adjudicative facts, therefore, the presumption seems to operate merely as a rule of evidence putting the burden of going forward upon the party challenging the statute.

Somewhat more rigorous than the presumption of constitutionality is the use of judicial notice. Here the Court itself vouches for the existence of the primary facts which sustain the constitutionality of legislation, and for the causal link which relates these facts to the constitutional objective; or the Court recognizes facts which invalidate the legislation. Nevertheless, the range and content of judicial notice are indeterminate. The Court itself has spoken of facts of which it *may* take judicial notice in order to sustain a statute,[74] and adverse facts of which it *must* take judicial notice[75] when a statute is challenged: evidently the first area is broader than the second. Nor does judicial notice always yield reliable data: often the facts noticed are highly controversial, and sometimes they are flatly untrue. To sustain statutes challenged under the equal protection clause, the Court has taken judicial notice of the facts that criminals throng to large cities,[76] and that night work threatens the morals of women in large cities.[77] It has noticed that itinerant vendors of patented articles have a "fluency of speech and carelessness regarding the truth of their representations" which justify special treatment.[78] Here the Court is noticing adjudicative facts, and of course it often sustains statutes by taking judicial notice of legislative facts which constitute a plausible and therefore conclusive hypothesis.

It is rather seldom that the Court has noticed adjudicative facts in order to invalidate a statute,[79] but it has often noticed legislative facts for this purpose. In striking down the first Railroad Retirement Act, the Court imported a psychology from some unknown source: "If 'morale' is intended to connote efficiency, loyalty, and continuity of service, the surest way to destroy it . . . is to substitute legislative largess for private bounty and thus transfer the drive for pensions to the halls of Congress and transmute loyalty to employer into gratitude to the legislature."[80] Critical to the argument holding the Agricultural Adjustment Act unconstitutional was the assumption that the prices a farmer receives reflect his costs,[81] a proposition no economist could tolerate.

One of the commonest sources of facts of which judicial notice has been taken is "common knowledge." Encyclopedias and other reference works have been used. Justice Brandeis used to develop extensive bodies of data from monograph literature, reports of government agencies, and the like and introduce them into his opinions by judicial notice.[82] But there are limits, albeit vague ones, to judicial notice. In *Chastleton Corp.* v. *Sinclair*[83] Justice Holmes for the Supreme Court took judicial notice of the fact that the housing emergency in the District of Columbia had ended, but remanded the case to the trial court to determine whether there had been an emergency at various earlier dates. In *Borden's Farm Products Co.* v. *Baldwin*[84] the Court refused to take judicial notice of conditions in the New York milk market and remanded the case to the trial court to determine those conditions.

Judicial notice is of course an indispensable tool.[85] But it has inescapable vices. It does not rest on testimony, which means that the party adversely affected has had no opportunity to disprove the often dubious data noticed. Nor can the question be argued on appeal, for it emerges only in the final opinion of the Supreme Court. When an administrative tribunal privately notices facts in this manner, it violates the due process clause.[86] This defect might be cured if a petition for a rehearing were granted, but rehearing has never been granted on the score of erroneous notice. In any case, it would be better to avoid the error than to cure it.

Judicial notice attempts to establish the relevant facts by some other means than presumption or conjecture. But within its limits it has grave faults; and there are areas of fact which lie altogether beyond its limits. Two other methods remain. Evidence on the facts has been received in the trial court both to attack and to sustain statutes. What is called the Brandeis brief is also used to establish facts; its use is principally to sustain statutes, since it undertakes only to demonstrate possibilities, and the proof of invalidity requires more than this.

State courts have rejected evidence on some specialized problems, such as the legislature's compliance with the procedural requirements of the state constitution, and have sometimes said more broadly that no factual evidence could be considered in a challenge to a statute except that of which the court must take judicial notice.[87] But for the most part these latter cases involved legislative facts; as we have seen, the Supreme Court itself has never considered adverse evidence when any plausible theory of causation would attribute a proper effect to the statute. Except for two recent cases, the Supreme Court has always required the consideration of adjudicative facts which would render a statute unconstitutional in application.[88]

State courts have even tried questions of legislative fact. In New York in 1885 expert testimony on the wholesomeness of oleomargarine was taken, and the Court of Appeals on this record concluded that the prohibition on the manufacture of this food was a denial of due process.[89] In the same year the same court considered adjudicative facts. It held that a statute forbidding the manufacture of cigars in tenements was unreasonable because the practice was not shown to cause any injury in the instant case: proof had been offered at the trial that the odor of tobacco did not escape from the manufacturer's room to annoy other tenants.[90]

In habeas corpus actions the consideration of adjudicative facts is inevitable.[91] In an equal protection case in 1885, on an uncontroverted record which showed discrimination against Chinese, the Supreme Court held that the administration of a San Francisco ordinance denied equal protection.[92] After 1890 it became usual to try adjudicative facts in due process cases.[93] Of course, the burden of proof is ordinarily on the challenger.

When the issues have been tried below, the Court arrives at its conclusions on the record, according appropriate respect to the findings of the trial court.[94] Or the relevant facts may be admitted by demurrer. In a series of cases between 1924 and 1938, when the trial court dismissed the complaint without taking evidence and the Supreme Court felt that a constitutional issue had been raised, it reversed and remanded the case for a trial of fact. This involved no doctrinal innovation, but the opinions showed more concern for facts than the Court has done before or since. In 1924 the Court remanded the *Chastleton* case[95] to the trial court to determine the adjudicative facts as to a housing shortage in the District of Columbia. In 1927 two equal protection cases were sent back for a determination of traffic conditions in Hammond, Indiana.[96] In 1934 *Borden's Farm Products Co.* v. *Baldwin*[97] raised an equal protection problem. The plaintiff had alleged a denial of equal protection in general terms but had pleaded no specific facts: the district court dismissed the complaint. The Supreme Court held that the constitutional issue had been adequately raised and remanded the case for a determination of the conditions in the New York milk market. A master was appointed; he found market conditions which justified the classification; the district court adopted his findings, and the Supreme Court affirmed.[98] This was a spectacular demonstration of the possibility of solving difficult constitutional questions by a trial of fact. In 1938 a due process question was sent back to the district court in Florida for a consideration of facts.[99] But in 1946 the Supreme Court upheld a New York court in refusing to admit evidence of adjudicative facts to show a denial of due process;[100] and in 1955, in a legal situation very like that in the *Borden* case, it dismissed certiorari instead of sending the case back for trial of the facts.[101] These decisions reflect the diminishing concern for facts.

Even in the nineteenth century appellate briefs instanced facts of which their authors hoped the Court would take judicial notice. The method emerged into prominence in 1877 in *Munn* v. *Illinios*,[102] when the Court accepted what might be called a reverse Brandeis brief. To show that the Illinois statute regulating grain elevators interfered with interstate commerce, plaintiff-in-error had supplied in his brief a detailed description of the industry, its magnitude, and its involvement in interstate commerce. Chief Justice Waite said, "We accept as true the statements of fact contained in the elaborate brief of one of the counsel of the plaintiffs in error,"[103] and held that these data showed the business to be one affected with a public interest and therefore subject to state regulation.

Those who complained for three decades of the decision in *Lochner* v. *New York*[104] were also admirers of the Brandeis brief. They overlooked the fact that Lochner, who challenged the limitation of the hours of bakers, supplied in his brief scientific data showing mortality rates and the health hazards of various trades, "all to the effect that the baking industry was at least average in the wholesomeness of its conditions."[105] The state offered no data but relied upon the naked presumption of constitutionality. The Court commented favorably on Lochner's data, and perhaps this suggested to Louis Brandeis the desirability of factual briefs in support of statutes. In *Muller* v. *Oregon*[106] Brandeis offered his famous brief in support of the limitation of the hours of labor of women. Gradually the Brandeis brief established itself, until today it is taken for granted.

Originally the purpose of the Brandeis brief was not to prove the existence of facts but of opinion: it was to show that reasonable men held or could hold the view of social and economic causation which underlay the statute. Likewise, when Justice Brandeis took judicial notice of data of the same sort, he represented it as evidence of nothing more than a hypothesis which would reinforce the presumption of constitutionality.[107]

The usefulness of the Brandeis brief depended upon the circumstances. Where the presumption of constitutionality obtained, the legislative facts which the brief supplied were enough to justify the statute. When it had become established that a limitation of the hours of labor was health legislation, the presumption attached and the Brandeis brief did the rest.[108] But when the minimum wage problem was subsumed under the doctrine of freedom of contract, a presumption of unconstitutionality obtained;[109] and in this case, as we have seen, a statute needs proof rather than a hypothesis to support it.[110] In the *Adkins* case on the District of Columbia minimum wage for women, Justice Sutherland found Felix Frankfurter's brief "only mildly persuasive."[111] Justice Holmes in dissent protested that it was meant to be nothing more; it was intended only to show that "the belief reasonably may be held."[112] But of course Justice Holmes had never accepted the proposition that restraints upon freedom of contract are presumptively invalid. It is quite possible that if Mr. Frankfurter had undertaken to supply proof of fact rather than of opinion he could have saved the statute.

Of course, the Brandeis brief may report genuinely reliable facts; it is more likely to be a conglomerate of fact and opinion. This is especially dangerous, for it facilitates what threatens to become a settled practice—plucking opinions from a Brandeis brief and treating them as fact by judicial notice. This has even happened with adjudicative facts. In the *Dennis* case[113] the majority of the Court took from the government's brief unproved allegations which had never been offered at the trial and which the defendants had had no opportunity to disprove, and used these ex parte assertions as solid evidence which supplied an essential element in the argument for affirming conviction.[114]

Presumably most people would agree that it is better to decide cases by facts than by opinion; but there can be no assurance that what the Brandeis brief offers is fact, or even informed opinion. No formal tests are applied to the material included in a Brandeis brief; anything in print can go in. It is common knowledge that printed matter, even from disinterested sources, is sometimes incomplete or erroneous, and that it may adopt completely mistaken interpretations. Whatever advantages the adversary procedure may offer for sifting out truth are not available in this method of presentation. Of course, the judges evaluate the materials with such expertness as they command; but if they possessed the knowledge requisite for an adequate appraisal they would not need the help of a Brandeis brief.

It seems especially inappropriate to employ congressional hearings and committee reports to supply the facts which determine the constitutionality of a federal statute. This is allowing one party to the litigation to build an ex parte record and then deciding the case on the basis of that record. But this is standard practice.

Since the close of the 1936 term, the Supreme Court has not held invalid anything that could be called economic legislation except state regulations and taxes challenged under the commerce clause, and a state tax challenged under the equal protection clause.[115] It first stated its new philosophy explicitly in 1941:[116]

> We are not concerned, however, with the wisdom, need, or appropriateness of legislation. Differences of opinion on that score suggest a choice which "should be left where * * * it was left by the Constitution—to the States and to Congress." . . . There is no necessity for the state to demonstrate before us that evils persist despite the competition which attends bargaining in this field. In the final analysis, the only constitutional prohibitions or restraints which respondents have suggested for the invalidation of this legislation are those notions of public policy embedded in earlier decisions of this Court but which, as Mr. Justice Holmes long ago admonished, should not be read into the Constitution.

This view has frequently been repeated or acted upon when the problem has been one of legislative facts.[117] The implication, however, that the new policy is confined to the area of economic legislation is misleading. The change was accomplished by the relaxation of tests of constitutionality, and necessarily the liberalized tests are applied in other fields as well.

When one considers that concern over the legal position of labor was a principal cause of the agitation that led to the revolution of 1937, the result is ironical. One of the most prominent consequences of the revolution has been the loss of the right to work. A state may in effect make the trade of pilot exclusive to and hereditary in a few families,[118] and may confine the occupation of barmaid to the wives and daughters of proprietors of bars.[119] It may make the trade of longshoreman dependent upon the discretionary approval of a waterfront commission which may exclude any person convicted of any of a number of crimes, a Communist or one who teaches communism, and any person who it thinks will be a bad influence on the waterfront.[120] New York may suspend the medical license of a doctor because he has been convicted in another jurisdiction of a crime which does not involve moral turpitude, has nothing to do with the practice of medicine, and is not an offense in New York.[121] Congress may exclude persons from employment in which they may interrupt the flow of interstate commerce if it has formed the opinion that they may take such action.[122] Congress may pass an antifeatherbedding statute aimed solely at James C. Petrillo.[123]

While the right to work has thus lost its constitutional status, right-to-work laws have been upheld. Under these the state may forbid the employer and his employees to contract freely; it may in substance, the Supreme Court held in the *Lincoln Union* case,[124] insert a term in the contract for the benefit of third persons who are not parties to the contract. In the latter case *Wolff Packing Co.* v. *Court of Industrial Relations*[125] was explicitly overruled, so that in case of disagreement between employer and employees in any industry the state may prescribe to the two parties the exact level of wages, hours, and working conditions.

The principal instrument of the new Court is the presumption of constitutionality. A "Green River" ordinance has been upheld when challenged under the commerce clause and the First Amendment because the municipality knew local conditions.[126] New York might well believe, because of local conditions, that it created a traffic hazard if the owner of a truck advertised the wares or services of another on the sides of his truck, but not if he advertised his own wares or services.[127] Scientific opinion will be accepted when it supports a statute, but when it does not, "the Due Process Clause does not require the legislature to be in the vanguard of science—especially sciences as young as human ecology and cultural anthropology."[128] Whereas in the past the Court regarded the fact that several legislatures had passed an act as evidence of the validity of the statute, Justice Frankfurter has discovered that the fact that eleven legislatures have rejected an act demonstrates that it should be upheld in other states where it is passed;[129] an appeal to the electorate is shown not to be hopeless. No doubt the legislature felt that the nepotism of the Louisiana pilot-licensing law was overbalanced by the benefits of "family and neighborly tradition."[130] Oklahoma probably had something in mind when she forbade fitting new frames to old lenses without a prescription while permitting the unsupervised sale of new glasses in ten-cent stores.[131] In the *Gobitis* case[132] the majority held that a reasonable man could believe that little Jehovah's Witnesses who were so unpatriotic as to refuse to salute the flag could be taught patriotism by expelling them from school and imprisoning their parents. This is the theory Archbishop Laud applied to the Puritans.

The use of the presumption on such questions of legislative fact is not novel, although the applications are sometimes startling. But the presumption has broken new ground in the field of adjudicative fact. Feiner alleged that three New York courts had deprived him of his rights under the First Amendment, but the Supreme Court denied this contention because all these courts had found it not to be true.[133] Because Congress heard ex parte testimony to the effect that Communists interrupted interstate commerce, the Court held that Congress might exclude them from office in unions certified by the National Labor Relations Board.[134] As we have seen, two cases have raised doubt as to the right of the aggrieved party to present evidence of adjudicative facts challenging a statute.[135]

Judicial notice has reached a new degree of particularity. Justice Jackson was particularly fond of the works of Claude Bowers and the *Encyclopedia of the Social Sciences;* he utilized the former in formulating a principle of statutory construction in *Collins v. Hardyman.*[136] His experience at Nuremberg supplied him with a rule of constitutional law in *Terminiello v. Chicago.*[137] Justice Frankfurter held that the closed shop was an evil on the basis of the utterances of Louis D. Brandeis of almost forty years earlier.[138] From Justice Frankfurter also we learn that "no one is better equipped than George F. Kennan to speak on the meaning of the menace of Communism and the spirit in which we should meet it."[139]

In the *Dennis* case Justice Frankfurter supplied the danger which justified the conviction of the defendants for conspiring to advocate revolution by taking judicial notice of six facts[140] which purportedly bore on their offense: (1) "The Communist doctrines which these defendants have conspired to advocate are in the ascendancy in powerful nations who cannot be acquitted of unfriendliness to the institutions of this country"; (2) "In 1947, it has been reliably reported, at least 60,000 members were enrolled in the Party"; (3) "A Canadian Royal Commission appointed in 1946 to investigate espionage reported that ... 'the Communist movement was the principal base within which the espionage network was recruited'"; (4) the English spy Dr. Klaus Fuchs was a Communist; (5) "Evidence supports the conclusion that members of the Party seek and occupy positions of importance in political and labor organizations"; and (6) "Former Senator Robert M. La Follette, Jr., has reported his experience with infiltration of Communist sympathizers into congressional committee staffs [in *Collier's*]." One wonders equally at the effrontery which supplies facts essential to conviction for felony by judicial notice and at the frivolous character of these facts. But this is not so bad as what Chief Justice Vinson did: he supplied the necessary danger by taking judicial notice of the fact that the defendants had organized a seditious conspiracy, an offense not charged or proved.[141]

On the other hand, the Court has on one occasion refused to take judicial notice of facts invalidating a statute. In a situation exactly comparable to the *Chastleton* case,[142] Justice Frankfurter said that such considerations were for the legislature.[143]

The Court has given some attention to fact in cases of coerced confessions, denial of counsel, and racial discrimination in the composition of juries.[144] In a few areas it has rejected the presumption of constitutionality. For a time, limitations of rights under the First Amendment were presumptively unconstitutional.[145] Legislation directed at persons of Japanese descent is in substance treated as presumptively invalid.[146]

In *Sweatt v. Painter*[147] the trial court found substantial equality between the Negro and white law schools, but the Supreme Court reversed because of facts "incapable of objective measurement but which make for greatness in a law school." In *McLaurin v. Oklahoma State Regents*[148] the Court found inequality in the record. In these cases the right to equal protection was said to be a "personal right"; the problem was one of adjudicative fact. In the *School Segregation Cases*,[149] however, the question was treated as one concerning a race, and the Court took judicial notice of legislative facts which overthrew the statutes.

No attempt has been made to rationalize the divergent policies which the Court is currently pursuing, but sooner or later the Court must establish formulae which discriminate between types of cases and justify differences in treatment.

Thus far we have discussed the problem in terms of the dichotomy of law and fact. The solution of questions involves distributing labeled sets of facts into appropriate legal cubbyholes; the judge is a mail clerk sorting mail. No doubt this conception has some validity; there are routine cases which call only for identification and not for thought. But the solution of new problems is an altogether different matter. According to John Dewey,[150] the act of thought is single, although it has many strands. It involves facts which prescribe a feasible goal, the erection of a conceptualized bridge from facts to goal, and the reciprocal adjustment of the criteria of factual relevance, the conceptual structure, and the goal, until thought comes triumphantly home with the problem solved. If this is true, the separation of the problem of constitutional adjudication into two independent stages misdescribes the process, and an attempt to employ it can have no other effect than to prevent an intelligent solution. The goal and the solution are the law, but relevance to fact and feasibility in terms of fact condition them both. The raw materials which require the achievement of the goal, and which are worked up into the solution, are the facts; but the relevance of the facts is reciprocally defined by the goal. The conceptual structure which intervenes between fact and goal is quasi-legal. It consists of formulations, at first tentative and provisional, of a logical order. They are always valid in the abstract, but they must be tested and rejected or adopted in terms of their relevance to the particular problem. The process of thinking is indivisible.

Nevertheless, our institutions have always accepted the law-fact dichotomy. They have assumed the feasibility of separating the determination of fact from the decision of questions of law. Complaint has been made that this analysis does not describe either the existing situation or any possible division of labor in the judge-jury relationship or in judicial review of administrative action.[151] In administrative law a series of cases has assigned the decision of questions of "mixed fact and law" to the administrative agency.[152] Analytically, these are all questions of pure law. In Dewey's terms, on the other hand, not merely these but all questions are questions of mixed fact and law. The real argument for deferring to administrative judgment on these questions is not "the specialized equipment of the Tax Court and the trained instinct that comes from its experience";[153] it is rather that a division of the function of decision frustrates solution of the problem. On the other hand, assigning the whole process to the administrative agency raises the possibility that that agency will build up a jurisprudence distinct from that of the ordinary courts, and seeking different goals. If we are to have a coherent legal order, the Supreme Court must supervise the processes of administrative agencies as well as those of the ordinary courts. Effective supervision cannot be achieved in terms of the law-fact dichotomy, nor can it be achieved by converting legal questions into questions of fact and exempting them from judicial scrutiny, as under the *Dobson* rule[154] —this is to make the administrative process quite aimless so far as the judiciary is concerned, although it need not, of course, be aimless from the point of view of the agency.

In reviewing the determinations of administrative tribunals and inferior courts, the Supreme Court has at any rate this recourse. If it concludes that the process has gone astray from the goal—perhaps this is what the "clearcut mistake of law" of the *Dobson* case means—it can reverse and remand for proceedings in the light of the goal as defined by the Court. The fact-finding process can be brought into line with the legal objective. But in judicial review of legislative action no such possibility exists. This seems to be an argument for the Court's accepting greater responsibility in determining the facts in constitutional cases.

Under the prevailing rules no effective scrutiny of legislative facts—no appraisal of the relation of the program to the goal—is possible. It would be better not to pretend to undertake it. Currently the principal effect of judicial review is to mislead the people by persuading them that a statute has undergone some sort of test and has demonstrated its validity in terms of constitutional goals, which is plainly untrue. If judicial review is to have any meaning, questions of legislative fact which are susceptible to solution should be solved; those not susceptible to solution should be relegated to the category of political questions. There is no possible excuse for not trying adjudicative facts if they are properly pleaded. To attempt to cope with constitutional questions without a reliable set of facts is to play with a twisted cue and an elliptical billiard ball.

But more is needed than facts and goal. The intellectual bridge between facts and goal is made of concepts, among which are the doctrines or dogmas we have repeatedly mentioned above. If particular concepts have not always been used selectively or appropriately, that is no reason for rejecting the tool. Hans Kelsen has said that "a jurisprudence is conceptual or it is nothing." The intellectual barrenness of constitutional law is a consequence of the scarcity of concepts—of a scarcity, that is, of instruments for the solution of problems. Properly contrived concepts could eliminate many problems of fact and go far toward reducing the disorderly world of fact to order.

If judicial review is to be practiced at all, it should undertake genuinely intellectual solutions to problems. Intellectual solutions will not always coincide with legislative solutions, and they will therefore be called undemocratic; but it is only in theory that the legislature represents the popular will, and in theory the Constitution represents it more truly than the legislature. Moreover, the invalidation of statutes which restrict the democratic process is more democratic than those statutes.[155] In recent years has democracy gained or lost when the Court upheld restrictions on freedom of thought and association, when it upheld gross inequalities in the size of legislative districts, when it refused certiorari to the victims of congressional inquisitions? On other issues which do not directly involve the political process, it seems unlikely that democracy will suffer any real injury if legislatures are required to observe due process and to afford equal protection of the laws.

9

HADDOCK v. CIVIL SERVICE COMMISSION

Justice Tergiversation delivered the opinion of the court: The petitioner Haddock applied for a restraining order against the Civil Service Commission, which has given him thirty-day notice of discharge from federal employment for failure to comply with the so-called Incubator Act passed by the 80½ Congress, January 1, 1949. The case comes before us by certiorari.

Counsel for the Commission urge that Haddock is a litigious person given to bringing nuisance suits and is not entitled to relief in equity. We take judicial notice that the petitioner has often vexed the British courts with impertinent suits. (See A. P. Herbert, *Misleading Cases at the Common Law; Uncommon Law; More Misleading Cases.*) Nevertheless, the petitioner here raises a substantial issue; and even a litigious Englishman is a person within the meaning of the Fifth Amendment.

It appears that Haddock has been employed by the Bureau of the Census to devise a system of questionnaires for the discovery of Communists, "fellow travelers," potential Communists, and potential "fellow-travelers," to be applied to the whole population in the 1950 census. It is planned to publish the names of the subversive characters thus discovered for the information of their employers, relatives, and friends. We have permitted the House Committee on Un-American Activities and a number of patriotic organizations to appear as amici curiae on behalf of Haddock. It is argued that Haddock possesses a special skill in the detection of unconventional views, that he is indeed a sort of human spectroscope, and that such a work of national importance should not be interrupted.

Briefly put, the Incubator Act provides that all employees in both the classified and unclassified services, with the exception of policy-forming officers, must under pain of discharge submit to an operation of sterilization to insure that they do not beget or bear children. The reason is obvious, but is in any case stated in the preamble. The government deserves and needs the undivided loyalty of its employees. It has long been recognized that family ties establish interests, preoccupations, and loyalties inconsistent with wholehearted devotion to the public good.

Haddock alleges that the act deprives him of life and liberty without due process of law. He argues that the right of procreation and the right to have a family are "natural" rights of which government may not deprive him. But we have already recognized that "these fundamental human rights are not absolute." *United Public Workers* v. *Mitchell*, 330 U.S. 75, 95, 67 S.Ct. 556, 567, 91 L. Ed. 754, 770 (1947). Compulsory sterilization statutes have been upheld. *Buck* v. *Bell*, 274 U.S. 200, 47 S.Ct. 584, 71 L. Ed. 1000 (1927). Here no one compels Haddock to accept federal employment. "The servant cannot complain, as he takes the employment on the terms which are offered him." Justice Holmes in *McAuliffe* v. *New Bedford*, 155 Mass. 216, 29 N.E. 517, 518 (1892). If the due process clause is not an insuperable barrier to compulsory sterilization, it is not such a barrier to that which is attached to a voluntary contract of employment.

To be sure, the due process clause will invalidate a statute which is not reasonably related to a public purpose. But as we said in *United Public Workers* v. *Mitchell, supra:* "Congress and the President are responsible for an efficient public service." It is not for this court to pass on the wisdom of the means employed to achieve this legitimate end.

With the wisdom of the policy adopted, with the adequacy or practicability of the law enacted to forward it, the courts are both incompetent and unauthorized to deal. The course of decision in this court exhibits a firm adherence to these principles. Times without number we have said that the legislature is primarily the judge of the necessity of such an enactment, that every possible presumption is in favor of its validity, and that though the court may hold views inconsistent with the wisdom of the law, it may not be annulled unless palpably in excess of legislative power. *Nebbia* v. *New York*, 291 U.S. 502, 537-8, 54 S.Ct. 505, 516, 78 L. Ed. 940, 957, 89 A.L.R. 1469 (1934).

Likewise, "Questions of policy are not submitted to judicial determination, and the courts have no general authority of supervision over the exercise of discretion, which under our system is reposed in the people or other departments of government.... Whether it will result in ultimate good or harm it is not within our province to inquire." *Green* v. *Frazier,* 253 U.S. 233, 240, 40 S.Ct. 499, 502, 64 L. Ed. 878, 882 (1920).

To come closer to the case in hand, we said in *United Public Workers* v. *Mitchell, supra:* "For regulation of employees it is not necessary that the act regulated be anything more than an act reasonably deemed by Congress to interfere with the efficiency of the public service." "The use of the constitutional power of regulation is for Congress, not for the courts." This would seem to close the question.

But it is argued on behalf of Haddock that the Incubator Act goes beyond what is necessary for the maintenance of the integrity of the public service. We encountered in *United Public Workers* v. *Mitchell* the argument that "Congress has gone further than necessary" by forbidding political activity not merely to administrative employees but to industrial workers whose views and actions could have no possible influence on policy. We replied: "When, in the judgment of Congress, actions of civil servants menace the integrity and the competency of the service, legislation to forestall such danger and adequate to maintain its usefulness is required."

To be sure, we recognized in that case the existence of limits on the power of Congress. But we pointed out that such limits were to be determined by the "general existing conception of governmental power," and this conception we found expressed in prevailing practice and a large professional literature.

On the side of practice, we call attention to the fact that many municipalities have refused to employ married women as teachers, which clearly shows that conditioning public employment on the absence of family is within the existing conception of governmental power. Marriage and procreation are not a private affair. "There are, in effect, three parties to every marriage, the man, the woman, and the state." *Fearon* v. *Treanor,* 272 N.Y. 268, 5 N.E. (2d) 815, 816 (1936).

There is likewise an impressive professional literature in support of the policy of the statute. It is well known that Plato in his *Republic* denied both property and the family to the guardians, the administrative class of his ideal state.

And this will be their salvation, and they will be the saviors of the state. But should they acquire homes or lands or moneys of their own, they will become good housekeepers and husbandmen instead of guardians, enemies and tyrants instead of allies of the other citizens; hating and being hated, plotting and being plotted against, they will pass their whole life in much greater terror of internal than external enemies, and the hour of ruin, both to themselves and to the rest of the State, will be at hand.

Procopius tells us in his *Anecdota* that during the reign of Justinian, only eunuchs were employed in the civil service of Byzantium. The absence of family encouraged them in their devotion to the public good, and removed a powerful incentive to private enrichment, nepotism, and other expressions of self-interest. It is well known that the Catholic church has found celibacy an important aid in the maintenance of an impressive administrative organization. It may well be true, indeed, that the coherence of the church would have broken down without this support.

We find nothing objectionable in the statute.

Affirmed.

Mr. Justice Comestible concurred:

In my opinion, the bill should have been dismissed. Nothing in the record shows that the petitioner Haddock is capable of procreation, and he is therefore threatened with the loss of no valuable right. A justiciable issue is not presented.

Nevertheless I approve the general tenor of the argument of the majority. "All these are questions of policy not for us to judge. For it can never be emphasized too much that one's own opinion as to the wisdom of a law must be wholly excluded when one is doing one's judicial duty." *Osborn* v. *Ozlin*, 310 U.S. 53, 66, 60 S.Ct. 758, 84 L.Ed. 1074, 1080 (1940).

10

PRESIDENTIAL WARS: THE CONVENIENCE OF "PRECEDENT"

The presidential wars in Indochina have been the least publicized events in American history. The war, or rather the unopposed career of carnage, in Laos has never been acknowledged; there has been negligible official, and scanty unofficial, reporting of the military adventures in Vietnam and Cambodia. So obscure has been the history of our involvement that Robert McNamara, then Secretary of Defense, commissioned a study to discover what had happened. To maintain public ignorance, the Nixon administration unsuccessfully sought to enjoin publication of the study.

There has been even greater official reticence on the constitutional questions involved. In 1966, a year after President Johnson's massive escalation of the war in Vietnam, the State Department supplied the Senate Committee on Foreign Relations with a memorandum, so slight as to be frivolous, in justification of executive warmaking. The present administration has been even less communicative. In various forums, Secretary of State Rogers, Solicitor General Griswold, and former Assistant Attorney General Rehnquist have defended Mr. Nixon's prosecution of the war; these brief statements exhaust the administration's apologies for its conduct. They do not say much, but they say more than can be defended.

The framers of the Constitution attempted to put the question beyond doubt. At the Constitutional Convention the committee of detail reported a proposal that the legislature be given the power "to make war." The

Reprinted from the *Nation* 215 (Oct. 9, 1972): 301-4. Used by permission of the *Nation*.

Convention changed the word "make" to "declare," so that the executive might be free "to repel sudden attacks." This meant that war could be initiated in two ways: by joint resolution of Congress, and by the attack of an enemy. On issues arising from the war with France, 1798–1801, the Supreme Court held that it was for Congress to initiate all hostilities, whether general war or limited war, and that it was illegal for the president to exceed the authorization of Congress. In 1863 in the Prize Cases, the Court held that the president's power to resist sudden attack included response to insurrection; but it said that he had no power to initiate war.

According to Secretary Rogers, it follows from the power to repel attack that "in emergency situations, the President has the power and responsibility to use the armed forces to protect the nation's security." The emergency in Vietnam which purportedly called for independent executive action has never been identified; in any case, the Constitution authorizes Congress, and not the president, to determine when the nation's security is imperiled and when it is appropriate to use the armed forces to protect it.

But the Nixon administration places its chief reliance on the commander-in-chief clause. This title was introduced in English military usage in 1639 and is still used by the British to describe the highest-ranking officer in a military or naval hierarchy; this officer has always been subject to political superiors. When the Continental Congress made George Washington commander in chief in 1776, it instructed him "punctually to observe and follow such orders and directions, from time to time, as you shall receive from this, or a future Congress of these United Colonies, or committee of Congress." The Constitutional Convention adopted the term in the light of this usage. In 1850 the Supreme Court said of the position of the president, *after* Congress had declared war: "His duty and power are purely military. As commander-in-chief, he is authorized to direct the movements of the naval and military forces placed by law at his command, and to employ them in the manner he may deem most effectual to harass and conquer the enemy."

The commander-in-chief clause does not supplant the war clause, which gives the power to initiate war to Congress. And it must be read together with the clauses of the Constitution which authorize Congress to raise and support armies, to provide and maintain a navy, and to make rules for the government and regulation of the land and naval forces. The Supreme Court has held that only Congress may raise armies, that the president may not require an officer to perform any duty not imposed on him by statute, that he may not alter a salary fixed by statute, that he may not discharge an officer contrary to statute, that court-martial jurisdiction over soldiers is limited to that authorized by Congress, that a soldier when drafted may be assigned duties only in the capacity which subjected him to the draft. Congress has obliged the president to assign command of troops to the highest-ranking officer in the force; it has authorized the use of troops for some purposes and forbidden it for others; on several occasions it has forbidden that troops be sent to specified areas; when Theodore Roosevelt took the Marines off naval vessels, Congress obliged him to restore them. As David Dudley Field put it: "To command an army is to give it its orders.... To do what? That, and that only, which the laws allow; and the laws are made, not by him but by Congress. His function is executive."

No judicial precedents support the claim that the commander-in-chief clause authorizes the president to undertake acts of war. But the apologists for the war in Vietnam rely on purported executive precedents. This argument developed in a curious way. In 1912 the Solicitor of the State Department, J. Reuben Clark, published a list of forty-one armed actions or displays of force abroad which had not been individually authorized by Congress. Two were illegal, but the other thirty-nine were naval actions to protect citizens. After "cursory consideration" Clark offered a legal theory to justify these actions, but he warned that "a more detailed and careful study" might not support it. This theory was the proposition that citizens were entitled to protection at international law, that international law was incorporated in the law of the United States, and that in protecting citizens the president was merely executing the laws of the United States. In 1934 the State Department republished Clark's study, updating the list of foreign interventions.

In 1941 there occurred a revolution in legal theory. Defending President Roosevelt's action in sending troops to Iceland, Senator Connally argued that the president as commander in chief might send troops wherever he wished, and cited the eighty-five cases from the 1934 revision of Clark's list as evidence. The commander-in-chief clause thus replaced the president's executive power; the limitation to the protection of citizens disappeared, and with it Clark's misgivings about even this narrowly defined action. In 1950 the State Department used Connally's list of eighty-five cases as precedents for President Truman's unauthorized entry into the Korean War. In 1966 the State Department asserted that there were 125 precedents for President Johnson's unauthorized entry into the war in Vietnam. In 1967 the State Department offered a list of 137 "armed actions taken by the United States without a declaration of war." In 1971 Solicitor General Griswold said that the United States had formally declared war six times and had engaged in hostilities on 155 other occasions as well. On December 18, 1971, Senator Goldwater asserted that he had compiled a list of "192 military actions undertaken without a declaration of war, eighty-one of which involved actual combat or ultimatums tantamount to the use of force."

It is time to set the record straight. Congress has passed not six but thirteen formal declarations of general war against a named adversary. On eight occasions Congress has authorized hostilities short of general war against a named adversary. On thirteen occasions Congress has rejected or ignored presidential requests for authority to engage in limited hostilities. On at least seven occasions the executive has refused to undertake hostile action on the ground that Congress had not authorized it.

In all the lists of purported executive precedents, about half the cases have been brief naval landings to protect citizens or their property in a foreign country in a time of riot or insurrection. All the lists are in error: there have in fact been 116 such landings, 13 before 1865 and 103 thereafter. The 13 were legally unauthorized, but in 1862 Congress empowered the secretary of the navy to make rules for the government of the navy, and the rules issued in 1865 contained carefully limited instructions to protect citizens in foreign ports in case of need. The 103 landings after 1865 did not rest on the president's executive power or the commander-in-chief clause. They rested on congressional authorization.

Only 56 of these 103 landings appear in the 1967 State Department list. Nine of the other cases listed also had statutory authorization. Of the 72 remaining cases, most were trivial. Some were merely minatory demonstrations at sea; some involved merely technical trespass. An unknown number were undertaken by army or navy officers without authorization from their superiors; if they prove anything about the war power, they prove that it belongs to every commissioned officer. On the other hand, some cases have been presidential usurpations of great magnitude: six protracted occupations of Caribbean states, the Korean War, the Vietnam War. These can be said to establish that the president possesses the war power only if the mere repetition of a crime legalizes a sequence of crimes.

However, the Nixon apologists do not rest solely on the commander-in-chief clause; they also argue that the president's "executive power" authorizes him to engage in war. Justice Holmes said: "The duty of the President to see that the law be executed is a duty that does not go beyond the laws or require him to achieve more than Congress sees fit to leave within his power." In the 1952 Steel Seizure Case, three Justices, led by Harry Truman's crony Chief Justice Vinson, argued that the President's executive power authorized him to seize the steel mills in order to maintain military production; but six Justices denied that he could act without a statute. In 1971 the President sought to enjoin the publication of the Pentagon Papers, but six Justices held that he could not do so without statutory authorization. The other three Justices took no position; they thought it premature to resolve the issues.

Apologists for executive warmaking invariably refer to what Secretary Rogers has called "the President's constitutional authority to conduct the foreign relations of the United States." Of course, no such grant is to be found in the Constitution. The president shares the treaty-making power and the power to appoint ambassadors with the Senate. He shares the power over foreign commerce and all the war powers with the full Congress. Only two powers in foreign relations are assigned to him alone. He is commander in chief; but he acts in this capacity by and under the authority of Congress. And he has the power to receive foreign ambassadors. Alexander Hamilton said that this function was purely ceremonial; but it has come to entail recognition, which has legal consequences. But the power of recognition does not entail the war power. Presidents Madison, Monroe, Jackson, Grant, Cleveland, and McKinley refused to recognize revolutionary governments in colonial countries because this might be regarded as an act of war by the mother country, and only Congress could authorize acts of war.

The 1966 State Department apology asserted that the SEATO treaty authorized, indeed obliged, the President to go to war in Vietnam. No one had noticed this feature of the treaty for twelve years after its negotiation in 1954. No treaty made by the president and the Senate can authorize war. In the Constitutional Convention Charles Pinckney proposed that the war power be given to the Senate, but he found no second; it was given to the full Congress. Nor, if the Senate had the war power, could it delegate it *in futuro* to the president. Finally, no word of the SEATO treaty requires or permits the president to do anything whatever except to consult with the other signatories. In time of common danger each signatory is to act "in accordance with its constitutional processes." Today no reliance is placed on the SEATO treaty. As far as this writer has been able to discover, only Presidential Assistant Harry Dent has offered the SEATO treaty as justification for President Nixon's prosecution of the war.

Obviously it is impossible to overcome the constitutional assignment of the war power to Congress. So the argument shifts. During the Johnson administration and the first two years of the Nixon administration, reliance was placed on the Tonkin Gulf Resolution of 1964, in which Congress said that the president might do whatever he liked, "including the use of armed force," to assist Cambodia, Laos, "the free territory of Vietnam," Australia, New Zealand, Pakistan, the Philippines, Thailand, Great Britain, and France in the maintenance of their freedom. Under

Secretary of State Katzenbach called this resolution a "functional equivalent of a declaration of war." But a declaration of war always names an adversary; it makes hostilities mandatory; it specifies whether the war is general or limited. Tonkin Gulf attempted to delegate the war power wholesale to the president, at least as far as Southeast Asia was concerned.

Early in our history Chief Justice Marshall laid down the law of congressional delegation. Certain functions are "strictly and exclusively legislative," and "these important subjects must be entirely regulated by the legislature itself." But Congress may authorize judicial or executive rule-making on matters "of lesser interest, in which a general provision may be made, and power given to those who are to act under such provisions to fill up the details."

Clearly the initiation of war is legislative. In 1835 the Senate unanimously adopted a resolution drafted by Henry Clay which rejected a request of President Jackson for contingent authority to make reprisals on French shipping because the war power could not be delegated. Congress rejected for the same reason eight requests of President Buchanan for contingent authority to intervene militarily in Central America and Mexico.

Suppose, however, we agree with the spokesmen for the Johnson and Nixon administrations that choosing an antagonist and launching a war is one of those topics of "lesser interest" on which Congress may delegate the power of decision to the executive. As Chief Justice Hughes said in *Schechter Poultry Corp.* v. *United States,* in making such a delegation Congress must "perform its function in laying down policies and establishing standards, while leaving to selected instrumentalities the making of subordinate rules within prescribed limits and the determination of facts to which the policy as declared by the Legislature is to apply." In the Tonkin Gulf Resolution Congress laid down no policy and established no standard; the resolution was, as Senator Fulbright, who sponsored it in the Senate, said at a later date, "a blank check."

But in a strange opinion of 1936 by Justice Sutherland in *United States* v. *Curtiss-Wright Export Corporation* the Court had said that the limitations of the Constitution did not apply in foreign affairs, and that Congress might delegate to the president the power to make rules over foreign commerce without "laying down policies and establishing standards." Both the Johnson and Nixon administration have argued that the Tonkin Gulf Resolution was a valid delegation of the war power because in foreign affairs the rule against delegation does not apply.

Sutherland's statement was not law but dictum, and has been rejected in every subsequent decision. In *Reid* v. *Covert* in 1956 the proposition that the Constitution does not apply in foreign affairs was expressly repudiated. In two cases involving foreign commerce (the issue in *Curtiss-Wright*) and five cases involving matters "of lesser interest" under the war power (a curfew, price controls, rent controls, and contract renegotiation), all decided since *Curtiss-Wright,* the Court has announced and applied the orthodox tests of the validity of delegation: Congress must lay down policy and establish standards. In *Zemel* v. *Rusk* (1965) Chief Justice Warren said that the *Curtiss-Wright* case "does not mean that simply because a statute deals with foreign relations, it can grant the Executive totally unrestricted freedom of choice." The dictum in *Curtiss-Wright* has neither paternity nor progeny.

In any case, the Tonkin Gulf Resolution was repealed on January 12, 1971. Solicitor General Griswold, deprived of this purported statutory authorization, has argued that congressional appropriations for the support of troops in Vietnam have amounted to an implied ratification of the war. If these acts are ratifications, they too are uncontrolled delegations. But the argument ignores the law of ratification by appropriation laid down by Justice Douglas for the Court in Ex parte *Endo:* "The ratification must plainly show a purpose to bestow the precise authority which is claimed." And it ignores the doctrine of the equity of the statute. This doctrine, which goes back at least to the sixteenth century, is the proposition that the policy of a statute must be given effect beyond its literal terms. As Justice Holmes said: "The Legislature has the power to decide what the policy of the law shall be, and if it has intimated its will, however indirectly, that will should be recognized and obeyed." A repealer statute repeals all statutes, though not named, which share the policy of the statute repealed. If earlier appropriation acts carried any implied endorsement of the war, the repeal of the Tonkin Gulf Resolution, to which the appropriation acts were tributary, revoked that endorsement.

Nor has Congress left this in doubt. In the National Procurement Authorization Act of November 17, 1971, Congress declared it the policy of the United States "to terminate at the earliest practicable date all military operations of the United States in Indochina, and to provide for the prompt and orderly withdrawal of all United States military forces at a date certain, subject to the release of all American prisoners of war...." President Nixon in signing the bill announced his intention of defying it. Since then he has repeatedly said that he will end military operations in Vietnam only after an agreement to political terms stipulated by him. The war is being continued, not without Congress but in defiance of Congress. None of the policy arguments for executive usurpation— "emergency" or "national security"—applies to this war. No constitutional provision and no executive precedent justifies the President in continuing a war against the expressed will of Congress. The case is unprecedented.

Since there is no legal case for the Nixon administration, its spokesmen have taken final refuge, not in the law but in the assertion that they are not accountable to law. The courts will not undertake to decide "political questions." Secretary Rogers has said: "There are relatively few judicial decisions concerning the relationship between the Congress and the President in the exercise of their respective war powers under the Constitution. The courts have usually regarded the subject as a political question and refused jurisdiction." Mr. Rogers must know that there are literally dozens of cases in which the courts have decided "concerning the relationship between the Congress and the President in the exercise of their respective war powers under the Constitution." It was never suggested until the Vietnam War that the war power raised political questions. Rogers himself names only three cases, all concerned with this war. The Court of Appeals for the District of Columbia wrote a brief, confused opinion in *Luftig* v. *McNamara* in which it said, among other things, that the legality of the Vietnam War was a political question which it might not decide. In *Mora* v. *McNamara* the same court followed this earlier decision without opinion. Rogers's third case is *Massachusetts* v. *Laird,* in which the Supreme Court refused to permit Massachusetts to file a bill of complaint to challenge the war. It wrote no opinion and we are left to guess what motive or motives may have prompted the majority. Justices Douglas, Harlan, and Stewart dissented.

The first and central test of a political question which the courts may not adjudicate is, to use the language of Justice Brennan in *Baker* v. *Carr,* the existence of a "textually demonstrable constitutional commitment of the issue to a coordinate political department." The Constitution nowhere commits the decision of the constitutional issue of the power of the president to initiate war, or for that matter of the power of Congress to delegate its war power, to the president or to Congress. These are justiciable matters for the courts, which have repeatedly asserted that the president may not initiate war, and that Congress may not delegate legislative power to the president.

But there is a political question of another order, one which demands judicial solution: it is nothing less than the continuance of our republican form of government. As Justice Davis said, in holding Lincoln's declaration of martial law unconstitutional, "Wicked men, ambitious of power, with hatred of liberty and contempt of law, may fill the place once occupied by Washington and Lincoln." Chief Justice Marshall in deciding, in *Cohens* v. *Virginia,* a question more dangerous politically to the Court than the war in Vietnam is to the present Court, said: "We have no more right to decline the exercise of jurisdiction which is given, than to usurp that which is not given. The one or the other would be treason to the Constitution." But our present Supreme Court continues to evade, by denial of certiorari, the most important constitutional question of the twentieth century.

PART TWO
POLITICS

11

MATCHED-DEPENDENT BEHAVIORALISM: THE CARGO CULT IN POLITICAL SCIENCE

Neal E. Miller and John Dollard, in their study of imitation,[1] identify a type which they call "matched-dependent behavior." They illustrate it with a story. The father told Jim, aged six, and Bobby, aged three, that he had hidden a piece of candy for each of them in the living room. Jim looked in the fireplace: no candy. Bobby looked in the fireplace: no candy. Jim looked inside the piano bench: no candy. Bobby looked inside the piano bench: no candy. Jim looked under a cushion on the sofa, found a piece of candy, and ate it. Bobby looked under the cushion: no candy. "Bobby was now helpless"; he could think of no other place to look. Finally his father gave him the candy. "On a succeeding trial of the same game, exactly the same thing happened. The younger child would look only in the places already examined by his older brother. He would not respond to place cues by looking for himself."

More than twenty years ago Gordon W. Allport, in an address as divisional president to the Division of Personality and Social Psychology of the American Psychological Association, complained that "many of us seem so stupefied by admiration of physical science that we believe psychology in order to succeed need only imitate the models, postulates, and methods of physical science."[2] The same stupefaction has gripped those political scientists who call themselves behavioralists. We may liken the physical scientist to Jim; the behavioralist, who emulates his models, postulates, and methods, is Bobby. Miller and Dollard called Bobby's

---

Reprinted from *Western Political Quarterly* 20 (1967): 809-40. Reprinted by permission of the University of Utah, copyright holder.

behavior maladaptive, but they were wrong, for he always got his candy. Similarly, the behavioralists have never found a piece of candy; but they are given their candy by the Ford Foundation.

Gordon Allport was not complaining of the undertaking of psychology, but of the diversion of that undertaking into imitative and unrewarding channels. There is no intention here to complain of the undertaking in political science, as old as Aristotle, to deal dispassionately and systematically with the data. In particular, there is no intention to condemn the use of psychology—or at any rate psychologies like Allport's—in the explanation of politics. But the use of psychology is not new; it goes back to Plato.

Harold D. Lasswell has said that the "behavioral upswing" dates from the work of Charles E. Merriam at the University of Chicago in the 1920s and early 1930s.[3] But in fact the method and the assumptions of Merriam were traditional. Behavioralism is novel; Robert A. Dahl has called it a successful revolution.[4]

Although the adjective "behavioral" was used occasionally in the 1930s, the term "behavioral science" appears to have been introduced by the Committee on Behavioral Sciences, an interdisciplinary group organized at the University of Chicago in 1951 under the leadership of a psychologist, James G. Miller, with the encouragement of Dean Ralph W. Tyler. Miller has recorded the "working assumptions" of the Chicago "theory group":[5]

> First, we agreed to accept as confirmation of theorems only *objective* phenomena available to public inspection by more than one observer, excluding private experience. Second, we tried when possible to state hypotheses quantitatively, so that they might be precisely testable and could subsequently be corrected. Third, we attempted to make statements capable of being disproved as well as proved, by *crucial experiments*. Finally, as will be explained below, insofar as possible we employed dimensions of natural science related to the centimeter-gram-second system.

The first assumption is negative rather than affirmative: it is the rejection, common to behavioralism and psychological behaviorism, of both subjective data and subjective method. The second and the fourth make a commitment to the mathematical method of natural science. The third appears to be a bow in the direction of Karl Popper.

But these were not in fact the controlling assumptions of the Chicago group. Miller says that "we have found most profit in *general behavior systems theory*," and he goes on to describe this. The term "systems theory" was introduced in 1945 by Ludwin von Bertalanffy when he offered an alternative to the analytical method of natural science.[6]

In the world view called mechanistic, born of classical physics of the nineteenth century, the aimless play of the atoms, governed by the inexorable laws of mechanical causality, produced all phenomena in the world, inanimate, living, and mental. No room was left for any directiveness, order, or telos. The world of organisms appeared a mere product of chance, accumulated by a senseless play of mutation at random and selection; the mental world as a curious and rather inconsequential epiphenomenon of material events.

This "scheme of isolable units acting in one-way causality has proved to be insufficient. Hence the appearance, in all fields of science, of notions like wholeness, holistic, organismic, *gestalt* and so forth, which all signify that in the last resort, we must think in terms of systems of elements in mutual interaction."[7] In short, Bertalanffy rejected "the inexorable laws of mechanical causality" in favor of an Aristotelian teleology. Lurking behind this teleology is a vitalism like that of Driesch. It is not an open-ended vitalism like Bergson's; it aims at a given "final state," an Aristotelian final cause.

Mathematical behavioralism, with its commitment to analytical method and to efficient cause, is at the opposite pole from general systems theory, built as it is on an Aristotelian or Thomistic foundation. Yet some behavioralists believe they can combine the two. David Easton, in a book entitled *A Systems Analysis of Political Life*,[8] says that his goal is "descriptive, empirically-oriented, behavioral, operational or causal theory."

In 1954 the Ford Foundation established the Center for Advanced Study in the Behavioral Sciences at Menlo Park, California, with Ralph Tyler from the University of Chicago as director. The Center became the first training place for behavioral political scientists. It still functions, but now many graduate schools offer the same training. At Menlo Park, however, an atomistic and reductionist approach by way of mathematics very largely displaced the holistic approach of Miller's general systems theory, and the latter now has its strongholds at the University of Chicago and the Mental Health Research Institute at the University of Michigan, to which Miller migrated.

Behavioral projects, principally mathematical, are carried on by the RAND Corporation and the Pentagon; others are financed by various organs of the national government; the Ford Foundation has been generous with financial assistance. We may offer a behavioral hypothesis that the number of pages of behavioral literature published varies directly with the cube root of the number of dollars spent.

Harold Lasswell has said of the Center for Advanced Study:[9]

> The chief intellectual stress was methodological.... The methodological concern was threefold—(1) to encourage mathematical thinking or comparably strict methods; (2) to stimulate thinking about social processes in human history by giving consideration to general biological theory; (3) to provide a setting appropriate to the planning of research on problems of importance that are neglected or pursued by inferior methods unless recognized and undertaken by interdisciplinary teams.

The third topic can be dismissed. There have been collaborations of behavioral political scientists with economists, but this has not pooled methods familiar to the two disciplines. Rather, these teams have invariably had recourse to the tools of the mathematicians. Apparently Lasswell's second topic is an understatement of the ambition of general systems theory. Many persons call themselves systems theorists—in addition to Bertalanffy and Miller, Talcott Parsons, David Easton, Morton Kaplan, Coleman and Almond, Bertram Gross, and others. Although there are vague resemblances between the formulations of these authors, there are greater inconsistencies, and it is not feasible to review this literature here.

The chief impact of behavioralism has been Lasswell's first topic, the adoption of new mathematical tools. This is often unaccompanied by any degree of mathematical sophistication; and frequently it is entirely unaccompanied by political sophistication.

Since Petty, at least, we have had political scientists who have used mathematics, but they have been, in the language of Karl W. Deutsch, "'shorthaired' social scientists, the counters and verifiers, who are too often and too thoughtlessly identified with the behavioral approach in social science."[10] No one, not even the behavioralists, would deny the utility of such sources as the reports of the Census Bureau, or the value of the many empirical studies, such as voting studies, that have been drawn from these sources. But these are humble projects. The behavioralists have a more ambitious goal. They attribute the success of the physical scientists to the use of mathematics, and they believe that if they adopt this tool they will be able to achieve comparable results.

This issue is not a new one. A very long time ago Aristotle observed that a young man might become an expert mathematician, but he would lack practical wisdom, which is "concerned with things human and things about which it is possible to deliberate"—that is, not with invariables but with matters of choice. Mathematics deals with abstractions, whereas practical wisdom comes from experience.[11]

In the latter part of the nineteenth century, Wilhelm Dilthey introduced the distinction between the *Naturwissenschaften,* which deal with the physical world, and the *Geisteswissenschaften* or the human sciences, which deal with meanings and motives.[12] The *Naturwissenschaften* employ laws of mechanical causality; the *Geisteswissenschaften* employ human understanding, *Verstehen.*

Through Rickert and Windelband the teaching of Dilthey passed to Max Weber, whose name is of course one of the most widely respected in the social sciences. For Weber sociology dealt with interpersonal action to which the actor attached subjective meaning.[13] This meaning was comprehended by *Verstehen.*[14]

A correct causal interpretation of a concrete course of action is arrived at when the overt action and the motives have both been correctly apprehended and at the same time their relation has become meaningfully comprehensible.... If adequacy in respect to meaning is lacking, then no matter how high the degree of uniformity and how precisely its probability can be numerically determined, it is still an incomprehensible statistical probability, whether dealing with overt or subjective processes.

In his very valuable examination of the methodology of social science,[15] Frederick A. Hayek contrasts the data of the natural sciences with those of the social sciences. Physical science breaks up sensory experience into elements which bear computable relations to each other. Mathematics is not merely an auxiliary tool, and quantification is not merely increased precision: "It is of the essence of this process of breaking up our immediate sense data and of substituting for a description in terms of sense qualities one in terms of elements which possess no attributes but these relations with each other."[16] In contrast with this objectivist approach, social science must use a subjectivist approach; the data are the subjective meanings and purposes of human beings. We understand these meanings because we know our own subjective experience.[17]

Robert MacIver is a determinist, but he has said:[18]

There is no point in trying to apply to social systems the causal formula of classical mechanics, to the effect that if you know the state of a system at any instant you can calculate mathematically, in terms of a system of co-ordinates, the state of that system at any other time. We simply cannot use such a formula. It fits into another frame of reference. On the other hand we have the advantage that some of the factors operative in social causation are *understandable as causes,* are validated as causal by our own experience. This provides us a frame of reference that the physical sciences cannot use. We must therefore cultivate our own garden. We must use the advantages we possess and not merely regret the advantages we lack.

Similarly Carl J. Friedrich has said:[19]

> The physicist can merely note that every so often an atom deviates from the norm, but he is at present completely at a loss when it comes to accounting for it. Far be it from me to belittle the achievements of modern natural science; they are the more imposing precisely because the naturalist has to work without the guide of common human understanding. However, it is thoughtless, indeed, to deprive ourselves in the social sciences of the invaluable aid which such human understanding can give us, merely because the natural sciences have had to evolve techniques for getting along without it.

Morton A. Kaplan, a behavioralist, identifies his approach with science and dismisses as "traditionalism" the view that "understanding, wisdom or tradition are required for areas where human purpose is involved."[20] It is certainly the case that subjective understanding has been the traditional reliance in the interpretation of politics. No one can read Merriam's *Political Power,* for example, without realizing that it relies throughout on the subjectivism of *Verstehen* and not the objectivism of behavioralism.

Of course, a man might impose upon himself the obligation of walking on his hands, and might succeed in walking a hundred yards in this manner. It is conceivable that a student might take on the very considerable handicap of studying politics without the aid of understanding and might nevertheless arrive at one or more useful propositions about politics. There is a widespread opinion among political scientists that this has actually occurred.[21] Whether or not this is true can only be determined by reviewing the principal mathematical practices engaged in by political scientists and the major contributions of the mathematical behavioralists.

TRANSLATION

One of the most popular enterprises has been to translate vulgar speech into mathematics. Of course this could yield no scientific proposition that was not implicit in the English; nevertheless, it is supposed that knowledge is advanced by converting statements into what Carnap called "physical language."

Herbert Simon has been the most active translator in the field of political science. For Simon mathematics is "the most dulcet of languages,"[22] and he enjoys his task. So he has turned a set of propositions from Homans's *The Human Group* into mathematics; similarly he has translated a formulation of Leon Festinger's.[23] In addition, he has set up schemata of his own and has restated them symbolically.

Simon does not mistake a translation for a demonstration. He recognizes that it is merely a restatement whose form offers certain advantages:[24]

(a) Knowing more precisely what mechanisms or structural relations are being postulated, and sometimes calling attention to the need for further clarification of the operational meaning of definitions and statements;

(b) Discovering whether certain postulates can be derived from others, and hence can be eliminated as independent assumptions; whether additional postulates need to be added to make the system complete and the deductions rigorous; and whether there are inconsistencies among the postulates;

(c) Assisting in the discovery of inconsistencies between the empirical data and the theories used to explain them;

(d) Laying the basis for further elaboration of theory, and to deductions from the postulates that suggest further empirical studies for verification;

(e) Aiding in handling complicated, simultaneous interrelations among a relatively large number of variables, with some reduction of the obscuring circumlocutions entailed by nonmathematical language.

This statement of advantages should be supplemented by a statement of disadvantages. Something is lost in the translation. The aureole of meaning that surrounds words is trimmed off when they become mathematical counters; or, conversely, it is possible that the central meaning is excised and a fragment of the aureole enters into the formula. On the other hand, the entire ambiguity of an English word may survive unimpaired in a symbol which gives it spurious precision: calling power P does not make this rich and untidy word suitable for definition in a single equivalence. Finally, mathematical formulation imports the assumptions of mathematics into the statement, and this may work an unobserved alteration in the meaning of the verbal formulation. The assumption of game theory, for example, that utilities can be deprived of their subjective and variable character and can be rank-ordered and even represented as multiples of some common unit of measurement, is made possible by the device of mathematical formulation of verbal statements whose original meaning does not authorize such a claim.

An instructive example of simple translation is an essay by Otto A. Davis and Melvin Hinich, "A Mathematical Model of Policy Formulation in a Democratic Society."[25] They state their problem verbally:[26]

Given the precisely defined ... and unchangeable preferences of the voters in the population, candidates for public office compete for votes by announcing before an election their exact position on each of the relevant issues. Each voter compares the positions taken by the various candidates and casts his vote for that particular candidate whose position is "nearest" ... his own most preferred position. It is assumed that, once elected, a (former) candidate will adopt those policies which he announced during the campaign. Thus the questions to be answered are whether, and under what conditions, dominant strategies exist for the candidates.

After elaborate manipulations of symbols the results are translated back into English. "In other words, if the first candidate selects the policies in his platform to be exactly the same as the mean of the policies desired by the individuals in the voting population, and the other candidate does not make the same choice, then the first candidate is certain to win the election."[27]

Given that one of the mutually exclusive and exhaustive groups "desires" one set of policies, that the other group "desires" another set of policies, and that there is no conflict between the two sets of policies since each refers to a mutually exclusive set of issues, then the politician can enhance his chance of winning the election by giving each group what it desires.[28]

Given a party system, the minority party will lose unless certain conditions are present. If there is a "'smaller range' of taste and opinion about policy" in the minority party, and the position of the candidate of the party lies closer to the positions of a sufficient number of voters of the majority party than that of the candidate of the majority party, the minority party will win.[29]

The authors confess that "simplifying assumptions" have been made. This is not necessarily a fault: the construction of models or ideal types may be useful, although it is certainly an error to assume that all are equally useful. The real infirmity of the argument lies in the very fact of mathematical expression; it is the assumption that people can be arrayed on a linear scale of preference on an issue, so that medians can be calculated and the diffuseness of positions determined. From this grows the related assumption that there exists a common unit of magnitude which can be used to reduce preferences on all issues to a common scale and ultimately to a single mean. It is not merely that as a practical matter these measurements cannot be taken. The fault is more serious: the very conception is, to use the most damning words in the behavioral vocabulary, operationally meaningless.

Robert A. Dahl has translated the "intuitive idea of power" into a formula with four elements.[30] The power of A over a with respect to x is the probability that if A does w, a will do x, diminished by the probability that a would do x even though A did not do w. This can be rendered

$$M(A/a : w,x) = P(a,x \mid A,w) - P(a,x \mid A,\text{not-}w)$$

To translate the English into symbols does not advance science any more than a translation into Greek or Spanish would have done. But the translation is not faithful. One reads "probability" in the English as subjective probability, an expectation or guess on the part of the observer with regard to an individual event. The probability in the formula must be an objective probability, the ratio of the number of cases in which the outcome occurs to the total number of cases in the class of events. Dahl gives us no method of computing the elements in this ratio in any real case; and surely this is impossible. But then the formula is operationally meaningless.

The translation of a theory into mathematics requires a theory: "First catch your rabbit." Once one has a theory suitable for expression in mathematical terms, translation may assist in exposing its meaning. The next step would be to test the theory by the use of empirical data.[31] Economists are accustomed to compare their theories with the actual behavior of prices. But the political world is more complex than the economic; and no one—neither Aristotle nor Machiavelli nor Hobbes nor Harrington nor Marx nor the inventors of utopias—has ever succeeded in building into a political theory all the relevant variables. This means that the theory will not accord with actual behavior.

Of course, physical theories do not state all the variables encountered in nature; but in physics it is very often possible to establish laboratory conditions which exclude the undesired variables and permit observation of the behavior of the variables expressed in the theory. When this cannot be done, the theory is unverifiable. If it is ever possible to set up laboratory tests for theories about politics, it will be for very trivial propositions about small groups.

This means that the term "political theory" is a misnomer. A theory must be susceptible to confirmation or disproof. Consequently the more modest term "model" is often used to describe such logical constructs as that of Hobbes and the formulations of mathematical behavioralists. Typically, a model is unicausal; at most, it embraces only a few of the relevant variables. Therefore it is likely to have little predictive value for the real world. It does not follow that it is useless. One judges the merits of a model not by what comes out of it but by what is put into it; the famous models have rested on shrewd if partial insights into psychology or social relationships, on *Verstehen*. This means that individually they each report one of the multifarious causes that collectively shape events. In political science a model is not and cannot be a law; at most, it is a tendency statement. Because of the action of excluded variables, the tendency reported by a model may not emerge into the light in a given case. This does not necessarily invalidate the model; of course, it does not validate it either.

Yet in debates about public policy tendency statements are continually offered as genuine cause-effect propositions which forecast practical results. In the case of economic proposals, these statements sometimes do indicate the direction, although not the magnitude, of change. So we can have some confidence as to the character of the results of deficit spending or the relaxation of credit restrictions by the Federal Reserve Board.

Such forecasting is not confined to economics. Since the beginning of politics men have predicted the future on the basis of auguries or other formulae. Currently it is argued that prayer in the schools will reduce juvenile delinquency. The domino theory contends that the recognition of a military or diplomatic defeat by the United States entails the triumph of communism throughout the world. John Kenneth Galbraith has asserted that economic concentration produces "countervailing power."[32] All these propositions purport to be theories and not models. They could easily be formalized and tested against empirical fact. Probably the greatest service that mathematical translation could perform would be the evaluation of such theories.

NOMINAL DEFINITION

In a real definition the right-hand term of the equation, the *definiens*, is an analysis of the meaning of the left-hand term, the *definiendum*. The analysis may be correct or incorrect; a real definition can be true or false. In a nominal definition the entire meaning lies in the right-hand term, the *definiens*. The left-hand term is not a *definiendum*, for it has no meaning to be defined: it is merely a name arbitrarily attached by the speaker to the contents of the right-hand term. Consequently a nominal definition is neither true nor false: it exists by intention, "by definition."

Very frequently mathematical behavioralists pretend to solve a problem by taking a term which is ordinarily used to describe actual phenomena, emptying out its empirical content, and then equating the shell to a mathematical formulation on the right side of the equation. This yields no real definition of the term, but only a nominal definition of the mathematical formulation. This elementary logical error is often disguised by calling the definition "operational," and appealing to the authority of Percy Bridgman, who invented this term.[33] This is unwarranted. What Bridgman asserted was that "we must always demand that physical concepts be stated in terms of *physical* operations."[34] He warned that mathematical operations "are mental operations, and have no necessary physical validity."[35] Moreover, he explicitly denied that any phenomenon could be successfully defined in terms of a single set of operations.[36]

"To define a phenomenon by the operations which produced it" involves unproved assumptions. It implies that the performance of the same operations will always be followed by the occurrence of the same phenomenon, and this statement is operationally meaningless unless there is some method of checking the truth of the statement. This again implies that it means something to say "same" phenomenon, which implies, unless we are dealing with a pure convention, that there is some other method of recognizing the phenomenon when it recurs than through the operation of the definition. Operational definitions, in spite of their precision, are in application without significance unless the situations to which they are applied are sufficiently developed so that at least two methods are known of getting to the terminus.

That is to say, a "definition" of a phenomenon by a single operational method gives merely a conventional or nominal definition of the operation; it is not a definition of the phenomenon.

Behaviorist psychologists have also appropriated the word "operationalism" from Bridgman. They have better reason than the behavioralists, for they do use it to describe external physical operations. Their purpose, indeed, is to reduce psychology to objective description of conduct, excluding mental states and consciousness. This elimination of all subjective phenomena has migrated into mathematical behavioralism. So both Dahl and March define power in terms of overt conduct: he who stimulates the response has power over the respondent.[37] It follows that the victim who incautiously displays a well-filled wallet has power over the thief who robs him. This does violence to the conception of power which one has by *Verstehen*, but here behavioralism meets behaviorism. And if one is satisfied with a merely nominal definition of power there is no objection to a definition that gives the victim power over the thief.

As we have seen, Robert Dahl has translated a verbal definition of power into a mathematical one, employing two probabilities which are operationally meaningless. When he came to make a study of power in a concrete case, therefore, he substituted certain events—votes—for the probabilities, and transformed his real definition into a nominal one.[38] He and his associates compiled the votes of thirty-four senators on roll calls on foreign policy and tax and economic policy during the years 1946-54. Each senator is paired with every other senator; the senator who more often votes with the majority is said to be the more powerful. The thirty-four senators are then rank-ordered.

A series of intellectual leaps is made. This table of data is treated as a probability table. Then the probability table is called a power index. But it cannot be that. According to Dahl's formula, Senator S has a power over the Senate which is the probability that if Senator S does w—votes for a bill—the Senate will do x—pass the bill, or if he does not-w—votes against the bill—it will fail. This means that when Senator S votes in the majority he has demonstrated power over the Senate, including Senator T. But Senator T has also voted with the majority; thus, he has demonstrated power over the Senate and over Senator S. Indeed, every member of the majority is simultaneously superior and inferior to every other member of the majority.

But the formula needs to be carried further. If we insist that the power of a senator really depends on the probability that his vote will determine the fate of the bill, all the senators are completely powerless on all roll calls except those yielding a majority of one or two. If there is a majority greater than two, it does not matter whether any Senator S does w or not-w; his vote cannot influence the outcome. Where there is a majority of one, every senator in the majority has complete power—what Dahl would call a probability of one—over the Senate, for the change of his vote would change the outcome. If the majority is two, every senator in the majority has the power to produce a tie—the power, that is, to give the vice president complete power over the Senate.

To put the matter mathematically, let P_{im} equal the power of a member of the majority. Then

$$P_{im}(n/2 + 3) = 0, \text{ and } P_{im}(n/2 + 1) = 1$$

If power is equated to probability, it cannot exceed unity. But here we have multiple probabilities and multiplied power. Let $P[(n/2) + 1]$ equal the power of all the numbers of a majority with a margin of 1. Then on a single vote $P[(n/2) + 1] = (n/2) + 1$. Clearly we are not talking of probabilities. Nor are we talking of power.

Dahl recognizes certain imperfections in his scheme: a senator may achieve a high rating by correctly anticipating the vote of the majority; or he may do so by aping a genuinely powerful member. These are not the most important weaknesses in the scheme. Very often the vote of a senator demonstrates not his power but his powerlessness. When the president or the floor leader or a group of constituents does w, the senator does x. To define power in terms of votes is to invent a purely nominal definition of power.

In a study that has become famous, L. S. Shapley and Martin Shubik[39] offered a method for the a priori evaluation of the division of power among the various bodies and members of a legislature or committee system. This is accomplished with simple fractions. Decisive power in a committee vote is attributed to the member whose vote completes the majority of one side or the other. If there are n members, each member has $1/n$th chance of being the pivotal member; therefore all members have equal power. The vice president, with his power to break a tie, has as much power as any senator, unless it happens that an odd number of senators are present. The power indices of Senate, House, and president are 5:5:2, figures which reflect their tie-breaking power. "The indices for a *single* Congressman, a *single* Senator, and the President are in the proportion 2:9:350."[40] These computations, we are told, are not able to catch "all the subtle shades and nuances of custom and procedure that are to be found in most real decision-making bodies."[41] Nevertheless, the a priori power index will serve as a standard the departure from which will constitute a measure of empirical factors.

Herbert Simon has said that this index consorts well with his intuitive notion of power,[42] and Richard C. Snyder regards it as a true report of "voting power."[43] This is odd. As we said above, a legislator's vote may be a response to power rather than the exercise of power. Moreover, it is rare that a measure carries by a single vote. Therefore it is seldom true that the member who first completes the majority is responsible for the passage of the measure; it would in any case be carried by one of the later affirmative votes on the roll call. Nor does it appear that the pivotal member actually contributes more to the passage of the bill than one of the earlier voters who has made his vote pivotal. But the most important shortcoming is the psychology of the scheme. Do legislators actually value the occupancy of a mathematically defined position in a series? Did any southern senator ever vote in favor of a civil rights bill because he discovered that his position in the roll call would enable him to carry the measure if he voted in the affirmative? What Shapley and Shubik offer us is a permutation index, called a power index by an act of nominal definition.

William H. Riker undertook "A Test of the Adequacy of the Power Index."[44] His purpose was to test the assumption that men seek power, "the kind of power that the index measures"—the status, that is, of "the last added member of a minimal winning coalition."[45] He calls his investigation an empirical test of the assumption; since the question is psychological, one would expect him to use opinions as data. Instead, he uses changes of party affiliation. He adopts the a priori method of Shapley and Shubik and complicates it by introducing political parties. The power of a party—the frequency, that is, with which a party occupies a pivotal position in a scheme of random voting—varies with the size of the party; but a weighted index for all the parties can be computed from the theory of games. The power of an individual member in a party of m members will be $1/m$ of the party's power, since he will occupy the pivotal position once out of m times in a scheme of random voting. The test itself is to measure the power of members who migrated from party to party in the French National Assembly before and after their change of parties. If the assumption is sound, such migrations should show an improvement in the power of the migrants. But the study shows an average power loss of 5.9 percent for each migrant. (By assuming that the party benefited by the migrant makes a payoff to the migrant of its "total gain" from the migration, Riker reduces the loss to 1.7 percent. In what currency the party makes the payoff we are not told. The only units of value in the system are the values of the position of pivot man in the party and the position of pivot party in the legislature. The party cannot alter either of these figures, which means that the values are not transferable.) These results seem to discredit the formula, but Riker finds fault with his empirical test. He rejects the suggestion that more than forty of the six-hundred-odd members of the National Assembly were moved by ideology; and for him the sole remaining motive is playing the role of pivot man. One objection to the test might be the fact that parties have different capacities for entering into coalitions, and the power indices are therefore inaccurate. Riker rejects this explanation. More plausible to him is the suggestion that the power computations were so complicated that the migrants made errors in their calculations. Both these obstacles seem so formidable that, aside from the frivolous character of the thesis, one wonders why Riker undertook the study, and why he published it when it failed. Or did it fail? Perhaps it demonstrated that the behavior of legislators is not controlled by the ambition to be the $(n/2)+1$ man on one side—no matter which—on a roll call.

Riker is also the author of "A Method for Determining the Significance of Roll Calls in Voting Bodies."[46] What is needed is a "quasi-objective scale of significance." A single observer, and a panel of observers, will suffer from bias. "But it is both impossible and foolish to attempt to eliminate bias from judgments of significance. Significance involves meaning; and meaning must have reference to some persons. The problem is not to eliminate subjective judgment, but to select the persons whose subjective judgment will be used to weight roll calls. It seems intuitively justifiable that the persons whose judgments are so used ought to be those who, by their actions, make the significance, that is, the members of the legislature themselves."[47]

Therefore I suggest the following definitions: the *most significant* roll call possible is one in which (1) all members vote, and (2) the difference between the majority and the minority is the minimum possible under the voting rules. Conversely, the *least significant* roll call is one in which (1) a bare quorum votes, and (2) the outcome is unanimous.

Riker then contrives a formula for significance in which the total number of members, the number voting on each side, and the quorum requirements are all represented.

A mathematical measure of significance is of course absurd. Mathematics measures magnitudes and not significance. The formula yields only a number, nothing more.

But it is worthwhile to examine the assumptions Riker put into the formula. Clearly he has equated significance with intensity of feeling. He thinks that a large vote indicates such intensity, although a large turnout is not inconsistent with indifference. It is of course also true that there may be a small turnout and yet every member may vote at white heat. He considers that a closely divided vote indicates high feeling on both sides. But this is not necessarily true; and it is possible that when there is a huge majority, as for a declaration of war, all the members are experiencing very intense emotions. In short, Riker's formula is a very unsatisfactory attempt at a real definition of the psychological state of agitation of the legislators. Specialists in this field have a more direct method; they measure the perspiration rate. But when a false definition of agitation is converted into a nominal definition of significance, it becomes impossible to complain.

A real definition of significance would have to take account of the fact that a judgment of significance is not merely an emotional experience. It involves an intellectual appraisal of the consequences of an action for one or another value. Judgments of significance—forecasts of the future—may therefore be in error. In the case of legislators, it is of course notorious that they often vote on bills without reading them and without making any forecast except of the consequences of their votes for their own personal fortunes. It would not be difficult to show that when they do make forecasts of the general consequences of their votes they are usually in error. Congressmen are poor judges of significance.

James G. March has given another mathematical treatment of the problem of power or, as he calls it, influence.[48] He sets up matrices concerning the probability of given outcomes when the incumbents of certain positions—say, the president and the speaker—support or oppose a bill. This elaborate exercise involves two solecisms: it is impossible to supply empirical values for the symbolically designated values, which would be necessary if the formulations were to be meaningful; and the mathematical concept of probability is inapplicable to unique events, which the outcomes would be if they were given an empirical content. But the argument is mathematically unexceptionable. If the president's influence in favor of a bill is a, and in opposition $-a$, if the Speaker's influence in favor is B and in opposition $-B$, then when they both favor the bill the sum is $a+B$; when the president favors the bill and the Speaker opposes it, the sum is *a–B,* and so on. We are given no reason why the influence of a president or a Speaker in favor of a bill should be of the same absolute magnitude as his influence against it; but since the formulations are operationally meaningless there is no need to quarrel with them. In fact, of course, what we have here is an exercise in arithmetic and not a scientific formulation about influence. As children we learned that if John has three apples and James has one apple, together they have four apples. This problem bears the same relation to the science of pomology that March's formulations bear to political science.

Charles D. Farris has given us a nominal definition of ideology.[49] There are, he says, three ways of dealing with this phenomenon: "verbalism about the meaning of the word"; postponement of research "until most members of the profession agree on what the word means"; and behavioral research by "operational criteria." Being, apparently, an impatient man, he adopted the last course.

Farris examined roll-call votes on five issues in the House of Representatives in 1946. There were "32 logically possible groupings of pro and con positions on five issues." Each of these he calls a distinct ideology. Another roll call would produce 64 ideologies; by the end of the session the number of ideologies would be astronomical. And the ideology of a legislator would change every time he cast another vote. But most of these ideologies were empty houses. Only 12 of Farris's 32 possible ideologies were represented in the House. What we have here, of course, is a report of voting clusters in the House, the smallest 0.9 percent and the largest 23.3 percent. These clusters become tenants of 12 of the 32 possible ideologies by an act of nominal definition. Certainly the *definiens* is operational—it is an exercise in the mathematics of combinations—but the *definiendum* is meaningless. One does not supply empirical content to the *definiendum* by putting an empirical content in 12 of the 32 empty boxes in the *definiens.*

These are some of the better-known nominal definitions. The reader can recall others; or, if he likes, he can invent new ones ad libitum.

GAME THEORY

In 1944 John von Neumann and Oskar Morgenstern introduced "decision-making" into economics under the name of game theory.[50] They were able to show that if two or more players competed with each other under agreed rules for an agreed good, or utility, and if adequate knowledge and data were available, there was, or might be, a preferred strategy or range of strategies for each. This could be computed in terms of probabilities of outcome.

Game theory has evoked more enthusiasm among political scientists than any other technique. But it has three fatal disabilities: it assumes the objectivity, measurability, and commensurability of values; it makes indefensible psychological assumptions; and, on the practical level, it assumes that it is possible to obtain the empirical data necessary to compute the probabilities.

In the application of game theory in economics, values are allowed to collapse into dollars, which have the convertibility and measurability which the theory demands, and which present the necessary appearance of objectivity. Of course, utility always has a subjective foundation; and for logical positivists like game theorists it is exclusively subjective. Insofar as they rest on subjective states of mind, utilities are not stable but variable. Northrop has shown that economics cannot be a science in the sense of the physical sciences because the central concept is value and values wax, wane, and change in time; science, however, requires invariability.[51]

Some political scientists attempt to use dollars as the values of a political system. So Buchanan and Tullock reduce politics to the bids and sidepayments of three farmers jockeying to obtain the most favorable location of a road, a location which has a precise dollar value for each.[52] But most political contests—including this one—cannot be expressed in dollars.

William H. Riker has constructed a *Theory of Political Coalitions*[53] by means of game theory. The purpose of a coalition is to despoil others. Rational calculation keeps the winning coalition as small as possible; this maximizes the share of each partner. Riker treats of costs in the building of a coalition, and recognizes that the cost may exceed the prospective gain from the coalition. Costs may be in money or charisma or love; payments may be in threats of reprisal or money or policy or promises or emotional satisfaction. Unfortunately these things cannot be computed: "Utiles are just a convention for theorizing, not an actual measure which real persons can use."[54] A formula in terms of such utiles is clearly not operational.

In discussing the conflicts for which coalitions are built—markets and elections and war—Riker ignores cost. The conflict is treated as a zero-sum game, one in which the whole loss of the loser is imputed to the victor, and the victor retains his original utilities, as in poker. The "payoff" is in money or power or success.[55] "Often, and especially now when there is threat of nuclear war, the game has seemed non-zero-sum, that is, the common benefits of peace and civilization have seemed greater than any possible gain from conflict."[56] Nevertheless, "total war," which apparently means nuclear war, can be treated as a zero-sum game because "the loss of the losers, i.e., their destruction, is the announced object of the winners. The gain is the exact reverse of the loss."[57]

No other author has been more successful in establishing standardized utiles for a political game. The theory is also weak on the psychological side. It is not only necessary that there be measurable objective utiles at stake in the conflict; the decision-maker must attach exclusive value to these utiles. Riker solves this problem by pointing out that government is conducted by trustees, and attributing a special character to a trustee: "The one duty of the fiduciary agent is to guard the position of the beneficiary of the trust."[58] He has "one overriding moral standard: promote the interests of the beneficiary."[59] It is curious that in other mathematical discussions of the actions of fiduciary agents, Riker attributes to them the sole motive of promoting their own interests, which are described as maximizing personal power. In fact, of course, the whole vocabulary of value and emotion is needed to describe the conduct of any man, whether he is a trustee or not.

It is perplexing that anyone with the slightest acquaintance with history could suppose that decisions are reached on the motives and by the calculations postulated by game theory. "At the sight of the actions of man displayed on the great stage of the world," said Immanuel Kant, "it is impossible to escape a certain degree of disgust":[60]

With all the occasional indications of wisdom scattered here and there, we cannot but perceive the whole sum of these actions to be a web of folly, childish vanity, and often even of the idlest wickedness and spirit of destruction. Hence, at last, one is puzzled to know what judgment to form of our species so conceited of its high advantages.

If the psychology of game theory were applicable anywhere, it would be in games, where the utiles are defined and definite, the player has no motive except to acquire utiles, and the probabilities are calculable. Yet the psychological studies of gambling show that players regularly behave with less than the complete rationality imputed to them by game theory.[61]

Even more impressive a defect of game theory in politics, perhaps, is the flat impossibility of computing the probabilities which are supposed to govern rational decision. At a time when such matters were infinitely more simple than now, Clausewitz wrote:[62]

In order to ascertain the real scale of the means which we must put forth for war, we must think over the political object both on our side and on the enemy's side; we must consider the power and position of the enemy's State as well as our own, the character of his Government and of his people, and the capacities of both, and all that again on our own side, and the political connections of other States, and the effect which the War will produce on those States. That the determination of these diverse circumstances and their diverse connections with each other is an immense problem, that it is the true flash of genius which discovers here in a moment what is right, and that it would be quite out of the question to become master of the complexity merely by a methodical study, it is easy to conceive. In this sense Buonaparte was quite right when he said that it would be a problem in algebra before which a Newton might stand aghast.

Whence, then, come the empirical data that game theorists sometimes build into their studies? The answer is simple: they are invented. Philip Green has shown that the computations of Herman Kahn for thermonuclear war lack both evidence and plausibility.[63]

Game theory is a branch of economics; its utiles derive from the hedonistic calculus of Utilitarianism. One is tempted to say, as Macaulay said of the Utilitarians, that game theorists do no particular harm: they might as well be game theorists as jockeys or dandies; "It certainly hurts the health less than hard drinking, and the fortune less than high play."[64] But in fact they are dangerous. The incredibly superficial outlook of game theory is mistaken for a foreign policy.[65] Officials of the RAND Corporation complain that Secretary McNamara has drafted so many of their experts to the Pentagon that they have not enough left to man the computers.

Richard Snyder considered that John Foster Dulles was an intuitive game theorist. In 1955 he wrote:[66]

It is interesting to consider the present problem confronting Secretary of State Dulles over the defense of Formosa. If the United States is considered to be in a two-person, non–zero-sum game with Communist China, the theory suggests that the optimum strategy for the United States is to move first and commit itself to a defense of Formosa by some sort of device that would make it impossible to reverse the decision. This is so because often in a non–zero-sum game both players can lose, especially if one of the pay-offs is war. If the Formosa situation were a zero-sum game, the early commitment of the United States to a strategy might not be desirable. Although in such a game it does not matter whether one is predictable or not, bluff may offer one's opponent an opportunity for error that can be turned into a gain.

On the contrary, bluff in a non–zero-sum game may tempt your opponent into the use of a strategy that results in a negative pay-off for both players. From the standpoint of the safest course of action in Formosa, an automatic defense of Formosa—perhaps triggered by some automatic mechanism—would be most desirable because the opponent (in this case Communist China) must know that the strategy cannot be altered.... If the Secretary's diagnosis happens to coincide with the diagnosis of the theory, it is probable that it coincided because his reasoning followed the pattern indicated by the theory.

Thus, game theory leads directly to Herman Kahn's Doomsday Machine. The United States, said Kahn, might deliver ultimata to the Soviet Union, and make them plausible by irrevocably activating nuclear devices capable of destroying the earth which would be triggered automatically by a violation of any ultimatum.[67] If the earth were destroyed, the fault would lie with the irrationality of the adversary. This proposal, which according to Kahn is technologically quite feasible, evoked little enthusiasm even in the Pentagon. It could appeal only to intellectual and moral cretins. But, as Snyder has pointed out, it is the logical culmination of game theory.

At least since the advent of nuclear weapons, it has been inappropriate for states to behave as Rome and Carthage behaved. Such a conception of national interest is operationally meaningless. No state any longer has an interest distinguishable from the interest of the whole world. As John H. Herz has said: "Under the standards of a new humanism which places the preservation of the human race above any and all partial interests, the same behavior pattern now emerges as indispensable to national policy if the entire race is not to perish." He warns that if we continue the pursuit of "national interest narrowly conceived,... a catastrophic blowup will become an almost mathematical certainty."[68]

The certainty is indeed almost mathematical, but the computations lie outside the mathematics of game theorists. In the course of a torrent of prescriptions for American foreign policy, Morton A. Kaplan, on the basis, no doubt, of his confidence in game theory, asks for evidence that arms races lead to war, and opines:[69]

> If one thing is clear about the present, it is that some aspects of the arms race have improved the stability of peace in the world we live in, have diminished the probability that a nuclear accident or a provocative situation will produce war, and have made it possible to control nuclear war, if it occurs. Perhaps much of the "detente" which we perceive can be attributed to this greater military stability. Whether a continued arms race would have similar felicitous consequences or whether these would be overbalanced by unfavorable aspects of the arms race is a matter for sober and cautious analysis.

Kaplan does not have the usual hospitable attitude of the behavioralist toward the other social sciences: "Practitioners would do well to avoid the half-digested contributions of psychologists, anthropologists, and sociologists to the problems of foreign policy."[70] But game theory rests on a psychology, one that has been obsolete for nearly a hundred years. To be sure, one cannot tell how far Kaplan accepts the psychology on which his system is founded. He finds the United States deficient in the qualities of the game theorist: "We lack the will to act, the coldness to engage in counterterror, and the skill to discriminate among the contenders for favor."[71] And he considers that the Communist leaders do not pursue the utiles of the game and do not behave rationally; they are "paranoids."[72] Under these circumstances, what is left of game theory? Game theory assumes the rationality of both parties. Responses intended to counter the moves of a rational adversary will be inappropriate against an irrational adversary. Whatever may be the proper strategy against paranoids, it is not game theory.

But of course game theory is not a discipline and cannot solve any political problem. Its real function is to restate the problem that faces the world. Certainly Utilitarian psychology and economics had a broader purpose, but they were used in the nineteenth century to justify the world view of Dickens' Gradgrind and thus foreclose attempts at the solution of social problems. Game theory employs the same psychology to argue for the inevitability of the cold war. The one real consequence of the adoption of game theory is to bottom the discussion of international affairs on the assumption of reciprocal intransigent hostility. Game theory is academically more respectable than the philosophy of the John Birch Society; but it performs the same social function. And it performs no other function.

JURIMETRICS

In 1941 C. Herman Pritchett introduced the "box-score" method of displaying the agreement and disagreement of the several Supreme Court justices in the 1939 and 1940 terms.[73] In 1951 the psychologist Louis L. Thurstone, after Spearman the author of factor analysis, applied this technique to divided votes in the 1943 and 1944 terms as "an exploration in scientific method on the problem of identifying the blocs or subgroups within a larger group as in a legislature, council, or court, in terms of the voting records of the members"; but he refrained from drawing any psychological conclusions.[74]

In the past decade several political scientists have used mathematical techniques to compare divided votes and pairs of justices; even more frequently they have exhibited the voting records of justices on a Guttman scale. When the data can be so scaled, they display a quite regular descending order of concurrence like a stairway.

A summary of data, mathematically or graphically presented, is authentic fact, and can be used for whatever this fact is useful for. The behavioralists believe that from past votes of justices it is possible to predict future votes. Prediction has not merely practical but scientific value; it is the "verification of theory."[75]

The most popular school of thought believes that it is also possible to establish the significant features of the personality structures of the participating justices by techniques of comparison. In this case, personality is the mediating factor between the past votes and the predicted judicial behavior.

The comparative method of the behavioralists is applicable only to divided votes. Nevertheless, Glendon Schubert, the chief of those who distill psychological attitudes from votes, has offered a psychological explanation for unanimity. He points out that more than 90 percent of the decisions of the Supreme Court are unanimous,[76] and attributes this fact to "the homogeneity of values common to the justices as a group"[77] and "high communality in perception of the issues deemed relevant."[78] No doubt this is true of those decisions that follow the rule of stare decisis, but decisions that make new law must be explained in other terms. When the Court unanimously overthrew "separate but equal" in *Brown* v. *Board of Education*,[79] it was not applying settled legal values. Clearly a majority of the justices were determined to introduce a new value, but it seems unlikely that all of them really desired this. Probably some concurred for political reasons—most important, perhaps, the desirability of presenting a united front in the battle that was sure to follow.

Schubert has enumerated some of the occasional and personal factors that may influence a judge.[80]

Out of the entire situation (including the record, briefs, oral argument, conversation with colleagues, newspaper and television commentary, law review articles, the competence of his clerk, the current state of mental and physical health of himself and his family, perhaps the war news from Viet Nam, et cetera, ad infinitum, plus the remembered and the sublimated historical antecedents of all of these events) a judge defines the issue to which he will react in his decision. Much of his training as a lawyer, and of his socialization as a judge, combine with the customs and institutional procedures for judicial decision-making to provide maximal (within the range of possible variation for human beings) assurance that his cognition of the situation will be highly structured, especially when he defines the question for decision.

In addition to the influences listed by Schubert, we might point to the diversity of the ideological factors that affect judges. Justice Holmes charged the majority of the Court with coining Herbert Spencer's *Social Statics* into law.[81] Holmes himself coined Darwinism into law.[82] Justice Field's conception of due process was derived from the Christian idea of vocation.[83] Justice Burton dissented from a decision upholding the dismissal of public employees for past membership in the Communist party because the law contravened the Christian doctrine of repentance.[84] And it is familiar that a great variety of ethical and social ideas have supplied the content of due process on such subjects as procedure, economic regulation, speech, picketing, obscenity, and freedom of religion.

The number and the diversity of these influences might make one despair; it might lead to the pessimism of the rule-skeptics among the legal realists. But Schubert is confident that the data can be ordered: "The number of basic attitudinal dimensions that are relevant to the decision-making of the United States Supreme Court is very small."[85]

The explicit reliance of such authors is on attitude psychology. But they do not undertake to establish the judge's personality structure by psychological evidence, and then relate his personality to his votes.[86] Like orthodox lawyers, they confine themselves to the decisions. They define the problem, sometimes in terms of the legal issue before the court, sometimes in terms of the legal or social roles of the litigants, and then they compare the votes of the judges. If the vote is unanimous, nothing can be concluded. A single divided vote tells nothing. But if a substantial series of cases involving the same problem, whether defined in terms of issues or of litigants, can be discovered, and if the votes of each judge are consistent, or fairly consistent, in relation to the votes of his brother judges, this is taken to demonstrate two things. The problem is a real problem in the sense that the factual determinant of judicial votes has been isolated. And the psychological determinant has also been isolated. The responses of the judges to the facts attest to the presence or absence of a psychological attitude. Sometimes the cases simply display a permanent division of the court into blocs, like the "liberal" and "conservative" blocs identified by Pritchett. Sometimes the cases in the series present not a single issue but a succession of graded issues, progressing from one extreme to another. In this case, each judge has a "break point" which represents the extremity of his attitude; his vote changes when this point is passed. The several judges will have different break points, so that their differential adhesion to the value in question can be exhibited on a Guttman scale.

No attitude psychologist has undertaken to explain reasoned decisions in terms of attitudes. Attitudes or dispositions or biases are raw materials that go into decisions; but there are involved also rational calculation of the relation of means to ends and a rational evaluation of the end itself—a weighing of alternatives, costs, and consequences. It is in this sense that a choice among values can be said to be correct or incorrect: the decision inevitably involves reasoning, and this may be in error.[87] The obvious explanation of the consistency of the votes of a judge on an issue is that he has arrived at a settled opinion on the merits. An attitude or attitudes contributed to this conclusion; but rational appraisal of the problem and the outcome entered in as well. More than one variable is involved.

Attitude *a*, coupled with propositions *m* and *n*, may lead to vote *v*; attitude *b*, coupled with propositions *x* and *y*, may lead to vote *v*. This is clearly demonstrated in some concurring opinions. Judicial behavioralists, however, believe that votes have a one-to-one correspondence to appropriate attitudes. So behavioralism puts on attitude psychology a burden beyond its powers.

There are two other difficulties. The attitudes employed by behavioralists are not established by any psychological test but are borrowed from political polemics; they are versions of the political formula of "liberal-conservative" applied to judges in the controversial literature of the 1920s and 1930s. Moreover, the method of judicial behavioralism requires that attitudes come in pairs—"liberal" and "conservative"—and constitute polar opposites between which judges can be arrayed on a scale. But in psychology the opposite of an attitude is the absence of the attitude; it is not another attitude. Richard S. Cruchfield has summarized the literature: "We have tended to call someone liberal if he rejected the values of conservatism.... All persons who reject conservatism may not be liberals, for as in the case of the "authoritarian-democratic" dimension, liberalism-conservatism may not be variables, paired in such a way that a high score on one necessarily signifies a low score on the other."[88]

Schubert's first venture in scaling arrayed the justices on the question: "How sympathetic are you to claims of the right to counsel under the Fourteenth Amendment?"[89] Such a sympathy is not one of the attitudes one encounters in psychological literature. Nor is a subjective experience like sympathy very accurately measured by a vote on the real question before the Court: "Shall this defendant have a new trial?" The ordering of the judges by their votes is not an ordering by greater and lesser quantities of sympathy; it merely discloses how judges have voted on the question of right to counsel in the immediate case. It is a report of outcomes and not of causes.

Right to counsel involves a highly specialized attitude. Subsequently Schubert generalized his scale to a liberalism-conservatism scale; but then he began to break it down topically, and now he recognizes at least seven attitudinal dimensions: liberalism and conservatism on civil liberties; economic liberalism and economic conservatism;[90] social liberalism and social conservatism; a fiscal scale, for cases between government and taxpayers; a judical activism-restraint scale; a federalism scale; and a scale on the authority of the Supreme Court over the inferior courts.[91] Harold J. Spaeth has divided the economic scale into two, one measuring attitude toward labor unions and one measuring attitude toward government regulation of business.[92]

Certainly this is moving in the right direction. If the business regulation scale were further divided topically, to distinguish, for example, between cases involving antitrust laws and cases involving fair-trade acts, even greater consistency would be achieved. But this process of analysis is not an increasingly accurate exploration of the personality structures of judges: it is a topical analysis of holdings in terms of legal categories. If the analysis is carried far enough we will have, not a psychology, but a legal text which reports the holdings on concrete problems and the dissenting votes.

In fact, the behavioral method of interpreting decisions comes down in the end precisely to the common law method. At common law, as for the behavioralists, the opinion is not the law, but only the holding on the facts of the case. In an early study Fred Kort analyzed the right-to-counsel cases in terms of the presence or absence of certain sets of facts.[93] There was no mention of attitudes or of psychology. Instead, Kort undertook to establish empirical constants for each relevant fact. If the facts, thus weighted, added to a critical sum, the Court would require that counsel be afforded. Subsequently Kort has argued that both simultaneous equations and Boolean algebra can be used "to obtain a *precise and exhaustive* distinction between combinations of facts that lead to decisions in favor of one party and combinations of facts that lead to decisions in favor of the opposing party."[94] These methods, however, cannot predict "doctrinal changes and the adoption of new rules of law."[95] Similarly, Stuart S. Nagel has recommended that the weights of sets of facts in right-to-counsel cases be determined by obtaining coefficients of correlation; when the sum of these weights in a particular case passes an empirically determined number, one expects the defendant to win.[96] Reed C. Lawlor has proposed the use of symbolic logic to relate facts to decisions.[97] Lawlor has quite correctly identified his method and Kort's and Nagel's as the practice of *stare decisis,* and has recognized that it is necessary to take account of "personal *stare decisis*"—the positions adopted on previous factual situations by individual justices.

This is a very reminiscent scheme; it is what Jerome Frank[98] called "legal fundamentalism." Like James C. Carter,[99] these authors believe that anyone who examines the facts and applies himself to the precedents is bound to arrive at the right conclusion. A legal problem is merely a problem of cognition. But if it is necessary to employ a computer to work the sums, may not a judge make an error? Joseph H. Beale, whom Frank made his principal target, was more realistic. He recognized that a judge might err in applying the precedents to the facts, in which case his decision simply was not law.

Schubert very properly rebukes these authors for ignoring psychological considerations, and for the artificial division between law and fact which is one aspect of the failure to consider psychology.[100] Lawlor asserts that it is unnecessary to make the personal factors explicit: "Even if the judge's personal inclinations are unknown, they are implicit in the equations."[101] Psychological factors, then, can be ignored: fact and law are linked in an invariable manner.

But in fact Schubert adds to Kort only an unwarranted assumption. He identifies the significant facts in the same way as Kort, and regards the vote of the judge as a direct response to this stimulus.[102] In addition, he assures us that what mediates between stimulus and response is a psychological attitude. But he confesses that his attitudes are not empirical; they are "logical inferences from sets of decisional responses."[103] At no point does Schubert offer evidence on the question of the personality structure of a judge. Operationally, he merely adduces data of two sorts. Like Kort, he shows that in many cases a given stimulus is followed by a given response; but no more than Kort does he supply the causal link between the two. And he shows that in many cases the responses of judges on an issue can be ranked; but he does not demonstrate that this ranking is in terms of differential quantities of a given psychological attitude.

If one could measure psychological attitudes (As) independently, and then relate them to a fixed stimulus and varying responses, so that the scale reads S-A_1-R_1, S-A_2-R_2, ... S-A_n-R_n, we could conclude, as Schubert does, that "the votes of judges are attitudinal responses to the public policy issues raised for decision by cases."[104] But Schubert offers us $A_1 = S$-R_1, $A_2 = S$-R_2, ... $A_n = S$-R_n. The As are not otherwise identified or measured. This is merely a series of nominal definitions of attitudes which begs the question as to whether decisions are in fact simply functions of psychological attitudes.

Still other behavioral explanations of judicial conduct have been offered. In a study of the 1936 term of the Supreme Court, Schubert identified a three-man bloc moved by a liberal attitude, a four-man bloc moved by a conservative attitude, and a two-man bloc consisting of Chief Justice Hughes and his supporter Justice Roberts—Schubert calls the bloc Hughberts.[105] Inexplicably, it is asserted that Hughberts is neither liberal nor conservative. Nevertheless, on all the occasions on which this was possible except two, Hughberts joined with the three-man liberal bloc to form a majority rather than with the four-man conservative bloc. Schubert offers two explanations. The first is in terms of the Shapley-Shubik power index. If the members are rotated, a member of a five-man bloc is the swing-man making up a majority once in every five times; in a six-man bloc, he occupies the prized position which carries power only once in six times. Hughberts has maximized his power by voting with the three-man bloc. The second explanation is not supported by mathematics, but one can accept it by *Verstehen;* by giving decisions favorable to the New Deal, Hughberts hoped to ward off legislation directed against the Court.

If one employed Schubert's usual method, he would explain the votes of Hughes and Roberts by attributing liberal attitudes to them. There is no more reason to ascribe an appetite for Shapley-Shubik power, which after all brings only mathematical satisfactions, to the two-man Hughberts bloc that joined the three-man bloc than to the three-man bloc that joined the two-man Hughberts bloc. And it appears that Hughberts was not moved by a lust for Shapley-Shubik power in the 1931-35 terms, for then he regularly formed majorities with the four-man bloc;[106] but perhaps he had not yet learned to calculate permutations.

In the Hughberts game only two justices sought Shapley-Shubik power by practicing game theory, but S. Sidney Ulmer has ranked all the justices on a Shapley-Shubik index.[107] And both Samuel Krislov[108] and Shubert[109] have offered abstract discussions of coalition-formation on the Supreme Court in Shapley-Shubik terms. This is less plausible than Riker's theory of coalitions: in Riker's scheme, the majority coalition can exclude and expel members, whereas on the Supreme Court any justice can leave the minority position of powerlessness and achieve a fractional share of majority power simply by changing his vote. Schubert makes no effort to reconcile the Shapley-Shubik psychology with his attitude psychology.

Schubert recognizes three contemporary schools in the study of public law: the traditional, the conventional or political, and the behavioral.[110] Traditionalists explain a judge's decisions in part in terms of an authoritative structure of norms, in part in terms of his legal philosophy. For the conventionalists the judge is "a transmission belt for the articulation of group (social) interests."[111] "Behavioralists assign a predominant weight to judicial personality as a source of substantive decisional norms."[112]

All three schools have a common purpose: it is to establish a causal explanation for judicial decisions. This would be a useful and gratifying accomplishment. But most students of public law belong to a fourth school; in the new literature they would bear the flattering name of "policy scientists."[113] They regard law not merely as a phenomenon but as an instrument. They are not primarily interested in the explanation of past events, or even in forecasting the future in terms of the past. They are interested in controlling the future. They study opinions rather than votes because the outcomes they are concerned with are not votes but the social consequences of decisions.

Law is the making of choices; to a degree, it is the shaping of society and of the future. Like ethics, law is concerned with goals, with objectives. A judicial opinion is a statement of values and a forecast of the consequences for one or another value of the policy adopted by the court. But constitutional decisions are problems; they are not always solutions. Often the judges are mistaken. What the social scientist has to contribute is an understanding of inherited values, or history; an account of the shaping of new values, through psychology and sociology; and a projection of the consequences of choice, by ideal types, developmental constructs, analogy, or *Verstehen*. Almost certainly this is not enough. But it is an enterprise of enormously greater importance than the exhibition of past events on a Guttman scale, or the calculation of the tactics by which judges can most frequently attain the position of swing-man on a vote.

THE GREAT LEAP UPWARD

Unlike the other schools described above, the jurimetricians concern themselves with empirical data. They report and correlate certain facts. Such an ordering of data is not a scientific achievement, but it may be immediately useful to one who is interested in these facts; and it may suggest a hypothesis and lead to further inquiry.

The compilation of mathematical summaries of empirical data is as old as taxation. The comparison of two series of events goes back at least to the seventeenth century; sophisticated techniques of correlation are more recent. Since many propositions in politics assert the existence of a correlation of one sort or another, devices for testing such propositions can be very useful.

Some branches of physics have found it convenient to describe their findings as statistical probabilities rather than deterministic laws. Behavioral political scientists sometimes talk as though social science were in an analogous position, and they too by the use of statistics of correlation could obtain something equivalent to a theoretically elaborated law.

But the analogy fails. Physics deals with the behavior of entities which have been reduced to identities. One hydrogen atom is indistinguishable from another hydrogen atom. No such reduction has been achieved in social science. Personality factors, cultural factors, differences in the immediate environment, and historical factors—the past, the present, and the anticipated future—make it impossible to treat the members of a voting population as interchangeable units. Considerations of the same order make it impossible to assume that the structure of one voting population will resemble the structure of another voting population. Until we know better, we shall assume that one population of hydrogen atoms will behave in the same way as another population of hydrogen atoms. Since we know that the members of one human population are identical with the members of another human population in only a few biological respects, we do not expect these populations to behave alike.[114]

A. A. Tschuprow emphasizes "the difference between statistical correlation and natural law."[115]

The regression equation of Y on X expresses the functional relationship between the conditional mathematical expectation of Y and X....

Yet the law of nature is always reversible. If Y is an explicit function of X one can express X as an explicit function of Y by means of formal-mathematical operations and suitable symbols: if $Y=X^2$, then X equals the square root of Y.... On the contrary, the regression equation of Y on X and the regression equation of X on Y are not deducible from each other.... By no ingenuity of mathematical reasoning can one equation be deduced from the other: each must be obtained independently by the consideration of the joint frequency distribution. This is itself by no means surprising, since the regression equations do not connect the same magnitudes: the one connects the conditional mathematical expectation of Y with X, the other, the conditional mathematical expectation of X with Y; they have just as little in common as an equation which connects X and Y with another equation which connects two variables, U and V.

To put it another way, a nomothetic formula is a logical proposition; a regression equation is a factual description—a report of the values an empirical Y can have, and their frequencies, when an empirical X assumes a given value.

Sometimes, when a table of empirical data reports varying outcomes, the fraction of the total which an outcome constitutes is called a probability. The Jury Verdict Research Company began in 1960 a two-volume loose-leaf service, *Verdict Expectancies* and a *Valuation Handbook.* Reviewing the data, Stuart S. Nagel[116] says that a pedestrian hit by an automobile at a point other than a crosswalk has a 34 percent chance of winning a lawsuit; a plaintiff bitten by a dog has a 46 percent chance of winning. The data, of course, show nothing about the chances of any litigant: they show that 34 and 46 percent of the persons who brought the specified actions within the specified period of time won. But some pedestrians and some victims of dog bites who might conceivably have won never contemplated suit; an unknown number who presumably would have lost were dissuaded by their attorneys from suing. Aside from this, all the conditions for assessing probability in an individual case are lacking. The only meaning of probability when a lawsuit is contemplated is the subjective estimate of an attorney concerning what he and the defense attorney can persuade an as yet unknown jury to believe and to feel.

William H. Riker and Ronald Schaps have undertaken to establish an "index of disharmony" in federal government and to validate it by correlation.[117] Using the Shapley-Shubik power index described above, they computed the power of the two political parties in the national government and in the states for the years 1937-56. When party A has a power index of more than 0.5 in the national government, an index of disharmony can be computed. This is arrived at by subtracting the power index of the same party for all the states from 1.0. If the remainder, the index of disharmony, exceeds 0.5, this means that rival parties dominate the national government and the states. The higher the index, the greater the power of party B in the states and, according to the hypothesis, the greater the disharmony between the national government, controlled by party A, and the states.

Riker and Schaps offered an empirical test for their thesis that parties are the source of harmony and disharmony in federal government. For the period embraced by their study, they counted the lawsuits which reached the Supreme Court, at least to the point of denial of certiorari, in which the United States was a litigant against a state or submitted a brief amicus curiae against a state as a litigant, and those in which the United States was a litigant and a state or states submitted a brief amicus curiae against the United States. Then these episodes of disharmony were reduced by subtracting from them cases in which the United States and a state were on the same side or one of them submitted a brief amicus curiae in support of the other. No reason for introducing these evidences of harmony is given, but it considerably improves the result.[118]

> Assuming that federal cases in the Supreme Court reveal the existence of actual federal disharmony, we counted the number of such events and correlated this number, by bienniums, with the index of disharmony. This calculation resulted in a coefficient of correlation of about +.79. Testing this coefficient against the hypothesis that it might have occurred by chance, it appears that the coefficient is just within the 2 percent level of confidence, which is to say that a correlation this high would occur by chance only in 2/100 of the possible correlations.

In fact, the authors assure us, "the correlation is more impressive than it appears."

Of course, lawsuits very frequently array national policies or interests against state policies or interests, and this is disharmony of a kind. Much more often than not these collisions occur in suits between private persons, or suits in which the national government or a state is involved, but not both. Riker and Schaps have rejected this body of data; they have limited their survey to cases in which both governments appear, if only as amici curiae. This must be because there have been two governmental decisions to participate in the immediate lawsuit. The next appropriate step would be to show that in suits between the national government and states, one party controlled the one and the other party the other, and that in suits in which they were on the same side the same party controlled both governments. This would be a more meaningful correlation between political parties and lawsuits than that of Riker and Schaps—a correlation between lawsuits and gross electoral results. But the considerations that array the national government and the states against each other in court, or on the same side, very seldom have anything to do with Republicans and Democrats.

We have here no real definition of disharmony, but two different nominal definitions. On the one hand, disharmony is equated with the situation in which the national government and a majority of the states are controlled by different political parties. On the other, it is equated with the occurrence of lawsuits between the national government and the states, whether or not these are controlled by different political parties. These nominal definitions are inconsistent with each other, since they name two different sets of data. But the authors believe that the two nominal definitions amalgamate and form a real definition because for a twenty-year period they found a high correlation between the two sets of data. The proper way to express their findings is to omit the word "disharmony" and to report the data: for a twenty-year period, when one party controlled the national government and the other controlled the states, the number of lawsuits in which the national government and the states appeared on opposite sides increased. But, in the absence of a showing that the lawsuits arrayed political parties as well as governments against each other, this can be nothing more than an accidental correlation.

In like fashion, unwarranted conclusions have been drawn from studies of the votes of legislators. George M. Belknap has shown that in their votes on amendments to the Taft-Hartley bill the senators can be roughly ordered on a one-dimensional scale.[119] Belknap avoids the assumption of personality types of liberal and conservative and falls back on more specialized attitudes: there are pro- and anti-labor attitudes. To the extent that the votes of senators express their attitudes, it is proper to infer the attitude from the votes, for the attitude is nothing more than a propensity to cast such votes. But of course a senator's attitude on the issue is only one influence on his vote; and it is often on the weaker side. Self-preservation may be a stronger motive. The general character of the senator's constituency affects his voting on labor questions. The voting behavior of Representative Keating from a conservative rural upstate district in New York differed markedly from that of Senator Keating from the urban state of New York; yet one doubts that his personality was restructured when he changed his constituency.

Dean R. Brimhall and Arthur S. Otis have introduced a variant on this method. They took the opinion of the editors of the *New Republic* as to whether a vote on each of eighteen issues was "progressive" or "conservative," and ranked senators and representatives in seven groups for each of four sessions.[120] They found that "there are 46 chances in 100 that a congressman's scale value will not change at all from any given year to the next; there are 83 chances in 100 that his scale value will not change more than one unit; and there are 95 changes in 100 that his scale will not change more than 2 units."[121] This is supposed to support the inference that there is consistency in voting behavior. It is true that in the case of congressmen whose averages placed them in the "progressive" classes 1 or 2 during the four sessions, one has a voting pattern—which does not necessarily yield an inference as to psychological type—which approaches the *New Republic*'s estimate of the merits of bills. In the case of those whose averages placed them in the "conservative" classes 6 and 7 for four years, one has a significant negative correlation with the judgment of the *New Republic*. These two groups account for 26 of the 96 senators. For the 70 senators in the intermediate classes 3, 4, and 5, there is no significant correlation with the judgment of the editors of the *New Republic*. The only "consistency in Congressional voting" shown by the study is the fact that the opinions of the *New Republic* do not relate in a significant way to congressional voting. This, of course, does not mean that consistency in voting is necessarily lacking. It does mean that the authors have chosen the wrong yardstick.

Considerably more ambitious is the attempt to establish a causal chain of several factors whose relations to each other and to the outcome are purportedly demonstrated by correlation. Hayward R. Alker, Jr., has offered alternative causal chains involving political participation, Communist vote, per capita gross national product, urbanization, literacy, polyarchy, and other topics.[122] Likewise he has identified voting clusters on roll calls in the United Nations, and has attributed these to causal factors.[123]

Arthur S. Goldberg took five characteristics of 645 voters in the 1956 presidential election and examined the correlation of these factors with each other and with the votes of the respondents.[124] The candidates and the issues, or the voters' opinions on these, were not included; campaign strategy was not considered; the contemporary state of affairs —economic conditions affecting the respondents, domestic and foreign political and social problems—and the respondents' perceptions of these, and their hopes and apprehensions about the future, were all omitted.

It is not surprising that Goldberg found it impossible to establish satisfactory correlations between his variables and the votes cast. He concluded that the contemporary scene must be included by building into the model an indeterminate number of perceptions of political events "as they arise in the political arena, probing in each case for evaluation of the party's handling of the events." Obviously an indefinite number of variable perceptions could not be built into a formula. We cannot expect regression equations to displace polling techniques.

Empirical correlations, like those of Alker and Goldberg, are mathematical descriptions of unique sets of facts. A description is not an explanation. Alker has said: *"Surely one can hypothesize that the coefficients in any statistical investigation of international behavior making additivity assumptions have 'realistic' or 'causal' significance. Until and unless some attempt has been made to verify the pattern of causal interdependence among the variables involved, however, these hypotheses must remain largely conjectural."*[125] Where are these hypotheses? The coefficients of correlation within a limited population of events are a set of statements about those events; they are not hypotheses about other events. Alker's hypotheses are not conjectural; they are unformulated.

Surely the most ambitious attempt to soar into the empyrean on wings composed of nothing more than mathematical reports of empirical data is an essay by William N. McPhee,[126] who is well known for voting studies. Given only the number of television programs surviving from year to year—given no standards for the classification of television programs into A, B, and C ratings, and the identification of no single program in terms of quality—he purported to establish what percentages of A, B, and C programs survived in the second half of the 1950s.[127] It was 81 percent for both A and B programs, 24 percent for C or inferior programs. If we redefine the symbols, the formulae will equally well support the conclusions that 24 percent of the best programs survived, and 81 percent of the intermediate and poor programs. One can do a number of things with an algebraic formula, but one cannot get milk from it, as McPhee has tried to do.

What is wrong with these studies, of course, is not that they use statistics. We shall never be able to dispense with counters and verifiers. But it is wrong to suppose that merely by compiling figures we can arrive at science. There is something wistful about the practice. During the last war the natives of New Guinea became accustomed to receiving goods from airplanes of which they knew nothing except that they came from the sky. After the war the planes came no more. Then there developed a new form of the "cargo cult": the natives built landing strips and facsimiles of airplanes on the ground, in the hope that they would attract planes loaded with cargo from the sky.[128] Mathematical behavioralists admire the natural sciences. They have built their facsimiles on the ground. But they have not drawn down bounty from the sky.

12

THE WALGREEN POLITICAL SCIENCE

In December, 1954, the Reece Committee on Tax-Exempt Foundations reported that the social sciences in the United States had been corrupted or dragooned by tax-exempt foundations into "an irresponsible 'fact finding mania.'"[1] Empiricism and experimentation threaten to bring national disaster. "Empiricism by the very nature of its approach ignores moral precepts, principles and established or accepted norms of behavior, and seeks to base conclusions solely upon what the senses will take in by means of observations."[2] This leads to moral relativism, and[3]

moral relativism and the cultural lag theory strike at the very root of the average American's traditional values. Promulgation of such unverified, pseudo-scientific theories dissolves the belief that religion gives us certain basic verities upon which we must construct a moral and ethical life, that certain basic and unalterable principles underlie our system of government and should be maintained faithfully for the preservation of our society.

Experimentation in the natural sciences is good.[4]

Experiment with human beings and their mode of living and being governed is, however, quite a different matter. If by "experiment" is meant trying to find ways in which to make existing institutions better or better working, that too would be admirable. If by "experiment" is meant trying to find ways in which other political and social institutions

---

Reprinted from *Indiana Law Journal* 30 (1955): 374–81. Used by permission of the Trustees of Indiana University and Fred B. Rothman and Company.

could be devised to supplant those we live by and are satisfied with—then such experiment is not a desirable use of public funds expended by private individuals without public accountability.

It follows that "some of the larger foundations have directly supported 'subversion' in the true meaning of that term, namely, the process of undermining some of our vital protective concepts and principles."[5]

It is a pity that the Committee did not examine the activities of the Charles R. Walgreen Foundation at the University of Chicago, for there it would have found comfort. After an initial period of uncertainty, the Walgreen Foundation has discovered its own political science—or political philosophy—one which rests on metaphysics rather than science, and which occupies itself with objective values rather than objective behavior. It is expressed in four volumes of lectures published by the University of Chicago Press: *Philosophy of Democratic Government* (1951), by Yves R. Simon; *The New Science of Politics* (1952), by Eric Voegelin; *Natural Right and History* (1953), by Leo Strauss; and *The Moral Foundation of Democracy* (1954), by John H. Hallowell. There are individual variations, but the four have a common source. This common source, the basis of the Walgreen political science, is the politics of St. Thomas Aquinas.

St. Thomas undertook to combine two sorts of truth: what he understood to be the teaching of Christian revelation and what he understood to be the teaching of reason. In the latter connection, he made extensive use of Aristotle, but necessarily a Christianized Aristotle who bore little resemblance to the pupil of Plato.[6] Even in Aquinas, reason and revelation were uneasy partners; and with later authors the emphasis shifted to one or the other element. Jesuit theology, launched by Molina in the sixteenth century and given definitive political expression by Suarez in the seventeenth, gave such attention to nature and reason as to overshadow revelation, and to expose the eighteenth-century Jesuits to the Jansenist accusation of infidelity. The Arminian Grotius went further and erected a rationalistic system independent not only of revelation but of deity. The Jansenists, on the other hand, adopted an approach resembling that of Calvin; for them revelation and the supernatural were virtually exclusive standards of truth and value.

Of our authors, Simon appears to occupy substantially the Jesuit position; he is certainly the closest to St. Thomas. Strauss seems to have the general intellectual orientation of Grotius, though, oddly enough, he does not discuss Grotius in his book. Without rejecting a supernatural approach to politics, he is satisfied with a naturalistic one, a position for which he has been chided by Hallowell.[7] Voegelin and Hallowell talk a great deal about "reason," but they both appear to be in the

Jansenist tradition. For them the supernatural is the essential and decisive element in politics. To Voegelin "the truth of man and the truth of God are inseparably one."[8] To Hallowell history is "a dialogue between God and Man."[9]

Our authors agree with the Reece Committee in rejecting empiricism as an approach to the study of politics. Voegelin makes a violent attack upon the collection of data without the guidance of "classical and Christian metaphysics."[10] Evidently the central metaphysical principle is soteriology, but an edited soteriology. Christian soteriology, says Voegelin, was in the beginning corrupted by gnosticism; and, in the twelfth century, it was again corrupted by the idea of progress in the "Everlasting Gospel" of Joachim of Flora. Voegelin dates from Joachim all historically oriented movements that look to the future for the betterment of human society, and these too he denounces as "Gnosticism": the Protestants, the Puritans, the Quakers, the Encyclopedists, the socialists, the existentialists, and, more generally, "progressivism, positivism, scientism,"[11] are the bearers of this vicious tradition. So it is to the Dark Ages that Voegelin looks for his political principles.

Strauss directs his principal attack against Max Weber, whose name is among the most prominent in the development of method in the social sciences. What the name of Weber stands for is, of course, the proposition that science must confine itself to the study of fact, without pretending to arrive at ultimate value judgments. The theoretical foundation of Weber's position is the epistemology of Kant, which is the basis of scientific method and therefore of positivism. Strauss sidles around the epistemological question and attacks Weber on minor grounds. He also raises a bogeyman: positivism undermines morals and somehow leads to Hitler.

Hallowell has the most detailed roster of purveyors of error. He does not reach back, as Voegelin, to Joachim, but, beginning with Helvetius in the eighteenth century, he excoriates Robert Owen, Freud, Pareto, William James, John Dewey, E. R. Bentley, Thurman Arnold, Harold Lasswell, and Hadley Cantril; he devotes a whole chapter to T. V. Smith. These men miss true rationalism by excess or defect. For Hallowell, as for Strauss, the intellectual errors of our time sum up in positivism. It was the "liberal, positivist jurists" who, "unwittingly it may be, prepared the way for Lidice and Dachau."[12] If his book demonstrated the philosophical unsoundness of positivism, it would certainly be the most important book of our generation; but, instead of argument, it offers only dubious propositions about historical causation like that quoted above.

Strauss, at least, believes in the possibility of excogitating an ethics, and the whole school attacks positivism as "irrational" because it insists that value judgments lie outside the range of demonstrable propositions. But, apparently, one can be too rational, for Hallowell reproves the *philosophes* for their "unbounded confidence in man's ability to be persuaded by reason to establish a just social order."[13] Hallowell's reason is "not that emasculated idea of reason which has infected post-Cartesian philosophy, a reason cut loose from love and debarred from vision, . . . but rather a reason directed toward God as its ultimate goal." It is a "seeing passion" which is "the love of God."[14]

It follows that—leaving Strauss aside—human society is comprehensible only in theological terms. Simon tells us that God has conferred spiritual power directly on the pope; temporal power He has vested in the people, who transfer it to their rulers. Even in a democracy, however, the power of decision does not rest with the people: it rests with "authority." Extremely grave abuses may justify the deposition of kings, or the coercion of elected officials by public opinion; but the latter step, like the former, is revolutionary.

This politics necessarily entails an attack upon individualism. Although our authors cite John Locke with approval when his prestige can be drawn to their cause, in fact they reject his whole system. The state, says Simon, is not an artificial creation aimed at convenience; it is the natural condition of man. The "common good," the object of this natural society, transcends the additive particular goods of the members. Authority determines this common good, and this is not inconsistent with liberty; liberty and authority are supplementary and indeed appear to be almost identical.[15] Hallowell tells us that freedom is not "the power to do what one wants," it is "service to God and one's fellow-men."[16] It is liberty in this sense that enters into the tables of democratic values which our authors sometimes supply. It is therefore natural that religious liberty is nowhere included as one of the democratic values.[17] In this system God accepts only one kind of service. Did not Aquinas say that "heretics not only may be excommunicated but also may justly be put to death"?[18]

Similarly, freedom of speech is confined, as in the Soviet Union, to a discussion of means. The ends toward which society is directed are not open to argument. Simon says: "Under fully normal circumstances the propositions relative to the very ends of social life are above deliberation in democracy as well as in any other system. Circumstances which make it necessary to deliver the principles of society, its very soul, to the hazards of controversy are a fateful threat to any regime, democratic or not."[19] Hallowell quotes this passage with approval,[20] and warns against the individual conscience that has "'freed' itself from the Christian revelation and the authority of the church."[21]

But suppose the majority of the society has already been corrupted by bad argument and led astray from the common good. Voegelin boldly faces up to the question of what is to be done with a democratic society in which "Gnosticism"—that is individualism, Protestantism, socialism, existentialism—commands the allegiance of the majority. In this case it is necessary to jettison democratic procedures in order to save the common good.[22]

> Theoretical debate can be protected by constitutional guaranties, but it can be established only by the willingness to use and accept theoretical argument [i.e., theology]. When this willingness does not exist, a society cannot rely for its functioning on argument and persuasion where the truth of human existence is involved; other means will have to be considered....
>
> ... A government has the duty to preserve the order as well as the truth which it represents; when a Gnostic leader appears and proclaims that God or progress, race or dialectic, has ordained him to become the existential ruler, a government is not supposed to betray its trust and to abdicate. And this rule suffers no exception for governments which operate under a democratic constitution and a bill of rights.... A democratic government is not supposed to become an accomplice in its overthrow by letting Gnostic movements grow prodigiously in the shelter of a muddy interpretation of civil rights; and if through inadvertence such a movement has grown to the danger point of capturing existential representation by the famous "legality" of popular elections, a democratic government is not supposed to bow to the "will of the people" but to put down the danger by force and, if necessary, to break the letter of the constitution in order to save its spirit.

Unfortunately, we are not told directly what course of action is proper when the government as well as the people is "Gnostic"; but perhaps Franco showed us the way in Spain.

One can perhaps understand why authors in possession of a precious truth which they infallibly know are unwilling to risk it on what Voegelin calls the "loaded dice"[23] of free discussion; but what explains their animus against the empirical method and experimental research? There is good reason. Science rests upon the Kantian distinction between fact and value, and this too is fatal to their truth. St. Thomas undertook to objectify value by asserting that what is is somehow a reflection of what ought to be; what ought to be, on the other hand, obtains its warrant from what is. The philosophy of natural law comes down to a simple semantic confusion; scientific method precludes this confusion.

We may suspect also another motive. Thomistic natural law has become the philosophy of conservatism because it represents whatever happens to exist as a mirror of what ought to be. But the seam in this comforting cloak can easily be rent in either of two directions. A dispassionate examination of facts reveals that there is not even an approximate correspondence between existing facts and any generalized ethical scheme. And there is an opposite danger. The enthusiastic adoption of an ethical program explicitly at variance with the existing facts—"Gnosticism" or any other reformist movement—threatens the monopoly of the existing church, which claims a divine sanction, and the existing state, which is said to have a natural sanction. The status quo can tolerate neither an analysis of the past nor a program for the future. It is for this reason that Simon must insist that "deliberation is about means and presupposes that the problem of ends has been settled."[24] The problem of ends must not be opened up. This leads to "Gnosticism" or to positivism. Indeed, it may, according to our authors, lead further. Simon tells us that "in times of social and political convulsions, a skeptical thinker, an agnostic intellectual, may reveal that his sense for the absolute, diverted from being by idealism, rendered acute by culture, and frustrated by doubt, has grown into a destructive frenzy."[25] According to Voegelin, "Totalitarianism, defined as the existential rule of Gnostic activists, is the end form of progressive civilization."[26] Strauss asserts that "the contemporary rejection of natural right leads to nihilism—nay, it is identical with nihilism," and that "the inescapable practical consequence of nihilism is fanatical obscurantism."[27] Hallowell assimilates the positivist to Plato's tyrant. "When the individual revolts against tradition and authority, when instinct and desire are exalted above reason, when intellect is subordinated to will, when all desires become lawful and no standard is left for choosing among them, then at last a master-passion '... takes madness for the captain of its guard....'"[28]

It is unlikely that the reader, who is probably "Gnostic," agnostic, or positivist, will recognize himself in these portraits. He will not be conscious of destructive frenzy, nihilism, or fanatical obscurantism. Indeed, it seems that these proscribed classes have a deeper devotion to rationality than the authors under review. Each of these authors is confronted by the epistemology of Kant, an obstacle that must be overcome if their position is to be validated philosophically. Answers to Kant have been contrived; they have not received general acceptance. But these authors do not undertake to answer Kant; they never mention him. Their only reply to the Kantian position is the assertion that it leads to socially undesirable results. Blasphemy is an offense of indeterminate dimensions, but surely a believer must count it blasphemy to offer as an argument for God the utilitarian consideration that the idea is a social convenience.

We must face up to the universe. It is not really profitable to dismiss the work of Freud and Bentley and Lasswell because it makes us uncomfortable, or because it damages the prestige of existing institutions. Nor does facing up to the universe inspire one with megalomania. Hitler was after all no positivist: on the contrary, he was an absolutist cut from the very piece of cloth our authors peddle. On the other hand, history's greatest skeptic, Anatole France, drew this compassionate moral from an unflinching survey of human society: "Let us appoint Irony and Pity the witnesses and judges of mankind."

Simon opens his book: "Communism and national socialism have come to resemble each other in so many respects that their historical diversity and their lasting opposition arouse wonder."[29] We may add a third to this list; it is what Voegelin has called "the new science of politics." This authoritarian creed is the enemy of free inquiry, of free thought, of the individual conscience. It will tolerate discussion only of means by those who accept prescribed ends; and these prescribed ends are determined by a prescribed religion. There is nothing new about this "science," and its history is a history of ceaseless persecution. One of the most disquieting things about the time in which we live is this revival of intellectual obscurantism.

13

MACROPOLITICS: AGGRESSION IN GROUP THEORY

It was the conviction of Hobbes and the Utilitarians that all social phenomena could be explained in terms of individual psychology. Their lack of success is often attributed to the narrowness of the base on which they built. But desire and aversion, pleasure and pain are not narrow concepts; they are extremely broad. The psychological experiences they sum up include as constituent elements appetite, gratification, privation, pain, frustration, resentment, fear, love, hatred, and aggression. It is not the narrowness but the breadth of the concept of motive in the Utilitarian psychology that makes difficulty. Narrowness and direction are essential to concepts if they are to be useful tools of thought. It may be that what is needed is a refinement rather than an expansion of the psychology. Specifically, the purpose here is to select out of the complex emotions we call pleasure and pain the ideas of frustration, resentment, and aggression, and use them as a ladder by which to rise from the level of individual behavior to social behavior. What results will be an experimental schema. As with other schemata, it may be as useful for what it leaves out as for what it includes. As with other schemata, there is the danger that the omissions will altogether destroy the utility of the analysis. What seems most likely is that the selection of data embraced in the schema will throw light on some aspects of group behavior while giving no help at all with other aspects.

Man is a desirous creature. He is born in want; he lives by wants; and he dies wanting. When a want is satisfied, it disappears, and apparently

---

Reprinted from *Audit* 1 (Feb., 1960): 3-9. Used by permission of *Audit*.

the gratification, too, soon vanishes; new wants arise and clamor for attention. Many desires are bound to be frustrated, but when they are frustrated they do not die; they enter upon a new life as resentments. Gratification and privation do not, however, exhaust man's relation to his environment. The environment is active: it inflicts pain, and pain generates fear. Appetite and apprehension accompany every man through life.

Apparently people are susceptible in varying degrees to frustration; the intensity of disappointment is a matter of personality structure. It appears also that there are cultural variations in this matter; what might be called the cultural threshold of frustration is reflected in the personality of the individual.[1] But all such differences occur within an invariable frame. As Bentham said, "Nature has placed mankind under the governance of two sovereign masters, pleasure and pain."

The frustration of desire—and in frustration we may here include pain—produces resentment. Since we have no instruments for measurement, we cannot demonstrate, but we can at least offer the hypothesis, that resentment is proportional to the subjective experience of frustration. Supporting evidence is afforded by introspection.

Resentment is a motive for action. The action which it produces is ordinarily called aggression.[2] We may say that invariably Frustration = Resentment; but it is not immediately or always true that Resentment = Aggression. There may be impediments which prevent the spontaneous or full manifestation of Resentment in the form of overt Aggression. The rule that Frustration, mediated by Resentment, equals Aggression constitutes an ideal rather than a necessity. It represents the primitive conception of justice, the *lex talionis*, an eye for an eye. Aristotle said that justice consists in giving to every man his due: that is, Frustration equals Aggression.[3]

Resentment is under a powerful compulsion to direct itself at a human object. Man is a moral being, which means that he must respond to frustration with blame, with the imputation of guilt. It is not possible to impute blame to nonhuman agents. Resentment at frustration from inanimate or animal sources may find partial outlet in aggression against a nonhuman object, by the kicking of furniture and the like, but fully satisfactory relief cannot be obtained except at the expense of a moral agent. There is a compelling impulse, a practical necessity, to attribute frustration to the guilt of some human agent.

This is not difficult. At near or remote distance in a chain of nonhuman causes which leads to misfortune can be discovered an act or omission of some human being: this becomes the true cause, and it is attributed to malice or willful negligence. The greater the frustration, the more imperative the need to discover guilt. In an acute case a causal analysis which has no plausibility whatever will be accepted, because it satisfies the need to attribute blame for frustration to some human being.

There is a strong tendency to assign guilt to some vulnerable agent upon whom resentment can be discharged with impunity. But it may be that the compulsion of fact or logic, or the beliefs or values of the frustrated man, will preclude this easy solution. He will then store up resentment, as a Leyden jar stores electricity. Most people go about partially charged most of the time. On some trivial occasion resentment may burst forth in a volume entirely disproportionate to the cause which released it. Lynchings and riots are a kind of social therapy in that they temporarily drain the participants of their frustrations and resentments.

Although the usual response to frustration is to direct blame outward, and to engage in overt aggression, some persons have inconvenient personality structures which cause them to direct blame inward. There are then no obstacles to aggression: the individual attacks himself, and in the ultimate case destroys himself, either by madness or by suicide.

One way or the other, resentment presses for release. Rather alarming quantitative considerations emerge. Given free circulation among like units, a frustration of A results in aggression against B. This produces in B a pain and frustration which is discharged upon C. C relays the charge to D, and D to E; it circulates indefinitely. But new frustrations from nonhuman causes are continually inflating the currency of aggression circulating through society. There may be some loss in transmission; and some of the currency is hoarded, so to speak, in the shape of resentment which is for the time being bottled up in the human Leyden jars. A certain quantity of this fatal currency will be taken out of circulation altogether whenever a man dies without discharging his Leyden jar, although his death may produce new pain and frustration among survivors. But such subtractions can hardly offset the steady flood of new currency which comes into the system from new frustrations of nonhuman origin. As the total quantity of frustration increases, it seems inevitable that aggression should also increase. Have we here an explanation of the increase of suicide and insanity, of juvenile delinquency, crime, and war?

Thus far we have discussed frustration at the level of interpersonal action, the level of the microcosm, of micropolitics, so to speak. Our problem is to rise from this level to the level of macropolitics—to employ the ideas of fear and frustration to explain group behavior.

Of those authors who have taken an individualistic psychology as their point of departure, only Peretz Bernstein, in his penetrating study of anti-Semitism, has succeeded in developing a group theory without abandoning his premises.[4] For Bernstein as for Alfred Adler, nature abounds in fear and frustration: these overmaster the individual, and he seeks strength in society. This may sound like Hobbes's social contract, but Hobbes merely offered us an abridgment of the truth. Let us put the matter another way. The individual enters society at birth, and he knows friendship and love as early as he knows pain and fear. He knows them as the converse of these evils and the defense against them. So love is the corollary of fear. The same thing can be put in still another way. The individual regards his society as an aspect of himself. His values are social values; in fact, as Charles Horton Cooley argued, personality itself is socially conferred.[5] In primitive times society was the kin group, but when the clan order was destroyed by the state larger groups became the carriers of social values. A basic and persistent principle of grouping is ethnic likeness, for physical similarities are easily identified. Linguistic and religious groups afford the shelter of the familiar. The state offers the opportunity of identification through the intermediary of a symbol or a man: common allegiance to this intermediary makes all the members of the state members of the same group.

Group membership greatly increases the strength of the individual, not only for defense but for aggression; and aggression is as real a need as defense. In fact, the impulse to aggression often outruns the desire for safety. Perhaps this supplies at least a partial explanation for fluctuations in group loyalties. Bernstein suggests that a group attracts loyalty in proportion as it affords an outlet for aggression. If we compare the individual to a Leyden jar, we may compare groups to drifting clouds through which static electricity pours into new concentrations at points which offer an opportunity for discharge. Sometimes an ethnic, sometimes a religious, sometimes a linguistic group, sometimes a group based on nothing more than dietary practices, moves into a posture of antagonism to another group. Great accumulations of frustration, welling up from multitudes of private lives, are drawn into the two adversary groups, increasing the tension and therefore the attractiveness of membership. When war, the ultimate expression of social hatred, occurs, the individual scraps all other loyalties—family, ethnic, religious, cultural—in favor of loyalty to the belligerent group which affords him the opportunity to discharge hatred in comforting unanimity with the group.

Group loyalty is therefore a function of social collision. The members of a group achieve self-consciousness, and group-consciousness, only by contrast with another group. Of course, the content of rival groups invites conflict; but it seems also that the fact of collision helps to create and define the groups. Collision is a part of group structure. Protracted conflict, however, is likely to transform the group. A group which persists in a position of violent antagonism may well take on the character of a state, or appropriate to itself an existing state, for the state is the most convenient vehicle of antagonism. It is thus that the state comes to have an ethnic, a religious, a linguistic, a cultural content. By summing up the likenesses and therefore the loyalties of its members, the state achieves a virtual monopoly of love and hatred.

But on occasion other groups within the state evoke loyalties which challenge that to the state itself. The state may, through aggression, overrun its original social base, and acquire dominance over ethnic, linguistic, or religious groups for whom the state remains alien. The Austro-Hungarian empire is a familiar example. Or conflicting groups may arise within the state, and if the state is associated with one of the belligerents the other will repudiate the state. This occurs in the case of protracted class struggle. But if the conflict achieves resolution, the victor becomes the state. Even a rebellious group for which the very form of the state is an enemy, as the Russian proletariat, is fated by a cruel destiny to become a state through victory.

It appears that not only group loyalty but social valuation is a function of group conflict. When great tension arises between the members of a single pair, the other pairs of groups in society are emptied of emotional content. They are now significant only as supports for one or the other of the two belligerents, and their values must be redefined in terms of this alien polarity. This distorts their structure and their content. The belligerents themselves build up elaborate ideologies to characterize themselves and each other. Since conflict situations change, valuations shift. With each change of antagonist it becomes necessary to redefine the values attributed to one's own group in such a way as to pair off against the new opponent; it will probably be necessary also to alter the characterization of the opponent, who may have been until recently an ally.

Whatever the content of social values, they are bound to have a standard structure. One's own group is virtuous. It is entitled to the same priority that the individual attributes to his own demands on the environment. It is not possible to hate the opposing group without attributing blame or guilt: therefore the antagonist is vicious. When ultimate good thus confronts ultimate evil, when the moral order of the universe is at stake, any means to victory is justified.

In the political relation, then, two groups are bound into coherence and conflict by the antagonism between them. This antagonism is composed of the attractive and repulsive forces of love and hatred, which reciprocally generate each other. Social values are the tension of the system. Behind the organized system, behind the interlocked groups, is the prime element, the raw undifferentiated stuff of which society is made, the fears and frustrations of multitudes of individuals, continually welling up, continually renewed.

It now becomes necessary to qualify this thesis in two ways. Thus far we have eliminated initiative in decision from political life: rolling clouds of hatred discharge their lightning in a mindless and mechanical way in the social world as in the natural. But politics is not completely irrational. The larger social groups are organized under leaders who can, to a degree, control the orientation of their groups. They can manipulate them into and out of positions of extreme antagonism. Our analogy to electricity in nature breaks down, for social electricity moves through circuits which can be broken. But the electricity is always there, and the leaders are often in a position to discharge it. Rational calculation dissuades them 99 percent of the time; rational calculation or miscalculation leads them on the hundredth occasion to press the key that closes the circuit.

Moreover, we have overstated the case in saying that belligerency transfers all group loyalties to the two belligerent groups. Other social groupings persist with varying degrees of vitality. There are affirmations of value too stubborn to yield to the hatreds of the moment. Some of these may be not group affirmations but individual ones, and they may include an unusual devotion to rationality.[6] It is not the case that only the leaders are capable of rational evaluation of a situation. For every ten thousand Stephen Decaturs there is a Henry David Thoreau.

And there are at least two forms of dissent that amount to repudiation of the whole social order that produces belligerency. The mystic transfers his expectations to another world, where frustrations do not exist; he ascends through a trap door to heaven. But if we reflect that Plotinus himself had this experience only four times in six years we will probably expect no large-scale results from this psychological phenomenon.

Religion offers still another escape from group hatred. In some systems it undertakes to separate those Siamese twins love and hatred, and to reorganize the world in terms of love alone. The logic of this proposal entails that there be neither Jew nor Gentile, that aggression be renounced, and that law and justice yield to love. This solution has been adopted by a few unusual men, who have thereby more often earned the martyr's crown than the saint's halo. What must occur psychologically in such men is a reorganization of the value system so extensive as to amount to a reorganization of the personality, the creation of a personality incapable of frustration. But cases of this sort have been so few as to have no effect upon history. It is a lamentable reflection that for nearly two thousand years one of the principal vehicles for the expression of hatred has been groups organized in the name of Christ.

14

A TYPOLOGY OF REVOLUTION AND IDEOLOGY

Like other associative human activities, politics is a blend of cooperation and dominance, of consent and coercion. David Hume said that all government rested on "opinion"—even the Turkish despot, whose principal prop was force, was dependent on the opinion of his Mamelukes. But in fact the Mamelukes could not have employed force successfully on his behalf without the uncoerced submission of the subject population. Sentimental attachment to the government may be useful in inducing submission, but it is not indispensable. The submission that is essential to society is merely the performance, reluctant, resigned, or willing, of the social routines which constitute the life of society. Power rests atop the enormous pyramid of use and wont. Ordinarily the principal sanctions which support the social order are not administered by the government. Anatole France said:

But it always surprises me somewhat to see the mature and even the aged led astray by the illusions of power, forgetting that hunger, love, death, all the mean, as well as the sublime necessities of life exercise so imperious a control over the mass of mankind that those who rule over their bodies are left with nothing more than power on paper and empire in words. And what is more wonderful still—the people believe that they have other rulers than their poverty, their desire, and their imbecility. He was a wise man who said: "Let us appoint Irony and Pity to be the witnesses and judges of mankind."

This essay is in part an abridgment, in part an expansion, of the author's *Class Struggle*. It was presented at the Conference on Revolution at the Center for the Study of Democratic Institutions, Santa Barbara, Calif., in May, 1969 and is used here with the permission of the Center.

178 / POLITICS

Nevertheless, government does administer important sanctions. And it dispenses important social goods. Perhaps the most important of these is justice or, it may be, injustice. These are normative conceptions about the proper structure and functioning of the social order. Except in times of revolutionary upheaval, the social order sustains government by consent, and the government employs force for the maintenance of the social order. The government is therefore committed to a particular version of justice, the propriety of the existing social order. But other versions may be entertained by other segments of society. To the degree that this occurs, the social cement of consent is weakened. The use of

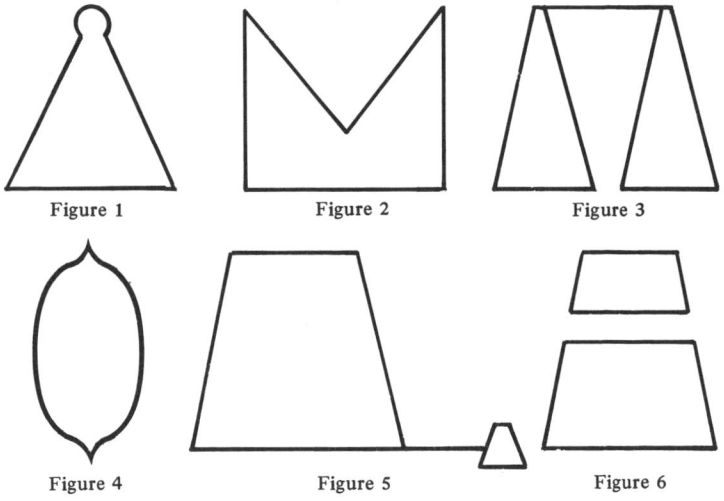

Figure 1   Figure 2   Figure 3

Figure 4   Figure 5   Figure 6

force as an integrating device must be correspondingly enlarged. This may provoke retaliatory force. Revolution may ensue.

The course of events varies in various social structures. These may take several forms. Critical in determining these forms, and in determining the course of events, are the quality of the consent which sustains the society, the social expectations which we call justice, and the changes in those expectations.

Figure 1 represents a society in which the government has so little command over the loyalty of its citizens as to be vulnerable to overthrow by a coup d'état. On the basis of historical evidence, it seems possible to recognize three such situations. In absolute monarchies the populace has no part in politics, and, if the society is static and stable, is likely to take no interest in politics. Obedience here is merely habitual, and the ties between crown and populace are tenuous. Such a monarchy is exposed to palace revolutions, for the people will accept without demur a new ruler. Palace revolutions afflicted Rome and Constantinople, and Turkish Istanbul; indeed, they have occurred in many absolute monarchies. Ordinarily the agency which carries out the revolution is the military establishment about the ruler, or some part of it. A palace revolution requires the use of very little violence; but it can also be defeated by a small amount of violence. An attempted coup d'état in Peru in 1939 was frustrated by the recalcitrancy of one officer of the palace guard. This is the level on which politics is practiced in absolute or dictatorial states.

The coup d'état also appears in another setting. Societies which have undergone rapid vicissitudes of rule fall into an apathy comparable to the political indifference found in despotisms, and submit readily to further change. In 1799, when Napoleon Bonaparte with ridiculous ease made himself First Consul of France, the country had experienced six governments in ten years; it did not mind another one. In 1660 the city of London, which had seen five national governments in twelve months, addressed the restored Long Parliament thus: "That the City did congratulate the happy return of the Parliament: That they found some persons for a monarchical, some for a commonwealth, some for no government at all: the last they did dislike: for the other, they would not direct, but should acquiesce, and submit to the determination of Parliament."

The third type of vulnerable government is the case put by Lenin in his "letter to Comrades" on October 29-30, 1917. He denied that to undertake a socialist revolution under existing conditions could be equated to the unpremeditated insurrectionism associated with the name of Blanqui:

A military conspiracy is Blanquism, *if* it is organized not by a party of a definite class, *if* its organizers have not analyzed the political moment in general and the international situation in particular, *if* the party has not on its side the sympathy of the majority of the people, as proven by objective facts, *if* the development of events in the revolution has not brought about a practical refutation of the conciliatory illusions of the petty bourgeoisie, *if* the majority of the recognized "plenipotentiary" or otherwise expressed organs of revolutionary struggle like the Soviets have not been conquered, *if* there has not ripened a sentiment in the army (if this is going on during a war) against the government that protracts the unjust war against the whole of the people, *if* the slogans of the uprising (like "All power to the Soviets," "Land to the peasants," or "Immediate offer of a democratic peace to all the belligerent peoples, coupled with an immediate abrogation of all secret treaties and secret diplomacy," etc.) have not become widely known and popular, *if* the advanced workers are not convinced of the desperate situation of the masses and of the support of the village, a support proven by a serious peasant uprising against the landowners and the government that defends the landowners, *if* the economic situation of the country inspires one with earnest hopes for a favorable solution of the crisis by peaceable and parliamentary means.

Figure 2 represents a society in which the pyramid of consent rises to two—there may be more—apices. In such a society the two authorities may come into collision, and each will draw upon its consensual support in the common social base. This will split the society and may produce civil war. The middle ages saw such collisions between church and state and between the baronage and the king. The American Civil War was in part a regional war, like that invited by the structure in figure 3; but it was also a contest between the national consensual structure on the one hand and state consensual structures on the other. In these cases conflict arose between institutions that had previously coexisted more or less amicably. But it is also possible that social discontent may generate an institution which divides loyalty with the government. In Italy the Mafia achieved a division of authority with the government. The Ku Klux Klan did much the same thing in many southern communities. In the Parliamentary Army in the years 1647-49 the common soldiers chose Agitators who forced their way into the Council of the Army. The spontaneous establishment of soviets in Russia in 1905 and in 1917 was a similar phenomenon. This occurrence persuaded Lenin that a social revolution was possible only through the development of a "dual state." It was useless to capture the existing government, for the old state and the old bureaucracy could not serve revolutionary purposes. It was necessary that a new state, the soviets, grow up alongside the old state apparatus and displace it.

Figure 3 represents a governmental arrangement which has been fairly common through history. Two or several societies maintain a more or less independent existence, but have a government, most often a royal government, in common. This was the usual means by which small kingdoms were aggregated in the late middle ages. The Christian kingdoms of Spain were thus amalgamated; the kingdoms of England, Ireland, and Scotland did not become a single body politic until the eighteenth century. The Hapsburg federation endured until 1918; this arrangement had advantages for the ruler. The emperor of Austria could call in Magyars against the Germans of Austria, and Germans against the Magyars; he could use both against the Czechs. It might also have advantages for subjects. Machiavelli observed that a king was likely to deal more moderately with colonies than was a republic, because he might need their support against the homeland. But there was always a tendency for a ruler to favor a single nation—the Hapsburgs, the Germans; the Romanoffs, the Great Russians. Moreover, the implicit antagonism in such a federation considerably reduces its stability.

With figures 4, 5, and 6, we come to the problem of social revolution. In this case the society divides along lines of economic cleavage. Accordingly, the appropriate representation of society is usually thought to be pyramidal, as in figure 6. The highest income groups are thought to have the fewest members; the pyramid broadens as income decreases, and the largest social class has the lowest income. Harold D. Lasswell has protested that this picture does not accurately represent the facts. There are comparatively few very wealthy and comparatively few very poor, and the largest concentration of numbers is in the middle of the income range; therefore figure 4 is a truer portrayal of society. Probably the proportionate distribution of income at different levels varies from society to society and from age to age. But certainly societies do often contain relatively small, severely deprived groups which lie below the broadest income stratum in the social order. However, it may be misleading to treat this group as the lowest level in an integrated society. Figure 5 suggests that in many cases, at least, it constitutes a separate society attached only externally to the principal society. Unfortunately, the figure cannot adequately represent the character of this attachment. One aspect, of course, is economic dependence; this normally involves also poverty beyond that found in the lowest stratum of the principal society. In addition, social deprivation is imposed upon the subordinate society; hatred and contempt are discharged upon its members by the members of the principal society. The status of members of the inferior society is not one of inferior worth; it is one of worthlessness, confirmed and enforced by legal and extralegal sanctions. The pariah caste in India is a familiar example; similar outcast or out-caste groups have existed in many countries. Jews have been subjected to such treatment throughout much of history. The black population has constituted and still constitutes such a group in the United States. Illuminating is the case of the *cagots*, who were formerly found in small villages along the Bay of Biscay from the mouth of the Loire to northern Spain. Like the Jews, they were emancipated by the French Revolution. When anthropologists made physical measurements of members of the group in the nineteenth century, they found no means of distinguishing them from their neighbors.

Historians have been at a loss to explain the origin of this group. Georges Clemenceau, however, himself a *cagot,* said that they were descended from the outriders of Attila's army, left stranded when the Huns were forced to retire after the battle of Châlons. We have records of them from the sixteenth century. Their neighbors explained that the maltreatment inflicted upon them was punishment for an ancient and forgotten sin. A *cagot* might follow no trade except that of stonemason. He might own no more than six geese; if he kept more, his dominant neighbors took all his geese. He must wear gloves in crossing a bridge because he might contaminate the handrail by touching it. *Cagots* were Christians but were required to enter the church by a separate door.

These cases suggest that the members of an outcast group are singled out for this status by racial difference. In his *Jew-Hate as a Sociological Problem* Peretz Bernstein has given a psychological explanation of the phenomenon. He does not cite Alfred Adler, but like Adler he considers the individual to be weak, fearful, and frustrated. He finds protection in the social group, and loves those who protect him. But pain and frustration persist. By a psychic alchemy these are converted into hatred, which seeks an outlet in aggression against any convenient object. It is not always safe to discharge hatred within the group; but the members of the group can hate the members of another group in the safety that comes with numbers. Social groups always come in pairs, but pairs of the same kind: linguistic group hates linguistic group; religion hates religion; race hates race. The state is the group organized for aggression: combat groups tend to become states. The ostensible causes of combat are not the basic cause. The basic cause is private frustration welling up from countless private lives; this is transmuted into public hatred.

When a defenseless minority group lives among a majority from which it is easily distinguishable, it affords a safe and easy target for majority hatred. Almost inevitably it receives this attention. It is given a permanent status outside the social order—in effect, outside the law. Members of the majority may discharge their frustrations upon the minority with impunity. Thus the minority performs a therapeutic function. Like the outrigger on a canoe, it stabilizes the society to which it is attached.

Various factors may reduce hostility between the groups; and individual members of both groups may altogether lack hostility. Two different attitudes may emerge in members of the minority group. Some of them, usually those at a higher income level, may desire admission into the society dominated by the majority. Others, usually those of lower income, feel the full force of social hatred and desire independence from the majority. The former are currently represented by the NAACP; the latter, by the advocates of Black Power.

However, what is usually regarded as the typical case of class struggle is the conflict of economic groups within a single society. This has occurred many times in history. It was chronic in the Greek city-states; it occupied the last century of republican Rome; it broke out with great violence in the late middle ages. The French Revolution brought about an association of the idea of class struggle with the new doctrine of progress and the equally new doctrine of equality, and nineteenth-century socialists identified all these as the pattern of history. But in the twentieth century the violent outbreak of fascism showed that an insurgent class might seek retrograde and anti-equalitarian goals.

Despite the frequency of class struggles, wars have been much more frequent. And the number of years in which any society has experienced class struggle is enormously smaller than the number of years in which the members of the several income strata of the society have lived amicably side by side. If class consciousness—the identification of oneself as a member of an income stratum arrayed in antagonism to another income stratum—is an essential feature of class, classes have not existed through most of history. A class comes into existence, and class struggle occurs, only when this subjective factor is added to the objective differences expressed in the legal and economic organization of society. Under what circumstances does this occur?

One of the ways in which values are acquired is by habituation. The members of a given economic stratum—let us call it for convenience a class—develop settled expectations of prestige. The members of an intermediate class are reconciled to the enjoyment of greater incomes and greater prestige by members of a superior class. They consider it only decent that members of an inferior class receive smaller incomes and less prestige. Social justice is the satisfaction of these established expectations.

In a static society, where long habituation has stabilized the expectations of every class and a static economy supplies to each class its habitual gratifications, no tension will exist. It is only when a shifting economy inculcates new wants and new standards in a class, or frustrates the established expectations of a class, that class action need be anticipated. Edward A. Ross formulated the rule thus: "A class struggle is precipitated by an economic or technological change which throws up a new class or threatens to ruin an old one."

So well settled are the values of a class that it is difficult to bring about an expansion of its material wants, unless endless covetousness is one of the properties of the class, as it may well be in modern society. In his *Social Psychology* Ross quoted an observer of the Mexican peon:

The experience of railroad companies and other employers of labor in Mexico has been that higher daily wages increase idleness, and that, if the day's wages for a day's work be doubled, the number of working days will be halved. It is also a fact confirmed by experience and observation of many employers that the amount of labor performed bears no direct relation to wages and that even when work is done by the task instead of by the day the promise of additional remuneration will seldom result in an increased output.

There is a famous passage in which Ferdinand Lassalle, the German socialist, berated German workingmen for their "accursed absence of needs": "French and English workingmen have to be shown how their miserable condition may be improved; but *you* have first to be shown that you *are* in a miserable condition. So long as you have a piece of bad sausage and a glass of beer, you do not notice that you want anything."

But even the Mexican peon may find his needs expanding, or his wants disappointed. The German workers, who were not long out of feudalism when Lassalle wrote, had acquired new standards of consumption by the end of the nineteenth century. It is a consequence of an expanding economy that the wants of the classes affected increase, perhaps to such a point that class values shift. At this stage envy and imitation come into play. Because of the hierarchical arrangement of classes, the values of the upper classes command the respect of the inferior. In a settled society this will not lead to rivalry or emulation. The lower classes will take over from the upper only those values intended for their consumption, as religious and legal observances. But when the strata have been warped by economic change, and the boundaries between classes have become somewhat permeable, the newly emancipated classes are likely to covet the goods of their betters. Their old values enfeebled by change, they aspire to the values of the class immediately superior. If no legal or political obstacles exist, the newcomers may fuse with the class above. The comparative peacefulness with which momentous social changes have occurred in England has been due to the easy accessibility of the title "gentleman," and the comparative unimportance of the peerage as a test of quality. In monarchical France, on the other hand, where nobility did not descend by primogeniture but extended to all children of noblemen, the possession of a legal title was the hallmark of gentility and was the key, moreover, to exclusive legal privileges. This closed social order could not accommodate itself to change, and was therefore overthrown by the bourgeoisie in the French Revolution.

Expansion of the desires of a class, then, may be a cause for class struggle. Whenever a rising class meets barriers which frustrate its new expectations, there is a probability of class action to remove these barriers.

This will invariably be accompanied, as we shall see, by an ideology which denounces the barriers as unnatural impediments to a natural and just ordering of society.

On the other hand, economic changes may withdraw the support to which a class has been accustomed, and cause it to descend in the social scale. This of course will shock the declining class, and once again an ideology will be formulated, this time to demonstrate the rightness of the previous order and the unnaturalness of change. Not infrequently the rise of one class will be accompanied by the decline of another, for social movements are in many cases reciprocal. Under these circumstances two classes will become revolutionary at the same time. They may, but they need not, be enemies. They may turn on each other, or they may make common cause against a scapegoat, as the rising bourgeoisie and the declining nobility in the years before the French Revolution joined in attack on the monarchy.

It was said above that the members of a class have common expectations of consumption and common expectations of prestige. Obviously these will be closely related, for each reflects the economic status of the class. But whereas habits of consumption are fixed by considerations internal to the class, prestige is relative to the entire social structure, and will alter when a change occurs in the distance between classes. Habits of consumption depend for their gratification upon what might be called absolute income, in the sense of real income in goods and services; prestige depends upon comparative income, or the ratio of the income of a given class to the incomes of adjoining classes. It becomes necessary to consider the circumstances under which a change in absolute income will provoke class action, and those in which a change in comparative income will have that consequence.

The proletariat, living on the margin of subsistence, is more responsive to change in absolute income than any other class. Raymond Postgate, one of the foremost students of revolutions, has this to say:

> It was also observed that certain conditions of the labor market were favorable to the revolutionary sentiment, and others not. The scattered comments on this phenomenon do not seem to have been ever coordinated; but the results of a rough survey of the facts seem to be that revolutionary sentiment reaches its peak when the condition of the working class, economically, is going sharply up or sharply down. That is to say, the "revolutionary urge" increases either when a steady rise in the standard of living is sharply checked and turned into a painful and obvious decline; or when a gradual rise in the standard of living comes after a period of great discomfort. In the latter case the workingman has recent memories of suffering and a small increase in comfort and leisure gives

him energy and strength to express his resentment. The history of the Chartist movement in Great Britain shows the latter process working with almost thermometrical exactitude. The General Strike of 1842 was directly caused by a sudden harsh trade crisis, of the usual Victorian kind, which brought savage suffering to the workers immediately after a more peaceful and easy period in which the bad conditions of earlier years had seemed to be slowly improving. The hysterical and helpless outburst of 1848, the last spasm of Chartism, came two years after the great misery and famine of 1846. The hideous wretchedness of that year was over, the working class was at once sore from its wounds and yet sufficiently recovered to think it had strength to seek its revenge.

A similar cycle may perhaps be observed in the latest history of British industrial convulsions.

Evidently a serious decline in absolute income will produce class action, though the response may be delayed until more favorable circumstances occur. A rise in the standard of living of the proletariat without a previous period of privation may engender new appetites and provoke strikes. These strikes, however, will be economic rather than political weapons, and it seems unlikely that they will assume the proportions of class aggression unless the bourgeoisie undertakes to arrest the progress of the proletariat by interposing a noneconomic barrier in the form of legislation or governmental coercion. This, of course, may easily happen; it is particularly likely to occur if the rise of the proletariat is synchronized with a decline in the absolute or comparative income of the superior class.

If it is the most sensitive to changes in absolute income, the proletariat is the class least likely to be affected by considerations of prestige. By virtue of its position at the bottom of the social scale, it is almost naked of prestige. A change in comparative income unaccompanied by a change in absolute income would probably elicit little response from the proletariat, though it might have serious repercussions in the adjoining class. But it seems at least theoretically possible for a proletariat equipped with new appetites by a rise in absolute income and brought within easy range of a superior class by a rise in comparative income to display social rivalry toward that class, and if repressed by artificial barriers to resort to class action for the removal of the barriers.

As the lowest class cannot lose prestige by a decline in income, so too it is true that an increase in absolute or comparative income cannot effect any considerable increase in the prestige of the highest class. It is probably also the case that an increase in income, absolute or comparative, will not increase the ambitions of the highest class, although it may and often does cause a demoralization of class standards. A decline in the absolute income of the highest class is not likely to be grave enough to be reflected in politics unless it is also a decline in prestige. Against such a relapse an aristocracy will fight bitterly; in fact, no aristocracy has ever been ousted from its primacy in a period of time short enough to make the process observable without serious bloodshed. The conflict of course is in the name of the ancestral culture, and the patricians, the Cavaliers, the *noblesse,* the Whites have often been quite sincere in professing these values.

Probably intermediate classes may be led to class action by a decline in absolute income which disappoints their expectations, or by such an increase as establishes new expectations inconsistent with the social order. But usually such a change is also a change in comparative income, and brings about a change in the social distance between classes. This raises the question of prestige, which may also be raised when comparative income changes without any change in absolute income. Hans Speier has made a brilliant analysis of this question in a study of the social dynamics of the Nazi movement, which drew its numerical strength from a declining lower middle class. Every class has what he calls a "social insecurity level" with relation to the classes above and below. When the social distance narrows, either because of the fall of the superior class or the rise of the inferior class, there is an increase in interclass tension and a possibility that the insecurity level will be crossed, with resulting political action. The significant thing is not the absolute stature of either class, but the ratio between the classes.

The increase in security resulting from an ascent in the social scale is not so great for either class when both an upper and a lower class rise together, nor is the decrease in security resulting from a descent in the scale so great when both fall together. And from this it follows that when a lower class rises and a higher class falls, the security of the higher class is disturbed more than the drop in its position would alone account for, just as the rise of a higher class coupled with the fall of the lower class aggravates the resultant actual insecurity of the lower class.

. . . For example, a falling lower class will be affected by its fall if a higher class is falling even more. Or the lower class may reach an insecurity level without change in its status if the higher class rises still further above it; and the higher class may reach an insecurity level without change merely by a rise in the lower class.

. . . If both classes move upward the entire social structure reaches a higher level than before, if they both move downward it takes a lower level, but there is no change in the relative position of the classes; the inner tension of the structure remains the same.

Speier qualifies these general rules by noting exceptional cases. During wartime the fervor of patriotism is likely to make considerations of social distance less compelling; here a larger cultural value overshadows class values. Furthermore, decline in class prestige and social insecurity can be in some measure offset by the creation of a prominent declassed group which is deprived of all rights and social standing to serve as butt and compensation for the rest of the population: it was remarked by many observers that anti-Semitism performed this function in Nazi Germany.

To summarize, a change in either the absolute or the comparative income of a class may be a forerunner of revolution. A decline in the absolute income of a class is likely to provoke resentment if habitual consumption is seriously curtailed. An increase in absolute income may cause a breakdown in the habitual standards of the class and perhaps produce rivalry toward a superior class. A decrease in the comparative income of a class, whether or not there is a change in absolute income, decreases the prestige of the class and makes it potentially revolutionary. An increase in the comparative income of a class arouses its prestige expectations, perhaps to such a point that it will undertake to rectify a social order which refuses to gratify them. And because, as Speier has pointed out, the classes are linked in a single structure, the movement of one class has significance not for that class alone, but also for the superior and inferior classes upon which it exerts tension.

To the rules which organize a society and assign place and function to its parts Aristotle gave the name distributive justice. Today we call the attribution of justice to a particular system an ideology. An ideology is a justification of an existing society or a recommendation of a new one. Not all governmental overturns are ideological. When Catherine the Great displaced her husband, her motive was not ideological, nor did the Russian ideology alter. Even large-scale contests need not be programmatic. In race riots and in massacres of members of minority groups there is an emotional prompting of hatred, and virtually no intellectual content. But there are also ideological struggles. Indeed, one usage confines the word "revolution" to ideological movements. On the other hand, some ideological movements are neither revolutionary nor counter-revolutionary; the state is irrelevant for their purposes.

What causes ideologies to emerge? What supplies their content? Two principal methods of study have been employed. The first is the historical method, which undertakes to explain a system of ideas by relating it to antecedent ideas. Too often historians seem to assume that an idea is a solid counter like a piece of currency which passes unchanged from the mind of one author to that of another, so that thought is a kind of money-lending and borrowing rather than creation. This leads to absurdities like the opinion of Thomas Hobbes that the English Civil Wars were caused by the reading of Roman literature which extolled republicanism.

Nevertheless, despite such abuses of the historical method, we must not overlook the obvious fact that for the most part a man inherits rather than invents the tools with which he thinks.

On the other hand, the method of causal explanation which may be called sociological, and which finds its most extreme expression in the sociology of knowledge of Karl Mannheim, regards every idea as a response to the immediate environment. Accordingly, although it is possible to classify ideological systems in terms of formal structure, this classification is a taxonomy and not a phylogeny. In the preoccupation with the establishment of causal links between the intellectual response and the nonintellectual stimulus, this approach ignores the continuity of human thought and whatever intellectual link there may be between generation and generation.

Nevertheless, it is obviously true that men think about their problems, and that their problems are contemporary with them, so that systems of ideas are necessarily responses to the environment. We must add that men formulate their problems in terms of their intellectual heritage—that in many cases, indeed, their status as problems is a function of the intellectual heritage—and that the equipment they bring to bear for their solution is likewise inherited. Culture has time dimensions as well as spatial dimensions. Both the historical and the sociological methods of explanation must be employed in any rounded account of intellectual history.

The use of the sociological method sets us the task of constructing a typology of ideology which relates each type to a particular structuring of society or a particular change in the social structure. The use of the historical method requires us to identify in our intellectual history generative ideas which mesh with our types of ideology.

If one applies the discriminating principle of history or time to the data, one arrives at a typology of ideology which recognizes six forms. What I shall call statism is timeless. What I shall call progressivism places its values in the future. Reaction finds its values in the past. Conservatism finds its values in the present. What I shall call, following Georges Sorel, the catastrophic myth anticipates passage into the future by a dramatic interruption of the present. What I shall call, from its principal manifestation, Christian anarchism finds the future in the present. I shall undertake to show that each of these is a distinct and appropriate response to a given environmental situation.

It would be too good to be true if we could find in our cultural heritage six distinct originals of these attitudes. It appears that there are three such originals, and that these are enough. One of them is what Arthur V. Hocart called the primitive religion of mankind, the worship of the divine king. The second is the linear conception of history. The third is the belief in the divinity of the individual man. The first of these generated the second and third.

The link between idea and ideology is the conception of history. Philosophies of history are multitudinous, but we may say that there are two major types.

The one is the cyclical theory, according to which history moves in a closed circle, forever returning to its point of origin. Usually this is a cycle of decay and regeneration. We are most familiar with it in the Golden Age and the ages of degeneration of Hesiod, in the cosmology of Plato, in the historical views of the Stoics. The other theory is one of linear historical development; this view regards history as an irreversible progress toward a goal. These two views appear to be mutually exclusive alternatives, but in fact they may well be versions of a single idea found in the primitive religious belief of mankind, what Eliade has called "the myth of the eternal return." Apparently the primitive religion of mankind was a magical rite to insure crops. A central feature was the ritual combat in which the king of the old year was slain and a new and vigorous king installed. This symbolized the death and rebirth of vegetation; it was, further, a poetic recognition of the conditions of life. It became the central feature in all interpretations of human existence. The cycle of the seasons, mirrored in the annual death and resurrection of the king—who is also the god—gives rise to the cyclical view of history, which follows the pattern of Mesopotamian agriculture through the verdant growing season into the maturity and the browning and decay of vegetation. This view of history reflects the annually or semiannually repetitive character of the ritual of the installation of the divine king.

But there is another view of history, one which extends a single performance of the ritual over the whole span of human destiny. The central figure is still what Frazer called the "dying and rising god," but the drama is enacted only once, and all of time is devoted to its consummation. We may conjecture that this adaptation was accomplished among people who had lost the institution of the divine king. Certainly it found its most striking development among the Jews, who apparently once knew and then lost the temporal divinity. When the ritual is extended over all of time, there emerges a linear progressive view of history, one which points toward a final goal or destination. So the cyclical theory and the linear theory are genetically identical. This is not perplexing when we reflect that a straight line is a circle whose center lies at infinity, and that the effect of substituting a single ritual for the annually recurring one is precisely to introduce infinity.

This is what is meant by saying that the Hebraic-Christian tradition is a historical tradition. The ritual of the installation of the divine king is spread out over all time: it then becomes a historical narrative. One of the features of the installation ceremony of the divine king at Babylon was the creation ceremony, by which the king enacted the role of the god Marduk and shaped the universe out of the carcass of the water-monster Tiamat. A derivative version is found in the book of Genesis. History then begins with the creation of the earth. The forward-looking orientation of Jewish thought may antedate the Exile, or it may be subsequent. What is certain is that it becomes a major theme only in the two centuries before the Christian era. In Jewish literature the principal emphasis is on the earthly emancipation of the Jewish people and the institution of the Kingdom of God on earth. In Christian thought the warrior-messiah of Jewish days more or less disappears, and salvation becomes an individual rather than a national goal. To the extent that this occurred, Christianity ceased to be a doctrine of uncompleted history, although it was still time-oriented. But the millennial heresy never disappeared. It found expression in the Everlasting Gospel of Joachim of Flora in the twelfth century; it was associated with political revolution in France, Italy, Bohemia, Germany, and England in the thirteenth through the seventeenth centuries; it is the mainspring of the Jehovah's Witnesses today.

More influential than this apocalyptic vision, however, has been the general forward orientation which was called above progressivism. The linear theory has supplied the principal framework for European and American political thought. In the eighteenth century it was secularized and became the doctrine of progress, which has been the chief prop of liberalism and democracy. Indeed, Marxism also seems to be a secularized version of Christian eschatology, with class struggle taking the place of Armageddon and the classless society serving as the Kingdom of God.

However, this does not exhaust the political effect of the cult of the divine king. The historical role of messianism is interesting. Wallis' count shows more than two hundred Christian, Jewish, and Moslem messiahs since Christ. For a long time the announcement of a new messiah or Mahdi was the usual way of initiating political revolution in the Moslem world. But more significant is the role of the divine king himself. The divine king was the generating and the sustaining force in society. He was in person the highest moral and ethical value. This character was transferred to his capital, which was, as Hugh Nibley says, the center of time and space. The worship of the divine king is timeless: time stands still, and Rome is the eternal city. Alexander the Great appropriated this role. The city of Rome made itself a divinity, and temples were erected to

Rome in the conquered cities of the East. When Rome acquired an emperor, he was virtually deified. And Christian Rome succeeded in maintaining its claim to be the center of the earth. Here we have one of the simplest and most pervasive of ideologies, the worship of state or church, which is, as Justice Frankfurter said in upholding the compulsory flag-salute, "a value inferior to none in our legal hierarchy."

At the same time, however, we should recognize the existence and persistence, at least since classical times, perhaps throughout history, of an antistate cult, the mirror image of official statism, but with the values reversed. The Roman Saturnalia was a deliberate inversion of the social order. In the middle ages there was an underground religion of devil-worship which practiced a reversal of Christianity. Witchcraft was the principal expression of this subterranean movement, and it was often a political expression. There is good reason to believe that Joan of Arc was a witch. It appears that Free-Masonry grew out of witchcraft, and it is interesting that the great sorcerer Cagliostro attempted to organize the Masons into a revolutionary order in the late eighteenth century. It will be remembered that the Free-Masons were active in the French Revolution and were the leading anticlericals of the nineteenth century.

There remains one inherited element to be discussed. The relation of this element to the divine king is not obvious but is real. The king was divine because the god was incarnated in him. But the divinity of the king was a function of magic, and magic could be used in other settings. The first professional practice of medicine consisted in the employment of rites borrowed from the installation ceremony of the divine king. By this means the patient was identified with the king and thus with the god, and the disease was expelled by the presence of divinity. By a similar means, the initiation ceremony that is so widespread, the common man acquired a soul—that is, divinity entered into him. In Hebrew religion, however, a ritual identification with god was not enough. Since Judaism was time-oriented, a soul was not saved simply by existing; it must look forward to a final judgment for its sins. But the coming of Christ brought a new dispensation. Christ had atoned for men's sins, and immediate participation in deity was available, not by ritual but by conviction. The divine king was so decentralized that all human institutions lost their sanctity. The individual man acquired individuality and became capable of what we now call human dignity. This, however, is a dignity that man has not enjoyed by simple virtue of his humanity either before or after Christ. Human dignity has been an aspiration rather than a postulate; it has been linked with progressivism since the Renaissance.

This idea also gave rise to the ideology which I have called Christian anarchism. Participation in deity has for some people required acceptance of the ethics of deity—that is, of the pacifistic anarchism of the Sermon on the Mount. The teaching of the Sermon on the Mount appears to be an ethics widespread throughout the East: it appears in the *Upanishads,* the *Bhagavadgita,* and the Dead Sea Scrolls, and emerged in this century in the Satyagraha of Gandhi.

I take it that these religious sources have supplied the inherited equipment from which political ideologies have been wrought. But history displays a great variety of ideologies. What accounts for the appearance now of one, now of another ideology? Here we turn to sociological explanation.

A certain amount of work has been done on the personality traits which cause one or another creed to appeal to a given person. No doubt character structure may predispose one toward a particular ideology. But we are interested in the larger question. What social conditions sweep the masses of men, regardless of their personality structures, into a single political movement?

If we begin with statism, we can easily explain its appeal. Men love what they are taught to love. They are born and live and die in allegiance to the state—or, it may be, the church. When the state is the final value, ethics is the interest of the state—or, it may be, the church. In the fifteenth century the Bishop of Verden said: "When the existence of the church is threatened, she is released from the commandments of morality. With unity as the end, the use of every means is sanctified, even cunning, treachery, violence, simony, prison, death. For all order is for the sake of the community, and the individual must be sacrificed to the common good." *Dulce et decorum est pro patria mori*—the individuals have usually been willing to be sacrificed, and the state has never hesitated to call upon them. Since the sixteenth century we have called the system of ideas which makes the interest of the state the paramount value "reason of state." Machiavelli did not invent this doctrine. Egoism is a property of organizations as well as individuals; perhaps it is more truly a property of organizations, for nothing is more common than for individuals to submerge their egos—and their morality—in the organization.

Statism is the ideology of a coherent, harmonious, one-valued society. But societies are not always harmonious and not always one-valued. What disrupts them? We have said that a man holds the values he has been taught. He forms expectations as the result of habituation, and he defines justice as the gratification of these expectations. The miller on the river Dee would not change his low degree for any other life.

But society may change while the social order stands still. A class or group may become equipped with new expectations which are frustrated by a static social order; or the society may withdraw its accustomed support and fail to gratify the established expectations of the class. A rising class equipped with new expectations looks to the future, to the horizon, for a just social order which will gratify those expectations. On the other hand, a declining class, one whose established expectations are disappointed, finds its values in the past and in this sense looks backward.

We have postulated a rising class which encounters a social barrier. This restriction will be denounced as unjust, and appeal will be made to freedom beyond the barrier. The principle of hierarchy and inequality which characterizes the old social order is regarded as a wilful and unnatural interference with a natural and just order. Appeal is taken from a fraudulently imposed inequality to a natural equality. A rising class is therefore equalitarian and libertarian.

The most familiar example is the rising middle class of the seventeenth and eighteenth centuries. Equipped with new demands by its economic advances, and frustrated in these demands, especially its prestige demands, by king, clergy, and nobility, the middle class in England, France, and America overthrew the survivals of feudalism in the name of liberty and equality, and prepared the way for democracy. But none of these was a final value, for there could be no final value. As James Russell Lowell wrote:

New occasions teach new duties; Time makes ancient good uncouth;
They must upward still, and onward, who would keep abreast of Truth....

The historical tradition which the progressivist ideology employs is the linear view of history. The Great Seal of the United States bears the legend *Novus Ordo Saeclorum*. The progressivist ideology looks beyond the existing state and church to a cosmic universal justice for free and equal individuals. The social contract doctrine, liberalism, democracy, socialism, anarchism are all expressions of the progressivism initiated by a rising class.

Suppose on the other hand a declining class, one whose habitual expectations are no longer gratified. Such a class will seek to regain its former position. It will attach value to hierarchy and inequality, and will define justice as the secure occupancy of an accustomed position within a hierarchical social order. Its values lie in the past, and it seeks to restore a vanished order. It seems appropriate to call such a class reactionary. A number of consequences follow from its social position. It is affirming as a final value, as universal justice, the hierarchical social order. Therefore it adopts an extreme nationalism, resembling in this respect the ideology of statism. But presumably the decline of this class was a result of an irreversible historical process. This means that its effort is foredoomed to failure. Of course, a declining class cannot afford to recognize irreversible historical processes, or history, at all. It therefore attributes its plight to the manipulations of a few evil men. The conspiracy theory of history, which explains massive social events as the outcome of sinister conspiracies, was popular with the admirers of the Old Regime which was overthrown by the French Revolution and with the German Nazis, both reactionary classes, and currently has a wide following among those who feel their positions threatened in the United States. Since history is irreversible, and the old order can never be restored, reaction involves progressively more harsh methods, more and more bloodshed, until the reaction itself is crushed by the wheel of change.

The best example of reaction is of course to be found in European fascism. We may use this convenient term to describe the efforts of the classes displaced by the French Revolution and the industrial revolution— the clergy and the nobility, who suffered through the political revolution, and the so-called lower middle class, the artisans, handicraft workers, and small manufacturers, who were displaced by capitalism in the course of the nineteenth century—to restore a vanished hierarchical order. The political theory of this group was first stated in 1800 by Fichte in his *Closed Commercial State,* which sought a stable, hierarchical order with the state as the final value. Hegel took up the argument, and in Hegel we find clearly expressed what might be called the time-dilemma of reaction. Values are prescribed by the past; they give direction to the present; they must be achieved in the future. The past must flow through the present into the future, which is then simply the maturity of the past. This view of history, which is certainly much more sophisticated than its alternative, the conspiracy theory, seeks change without novelty; the future is simply a purified past, the past raised to a higher power. To the progressive philosophers of the Enlightenment, history was, as Gibbon said, the record of the follies, vices, and crimes of mankind. The bright new day would break with history. To Hegel there was no bright new day: the brutal flow of the past was self-vindicated by its extension into the future.

German fascism taught reaction: the return of women to the kitchen; the abolition of democracy; the restoration of inequality in all aspects of life. Austrian clerical fascism taught the corporative state, a frozen economy in a frozen society. Always fascism places final value in this hierarchical society.

We have defined progressivism as a creed looking to the future, reaction as one looking to the past, conservatism as one which finds its values in the present. Who feels impelled to make an affirmation of the values of the present? The circumstances are very limited, for usually the admirers of received values become vocal only when their supports have been cut away, and this makes them the apologists of reaction. Edmund Burke is usually regarded as the oracle of conservatism. He defended the values of the past while they still existed in England; he was impelled to become articulate in their defense by the French Revolution, which pulled down old institutions on the continent and threatened by the force of its example to produce the same result in England. Faced with a program for the rational reorganization of society, Burke was forced to deny the possibility of rational management of human affairs. Faced with the universal values of Liberty, Equality, Fraternity, Burke was forced to deny the validity of universal values, and to insist that value attached only to that part of the past which survived into the present. This involved a radical moral relativism. Finally, Burke was forced to deny that final value attached to the state, which was the great organ of change in France, and to attach value to society, viewed as the quiescent routine of inherited behavior. In this he differs from the reactionaries, who have a program to be effectuated and are therefore obliged to exalt the state. He does, however, resemble the statists, and conservatism might be regarded as one form of statism.

Next is the tradition which I have called the catastrophic myth. Let us suppose, not a class within a society which is rising or declining relatively in that society, but an entire society which is threatened with destruction. Its values are yielding to the impact of a more powerful culture. The case is beyond human help. Such a society may make either of two responses, or both in sequence. The first is defiance; the second is surrender. Since men initially believe that their society is natural and inevitable—since they are initially statists—they cannot accept the possibility of its extinction. Therefore they predict direct divine intervention and a catastrophe by which God will overwhelm the conquerors and restore the conquered. The intervention may be that of a divinely designated warrior-king, and it will be remembered that the Maccabees, Simon Bar-Kochba, and others claimed to be the Jewish Messiah about the time of Jesus. Or the Messiah may be an angelic figure, or God Himself. The apocalyptic literature is full of alternatives, but in every case superhuman effort is needed to restore Israel. Apocalypse entered into the New Testament in the Book of Revelation. In modern times we have repeatedly seen colonial peoples threatened with extinction have recourse to the catastrophic myth. Most familiar to Americans is the ghost-dance religion of the American Indians in the 1870s, 1880s, 1890s. There were predictions that the heavens would fall and crush the whites, that the dead would return and expel the whites, that the buffalo would spring up again. The T'ai-p'ing rebellion in China was an attempt to expel foreign devils and was sustained by a catastrophic myth: there was something similar in the Boxer Rebellion at the close of the nineteenth century. In South Africa in 1857 the Kaffir tribesmen expected two suns to rise, the skies to fall on the whites, the dead to rise to war on the whites, and the earth to be covered with wheat and cattle. They killed and consumed all their cattle in anticipation of the day, and the tribes were broken by starvation. A number of instances of the catastrophic myth have occurred in Nigeria, South America, New Guinea, and the Pacific islands.

These phenomena are called messianism by the anthropologists, but usually there is no messiah. There is almost always some borrowing of Christian eschatology, and the myths are sometimes treated as simple cultural borrowing. But they are more than that. They express the final protest of a dying people or a dying culture, the appeal to the supernatural for salvation. Observe that the catastrophic myth, since it aims at the overthrow of the oppressors, is impliedly libertarian and egalitarian. It is for this reason that the literature of the Jewish apocalypse has contributed to progressive ideology, which, although it is optimistic rather than despairing, is also egalitarian and libertarian.

A colonial people occupies a relation toward the dominant power very like that of an outcast group to the principal society represented in figure 5 in the preceding pages. In both cases the oppressed group experiences privation inflicted by the oppressors. The experience of privation generates resentment. But there are differences. A colonial people is not integrated into the culture of the dominant power. It seeks not assimilation but emancipation and the revival of its native culture and values. An outcast group, on the other hand, is functionally related to the major society. There is a scheme of distributive justice, theoretically obligatory on both societies, which defines the minor as an integral part of the major. Some members of the minor society are likely to achieve a measure of economic success within the major society and to feel entitled to a proportionate measure of prestige. These upward-mobile individuals have the psychology and the ideology of members of a rising class. They consider the barriers to achievement and acceptance to be unnatural and arbitrary limitations upon a natural liberty and equality. The native culture of their group, which is separatist and statist, seems to them almost as objectionable. A number of *cagots* broke the prohibition on intermarriage in France in the eighteenth century, and one even bricked up the *cagot* door in the parish church. The abolition of the ghettos by Napoleon played an important part in bringing

Jews into the main currents of European politics. Many of the most dedicated and ablest leaders of progressive movements have been Jews. In the twentieth century, in America, educated and prosperous blacks have moved into the forefront of the progressive movement.

But oppression can also turn an outcast group in upon itself, so that it seeks emancipation rather than assimilation. This process finds ideological expression in a catastrophic myth. There were repeated messianic outbreaks in the Jewish ghettos in the middle ages. A powerful movement in the black ghettos today repudiates white society and white culture. Nat Turner had messianic delusions, and religious messianism animates the so-called Black Muslims. Even more widespread is what might be called cultural messianism. The slave society did not supply a system of values appropriate to the ambitions of black secessionists. Therefore it was necessary to go to the distant past to discover an independent culture, to adopt African dress and to study Swahili.

There remains one type of ideology, the doctrine of Matthew 5:39: "Resist not evil." Two passages in Proverbs look in this direction, and a few passages in the Talmud, but nothing like the extremity of the Sermon on the Mount is to be found in Jewish literature. It has, however, analogues in Eastern literature, and from this tradition Gandhi forged the powerful political weapon of nonresistance. This is the creed of Christian anarchism. It flourished greatly in czarist Russia: there it was linked with the messianism that produced a series of Russian messiahs. Count Tolstoy is its most famous Russian exponent. The Doukhobors have brought it to this continent. The western forms are creeds of the Quakers and the Mennonites. It is curious that the Quakers, who live in a new dispensation, reject the authority of the text, and are guided only by the inner light, should arrive at the same result as the Mennonites, who are fundamentalists and follow the text of the Bible literally. A result that can be achieved by these two different roads must be an important truth about Christianity.

One of the most instructive manifestations of what I have called Christian anarchism is the religion of peyote. This cult was borrowed from Mexico in the 1840s and was taken up in a number of tribes of Plains Indians. The ritual is not elaborate; the principal feature is eating the root of peyote or drinking peyote tea, and by the use of this drug achieving communion with God. This communion is sometimes gained through the aid of Peyote, a personification of the root and an intermediary to God. The ethical conviction that results is love and pacifism: "We should all feel sorry for one another" is one Indian's version. Christian elements have entered in, and Indians sometimes speak of Jesus as "the white man's Peyote."

Peyote emerged in the defeat of a culture. Unlike the catastrophic myth, Christian anarchism does not appeal to arms for restoration. It surrenders and finds a new orientation in relation to God. It has been suggested that peyote was a sequel to the ghost-dance religion—collapse following defiance—but in fact the tribes that have taken up peyote are not the tribes that practiced the ghost-dance religion. Some of them had been broken long before. Quite possibly the native structure of the society and of the personality instilled by the society determines the response.

These six types of ideology fall into two classes. Statism, conservatism, and reaction affirm the primacy of society and attach value to hierarchy and inequality. Progressivism, the catastrophic myth, and Christian anarchism all seek a break with established society. They are future-oriented and are libertarian and egalitarian.

15

THE PRESIDENCY AS AN IDEAL TYPE

James MacGregor Burns, who has been one of the principal extollers of the strong presidency, said: "I do not contend that the White House exercises a kind of divine magic over the incumbent and invests him with magical power." Rather, he said, the presidency brings out the "potentially great" in men: "We do have by now ample indication that the Presidency, with its spacious view of the world, its command of talent, and above all its historic role—does work its way on the men in the oval office."[1]

The word "great" covers a broad territory. Attila, Genghis Khan, and Napoleon have been called great. The practice of historians seems to have assigned the adjective to two classes of American presidents. A president whose name is identified with a great national crisis is great, not because of his conduct but because events have made him a symbol of the nation. George Washington is not regarded as a great president because of his administration of the office (although he should be) but because he was commander-in-chief during the Revolution. Abraham Lincoln, whom Wendell Phillips called a "first-rate second-rate man," conducted the Civil War with a curious mixture of irresolution and imprudence, and won only because the side he commanded enjoyed a great preponderance of men and resources; but he is called a great president. Woodrow Wilson, although he was "too proud to fight," involved the country in the First World War, and thereby wrapped himself in the flag.

Reprinted from *Fortuna* 2 (Jan.–Feb., 1976): 18-34. Used by permission of *Fortuna*.

If the Mexican War and the Spanish-American War had put the nation in hazard, Polk and McKinley would also be regarded as great presidents. Harold Laski said that in every crisis the American people have found a president equal to the occasion. Rather, it is the case that in every tragic drama the dimension of heroism is ascribed to the actors.

Second, greatness is attributed to presidents who have magnified the office, whether by usurpation, self-assertion, or the sponsorship of an ambitious legislative program. Apparently Andrew Jackson believed that the world was flat.[2] He is not known to have read more than one book in his life.[3] John Quincy Adams did not exaggerate greatly when he said that Jackson "hardly could spell his own name."[4] Nevertheless, a large literature of adulation has grown up about Jackson, and his name appears in every list of great presidents. The reason seems to be that Jackson was arrogant, contentious, and violent, and embroiled himself frequently with Congress. The names of Woodrow Wilson and Franklin Roosevelt are associated with extensive domestic programs as well as with foreign wars. The fame of Grover Cleveland seems to rest on nothing more substantial than his challenge to Congress, principally by the veto of innumerable private bills. But it is not necessary that a president accomplish something significant in order to be called great. It is only necessary that he strike a dramatic posture—"Perdicaris alive or Raisuli dead"—and that this succeed in the sense that it does not produce an immediate failure. If by some miracle Lyndon Johnson's Vietnam adventure had succeeded—but no president has a right to expect miracles—he would be regarded as a great president. Of course, other nations make their heroes in the same way.

Probably a more reflective view of greatness would emphasize other values and other traits of behavior. A great president would subordinate personal interests and personal fame to a larger social interest. He would not support predatory groups in the exploitation of the public at large. He would judge policies in terms of a long-range calculation of social consequences rather than a short-range calculation of political advantage; and he would perform this calculation aright. He would be a man of personal integrity.

Perhaps no one would deny that George Washington and John Quincy Adams at least approximated this definition of greatness. Probably everyone would agree that the majority of our presidents have not come within bowshot of it. Concerning the eligibility of the remaining presidents there might be debate, for partisanship never fails to extol those who are identified, even distantly, with a partisan name or cause.

The early literature of republicanism argued that the electoral process would bring to office men possessed of republican virtue, whereas in hereditary monarchies the character of the king was a matter of chance. But it appears that virtue is a positive handicap in the selective process of American politics. One need not agree with H. L. Mencken that servility and opportunism are the sole qualities of the politician. Nevertheless, one who lacks these qualities enters upon a political career under a great competitive disadvantage. Moreover, politics is conflict. A combative personality is an initial asset; the practice of politics confirms and reinforces this trait. For the combative man victory in the struggle is the central issue. Other considerations become merely means to this end. Ruthlessness is added to servility and opportunism.

When Theodore Roosevelt declared for the Republican nomination for the presidency in 1912, his close friend Elihu Root wrote sorrowfully in a private letter:[5]

He is essentially a fighter and when he gets into a fight he is completely dominated by the desire to destroy his adversary. He instinctively lays hold of every weapon which can be used for that end. Accordingly he is saying a lot of things and taking a lot of positions which are inspired by the desire to win. I have no doubt he thinks he believes what he says, but he doesn't. He has merely picked up certain popular ideas which were at hand as one might pick up a poker or chair with which to strike.

And later he said of Roosevelt: "Combativeness was his essential characteristic."[6]

William Howard Taft had been lifted up and thrust by Roosevelt into the presidency, and could not hold his ground against his former sponsor, although he made pathetic boast of his resolution: "Even a rat in a corner will fight."[7] Root's forecast proved true: "I don't think Roosevelt will succeed in getting the nomination. He will, however, succeed in so damaging Taft that he can't be elected."[8]

A schoolmate recalled of the young Richard Nixon: "He was combative rather than conciliatory. He had a nasty temper."[9] Nixon's campaign style was always one of personal assault. He began by unseating first Jerry Voorhis and then Helen Gahagan Douglas by campaigns of vilification. His role in the 1952 campaign was to slander Truman's principal advisors. So unsavory did his reputation become that in 1967 Raymond K. Price, who was to be his most prominent speech writer, advised that it was necessary to allege that Nixon had grown, mellowed, and matured.[10] Newspaper columnists speculated as to whether there was in fact a "new Nixon," and on television the candidate confirmed that he had indeed changed and matured. In the 1968 campaign the cruder tasks were assigned to his running mate Agnew, but Nixon's own campaign followed his usual pattern. He ran against the Supreme Court, and more especially against Johnson's attorney general, Ramsey Clark, whom he blamed for an alleged breakdown of law and order, although he knew that the Department of Justice had neither the responsibility nor the authority to deal with "crime in the streets" and he privately thought that "Ramsey Clark is really a fine fellow. And he's done a good job."[11]

It is possible to enter politics without such a natural endowment, and even to achieve high office without acquiring the aptitude. A candidate from an influential family may enter politics in a safe legislative district, and may rise a certain distance without learning the elementary political skills. But he is defenseless when he encounters a practitioner of gutter politics, as Millard Tydings was defenseless when Joe McCarthy attacked him.

It is even possible to enter politics at the highest level, to become a candidate for president without serving a political apprenticeship and becoming a politician. But such a man does not win the nomination; it is given to him by professional politicians, and they choose a man whom they expect to serve their purposes. Dwight D. Eisenhower was enlisted by Thomas E. Dewey, the political representative of eastern financial interests, to champion their foreign policy against the claims of midwest industry represented by Robert A. Taft. Probably Eisenhower had encountered politics even in the structured bureaucratic life of the army, but the skills he had acquired were not those of electoral politics. Nevertheless, he tolerated the sharp practice that won him the nomination at the Republican convention in 1952 and the red-baiting his party carried on in the ensuing campaign; he even abandoned his friend General Marshall, to whom he owed his military career, when Marshall was traduced by Senators McCarthy and Jenner.

Machiavelli said:[12]

For there is such a difference between the way men live and the way they ought to live that he who prefers what ought to be done to what is actually done learns the way to ruin rather than to self-preservation; for a man who may desire to profess virtue in every matter insures his ruin among so many who are not virtuous. Whence it is necessary for a prince who wishes to survive to learn to be dishonest, and to be honest or dishonest according to the circumstances.

As we have said, an elective prince will have already learned this lesson. But is there not, as Burns says, something in the presidency that produces change in the man, that evokes new behavior, that liberates "potential greatness"?

Since Aristotle we have known that character is formed incrementally, by a long succession of decisions. The politician who remains in the race is obliged to make a series of choices between principle and expediency. He must reward his followers at the public expense. On one or more occasions he may be forced to break faith with his friends and allies. Like the boy in Grimm's fairy tale who paid his way with his golden brains, the politician pays his way with his character. He may arrive at the presidency with his heritage entirely spent. Henry Adams, "stable companion to statesmen," as he called himself, has recorded the regret with which he saw John Hay yield to McKinley's summons to come to Washington as secretary of state. "No one in his experience had ever passed unscathed through that malarious marsh."[13] Office was poison; this "poison was that of the will—the distortion of sight—the warping of mind—the degradation of tissue—the coarsening of taste—the narrowing of sympathy to the emotions of a caged rat."[14]

Once formed, character is not very malleable. A psychiatrist does not undertake to reform it entirely but to undo a single quirk, and even in this he is not likely to succeed. Nevertheless, behavior is a function not only of character but of the situation. A change in status may alter the problems which face a man and thus may elicit new behavior patterns. When a politician is appointed to the Supreme Court, he often turns out better than most observers expect. He has abandoned the combative posture. His role is now dictated by the value system of the law. He will see this system, to be sure, through personal spectacles, but it will have a stability altogether lacking in the kaleidoscopic environment to which the politician must continually adjust himself. In this sense, the office changes the man.

Does anything of the sort occur to the president? He does not escape from political life into another system of values. Rather, political life rises to a higher pitch of intensity. Henry Adams explained Theodore Roosevelt in impersonal terms:[15]

Power is poison. Its effect on Presidents had always been tragic, chiefly in an almost insane excitement at first, and a worse reaction afterwards; but also because no mind is so well balanced as to bear the strain of seizing unlimited power without habit or knowledge of it; and finding it disputed with him by hungry packs of wolves and hounds whose lives depend on snatching the carrion.

But individual men are individuals; each one is unique. Obviously we can make no confident forecast about an unidentified individual case. This need not terminate inquiry. The question is about the office and not the man. Can we offer a sociological account of the character structure appropriate to the official role, the behavior pattern the office may be expected to generate, leaving aside questions of personal biography?

Max Weber has described the method of "ideal types."[16] An ideal type is an abstract description of the implications of a social situation. It is not an empirical generalization; but it is constructed by the use of our empirical knowledge of human nature. It is the work of *Verstehen,* of empathic understanding. It is the only tool we have for calculating the consequences of adopting institutions of one sort or another. It is not an instrument of prediction; but it is an account of tendencies.

The man who achieves the presidency does change his status, and does acquire greatness of a special sort. He stands at the pinnacle of power, not only in the nation but in the world. He is flattered and adulated. Lord Acton said that all power corrupts. Adam Smith gave a description of the process that is worth quoting at length.[17]

> Of the persons who, in estimating their own merit, in judging of their own character and conduct, direct by far the greater part of their attention to the second standard, to that ordinary degree of excellence which is commonly attained by other people, there are some who really and justly feel themselves very much above it, and who, by every intelligent and impartial spectator, are acknowledged to be so. The attention of such persons, however, being always principally directed, not to the standard of the ideal, but to that of ordinary perfection, they have little sense of their own weaknesses and imperfections; they have little modesty; are often assuming, arrogant and presumptuous, great admirers of themselves, and great contemners of other people. Though their characters are in general much less correct, and their merit much inferior to that of the man of real and modest virtue, yet their excessive presumption, founded upon their own excessive self-admiration, dazzles the multitude, and often imposes even upon those who are much superior to the multitude. The frequent, and often wonderful, success of the most ignorant quacks and imposters, both civil and religious, sufficiently demonstrates how easily the multitude are imposed upon by the most extravagant and groundless pretensions. But when these pretensions are supported by a very high degree of real and solid merit, when they are displayed with all the splendour which ostentation can bestow upon them, when they are supported by high rank and great power, when they have often been successfully exerted, and are, upon that account, attended by the loud acclamations of the multitude; even the man of sober judgment often abandons himself to the general admiration. The very noise of those foolish acclamations often contributes to confound his understanding, and while he sees those great men only at a certain distance, he is often disposed to worship them with a sincere admiration, superior even to that with which they appear to worship themselves....
>
> Great success in the world, great authority over the sentiments and opinions of mankind, have very seldom been acquired without some degree of this excessive self-admiration. The most splendid characters, the men who have performed the most illustrious actions, who have brought about the greatest revolutions, both in the situations and opinions

of mankind; the most successful warriors, the greatest statesmen and legislators, the eloquent founders and leaders of the most numerous and most successful sects and parties; have many of them been not more distinguished for their very great merit, than for a degree of presumption and self-admiration altogether disproportioned even to that very great merit. This presumption was, perhaps, necessary, not only to prompt them to undertakings which a more sober mind would never have thought of, but to command submission and obedience of their followers to support them in such undertakings. When crowned with success, accordingly, this presumption has often betrayed them into a vanity that approached almost to insanity and folly. Alexander the Great appears, not only to have wished that other people think him a god, but to have been at least very well disposed to fancy himself as such. Upon his deathbed, the most ungodlike of all situations, he requested of his friends that to the respectable list of deities, into which he himself had long before been inserted, his old mother Olympia might likewise have the honour of being added. Amidst the respectful admiration of his followers and disciples, amidst the applause of the public, after the oracle, which probably had followed the voice of that applause, had pronounced him the wisest of men, the great wisdom of Socrates, though it did not suffer him to fancy himself a god, yet was not great enough to hinder him from fancying that he had secret and frequent intimations from some invisible and divine Being. The sound head of Caesar was not so perfectly sound as to hinder him from being much pleased with his divine genealogy from the goddess Venus; and, before the temple of this pretended great-grandmother, to receive without rising from his seat the Roman senate, when that illustrious body came to present him with some decrees, conferring upon him the most extravagant honours. This insolence, joined to some other actions of an almost childish vanity, little to be expected from an understanding at once so very acute and comprehensive, seems, by exasperating the public jealousy, to have emboldened his assassins and to have hastened the execution of their conspiracy. The religion and manners of modern times give our great men little encouragement to fancy themselves either gods or even prophets. Success, however, joined to great popular favour, has often so far turned the heads of the greatest of them, as to make them ascribe to themselves both an importance and an ability much beyond what they really possessed; and, by this presumption, to precipitate themselves into many rash, and sometimes ruinous adventures. . . .

In the humble projects of private life, as well as in the ambitious and proud pursuits of high stations, great abilities and successful enterprise in the beginning, have frequently encouraged to undertakings which necessarily led to bankruptcy and ruin in the end.

No special dispensation exempts presidents from the intoxication of power. David Lloyd George has recorded the "most extraordinary outburst" of Woodrow Wilson at the Paris Peace Conference.[18]

"Why," he said, "has Jesus Christ so far not succeeded in inducing the world to follow His teachings in these matters? It is because He taught the ideal without devising any practical means of attaining it. That is the reason why I am proposing a practical scheme to carry out His aims." Clemenceau slowly opened his dark eyes to their widest dimensions and swept them round the Assembly to see how the Christians gathered around the table enjoyed this exposure of the futility of their Master.

In *The Twilight of the Presidency* George Reedy, who served as press secretary and special assistant to President Johnson, says that the office itself engenders such an attitude. The president "is treated with all the reverence due a monarch,"[19] he is a "semidivinity."[20] Consequently he regards himself with awe, and "can easily slide into a feeling of divinity."[21] Those who surround him are sycophants, and he is isolated from the people. Unless he is a "weak president" or an unusually wise one, his advisors will merely reflect back his own opinions and biases.[22]

Probably the self-made man is more vulnerable to megalomania than one born to the purple. He ascribes to his personal star or his personal destiny the preeminence which the latter is satisfied to ascribe to his station. Consequently he is led on to further and further adventures; in the end he is likely to come to disaster. Napoleon and Hitler are examples.

But perhaps we should distinguish between kinds of self-made men. Machiavelli said that "the prince must know how to play the beast as well as the man," and should emulate both the lion and the fox.[23] The lion is strong but is vulnerable to snares; the fox, although physically weak, succeeds by deceit. Pareto[24] made the lion and the fox alternative types of statesman. The lion characteristically employs frontal assault; the fox relies upon cunning. There is something to this. Caesar Augustus and Oliver Cromwell were extraordinarily clever manipulators; in our own day, there was Stalin. It does not appear that Stalin himself was deceived by the "cult of personality" which virtually deified him. Rather, the emergence of such a cult seems to be a condition of the survival of a nation which is in a process of rapid social change. In a stable society, the coherence of the society is guaranteed by settled institutions and cultural practices which give the citizenry assurance and security. But in Stalin's day the institutions and the culture of the Soviet Union were in a state of rapid and bewildering transformation. The only focus for social cohesion was the figure of Stalin himself. The very ruthlessness with which Stalin destroyed the impersonal supports of the social order threw the society into dependence upon his person for emotional orientation and confidence. The same phenomenon is observable in other colonial countries in a period of rapid dissolution of institutions. The cult of personality emerged in China with Mao Tse-tung, in Indonesia with Sukarno, in Egypt with Nasser, in Cuba with Castro, in Ghana with

Nkrumah, and in other African countries with other leaders. A similar development has occurred in industrialized societies in time of social collapse. The Great Depression destroyed the economic supports of the petty bourgeoisie in Germany, reducing them, to use Trotsky's striking expression, to "human dust." Unanchored and lost, they accepted the leadership principle and restored social structure in the form of a cult of Hitler.

If we accept the types of the lion and the fox, it appears that self-confidence and recklessness are more likely to characterize the lion than the fox. The fox succeeds by intrigue, which means that he consciously employs the strength of others. Stalin, who achieved power by manipulation, was enormously cautious. His goal was "socialism in one country," and often this seemed to entail opposition to socialism in any other. He attempted actively to discourage the rebellion of partisans and Communists against the British and the monarchy in Greece which Harry Truman in 1947 made the occasion for the pronouncement of the Truman doctrine for the repression of the supposedly insatiable expansionist appetite of Stalin. He endorsed Chiang Kai-shek in China and tried to hold back Mao Tse-tung. But if supreme power did not induce megalomania in Stalin, it worked other unfortunate consequences. Acutely aware of the precarious tenure of power in a state in which it was so little routinized by institutions as in the Soviet Union, he developed suspicion and fear of his colleagues which progressed into paranoia and produced bloody purges.

On the other hand, there is certainly no assurance that a man whose career has hitherto been that of a fox will not upon achieving supreme power develop the hubris of a Caesar or a Napoleon. Lyndon Johnson had been a skillful manipulator, and achieved the presidency by the arts of the fox. But apparently his staggering victory over Goldwater in 1964 induced a self-confidence which led him to catastrophe. His language became as rash as his actions. Speaking at Omaha on June 30, 1966, he laid claim to the war power of Congress: "Now there are many, many who can recommend, advise, and sometimes a few of them consent. But there is only one that has been chosen by the American people to decide."[25] At Des Moines, on the same day, he seems to have felt that he was being crucified by the "strident voices" that opposed his war, for he said: "I am not angry; I am not even sorrowful. I sometimes think of the words, 'God forgive them, for they know not what they do.'"[26] He was in better spirits in Lancaster, Ohio, on September 5, 1966 when he assured the American people: "If you make these sacrifices for your country, you make these sacrifices for me."[27]

Power and responsibility entail other consequences. The duties of office produce exhaustion, which may have immediate effect. Theodore Sorensen says: "I saw first-hand, during the long days and nights of the Cuban crisis, how brutally physical and mental fatigue can numb the good sense as well as the senses of normally articulate [sic] men."[28] Over a long term the strain of effort and of hope, apprehension and uncertainty induces tension. Physical and mental health are eroded.

The physical demands of a chief magistracy exceed the resources of most men. Before he was elected to the presidency, Wilson said that we must choose the president "from among wise and prudent athletes";[29] Harold Macmillan said that a prime minister must have the constitution of an ox.[30] But ordinarily a man achieves a leading position in politics only in his later fifties or even his sixties, an age at which most men, even athletes, have incurred permanent maladies of one sort or another. These maladies, aggravated by the strain of office, may have not merely physical but psychological consequences. They may distort perception or impair the judgment. In 1960 Dean Rusk, later secretary of state, said: "The international list of those who have carried great responsibility while ill is a long one and there are fleeting glimpses of decisions which good health might have turned another way."[31] An English physician, Dr. Hugh L'Etang, who has canvassed all the available sources, has summarized his findings: "The list of international statesmen, senior officials who have borne supreme responsibility, while in the grip of disabling and debilitating illness, is certainly long and forbidding. In many cases a plausible case can be made for a link between their physical and mental handicaps and impairment of performance, judgement and power of decision."[32] L'Etang points out that "since 1908 eleven out of thirteen British premiers and six out of ten American Presidents have had illnesses in office which have incapacitated them to some degree."[33] As early as 1906 Woodrow Wilson was advised to retire because of arterial degeneration. In 1913 Dr. Mitchell advised him that it was doubtful that he could retain his health through his first term.[34] Personality change seems to have begun as early as 1917.[35] In 1919, on the platform at Pueblo, Colorado, Wilson was disabled by what may not have been his first stroke.[36] The remainder of his career was tragic: "Wilson, isolated by his intimates and handicapped by increasing obstinacy, mental deterioration and failure of judgment, destroyed any hope of attaining even some of the objectives for which he had ruined his health."[37] So distorted was his judgment that he attempted to obtain the Democratic nomination for an unprecedented third term in 1920, at a time when he was ill and partially paralyzed and had suffered decisive political defeat in the Senate.[38]

Franklin D. Roosevelt was seriously ill by 1944 and died, apparently from a cerebral hemorrhage, in 1945.[39] President Eisenhower had a heart attack and a stroke while in office.[40] He worried about his capacity to perform the duties of his office and made arrangements to be replaced by the Vice President in case of total disability.

James Forrestal, secretary of defense under President Truman, resigned at the President's request in 1949. For some months, at least, he had believed that he was the victim of a conspiracy of Communists, Jews, and sinister figures in the White House.[41] If, as Drew Pearson reported, a few days after his removal Forrestal upon hearing a fire engine rushed into the street in his pajamas shouting that the Russians were attacking,[42] we must conclude that it was a fortunate accident that he was not secretary of defense at that time. Forrestal committed suicide a few days later.

From 1930 on Ramsay MacDonald suffered physical and mental impairment; he continued as prime minister until 1935, although in June of 1933 his friend Lord Salter considered that "he was already no longer in a mental and physical condition to be capable of the continuous and exacting responsibilities of high office."[43]

Winston Churchill was sixty-five when he became prime minister in 1940. He suffered various illnesses but did not begin to lose his physical and mental powers until 1944.[44] He lost office in 1945. He held the premiership again from 1951 to 1955, but he had a mild stroke in 1949 and suffered a serious one in 1952. His physician's report seems to indicate that he was not equal to his responsibilities in 1951, and after another stroke in 1953 he was clearly unfit to hold office. However, he resisted all advice and pressure to retire to the House of Lords until 1955.[45] His successor, Anthony Eden, experienced illness and political crises which apparently aggravated each other, and he was forced to retire in 1957.[46]

Dr. L'Etang surveys a multitude of similar cases and concludes with the modest proposition that great men are no less prone to illness than others. It does seem that the pressures and tensions of office make principal political figures considerably more vulnerable to disorders of the circulatory and nervous systems than are ordinary men. It is precisely these diseases that threaten the capacity of a ruler to weigh a multitude of factors and make a wise judgment in a difficult case.

Where there is illness, there is medication. Malcolm Muggeridge said that Anthony Eden was overcome "by excessive doses of sedatives, pep-pills, and John Foster Dulles."[47] It appears that the administration of tranquilizers, not only to chiefs of state but to other political figures, has now become standard medical practice. But the official must meet people, he must make decisions; for these purposes he is roused and sharpened with stimulants. In times of great trial he bounces back and forth like a pingpong ball. We are governed, as Harvey Wheeler has said, by a "chemical man." Some medications have side effects. In many cases, for example, cortisone produces a false euphoria and an unfounded optimism. The abuse of cortisone causes messianic delusions. President Kennedy was treated regularly with cortisone after 1954.[48] He may also have been treated with amphetamines.[49]

The fear that the president may become hopelessly irrational was the unexpressed motive for the proposal of the Twenty-fifth Amendment.[50] Unfortunately, the amendment does not meet the problem. Either the president, or the vice president together with a majority of the department heads, may certify his disability. But the president may resume office simply by giving notice to the two houses of Congress. He can be overruled only if the vice president and a majority of the department heads make a report of continuing disability to Congress and two-thirds of both houses confirm this finding. There seems to be no likelihood that a president will willingly surrender office. Nor will a majority of the department heads, who are his appointees and his political partisans and whose tenure of office depends on the president, vote him out unless his disability is as notorious as that of George III, whose insanity was recognized by act of Parliament. Moreover, the president may overrule any adverse finding and maintain his tenure of office unless two-thirds of both houses vote against him, which is improbable in the extreme.

In the British system the cabinet colleagues of the prime minister could surely displace him in case of disability, although a tense political situation might arise if he appealed to the House of Commons. But this has never occurred. Sir Henry Campbell-Bannerman was incapacitated by a heart attack as early as November, 1907, but he continued to hold the premiership. After a second heart attack on February 12, 1908, he was confined to his bed, but he did not resign until April 3, nineteen days before his death.[51] As early as 1952 some of Winston Churchill's associates tried to persuade him to surrender the premiership and take a seat in the House of Lords, but he refused to do so until April 6, 1955, by which time he was spending most of the day in bed.[52]

After much experience with politics and intimate acquaintance with the White House, George Reedy said:[53]

> A highly irrational personality, who under other circumstances might be medically certifiable for treatment, could take over the White House and the event never be known with any degree of assurance.
> ... I do have some experience with the reaction of human beings to irrational behavior, and it is clear to me that where presidents are concerned, the tolerance level for irrationality extends almost to the point of gibbering idiocy or delusions of identity.

To put it more simply, no one is going to interfere with the presidential exercise of authority unless the president drools in public or announces on television that he is Alexander the Great. And even in these extreme cases, action would be taken hesitantly indeed.

... He will still have the authority to drop the atomic bomb on another nation even though in the privacy of Senate cloakrooms experienced men are whispering that "the president is nuts."

What this means is that the presidency, like other autocracies and semiautocracies, embodies a permanent danger. But this danger is *in posse* rather than *in esse;* and in fact we have never, so far as we know, had a president who was authentically mad. Consequently the problem of insanity is not a feature of the presidency as an ideal type. An ideal type is a projection based upon features intrinsic to a social situation, a forecast which our knowledge of men and institutions leads us to expect as a normal response to the situation.

As a sociological concept, the ideal type cannot be a portrait of any actual man. Every man has his idiosyncrasies, and these may produce consequences not accounted for by, or even at variance with, the ideal type.

In some cases personal characteristics may mitigate the harsh outlines of the ideal type. Obviously it is possible and it does occur that some men survive the political struggle without collapsing into moral bankruptcy; they may win contests without becoming mere fighting-cocks. An acute and dispassionate intelligence, a firm footing in humility, perhaps even a well developed sense of humor may save a leader from megalomania. The leader may have an unusually sound body. But in contriving institutions we cannot take into account the unknown good qualities of unknown future incumbents. We must expect that incumbents will in the main fulfill rather than frustrate the potentialities of the institutions.

We should also recognize that a president may have personal traits which are not necessitated by the office but which may work damage in the office. The arrogance and self-righteousness of Woodrow Wilson were sources of weakness rather than strength. The character of Warren G. Harding colored his whole administration. Calvin Coolidge was temperamentally inclined to inactivity. Despite the cult of the "strong president," a Coolidge is likely to be less dangerous than a president given to self-dramatization. Theodore Roosevelt was addicted to posturing: this was clearly an overcompensation for childhood feelings of inadequacy. In the early years of the twentieth century Roosevelt's taste for the rash and the theatrical did little harm; but the vaulting ambition of John F.

Kennedy produced very grave problems. The British journalist Louis Heren identified one of them.[54]

> The President often feels compelled to initiate a new policy, even when one is not absolutely called for or when insufficient time has been given for consideration.... If this is regrettable, it is a fact of American political life that a President has a set period in which to make his mark, theoretically four years, or eight years at most, but it can be less if he loses majority support in Congress or public confidence. Moreover, he ascends to his awful throne of power with little or no intimate experience of foreign affairs. Unlike a British Prime Minister, he has not shared collective Cabinet responsibility and experience. He has rarely been a party to decision-making. Professor Schlesinger claimed for President Kennedy a most varied and extensive international experience. As a young man, the professor solemnly reported, he had talked to Franklin D. Roosevelt, Neville Chamberlain, and Stanley Baldwin. Unimpressive as this early experience may strike readers, it was more than that of some other presidents.

Heren illustrates this weakness of the system in which "a new President finds that he is to be tested in a field of which he has little or no experience, under the compulsions of public expectation and the personal desire to make his mark" by referring to the very instructive case of the Bay of Pigs. It is not true that responsibility lay with Kennedy's subordinates. "The fact of the matter, as admitted by one member of his staff who did not seek quick fame and fortune in memoir writing, was that President Kennedy, although new to office and with almost no experience, wanted to invade Cuba. When a President wants to do something badly, it is very difficult for a subordinate to oppose him."[55]

John E. Ullmann believes that this initial motivation persisted: "Kennedy, of course, did give up on the Bay of Pigs when it flopped, but there is strong evidence that his escalation of the defense budget, his intervention in Vietnam and his enthusiasm for the space race were all attempts to prove his *machismo*."[56]

Of course, this may be a misreading. Schlesinger assures us that Kennedy drifted into the Vietnam War because "he had never really given it his full attention."[57] But this confirms our central point. It means that the most fateful decisions are functions of the perceptions, the misperceptions, even the inattention of a single man. Neither the recruitment process nor the office provides any defense against the idiosyncratic weaknesses that are bound to be a part of the personality of any individual.

In the middle ages the literature of advice to kings urged upon them humility and self-abnegation. This probably did little good, but it did no harm. The contemporary literature of the presidency extols self-assertion and domination. The public at large applauds these traits. Unless he is immunized by an unusual character structure, as was Dwight Eisenhower, the president responds to this heady brew. The twentieth century has seen Mussolini, Hitler, Franco, Stalin, and a host of lesser figures faithfully fulfill the promises of power. We should expect that sooner or later a conjunction of the circumstances, the office, and a man will produce the same consequence in the United States.

16

THE INTERNATIONAL POWER ELITE

A cogent editorial in the May, 1959 *Monthly Review* ("Whom the Gods Would Destroy") argues that the European policy currently followed by the United States is self-defeating. The United States can have influence in Europe only by joining the Soviet Union in the repression of Germany. Our policy of promoting German hegemony in western Europe will enable Germany to emancipate herself. The Soviet Union will then settle the European question with Germany; and Germany will turn westward, challenging the United States for the domination of the capitalist world.

In terms of the traditional assumptions of American foreign policy, the argument is sound. We did not fight two wars to prevent the unification of Europe under German auspices merely because of revulsion at German *Kultur,* although it was of course necessary for the molders of opinion to arouse such revulsion. What moved our decision-makers was the obvious consequence of a German victory. If western Europe were organized and directed by Germany, the world power structure would be radically altered. More especially, Latin America, the Achilles' heel of the United States, would be irresistibly drawn into the European orbit. The European and Latin American economies are complementary. Only with difficulty have we maintained the political neutralization of Latin America at which the Monroe Doctrine aims, against the gravitational pull of a divided Europe. A western Europe united under Germany would outweigh

---

Coauthor, Hobert P. Sturm.
Reprinted from *Monthly Review* 11 (1959): 282-87. Reprinted by permission of Monthly Review Press.

us. When war broke out in 1914, Walter H. Page, our ambassador in London, wrote to Colonel House: "If Germany should win, our Monroe Doctrine would at once be shot in two." Similar considerations led the British to follow their historic policy of maintaining the division of Europe. No more than Latin America could the British empire resist a Europe united under a single command, whether that of Napoleon, Wilhelm II, or Hitler. This coincidence of interest made the United States and Great Britain allies in two anti-German wars. Why has the United States made a sharp break with its settled policy and its obvious national interest?

The editors of *Monthly Review* conclude that our ruling class has lost all grip on reality. It is defeated and declining and like all declining classes invents an imaginary world and contrives an aberrant program.

If we took the statements of apologists for official policy at face value, certainly no explanation short of insanity could be found. There is no important difference between the more sophisticated versions and those aimed at the semiliterate. We are told that war and conquest were invented by Stalin, perhaps also by Marx, Lenin, and Khrushchev. The explanation of international dissension is a new ideology which has destroyed the Golden Age of Christianity and democracy in Russia, China, and central Europe, and presses unrelentingly on the frontiers of what remains of Eden. The Free World has a common interest in maintaining its heritage: NATO, SEATO, and the rest attest it.

Formal apologies for a policy are seldom scrupulously true; but ordinarily there is a policy behind them. The policy need not be stupid or insane merely because an intelligent and informed man cannot believe the apologies. It can be argued that the new policy of the United States reflects a new interest on the part of those in the seats of power, an interest which will be served by European unification and the scrapping of the Monroe Doctrine. It certainly can be shown that the prevailing ideology is faithfully tailored to the service of such an interest.

C. Wright Mills has described the eclipse of local elites in the United States and the emergence of a national power elite. This elite has only imperfectly institutionalized itself. It has found lodgment in the executive branch of the government and the military. This fact, coupled with the acquiescence of the legislature in its own impotence, produces the executive usurpation which has replaced constitutional government since the latest war.

But is there not an international power elite, which has already displaced the national power elites of Mills? The United States became a creditor nation with World War I: the tendrils of finance reached out at that time and intertwined with British and French interests. But

Germany was the destined partner. The intrinsic strength of German industry led to the formation of international cartels which endured even the strain of World War II. At the same time her financial vulnerability after defeat in two wars exposed her to the invasions of finance capital. During the 1930s British financial interests believed that they could find expression through Germany as well as Great Britain: Munich seemed to promise a political reorganization of central Europe by Germany along with a financial reorganization by the City of London. These hopes had their German counterpart, as the flight of Hess to Great Britain at the height of the war showed.

American capital also courted the German *Fräulein,* who so suddenly became an Amazon. John Foster Dulles, apologist in the 1930s for the Axis powers, was the liaison man between the Germans and the American aspirants to the status of international elite. But these did not yet have power even in America. The death of Roosevelt and the succession of two puppet presidents made possible the achievement of Dulles—the abandonment of the Monroe Doctrine and the preparation of the European union for which Whilhelm II and Hitler strove.

Precise data are not available, but it is known that Italian industry is in great part American-owned, and that German industry and segments of American industry and finance are closely linked. The stream of ownership and association passes discreetly through Switzerland, which according to news reports is overrun with men in Brooks Brothers suits.

If there is an international power elite, a colossus with one foot in the United States and one foot in Germany, from the point of view of this elite the Monroe Doctrine is obsolete. A collision of interest between the United States and Germany is, from this point of view, a meaningless conception. Only at a subaltern level do Chevrolets compete with Pontiacs; General Motors profits from either.

We are accustomed to attribute to a power elite a stable and ordinarily a recognized position in a more or less rigid social order. Since no international power elite has yet achieved such secure tenure, we are likely to doubt its existence. But in fact a power elite is not necessarily the top stage of a static social pyramid. The power of making decisions is a function not only of the strategic position of the decision-makers but of the flow of events which call for decision, and the complex social response to this flow of events. Circumstances may produce problems which an elite is by its very nature incapable of solving. In this case, barring social collapse, it is displaced by another elite. The rapid succession of elites during the French Revolution was a consequence of shifts in problems, principally in international relations: the monarchy, the Girondins, and the Jacobins were in turn confronted with issues which they could not have mastered except by surrendering their power; and they fell.

Conversely, a favorable conjunction of affairs creates a new elite. In 1679 the allegations of Titus Oates brought the Whigs to power in England; in 1683 the allegations concerning the Rye House plot brought the Tories in. The power elite which currently dominates the United States and West Germany owes its position to the Cold War and the policies that war implies. The elite created and perpetuates the Cold War.

A power elite need not represent the bulk of property in a society. As a matter of fact, the great weight of industrial and financial capital in the United States lies outside the strategically placed interests—Wall Street, Big Steel, chemicals, and oil—that dominate American policy. Spokesmen for domestic interests—Ernest Weir of Little Steel, Cyrus Eaton of transportation, Marriner Eccles of western banking—have protested in vain against a foreign policy which sacrifices native American interests. While he lived, Senator Taft was the representative of an "isolationism" which would have preferred American interests to a spurious "internationalism" dressed in the shroud of Woodrow Wilson—an internationalism which is the expression of an international power elite. Nevertheless, our current power elite has held our society captive by two means.

Our economy suffers from a systemic disease which requires huge—and apparently increasing—government expenditures, if a tolerable level of employment of resources and labor is to be maintained. Since the objects of these expenditures were originally determined by the exigencies of war, it is the war industries, such as aircraft, that are prosperous enough and powerful enough to dictate appropriations. In the same industries unions are strong; and to maintain employment the unions also demand defense expenditures. But none of this would be possible without the Cold War. Domestic manufacture and labor are thus made tributary to the power elite. Whereas the international power elite itself is in the main Republican, the Democrats have been the eager agents in the popular cause of wasteful expenditure and have delivered over industry and votes to the power elite.

The irrationality of the armaments race can easily be demonstrated on the intellectual level; but matters never reach this point. Patriotism is the first test of fitness for employment in the communications industry, and the only universally acceptable content of patriotism is hatred of an external enemy. Since President Truman's message on Greece in 1947, patriotism has meant hatred of the Soviet Union. Since that date the popular press, radio, and television have promoted the Cold War with a single voice. Of course the people respond. The suggestion that hatred will not solve international problems is enough to doom a politician. It is easier to understand the ready capitulation of professional communication, which is after all a branch of the entertainment industry, than the abject surrender of social scientists; but for the most part these too have embraced with eager servility a view of the world compounded of Walt Disney and J. Edgar Hoover. This command of opinion is the second prop of the position of the international power elite.

Installed and entrenched by the Cold War, the power elite is not moving into a decline: it is entering its greatest day. We should look forward, as William Benton advises, to a defense and foreign aid budget of twice the present size within five years, with its prosperous consequences for the few. We may anticipate the rationalization of the European economy and the cartelization of the "Free World." This will involve the orderly—i.e., noncompetitive—exploitation of the resources and markets of the colonial world. It seems likely that the colonial countries, progressively impoverished and burdened with unsupportable populations, will resist, and in a bipolar world will seek the assistance of the Soviet Union.

It is altogether futile to expect our power elite to agree to the termination of the Cold War or even the relaxation of tension. This would bring them down. In view of the command they hold over the expression of opinion in the United States, it is hardly foreseeable that they and their policy will be unseated here. But Great Britain has consumed her capital in two wars and has no place in the international power elite; she has more reason than ever to resist the unification of Europe. France might conceivably summon the resolution to resume the pro-French policy last expressed in the rejection of the European Defense Community. It is possible that a native base of power might be reestablished in Germany, in which case the forecast of *Monthly Review* would prove to be correct, and the United States would pay the penalty for abandoning the Monroe Doctrine.

But as matters stand, the Free World, NATO, SEATO, the Baghdad Pact, the Eisenhower doctrine are not simply shams. Behind the jargon of freedom and the pretense of military effectiveness lies the reality of increasing economic integration, directed not in any real sense by the United States but by interests genuinely cosmopolitan. Imperial Rome saw her capital shifted to Byzantium; we may see the center of our world move to Geneva or to Bonn.

17

THE DOMINO THEORY

John Foster Dulles was the author of the "domino theory." This is the proposition that not only the first but the last defenses of America lie on the perimeter of her influence. If any outpost topples—South Korea, said MacArthur; Indochina, said Dulles; Formosa, said Eisenhower—there can be no effective defense at any closer point: the first domino brings down the last. The fate of the Pentagon and the White House is dependent upon the survival of such rulers as Syngman Rhee and Chiang Kai-shek and Ky.

A logical corollary of the domino theory is brinkmanship. If national survival turns on control of the sandbars of Quemoy and Matsu, then the whole nation must be put in hazard to maintain that control.

If this is correct, we might well wish we had not so many dominoes; we might profit by reducing their number. We have staked our national life on dozens of teetering dominoes that we have erected throughout the world, and any one may ruin us.

But the domino theory contradicts the conception of "core interests" which has hitherto controlled the practice of nations. The cost of enforcing marginal claims and interests may exceed their value; when this reckoning is clear, nations abandon such marginal interests. So France did not fight to the death to keep India from the British; the British did not fight to the death to keep it from the Indians. Ordinarily it is only for core interests that a nation hazards the core.

Reprinted from *Blaetter fuer Deutsche und Internationale Politik* 12 (1967): 212-13 (in German). Used by permission.

The primary core interest of a nation is sovereignty within its own territory. Not only the national resolution but the national strength increases as an enemy approaches this core. A distant war for a marginal interest requires huge expenditures for transportation and communication, and introduces inflexibility in the disposition of resources. Against the underdeveloped nation of 35 million Vietnamese the United States has put forth an effort which matches its effort against Germany in World War II; the Vietnamese, defending a core interest, have lost hardly a square yard of soil.

Yet there is some point to the domino theory; if it is given a realistic interpretation, Vietnam could topple other dominoes. If Vietnam successfully defies the United States, the rebels against American puppet governments in Venezuela and Colombia and Brazil and throughout the world will take heart; and we cannot repress them all. The continued extraction of oil and minerals, the domination of the economies of these countries by American firms, will be in jeopardy. We drop bombs and napalm on the Vietnamese to make an example of them.

We have no political stake in Vietnam. We are told that we are teaching China and the Soviet Union a lesson. If they are the adversary, every day the war continues is a victory for them. We have had 45,000 acknowledged casualties; they have had none. The war costs us many billions each year. Whatever they contribute to the Vietnamese cannot be 2 percent of our expenditure. Nor are we actually deterring them from starting similar wars in Laos and Thailand and India. If they have the power and the will to do this, now, when we are bogged down in Vietnam, is the very moment.

We have no economic interests in Vietnam. The plantations we defoliate are not American-owned. But from the point of view of the domino theory this is ideal. There is no impediment to the destruction of the whole country. And destruction is the policy. We drop napalm on the villagers. We destroy the crops of South Vietnam and the industrial resources of North Vietnam. We are engaged in genocide on the installment plan. This could not be expected to convert the Vietcong; but undoubtedly it makes a great impression in Chile and Peru.

The war is not really about Vietnam; it is a war, as we are often told, for the hearts of men. When the Nazis adopted this way of winning the hearts of men, they called it *Schrecken*—frightfulness. We call it pacification. Vietnam will be pacified, and the war will be won, when the whole country is one smoking cinder. This is within our power. It is appropriate that Dulles, apologist in the 1930s for Nazism, should have invented the domino theory. And there is a sense in which the domino theory is true. Core interests are at stake. But they are the interests of

American companies whose concessions and investments abroad are protected by American-paid military dictatorships. They are not the interests of the American soldiers and taxpayers who pay the price.

18

THE POLITICS OF BEDLAM

At the opening of the Revolution of 1848, Lamartine said of universal suffrage, "Il est un énigme et il contient un mystère."[1] Perhaps we will not be charged with plagiarizing from the erudite statesman Winston Churchill if we say that American foreign policy is "a riddle wrapped in a mystery inside an enigma."

Not that there is any doubt as to what the policy is. The policy is clear. Perplexity arises because it is, as Bertrand Russell has said, "the politics of bedlam."[2]

George F. Kennan, as a designated unofficial spokesman, described American foreign policy in his famous anonymous article "The Sources of Soviet Conduct," in *Foreign Affairs* in July, 1947. Marxism assumes hostility between capitalism and socialism, and the eventual overthrow of tottering capitalism by socialism through violence, though it be but a push.[3] There is no timetable, but historical inevitability requires the Soviet Union to maintain "a cautious, persistent pressure" upon the capitalist world. This idea generates a corollary, the "fiction" of "capitalist encirclement," the "semi-myth of implacable foreign hostility." This fiction is indispensable to the Soviet Union; it has become the main prop of the domestic power structure. The hardships of socialization necessitated dictatorship; and the population would accept dictatorship only if persuaded of the hostility of the external world. The myth of

---

Originally published in a shorter version in *Bulletin of the Atomic Scientists* 19 (Dec., 1963): 28–30. Reprinted by permission of the *Bulletin of the Atomic Scientists*. Copyright 1963 by the Educational Foundation for Nuclear Science.

223

encirclement was more important for the support of the dictatorship than was the iron discipline of the party or the severity and ubiquity of the secret police.

In view of this built-in intransigency, the appropriate American foreign policy was a "long-term, patient but vigilant containment of Russian expansive tendencies." The Soviet population was skeptical or alienated; the economy showed no "real evidence of material power and prosperity." Consequently "the United States has it in its power to increase enormously the strains under which Soviet policy must operate, to force upon the Kremlin a far greater degree of moderation and circumspection than it has had to observe in recent years, and in this way to promote tendencies which must eventually find their outlet in either the break-up or the gradual mellowing of Soviet power." This should take ten or fifteen years.

The Soviet Union has been contained by some hundreds of plane and "soft" missile bases on its borders; by "hard" missile bases and Polaris submarines; by NATO; by SEATO; by CENTO; by the Korean War; by the leashing of Chiang Kai-shek; by the Formosa Resolution; by military intervention in Laos and South Vietnam and Lebanon and Cuba; by the expenditure of $650 billion in military appropriations and foreign aid. The fifteen years have elapsed. Yet matters have not turned out precisely as Mr. Kennan anticipated. Indeed, it was foreseeable that the policy of containment would appear to the Soviet Union to validate the thesis of encirclement which, according to Kennan, was the principal source of strength and the defining characteristic of the Soviet regime; that pressure would reciprocally generate pressure; that the costs and the stakes would mount higher and higher; that eventually the tensions would become intolerable and the system of mutual hostility would explode into war.

So clear does this seem that one is curious about the mentality of containment. Here Mr. Kennan gives us valuable assistance in his recent book *Russia and the West under Lenin and Stalin*.[4] A kind of instinct has led him back to the Allied intervention in Russia in the years 1917-20; this was indeed the root of containment. He devotes more than a hundred pages to this period, but nowhere suggests the magnitude of the intervention; it was a regrettable minor incident which the "egocentricity which has characterized the Russian Communists down to the present day" has blown up out of all proportion. In any case, the invaders were morally superior to the Bolsheviks: their hostility was confined to "isolated manifestations," whereas the Communists hated all capitalists on principle.

Considerably more illuminating on the intervention is Richard H.

Ullman's *Intervention and the War*.[5] The British intervention is described in detail; less attention is given to the activities of the French, Japanese, and Americans. On September 7, 1917, when Kornilov marched on Moscow against Kerensky, a British armored-car squadron, dressed in Russian uniforms, participated. The British support of separatist movements in the Ukraine and Siberia, and the lavish financing of White generals and bandits; the British invasions at Murmansk and Transcaspia—these are candidly acknowledged. The various Allied justifications for intervention are described and discredited; but Ullman offers no alternative explanation of his own. Actually, there seems to be no difficulty in determining the true motives. Initially the British and the French were foolish enough to believe that they could restore the eastern front. This hope cannot have endured very long; but the French and the Americans continued to strive to extricate the released Czech prisoners in order to put them back in the war on the Allied side. The British saw a larger opportunity; they could complete the Crimean War and remove the Russian pressure on India and Iran by dismembering Russia. They did not really believe that Japanese troops could or would cross Asia and attack Germany from the east—for one thing, the Japanese told them repeatedly that they would never pass the Amur River; but they wanted Japan to amputate a section of Siberia. The United States, with its Pacific interests, could not with equanimity watch a great accession of strength to Japan; the American troops were sent to Vladivostok to hold the Japanese in check.

What is surprising is that the intervention is usually called a failure. It was a considerable success. From the body of Russia were detached Finland, Estonia, Latvia, Lithuania, Russian Poland, and Bessarabia; Russia was deprived of its treaty rights in Iran and expelled from the councils of Europe. The Soviet Union became, for the time, politically negligible.

This was only a part of a wholesale scuttling of the balance of power. This formula, which had guided British policy in the nineteenth century, dictated and required that the number of powerful states be maintained rather than reduced, and that no large state be dismembered. But in 1919 the Ottoman Empire, which Disraeli had saved in 1878, was shared out among the victors; the Hapsburg Empire was dismantled. Germany, of course, lost not only its colonies but 13 percent of its European territory and 10 percent of its native population. If we ignore France and Italy, there were in 1914 seven major powers in the world. In 1919 there remained but three, Great Britain, the United States, and Japan.

This posture of affairs is the world-view of George F. Kennan. For him the normal condition of international politics is that of the 1920s, when Germany was a submissive junior partner of Great Britain and the United States, and the Soviet Union was in effect nonexistent. He speaks with admiration of the Weimar Republic, whose only characteristic, of course, was a total incapacity for political initiative.

Pitt and Disraeli would have been aghast at the picture which Europe presented in the 1920s. Neither Germany nor the Soviet Union could long be repressed. If they combined, the West was helpless, as was demonstrated as early as Rapallo and again in 1939. When Germany became the mortal enemy of the West, the only sane course was to call in the Soviet Union as a balance. But the outlook of the 1920s was too strong. Rather than give the Soviet Union a voice in European affairs, Great Britain and France betrayed the Czechs at Munich; and in 1940 only the recalcitrancy of Sweden prevented them from putting themselves at war simultaneously with Germany and the Soviet Union.

The containment policy is the Soviet policy of the western states between the two wars, revived and applied in an even less appropriate setting. It reflects the same incapacity to do elementary political arithmetic. How far is it attributable to hostility to the domestic institutions of the Soviet Union? The primary purpose of British intervention in 1917 was merely to weaken Russia; the British would have hamstrung the czar with as little compunction. But Ullman tells us that Churchill eventually turned it into an anti-Bolshevik crusade. Although Kennan denies it, it seems clear that one of the factors shaping western policy between the wars was moral distaste for socialism. Certainly Kennan himself gives Marxist doctrine as the sole reason for the policy of containment after the second war. But he refutes his own argument. For most of the period covered by his book, the years 1925-53, the policies of the Soviet Union, foreign and domestic, so he says, were shaped in complete disregard of the international interests of Communism and of the national interests of the Soviet Union; they were designed to the sole end of protecting the position and power of Josef Stalin. Marxist doctrine in this period was not a coherent and systematic creed; it was a series of improvisations by Stalin which had no other purpose than to justify his successive barbarities. Containment, then, according to Kennan himself, was not intended to confine a bona fide Marxist-Leninist state. But the state of Stalin did have something in common with the state of Lenin and that of Khrushchev, and with Communist China: Kennan speaks of them collectively as "the Devil." The one thing they had in common, of course, was socialism.

But after he passes the year 1949, when the Soviet Union exploded an atomic bomb, Kennan changes his tone. No one is all bad; and there is some bad in the best of us. The policies of the Soviet Union are not shaped exclusively by Marxism-Leninism. We have a common interest with the Soviet Union, the prevention of the war which will destroy civilization. But he does not tell us how to prevent it. Exhortation without plan is futile.

Probably not the atomic bomb, but certainly the hydrogen bomb, has completely altered the structure of international politics. No defense is available or in prospect. So the United States and the Soviet Union can mutually destroy each other; Great Britain and France are at least partially eligible to the suicide club. In 1960 the National Planning Association estimated that twelve other countries had the necessary capacities to acquire nuclear weapons in the near future; eight more stood at a slightly greater remove in time; the next six probably could not qualify before 1965.[6]

A whole new discipline has grown up about the subject of thermonuclear war. We have had to acquire a new vocabulary. A kiloton equals a thousand tons of TNT; a megaton, now a small unit of measure, equals a million tons of TNT. A gigaton is a thousand megatons. Roughly speaking, one megaton equals a million deaths, or one megadeath, although the yield falls off at the level of six or eight megatons because one begins to run out of people. A Beach—the name comes from Nevil Shute's novel—is a quantity of fission energy sufficient to destroy half the population of the earth by fallout. In 1960 the United States had only four-tenths of a Beach in its stockpile, but by 1970 it will have 1.3 Beaches.[7] Fallout has made us familiar with other names: strontium 90, which accumulates and produces cancer, and cesium 137, which produces monsters in future generations; iodine 131, barium 140, strontium 89, and the other "short-lived" cancer-producing isotopes. Nuclear strategy has introduced still other terms: preventive war, initiated in the present to avert a war at some future date; pre-emptive war, or an attack in anticipation of an impending enemy attack; counterforce, or nuclear attack upon enemy nuclear capability; punitive war, a counterforce stroke coupled with the destruction of one or more Russian cities in retaliation for Soviet aggression somewhere in the world, the number of cities being proportional to the gravity of the offense; mutual deterrence or nuclear stalemate, the abstinence from nuclear attacks because of the ability of both powers to inflict "unacceptable" civilian losses upon each other; limited atomic war, fought on battlefields with weapons in the kiloton range in the expectation that mutual deterrence will prevent the use of megaton bombs against civilian populations; escalation, or the ascent from kiloton to megaton warfare at the option of the losing party; catalysis, or the precipitation of an atomic war between the two giants by an unsuspected third power which, for one reason or another, attacks one of them.

A spurious lexicon has supplemented this grisly one. Oskar Morgenstern has said: "Terms are frequently employed that have the appearance of authority while behind them there is exactly nothing. 'Sound military decision' and 'calculated risk' are some of these phrases. The first is entirely empty and the second never indicates what the risk is, how it is measured and what the alleged calculation actually consists of."[8]

Other terms, long familiar, linger on in our vocabulary; but they have become meaningless. There can be no balance of power when infinite power rests in each scale. Security, if it means a reduced degree of vulnerability, is gone. Defense no longer means a capacity to avert harm; as the term is used today, it means the retaliatory mortal blow of the fatally stricken.

Since 1945 all American military thinking has assumed Communist superiority in a conventional war fought anywhere in Europe or Asia. Neither NATO, SEATO, nor CENTO possesses any significant military component except the American. Consequently American strategy has been and must be nuclear. The present Pentagon policy is "the Mix," simultaneous reliance on counterforce, mutual deterrence, and limited war.[9]

Counterforce envisages a nuclear exchange with nuclear weapons as the targets. Russian bases will be destroyed, and our atomic opulence will survive Russian attacks on our bases; we can then oblige them to surrender by threatening to attack their cities. An extensive shelter program is implied; one formula envisages an ultimatum to the Soviet Union, the evacuation of cities to shelters in the country, and then the launching of an attack at Soviet bases if the time expires without Soviet compliance. This seems to invite pre-emptive war from the Soviet Union. In any case, only known and fixed bases are vulnerable to counterforce. But the Russians believe that some at least of their land bases are unknown—this is the reason for their sensitiveness to espionage and inspection; and it is supposed that they too have Polaris submarines.

Mutual deterrence proceeds on precisely the opposite assumption. A nuclear attack by either party will provoke intolerable retaliation; therefore we are in a condition of nuclear stalemate. But nuclear stalemate cannot prevent collisions, and these will give rise to limited wars. In a land war in Europe or Asia the western forces will be outnumbered; they must therefore employ tactical atomic weapons on the battlefield which will increase their firepower and deprive their opponents of the advantage of numbers. Perhaps the Russians have only large bombs, and will not dare use them, for fear that the United States will use large bombs against their cities; therefore they will lose the war. In 1962 President Kennedy twice said that if we were fighting a conventional war and losing it we would resort to atomic weapons, presumably atomic artillery on the battlefield; and Secretary McNamara also announced that we would use nuclear weapons in any European war. Let us suppose that the Russians, having no kiloton weapons, in a war in West Germany reply to kiloton shells with megaton rockets. This would mean the end of the bone of contention; 2,000 megatons (this is called a "moderate strike") would create a firestorm converting Europe from the Bay of Biscay to the Elbe into one vast Dresden, and the entire population would be cremated in their shelters. Would our president then initiate a nuclear attack on the Soviet Union, involving that country and our own in the same disaster? It seems unlikely.

Military victory is out of the question. Currently our politicians advocate what Herman Kahn has called "rationality of irrationality" strategies. The United States should commit itself irrevocably to war unless its wishes on a given issue prevail. The Soviet Union, persuaded that this resolution is irrationally immutable, behaves rationally; rather than involve itself and the world in destruction, it accedes or recedes on the point in question. Political leaders of the United States have practiced this strategy over Berlin and Cuba. The weakness of the strategy is that on some occasion the Soviet Union may not believe in the irrationality of our leaders, and may accept the challenge; the United States will then be faced with the alternatives of behaving irrationally by precipitating war and behaving rationally by surrendering on the issue. Kahn says, "One can almost confidently predict that unless arrangements are made for adjudication or arbitration, somebody is going to play the international analogue of Chicken once too often."[10]

The weakness of rationality of irrationality strategy is the lack of "credibility." To say that we would prefer nuclear war to a treaty over Berlin sounds like a bluff; and if it is treated as one we lose whatever advantage a treaty might give: we are faced with surrender or the holocaust.

Kahn describes a way of restoring credibility, the Doomsday-in-a-Hurry Machine, which he says is technically feasible though difficult and expensive to construct.[11] An apparatus which will destroy the world is buried in the earth. It is connected with thousands of sensory devices which will be activated automatically by appropriate Soviet misdeeds. Then the Soviets are informed of the provisions of the Soviet Criminal Code, any single violation of which will blow up the world. Thus they will be "contained" within any limits desired. The idea appealed, Kahn says, only to a few scientists and engineers in the Pentagon. Yet it is the perfect technological expression of American policy. It accomplishes the goal of containment with the only instrument we unquestionably command, the threat of the destruction of the earth; and it eliminates the rationality which has hitherto impaired the credibility of the policy.

Despite these flirtations with planned nuclear war, it is generally agreed that the danger of war by accident is at present greater. Given the vulnerability of air fields and missile bases, a response must be launched as soon as the radar warning is received; and radar has reported the moon and flocks of geese as flights of enemy bombers. A meteor can be mistaken for a bomb even after impact. The Pentagon has expressed confidence in its "fail-safe" procedure; but we do not know that the Soviet system is foolproof.

Writing in 1961, the British scientist Sir Charles Snow said: "Within at the most ten years some of those bombs are going off. That is certainty." Lord Hailsham, the Conservative minister of science, has said that "sooner or later there will be war."[12] American nuclear scientists and strategists agree. Harrison Brown says: "In the absence of meaningful agreements between the United States and the Soviet Union we are destined to blow each other out of existence. Perhaps tomorrow will be the day."[13] Herman Kahn says: "If we are to reach the year 2000, or even 1975, without a cataclysm of some sort, we will almost undoubtedly require extensive arms control measures in addition to unilateral security measures."[14] Donald Brennan says: "The chance of a general war within the next year is not zero, and, assuming the present course of events continues, the likelihood of a general war within the next ten of fifteen years appears very disturbing."[15] The German strategic expert Helmut Schmidt says: "It is hard to imagine how world peace can be preserved through the sixties if the arms race continues."[16] It is probable that civilization is in its last decade.

Nuclear war is a much greater enemy of the United States and the Soviet Union than either is of the other. This fact has supplied an incentive to disarmament which was lacking in the 1920s and 1930s. Since 1946, in one arena or another, the United States and the Soviet Union have discussed disarmament. At the same time the arms race has continually spiraled higher, so that peace is more expensive than war used to be. Several books have reviewed and evaluated the disarmament negotiations; they have made different assessments of the problems and of the sincerity of the parties.[17] It seems to this reviewer altogether impossible to achieve a significant reduction of armaments at the present time. Hydrogen bombs are small objects, easily concealed; and both the United States and the Soviet Union have ample room for secreting them in their own territories, to say nothing of those of their neighbors and the spaces under the sea. Knowing that an inspection system must fail, each country would expect the other to conceal bombs, and would therefore hide a part of its own stockpile. Probably a disarmament agreement would have no other effect than to introduce instability in the present balance of terror. To be sure, a solution might be found if, as has been proposed, both nations transferred their declared armaments to the United Nations, to be employed against an aggressor. But it would certainly be politically impossible for the United States, at the present time, to agree to the creation of another nuclear power, potentially hostile to its interests and at least theoretically superior in armaments. Most of the population would fear a United Nations equipped with nuclear weapons even more than they fear the Soviet Union. Likewise there seems to be no inducement for the Soviet Union to exchange a known danger for an unknown.

An agreement against testing, on the other hand, might at least put an end to weapon development and the instability which technological innovation introduces. It would save a substantial number of persons from cancer and would prevent predictable cases of stillbirth and malformation. It has been impossible to arrive at an agreement on testing because of Russian refusal to accept American proposals for inspection. A layman cannot arrive at firm conclusions on a technical subject such as this; but a survey of the evidence can hardly fail to convince him that the Atomic Energy Commission has engaged in systematic deception of the American public on the questions of the feasibility of detection of explosions and the dangers of testing.[18]

The discussion of the problems of war, disarmament, and testing has been pretty well monopolized by a new breed of scholars. Strategy used to be the property of military men, but now it is the province of civilians. Some, like Teller, derive their credentials from Los Alamos and Livermore; others, like Brodie, Kissinger, and Schelling, were apprenticed in the social studies. Their lucubrations are financed by RAND and other foundations; they dispense their learning at the war colleges. Most of these experts make two claims to proficiency: the services and the AEC, for their own reasons, have given them access to classified data; and they practice game theory with these data. Roger Fisher, for example, says: "The science of game theory has shown that an understanding of international relations may be acquired by comparing the rules of governmental conduct to those of a game."[19] At a time when problems were immensely simpler, Napoleon observed that mathematical calculation of all the elements that enter into war "would be a problem in algebra before which a Newton might stand aghast."[20] But mathematical computation, if it were possible, would be only the beginning. In politics as in poker, psychology is more important than mathematics. Although none of the game theorists has spelled it out, they all assume a standardized Soviet psychology. They agree with Herman

Kahn: "I concede that, aside from the ideological differences and the problem of security itself, there do not seem to be any other objective quarrels between the United States and Russia that justify the risks and costs to which we subject each other."[21] But the Soviet ideology fixes an exclusive goal, "world domination to be achieved by the use of military force." One gathers that the Soviet Union would not accept world domination if it were tendered pacifically: it would insist, as Kennan says, on giving a final push. Here is the confusion between strategic aims and tactical means which is exploited by all the paladins of the Cold War. Certainly Communists, like Christians, expect the eventual triumph of their ideology; but the route of the former is not marked in the detail currently attributed to it. Nothing in Marx is useful to Cold War argument, for he spoke exclusively of class struggle within a single society, and conceded that in a state where the working class had the vote, as in Great Britain and the United States, the proletariat might come to power legally. Consequently certain familiar quotations from Lenin, which are supposed to make anticapitalist war orthodox Communist doctrine, are offered. Of these a leading Soviet expert, Fred Warner Neal, says that "Lenin's inferences that the Soviet Union might use military means to foster ideological goals are often quoted out of context. When he made them, just before and during the Revolution, he was anticipating the early collapse of capitalism on a world scale, and his more aggressive statements were made while actually fighting a war of invasion brought on by capitalist powers."[22]

Marxism-Leninism is supposed to be so detailed and unambiguous that all its adherents agree on questions of policy and tactics: they constitute the "international Communist conspiracy." It was possible, no doubt, to ignore the emergence of national Communism in Yugoslavia, Hungary, Albania, and Poland; but the theory is considerably tattered as a result of the open division on questions of policy between China and the Soviet Union.

It is not unfair to say that the new breed of strategists undertake to deal with the gravest historical problems without any acquaintance with history: for this they substitute the postulated antagonism of game theory, made rigid by the vulgarized Marxism of the House Un-American Activities Committee. The shape of the 1930s, the occurrence of and participants in the Second World War, were apparent to any man of education and discernment by 1931; but Herman Kahn says of himself and "my colleagues" that if they had not lived through it "most of us would need to have much more knowledge of history than in fact we possess" to believe it.[23] He proves his point by writing in 1960, in his *On Thermonuclear War,* an account of the 1930s which omits all the decisive causative factors.[24]

It is still true that history is the key to politics. The Cold War is not an exercise on the chessboard; it is the outcome of the past, and it carries with it a future which cannot be controlled by the most skillful player. It can be understood only historically. Several short studies of the Cold War have been published;[25] but only D. F. Fleming's massive work, *The Cold War and Its Origins, 1917-1960*,[26] achieves the dimensions and the detail of history. This is a remarkable book to have been written and published in a period of crisis: it is as though Fay had written his *Origins of the World War* in 1912 rather than 1928. Fleming began the study in 1947, "when it seemed more than probable that we would go into a third world war within one lifetime." This forecast should be contrasted with the confident words which Kennan wrote in 1947.

Fleming describes the Allied intervention which greeted the new Soviet state in 1917 and the policy of containment from which it partially escaped in the 1930s. He agrees with Kennan that Stalin was not motivated by doctrinaire Marxism; he finds in Stalin's conduct a consistent pursuit of Russian national interests. The appeasement of fascism had anti-Soviet motives; but Stalin succeeded in turning Hitler to the west.

At Yalta Stalin insisted upon a system of spheres of influence which would afford friendly governments on Russia's western frontiers. But with the death of Roosevelt the policy of containment was revived by Churchill and Truman. Of course, it was impossible to deny the Soviet Union the influence it demanded, for its armies had conquered the entire territory; over a period of two years, after violent interchanges which embittered both sides, and made the security of its frontiers seem even more urgent to the Soviet Union, Stalin installed client governments in all the conquered countries except Finland, and amputated enough territory from Finland to prevent its use as an access route for invasion.

Not without initial misgivings, but soon with enthusiasm, the American press and public followed its leaders and the Cold War was launched. Acheson reformulated containment as a policy of "negotiation from strength": the United States would not discuss substantive issues with the Soviet Union until it had achieved such a preponderance of strength as to dictate the terms of settlement. What those terms would be was announced by Dulles: it was "rollback" of the Soviet Union from the central European territories over which the dispute originated.

Thus far the execution of the policy of containment has involved American participation in war only twice, in Korea and in South Vietnam. But it implies a continual readiness, fully spelled out in treaties and appropriations, to fight on every frontier of the Soviet Union and China, and elsewhere if the proper political complexion can be put on a dispute. To persuade the American public of the necessity of participation in distant quarrels in which the merits are at best obscure and no vital American interests are discernible, Dulles invented what Fleming calls the "domino theory"—the fall of any anti-Communist outpost anywhere, no matter how insignificant in itself, would be a toppling domino which would knock down all others in turn, ending with Fort Benning and the White House.

As Oxenstierna remarked three hundred years ago, the world is ruled by men of little prudence. With painstaking detail, and with deep anguish, Fleming traces the history of the Cold War and the arms race, which together have brought us to the edge of nuclear disaster. Even the strategists, without having mastered the history, can now see the outcome. Their usual proposal is arms control. Herman Kahn considers the limitation of armaments the only way of averting war.

But the arms race is an integral part of the Cold War. Although it may serve as a causative factor in producing the final explosion, it is not self-generating; at bottom it is a symptom of the Cold War and not its cause. Neither the arms race nor the Cold War can be terminated without a resolution of the substantive issues which divide the United States and the Soviet Union. On the western side, this would require abandonment of the policy of negotiation from strength and acceptance of the necessity of negotiating in the posture in which we find ourselves. We would have to reconcile ourselves to the existence of Communist positions of strength in central Europe and China. We would have to abandon the domino theory, which currently is the only justification for maintaining what President Eisenhower called the abnormal situation in West Berlin. We would have to recognize the fact of change, continually accelerated, which is bringing a world in which neither Marxism nor anti-Communism is a rational guide.

Of course, this is unthinkable. Charles Dodgson, who not only was superior to our present guides in strategy as a mathematician but was an unprofessional social scientist as well, described our species in its true habitat of Wonderland. When Alice asked the Cheshire Cat, "What sort of people live around here?" the Cat directed her to the Hatter and the March Hare: "Visit either you like; they are both mad." And when Alice protested, "I don't want to go among mad people," the Cat said there was no alternative: "We're all mad here."

NOTES

2: ARISTOTLE ON LAW

1. *Politics,* III, 16, 3 (Benjamin Jowett trans.).
2. "Rule of Law," *Encyclopedia of the Social Sciences* (Macmillan, 1931).
3. St. Joseph Stockyards Co. v. United States, 298 U.S. 38 (1936).
4. 75th Cong., 1st Sess., Report No. 711, p. 15.
5. *The Good Society* (Little, Brown, 1937).
6. *The Road to Serfdom* (Chicago, 1944).
7. See, for example, John Dickinson, *Administrative Justice and the Supremacy of Law* (Harvard, 1927), pp. 80, 127n.
8. *De Anima,* III, 10, 1.
9. *Nicomachean Ethics,* 1139b, 4.
10. Ibid., II, 5. Cf. *Categories,* 8.
11. Ibid., II, 1.
12. Ibid., VI, 12, 6 (David Ross trans.).
13. Ibid., VI, 13, 6.
14. Ibid., VI, 1-4.
15. Ibid., I, 3; II, 2.
16. Ibid., 1107a, 1.
17. Ibid., VI, 7, 7.
18. Ibid., VI, 8.
19. *Politics,* III, 4, 17.
20. *Nicomachean Ethics,* X, 9; *Politics,* VIII, 1. The father of the family has an advantage over the legislator because he can prescribe a regimen more immediately suited to particular needs, just as the physician in private practice can prescribe the treatment appropriate to the individual, and the boxer can train his pupil in a style of fighting peculiarly suited to him. *Nicomachean Ethics,* loc. cit.
21. Ibid., 1134a, 30.
22. Ibid., X, 9, 9.
23. *Politics,* II, 8, 24 (Jowett).
24. Ibid., II, 8, 18.
25. Ibid., II, 8, 20. And see *Metaphysics,* II, 3.
26. *Politics,* VII, 14, 15.
27. Ibid., V, 9, 12.

28. Ibid., VII, 2, 9.
29. *Laws*, 875.
30. *Republic*, 439-41.
31. *Nicomachean Ethics*, VI, 18, 5 (Ross).
32. X, 9. 12. For a contrary gloss on the passage, see J. Cook Wilson, "On the Meaning of *Logos*," *Classical Review* 27 (1913): 113, 116.
33. X, 8, 3.
34. *Rhetoric*, I, 1, 7 (John H. Freese trans.).
35. II, 9.
36. *Statesman*, 293-95.
37. *Politics*, III, 16, 7.
38. *To Philip*, 14, 127, in *Isocrates* (George Norlin trans.).
39. *Nicomachean Ethics*, IX, 2.
40. Ibid., V, 10. And see *Rhetoric*, I, 13, 11-19.
41. Since equity builds on the law, it will rest on the same moral base as the law itself. It is a more accurate implementation of the moral assumptions of the law; it corrects the law in its application rather than in its inception. See John A. Stewart, *Notes on the Nicomachean Ethics* (Clarendon, 1892) 1: 529.
42. *Nicomachean Ethics*, 1137b, 27-32 (Ross).
43. *Rhetoric*, I, 1, 7.
44. *Politics*, 1292a.
45. *Rhetoric*, I, 13, 13-19.
46. Ibid., I, 13, 19.
47. Ibid., I, 13, 12.
48. 863ff., in *Sophocles* (Francis Storr trans.).
49. *Antigone*, 454ff., ibid.
50. Sec. 10, in *Lysias* (Walter R. M. Lamb trans.).
51. *The Quality of Mercy* (Yale, 1940), pp. 111-12.
52. IV, 4, 19.
53. 1422a.
54. *Andromache*, 244. See Reginald B. Appleton, *Euripides the Idealist* (Dutton, 1927), p. 82.
55. *Rhetoric*, I, 10, 3.
56. Ibid., I, 13, 2.
57. See *Nicomachean Ethics*, V, 7. Cf. Herodotus III, 38: The Greeks burn their parents' corpses, and the Indians eat theirs; each nation regards the other's practice as revolting. "*Nomos* is king of all."
58. *Rhetoric*, I, 15, 3-6 (Freese).
59. Ibid., I, 12.
60. V, 7, I. See V, 9, 12; VIII, 13, 5.
61. Jacques Maritain is only the latest to say that the idea of natural law goes back to "the great moralists of antiquity and its great poets, particularly Sophocles. Antigone is the eternal heroine of natural law, which the Ancients called the *unwritten law*, and this is the name most befitting it" (*Les Droits de l'homme et la loi naturelle* [Maison Française, 1942], p. 78). The unwritten law of Sophocles was the complete opposite of M. Maritain's natural law. It was to Sophocles a conscious symbol of opposition to the new humane and rationalistic spirit represented by Euripides.
62. 2: 120-21.
63. *Aristotle's Theory of Conduct* (1905), p. 304.
64. *Nicomachean Ethics*, I, 7, 10-12.
65. Ibid., X, 2, 4.
66. See Octave Hamelin, *Le Système d'Aristote* (L. Robin, 1931), p. 302.
67. *Politics*, 1278b, 20.
68. Ibid., I, 2.
69. *Physics*, 193b, 28.

70. Ibid., 194a, 28.
71. Rhys Carpenter, *The Ethics of Euripides* (Columbia, 1916), p. 29.
72. II, 10, 25; 10, 27.
73. VII, 6, 13. Less striking are II, 8, 14-15; VIII, 3, 7-8.
74. III, 7, 11.
75. II, 1.
76. 641a, 34-641b, 10.
77. VII, 1.
78. *La Doctrine de l'intelligence chez Aristote* (J. Vrin, 1934), p. 16.
79. IX, 5.
80. III, 3, 7.
81. *Physics*, 193b, 8.
82. *Nicomachean Ethics*, II, 1.
83. Ibid., VI, 13, 1; VII, 8, 4.
84. Ibid., III, 8, 12. L. H. C. Greenwood, *Aristotle: Nichomachean Ethics: Book VI* (Cambridge, 1909), p. 56, regards the natural virtues as states of desire preliminary to virtue. See Plato, *Republic*, 375e, 530c; *Laws*, 963e.
85. VII, 7, 1-4.
86. VII, 15, 7. See Plato, *Statesman*, 309-10.
87. St. Thomas thought so in his commentary on V, 7, of the *Nicomachean Ethics*. See also Edward M. Cope, *An Introduction to Aristotle's Rhetoric* (Macmillan, 1867), pp. 239ff.; E. Zeller, *Aristotle and the Earlier Peripatetics* (Longmans, Green, 1897) 2: 176; Van Johnson, "Aristotle on *Nomos*," *Classical Journal* 33 (1938): 351.
88. 173a, 7-19.
89. Cf. V, 9, 12, and VIII, 13, 5.
90. *Nicomachean Ethics*, VII, 10, 4; 14, 4.
91. Ibid., VII, 10, 5.
92. Ibid., VI, 3; *Posterior Analytics*, II, 19.
93. *Nicomachean Ethics*, I, 4, 5-7; 7, 21; VI, 7, 6-7; *Movement of Animals*, 7.
94. For discussions see Sir Alexander Grant, *The Ethics of Aristotle* (Longmans, Green, 1885) 1: 487n.; Stewart 1: 4, 17, 173, 174, 202, 206-7; 2: 4-5, 24, 107; John Burnet, *The Ethics of Aristotle* (Methuen, 1900), pp. 79n., 80n., 247, 252n., 286n.; Greenwood, pp. 167-68; J. Cook Wilson, "On the Meaning of *Logos*," *Classical Review* 27 (1913): 113; J. L. Stocks, "On the Aristotelian Use of *Logos*," *Classical Quarterly* 8 (1914): 9; Leon Robin, *Greek Thought* (Kegan Paul, 1928): 264; H. W. B. Joseph, "Aristotle's Definition of Moral Virtue," *Philosophy* 9 (1934): 168, 176-77n.
95. Grant has collected instances, loc. cit.
96. Burnet, p. 79n.
97. *Nicomachean Ethics*, 1139a, 25, 31.
98. Ibid., VI, 13, 5.
99. Rudolf Hirzel, *Untersuchungen zu Cicero's Philosophischen Schriften* (Hildesheim, G. Olms, 1877) 2: 10ff.; Emile Brehier, *Chrysippe* (Alcan, 1910), pp. 101ff.
100. *Politics*, II, 1, 1; VII; VIII.
101. Ibid., IV, 1, 3; 11, 21.
102. Ibid., II, 6, 16; IV, 11, 1.
103. Ibid., III, 18; IV, 7, 2. Cf. III, 4, 4-5.
104. Ibid., III, 4, 4.
105. Ibid., III, 4. 3.
106. *Nicomachean Ethics*, I, 2, 8.
107. *Politics*, III, 11, 20-21; IV, 1, 9-10.
108. Ibid., IV, 8, 1.
109. *The Dialogues of Plato* (Oxford, 1892) 4: 441, 447.

3: ASTRAEA AND DIKÉ

1. Robert W. and Alexander J. Carlyle, *A History of Mediaeval Political Theory in the West* (Blackwood and Sons, 1903) 1: 55-56. And see p. 61, where the Carlyles say of the Roman lawyers: "They hold with Cicero that the civil law is organically related to the ultimate law of reason and justice; that it is not merely the expression of the capricious will of the lawgiver, but constantly tends, at least, to embody, to apply to the actual conditions of life, principles which are of perpetual obligation." One passage in Cicero does seem to suggest this outlook. *Laws*, I, v, 17.
2. Paulus said that the word *ius* was used in several senses. One, that which is always equal and good, is natural justice. *Ius civile* is that which is useful to all or most people in a single city. *Digest*, I, i, 11. Public law is that concerned with the Roman state; private law looks to the utility of individuals. *Justinian's Institutes*, I, 1, 4.
3. Francis M. Cornford, *Principium Sapientiae* (Cambridge, 1952), p. 192.
4. *Theogony*, 901-6.
5. Arthur O. Lovejoy and George Boas, *Primitivism and Related Ideas in Antiquity* (Johns Hopkins, 1935), p. 35.
6. Cicero recognized no Golden Age; see *De Inventione*, I, ii, 2. However, there is no private property by nature. *De Officiis*, I, vii, 21; I, xvi, 51.
7. *Metamorphoses*, I, 76-215. See Lovejoy and Boas, pp. 43-49.
8. Lovejoy and Boas, pp. 87-89.
9. *Epistulae Morales*, XC; Lovejoy and Boas, pp. 263-74.
10. George Boas, *Essays on Primitivism and Related Ideas in the Middle Ages* (Johns Hopkins, 1948), pp. 7-14.
11. Lactantius, *Divine Institutes*, I, xi; V, v. See Boas, pp. 33-41.
12. A full bibliography is given in William C. Greene, *Moira: Fate, Good and Evil in Greek Thought* (Harper & Row, 1963), pp. 410-13.
13. Plato, *Protagoras*, 337C (Benjamin Jowett trans.).
14. See Max Hamburger, *The Awakening of Western Legal Thought* (Allen & Unwin, 1942), p. 96.
15. Diogenes Laertius, *Lives of Eminent Philosophers*, VI, 63.
16. "Against Andocides," in *Lysias* (Walter R. M. Lamb trans.), sec. 10. The speech is not by Lysias. Ibid., p. 112.
17. See Grace H. Macurdy, *The Quality of Mercy* (Yale, 1940), p. 112.
18. I, 10, 3; I, 13, 2. Cf. *Nicomachean Ethics*, V, 7, 1; V, 9, 12; VIII, 13, 5. This writer has argued elsewhere that Aristotle had no idea of a natural law. "Aristotle on Law," in Milton R. Konvitz and Arthur E. Murphy (eds.), *Essays in Political Theory Presented to George H. Sabine* (Cornell, 1948), pp. 45-61.
19. II, 8, 14-15.
20. II, 10, 25, 27; III, 7-8; VII, 6.
21. 1421b37-1422a3.
22. Diogenes Laertius, VII, 88 (Robert D. Hicks trans.).
23. *De Partibus Animalium*, I, 5 (William Ogle trans.).
24. Epictetus, *Discourses*, III, vii, 2. See Marcus Aurelius, *Thoughts*, XII, 3: Man is composed of a little body, a little breath, and intelligence. The first two are his responsibility; only the third is properly his.
25. Cicero, *Republic*, VI, xiv-xx.
26. Marcus Aurelius, IV, 41.
27. Ibid., VIII, 24 (George Long trans.).
28. Cicero, *De Officiis*, I, iv, 12; I, vii, 22; Marcus Aurelius, X, 6; Seneca, *De Ira*, III, v; "Fragment of a Letter to a Priest," in *Works of the Emperor Julian* II: 297 (Wilmer C. Wright trans).
29. Ibid., IX, 9.
30. Epictetus, IV, i, 111.
31. Ibid., IV, i, 127.

NOTES / 239

32. Ibid., IV, i, 128.
33. Cicero, *De Finibus,* II, x, 31-32; III, v, 16-vi, 20. Cf. *De Officiis,* I, xxx, 107.
34. Seneca, *De Consolatione,* VI, vii.
35. See E. Vernon Arnold, *Roman Stoicism* (Humanities Press, 1958), chap. 12; Robert D. Hicks, *Stoic and Epicurean* (Russell & Russell, 1962), chap. 3; Cicero, *Academica,* I, x.
36. III, xxii.
37. VI, viii.
38. Charles H. McIlwain, *Constitutionalism Ancient and Modern* (Cornell, 1940), p. 40.
39. Huntington Cairns, *Legal Philosophy from Plato to Hegel* (Johns Hopkins, 1949), p. 137, has pointed out that Lactantius, who is our only source, uses this expression.
40. III, xx, 49. And see *De Inventione,* II, liii, 161-liv, 162.
41. IV, i, 127.
42. *De Otio,* iv. Cf. Epictetus, II, v, 26.
43. iv, 4.
44. Ibid., iv, 23.
45. *Thirty-sixth Discourse,* 22.
46. *Eightieth Discourse,* 5.
47. *Thirty-sixth Discourse,* 23. At 27 a hearer contrasts the mortal city with the divine city.
48. "To the Cynic Heracleios," VII, 238 B, C.
49. "Against the Galilaeans," ibid., III, 347. Climate and geography shape human nature. Ibid., 357.
50. *De Natura Deorum,* II, xxi, 56.
51. *Academica,* II, xlv, 137.
52. *Republic,* I, xvii, 27.
53. *Laws,* II, v, 12-13.
54. For a contrary view, see Charles H. McIlwain, *The Growth of Political Thought in the West* (Macmillan, 1932), p. 116.
55. *Republic,* I, xxv, 39.
56. Ibid., I, xxxii, 49.
57. *De Inventione,* I, v, 6. Here *civilis ratio* does not refer, as later in legal writings, to *ius civile;* it means "political science."
58. Cicero, *Republic,* III, xxxi, 43.
59. Ibid.
60. *The City of God,* II, xxi.
61. Ibid., XIX, xxi.
62. *De Officiis,* III, xvii, 69; *Republic,* I, ii, 2.
63. *Digest,* I, i, 9.
64. *The Question of Prohibitions,* 12 Rep. 64 (1607).
65. *Digest,* VII, 5, 2. Cf. ibid., I, iii, 14. Paulus: What is received in the law contrary to the reason of the law should not be extended to its logical consequences. 15. Julian: In those matters where the emperor has established a constitution contrary to the reason of the law, we cannot follow the rule of the law.
66. *Institutes,* II, 66; *Digest,* XLI, 1, 9, 3; *Institutes,* II, 65.
67. *Institutes,* I, 158. See also *Justinian's Institutes,* I, xv, 3.
68. Carlyle, p. 38.
69. *Digest,* XLI, i, 9, 3.
70. *Digest,* I, i, 1, 3-4.
71. *Digest,* I, i, 4. And see ibid., L, 17, 32.
72. *Digest,* I, i, 4.
73. Ibid., I, v, 4.
74. Ibid., XII, vi, 64.
75. Ibid., I, 1, 5.

76. *Justinian's Institutes,* I, i, 4.
77. Ibid., I, ii.
78. Ibid., I, ii, 1.
79. Ibid., I, ii, 2; I, iii, 2.
80. Ibid., I, ii, 2. This whole account follows Hermogenianus, supra, note 75, even to the reservation that some relationships were introduced by *ius civile.*
81. Ibid., II, i, 11.
82. Ibid.
83. Ibid., II, i, 12.
84. Ibid., II, i, 22.
85. Ibid., II, i, 7.
86. *Institutes,* IV, 16. It seems likely that Gaius is wrong, and that these rituals derive from wager of battle; but it also seems likely that he is reporting a traditional interpretation.
87. *Justinian's Institutes,* I, ii, 11; II, i, 1, 11, 41.
88. Ibid., I, xv, 1.
89. Ibid., I, xv, 3.
90. Ibid., III, i, 9.
91. Ibid., IV, i. 1.
92. This filiation is traced by Norman Cohn, *The Pursuit of the Millennium* (Harper, 1961), pp. 203-5.
93. Georges de Lagarde, *La Naissance de l'Esprit Laique au Déclin du Moyen Age* (Librairie E. Droz, 1946) 6: 140-85.

4: RETURN TO THE MIDDLE AGES

1. Eduard C. Lindeman, "Introduction," *The Scientific Spirit and Democratic Faith* (King's Crown Press, 1944), pp. ix-x.
2. *Letters on a Regicide Peace,* in *Works* (Harper, 1955) 1: 237.
3. *Reflections on the Revolution in France,* ibid. 1: 489.
4. Ibid., 471.
5. *Substance of the Speech on the Army Estimates,* in *Works* 1: 452-53.
6. Robert R. Palmer, "Man and Citizen: Applications of Individualism in the French Revolution," in Milton R. Konvitz and Arthur E. Murphy (eds.), *Essays in Political Theory Presented to George H. Sabine* (Cornell, 1948), pp. 132-33.
7. Alfred Diamant, "Forerunners of Austro-German Fascism" (thesis, Indiana University), contains elaborate statistical data. It should be recognized, however, that the "new middle class" of white collar employees played a prominent part in the fascist revolution. See Emil Lederer, *The State of the Masses* (Norton, 1940).
8. *German Theories of the Corporative State* (McGraw-Hill, 1947).
9. Ibid., p. 86.
10. Ibid., p. 81.
11. Ibid., pp. 89, 92, 96.
12. Joseph Husslein, *Social Wellsprings,* vol. 1, *Fourteen Epochal Documents by Pope Leo XIII* (Bruce Publishing Co., 1940), p. 167.
13. Husslein, vol. 2, *Eighteen Encyclicals of Social Reconstruction by Pope Pius XI,* p. 177.
14. Diamant.
15. Husslein, vol. 2, p. 175.
16. See Charles A. Gulick, *Austria from Hapsburg to Hitler* (California, 1948) 2: 1454-557.
17. *"Quadragesimo Anno,"* in Husslein, vol. 2, p. 213.
18. On La Tour-du-Pin, see Charlotte T. Muret, *French Royalist Doctrines since the Revolution* (Columbia, 1938), pp. 200ff.
19. Shepard B. Clough, "The House that Pétain Built," *Political Science Quarterly* 49 (1944): 30-39.

20. Anthony T. Bouscaren, "The European Christian Democrats," *Western Political Quarterly* 2 (1949): 61ff.
21. Gabriel Almond, "The Christian Parties of Western Europe," *World Politics* 1 (1948): 37.
22. Ibid.
23. Ibid., p. 35.
24. Alfredo Mendizábal, "Catholicism and Politics," in Feliks Gross (ed.), *European Ideologies* (Philosophical Library, 1948), p. 518.
25. The relation between the two ideas is spelled out by Pius XI in *"Quadragesimo Anno,"* in Husslein, vol. 2, pp. 193-205.
26. Emil Brunner, *Justice and the Social Order* (Harper, 1945), p. 6.
27. Ibid., p. 7.
28. Ibid., pp. 134, 194.
29. *Les Droits de l'Homme et la Loi Naturelle* (Maison Française, 1942).
30. Heinrich A. Rommen, *The State in Catholic Thought* (Herder, 1947), p. 313.
31. Hans Kelsen, *General Theory of Law and State* (Harvard, 1945), p. 428.
32. See, for example, Mendizábal. Jacques Maritain in his *Christianity and Democracy* (Scribner, 1947) makes it clear that for him a supernatural interpretation of human life is a precondition of democratic belief. Accordingly, "The sources of the democratic ideal must be sought many centuries before Kant and Rousseau" (p. 59.) He finds himself in agreement with Maistre on the basis of the state.
More candid is Rommen, p. 488: "There is little doubt that historically the modern democratic movements, especially the revolutionary ones on the European continent, were born of the wrong philosophies."
33. Rommen, p. 581, citing the encyclical *Sapientiae Christianae* of Leo XIII.
34. *Liberty against Government* (Louisiana, 1948).
Thomas Hobbes pointed out long ago, in his *Dialogue of the Common Laws*, that the imperative theory of law, according to which one is free to do anything not prohibited by the sovereign, affords more liberty than a jurisprudence like that of Sir Edward Coke, which professes to contain prescriptions for the whole range of human life.
35. Kay v. Board of Higher Education of the City of New York, 173 Misc. 943, 18 N.Y.S. 2d 821 (1940).
36. See Guido de Ruggiero, *The History of European Liberalism* (Oxford, 1927).
37. Kelsen, p. 427.
38. Wilfrid Harrison, introduction to Bentham's *A Fragment on Government* (Macmillan, 1948), p. xlvi. On Locke, see the careful study of Willmoore Kendall, *John Locke and the Doctrine of Majority Rule* (Illinois, 1941), p. 104.
39. A curious example of this literature is Harold R. McKinnon, *The Higher Law* (Gillick Press, 1946), which places in a single tradition Sophocles, Plato, Aristotle, Cicero, St. Paul, St. Augustine, St. Thomas, Bellarmine, Suarez, Hooker, Sidney, Blackstone, Pollock, and Roscoe Pound, with others too numerous to mention.
40. *Lectures on Jurisprudence*, lectures 1-2.
41. See John A. Ryan and Francis J. Boland, *Catholic Principles of Politics* (Macmillan, 1947), pp. 6-7.
42. *Summa Theologica*, II-II, Q. xi, ad 3.
43. See also the encyclical *"Immortale Dei"* (1885) in Husslein 1: 65.
44. See his *A Better Economic Order* (Harper, 1935).
45. Ryan and Boland, p. 314.
46. Abrams v. United States, 250 U.S. 616, 630 (1919). It is only "when men have realized that time has upset many fighting faiths" that they "come to believe even more than they believe the foundations of their own conduct that the ultimate good desired is better reached by free trade in ideas."
47. Sir James Fitzjames Stephen, in attacking Mill's *On Liberty* in his *Liberty*,

Equality, Fraternity (Smith, Elder and Co., 1873), p. 37, says that it is possible to be absolutely certain of the existence of London Bridge. This, he thinks, justifies censorship. Yet it would be possible for an absolute political power, custodian of absolute truth, to persuade most of the people of the earth that London Bridge did not exist. Much more extraordinary feats have been accomplished.
48. Brunner, chap. 1; McKinnon; Edgar Bodenheimer, "Recent Trends in European Legal Thought: West and East," *Western Political Quarterly* 2 (1949): 48; Lon L. Fuller, *The Law in Quest of Itself* (Foundation Press, 1940), p. 122.
49. Muret, p. 217.
50. The dissatisfaction of industrialists with Section 7a, which permitted unionization of employees, should not be permitted to obscure their gratification at suspension of the antitrust laws and at the opportunity of framing codes for the elimination of "unfair" competition within the industry.
51. Supra.
52. On the illegality of the pact, see Franz B. Schick, "Peace on Trial: A Study of Defense in International Organization," *Western Political Quarterly* 2 (1949): 1.
53. Nathaniel Peffer, "Democracy Losing by Default," *Political Science Quarterly* 63 (1948): 338.

6: LEARNED LEGERDEMAIN

1. Harry Barnard, *Eagle Forgotten* (Duell, Sloan and Pearce, 1938), p. 227.
2. In Dennis v. United States, 341 U.S. 494, 562-3 (1951), Justice Jackson takes judicial notice of the "fact" that the Haymarket bombing was a fruit of anarchist preaching. He cites the decision of the Illinois Supreme Court affirming the convictions in the *Spies* case as evidence.
3. Motion to quash the indictment denied, United States v. Foster, 80 F. Supp. 479 (D.C. 1948); convictions affirmed, United States v. Dennis, 183 F.2d 201 (C.A. 2d Cir. 1950); convictions affirmed, Dennis v. United States, 341 U.S. 494 (1951); petitions for rehearing denied, 342 U.S. 842 (1951).
4. O. John Rogge, *Our Vanishing Civil Liberties* (Gaer Associates, 1949), p. 225.
5. 18 U.S. Code Sec. 601; 22 U.S. Code Sec. 611.
6. 18 U.S. Code Sec. 2386.
7. 18 U.S. Code Sec. 2383.
8. 18 U.S. Code Sec. 2384.
9. 18 U.S. Code Secs. 2151-6.
10. 18 U.S. Code Secs. 791-7.
11. 18 U.S. Code Sec. 371.
12. 18 U.S. Code Sec. 2385. This act, adopted in 1940, makes it criminal "knowingly or wilfully" to "advocate, abet, advise, or teach the duty, necessity, desirability, or propriety of overthrowing or of destroying any government in the United States by force or violence," or "with intent to cause the overthrow or destruction of any government in the United States" to "print, publish, edit, issue, circulate, or publicly display any written or printed matter advocating, advising, or teaching the duty, necessity," etc., or "to organize or help to organize any society, group, or assembly of persons who teach, advocate, or encourage the overthrow or destruction of any government," etc., or to become a member or to "affiliate with any such society, group, or assembly of persons, knowing the purposes thereof."
13. The indictments are printed in George Marion, *The Communist Trial* (Fairplay Publishers, 1950), pp. 189-91.
14. Presumably Karl Marx was a "Marxist-Leninist"; at any rate, his writings were introduced to prove the doctrine. It is of course familiar that Marx himself conceded the possibility of a peaceful and legal institution of socialism in Great Britain and the United States, where the working class had the vote, and that the Marxism of the late Harold J. Laski led him into the Labour party rather than the

Communist party. Nevertheless, Judge Learned Hand in the Court of Appeals ruled as a matter of law that the mere conjecture of peaceful change was "absurd" to a Marxist-Leninist. United States v. Dennis, 183 F.2d 201, 206 (1950).

15. *State and Revolution* argues that it is impossible for a revolutionary socialist movement to take over and use the old state apparatus. A new state form—the soviets—must grow up alongside the old state and then overthrow it.

16. Marion, pp. 64-69. Four of the defendants were permitted to testify that the term "Marxism-Leninism" in the Communist party constitution did not imply the advocacy of revolution; but Judge Medina refused to permit the defendant Thompson to answer the question, and held his attorney in contempt for persisting in it (ibid., pp. 91-92). On appeal Judge Hand observed that "without more the ruling might indeed have unduly restricted Thompson's testimony, though it would scarcely have required a reversal"; but he held that the error was cured when Thompson defied the court and reported to the jury a conversation in which he had stated his views. United States v. Dennis, 183 F.2d 201, 232 (1950).

17. The defendants were also permitted to offer excerpts, but only if they bore on revolution. They were not permitted to build up an affirmative picture of Marxism-Leninism; Judge Medina ruled that the only statements relevant to the indictment were those advocating or disavowing revolution. The jurors were permitted to leaf through the books during intermission, but not to take them home overnight. Marion, p. 76.

18. The non-Communist affidavit in the Taft-Hartley Act was upheld by the Supreme Court on the basis of Mr. Budenz's testimony that in 1940 a strike was called by Communists to impede defense production in the Allis-Chalmers plant, in the face of testimony by a vice president of the company which seems to say that the company had no defense contracts. The case is American Communications Association v. Douds, 339 U.S. 382 (1950). See the present writer's comment, "Legislative Disqualifications as Bills of Attainder," below. The *Douds* decision appears to have stricken the bill of attainder clause from the Constitution at Mr. Budenz's behest, and the *Dennis* case does much the same thing for the First Amendment.

19. Selections from the testimony are reproduced in Marion, passim.

20. 19 *Law Week* 3166 (1950).

21. This question appears to have been discussed, not in connection with the statute, which seems to be the appropriate place, but in consideration of the defendants' intent. At the argument in the Court of Appeals, Chief Judge Hand observed that delay in execution did not alter the quality of an intent: "Nobody wants to do a thing before he can do it." Quoted in John Raeburn Green, *Separate Petition of Petitioner John Gates for Rehearing in No. 336, Supreme Court, October Term* (1951), p. 44n.

22. United States v. Dennis, 183 F.2d 201, 206 (1950).

23. Complaint has been made that the government's view of Marxism-Leninism, which Judge Hand adopted, regards it as a doctrine of "hand-made revolutions" (Marion, p. 98). The government did ignore one of the most characteristic features of revolutionary Marxist literature, the requirement of catastrophe as a preliminary to revolution. For Marx the catastrophe was to be the collapse of the lower middle class; for Engels it was a hopeless depression; for Lenin it was defeat in war, coupled with inflation, strikes, lockouts, peasant insurrection, and general despair. The hypothesis of Judge Hand resembles the unhistorical insurrectionism which Lenin in his famous *Letter to Comrades* denounced as Blanquism. And see Lenin's *Left-Wing Communism, an Infantile Disorder*.

24. Schenck v. United States, 249 U.S. 47, 52 (1919).

25. Herndon v. Lowry, 301 U.S. 242 (1937); Thornhill v. Alabama, 310 U.S. 88 (1940); Cantwell v. Connecticut, 310 U.S. 296 (1940); Bridges v. California, 314 U.S. 252 (1941); Taylor v. Mississippi, 319 U.S. 583 (1943); West Virginia State Board of Education v. Barnette, 319 U.S. 624 (1943); Thomas v. Collins,

244 / NOTES

323 U.S. 516 (1945); Pennekamp v. Florida, 328 U.S. 331 (1946); Craig v. Harney, 331 U.S. 367 (1947).
26. In upholding the action, the majority of the Supreme Court disapproved of the statement in Pierce v. United States, 252 U.S. 239, 250 (1920), that the question belonged to the jury. Dennis v. United States, 341 U.S. 494, 514 (1951). See the protest of Justice Douglas at p. 587.
27. This is made clear by the charge that the teaching must be "by language reasonably and ordinarily calculated to incite persons to such action, all with the intent to cause the overthrow or destruction of the Government of the United States by force as speedily as circumstances would permit." Quoted in Dennis v. United States, 341 U.S. 494, 512 (1951).
28. United States v. Dennis, 183 F.2d 201, 212 (1950).
29. In terms of the precedents, it would certainly be unsound. Judge Hand's statement about Justice Brandeis's classic formulation of the clear and present danger rule in Whitney v. California is flatly untrue. Brandeis made the imminency of danger a precondition of punishment of speech. "If there be time to expose through discussion the falsehood and fallacies, to avert the evil by the processes of education, the remedy to be applied is more speech, not enforced silence. Only an emergency can justify repression." Whitney v. California, 274 U.S. 357, 377 [1927]).
30. United States v. Dennis, 183 F.2d 201, 212-3 (1950).
31. Dennis v. United States, 341 U.S. 494, 581-2 (1951).
32. If two or more persons in any State or Territory, or in any place subject to the jurisdiction of the United States, conspire to overthrow, put down, or destroy by force the Government of the United States, or to levy war against them, or to oppose by force the authority thereof, or by force to prevent, hinder, or delay the execution of any law of the United States, or by force to seize, take, or possess any property of the United States contrary to the authority thereof, they shall each be fined not more than $5,000 or imprisoned not more than six years, or both. [18 U.S. Code Sec. 2384]
33. Dunne v. United States, 138 F.2d 137 (1943), certiorari denied, 320 U.S. 790, 814, 815 (1943, 1944).
34. Dennis v. United States, 341 U.S. 494, 546-8 (1951).
35. Gitlow v. New York, 268 U.S. 652 (1925).
36. Korematsu v. United States, 323 U.S. 214 (1944).
37. Actually, it had been applied to speech by groups as substantial as labor unions, as in Thornhill v. Alabama, 310 U.S. 88 (1940). In American Communications Association v. Douds, 339 U.S. 382, 396, 412 (1950), the chief justice himself seemed to concede its applicability to the Communist party.
38. United States v. Dennis, 183 F.2d 201, 214 (1950).
39. United States v. L. Cohen Grocery Co., 255 U.S. 81, 92 (1921).
40. Evidently Justice Jackson feels a little uncomfortable about this, since he later says: "I do not suggest that Congress could punish conspiracy to advocate something, the doing of which it may not punish." This does not quite agree with his earlier insistence that "the basic rationale of the law of conspiracy is that a conspiracy may be an evil in itself, independently of any other evil it seeks to accomplish.... So far does this doctrine reach that it is well settled that Congress may make it a crime to conspire with others to do what an individual may lawfully do on his own." It is submitted that Justice Jackson gives us little reason to treat speech cases differently from antitrust cases. See Green, pp. 21-22:
> The conspiracy proposal, no matter how much Mr. Justice Jackson himself would attempt to limit it, puts an end to enforcement of any of these freedoms, except for extraordinary cases of individual speech. Few, if any, of the numerous First Amendment cases with which this Court has dealt were cases of an individual speaking for or by himself alone, without prior consultation with anyone. In our modern world scarcely anything is done without 'conspiracy,' that is, without a planning, agreement or understanding of two

or more persons. It is obvious that this is true of the free exercise of religion and of freedom of speech and of the press. A newspaper produced by only one person would be novel; a religion with only one adherent equally so; picketing almost always involves concerted action; and a labor union presupposes more than one member.
41. P. 29. Since Senator McCarthy has made invidious comment upon Mr. Green's participation in the case, it seems proper to quote another passage from the brief: Since the circumstances are unusual and since the positions taken in this petition may differ from positions taken in the joint petition for rehearing, or otherwise, by petitioner's former counsel, it is perhaps proper to inform the Court that present counsel is appearing pursuant to a written understanding with petitioner John Gates to the effect that present counsel (1) will accept no fee, and (2) will have complete control over the positions to be taken in this petition and be free to take whatever positions counsel may deem advisable. The petitioner has stated in writing that he is aware of present counsel's utter disagreement with petitioner's political views and with Communism. [Ibid., p. 2]
42. Supra, n. 40.
43. "The Spirit of Liberty" (1944), in Irving Dilliard (ed.), *The Spirit of Liberty* (Knopf, 1952), pp. 189-90.

7: LEGISLATIVE DISQUALIFICATIONS AS BILLS OF ATTAINDER

1. See Francis D. Wormuth, *The Origins of Modern Constitutionalism* (Harper, 1949), chap. 8.
2. Ibid., chaps. 7, 18.
3. 1 *Blackstone's Commentaries* *155.
4. J. Allen Smith, *The Spirit of American Government* (Macmillan, 1907), p. 27.
5. Thomas Jefferson, *Notes on Virginia,* Query 13 (1784).
6. Ibid.
7. *The Federalist,* no. 48 (James Madison). The following statement is, at the least, an enormous exaggeration: "It was mainly for the purpose of arresting the tendency toward political democracy that the system of checks and balances in the federal Constitution was devised." J. Allen Smith, *The Growth and Decadence of Constitutional Government* (University of Washington Press, 1930), p. 81.
8. John Locke, *Two Treatises of Government: Second Treatise,* Sec. 142 (1690).
9. 1 *Blackstone's Commentaries* *44.
10. In his argument in Dartmouth College v. Woodward, 4 Wheat. 518, 579-82 (1819).
11. The early doctrine of vested rights rested on the ideas expressed by Webster. See Edward S. Corwin, "A Basic Doctrine of American Constitutional Law," *Michigan Law Review* 12 (1914): 247. For a time it found support in the eminent domain and due process clauses, Wynehamer v. People, 13 N.Y. 378 (1856); but it perished in Mugler v. Kansas, 123 U.S. 623 (1887), with the holding that eminent domain did not apply and the due process clause did not afford absolute protection to vested rights in property. The bill of attainder clause is of course absolute.
12. Charles H. McIlwain, *The High Court of Parliament* (Yale, 1910), p. 153.
13. Joseph Story, *Commentaries on the Constitution* (5th ed.; Bigelow, 1891), Sec. 1344.
14. 4 Wall. 277 (1867).
15. 16 Wall. 234 (1872).
16. See in accord, Davis v. Pierse, 7 Minn. 13, 82 Am. Dec. 65 (1862); Kyle v. Jenkins, 6 W. Va. 371 (1873).
17. 4 Wall. 333 (1867).
18. However, in Dent v. West Virginia, 129 U.S. 114, 128 (1889), Justice Field

asserted of the *Cummings* and *Garland* cases: "The constitution of Missouri and the act of Congress in question in those cases were designed to deprive parties of their right to continue in their professions for past acts or past expressions of desires and sympathies, many of which had no bearing upon their fitness to continue in their professions."
19. 328 U.S. 303 (1946).
20. Even the suspicion of subversiveness will justify administrative removal. Friedman v. Schwellenbach, 159 F.2d 22 (D.C. Cir. 1946), cert. denied, 330 U.S. 838 (1947); Washington v. Clark, 84 F. Supp. 964 (D.C.D.C. 1949).
21. 339 U.S. 382 (1950).
22. 61 Stat. 143 (1947), 29 U.S.C.A. Sec. 159 (Supp. 1950).
23. 339 U.S. at 413.
24. See Doe *ex dem.* Gaines v. Buford, 31 Ky. (1 Dana) 481, 510 (1833):
   A bill of attainder is not necessarily an *ex post facto* law. A British act of parliament might declare that if certain individuals or a class of individuals, failed to do a given act by a named day, they should be deemed to be, and treated, as convicted felons and traitors. Such an act comes precisely within the definition of a bill of attainder, and the English courts would enforce it without indictment or trial by jury....

In the case of Proclamations, 12 Co. Rep. 74, 75, 77 Eng. Rep. 1352 (K.B. 1610), Chief Justice Coke said: "But 9 Hen. 4 an act of parliament was made, that all the Irish people should depart the realm, and go into Ireland before the Feast of the Nativity of the Blessed Lady, upon pain of death, which was absolutely *in terrorem,* and was utterly against the law." This was not an attainder in the British sense because there was no corruption of blood.

Under the view adopted in this article, a disqualification based upon a legislative judgment of faulty character is a bill of attainder, whether the legislature grounds its action on past conduct, on other evidence, or on no evidence at all. It seems more improper to disqualify on conjecture than on past conduct.
25. United States v. Lovett, 328 U.S. 303, 326 (1946).
26. Ernst Freund, *Administrative Powers over Persons and Property* (Chicago, 1928), p. 100.
27. Story, Sec. 1344.
28. Requiring professional competence of physicians is not a bill of attainder. Dent v. West Virginia, 129 U.S. 114 (1889). Increasing the qualifications for the practice of drugless healing is not a bill of attainder even as to persons presently licensed. Butcher v. Mayberry, 8 F.2d 155 (W.D. Wash. 1925). A statute forbidding the practice of naturopathy is not a bill of attainder even as to persons already licensed to practice. Davis v. Beeler, 185 Tenn. 638, 207 S.W. 2d 343 (1947), *Vanderbilt Law Review* 1 (1948): 451, appeal dismissed, 333 U.S. 859 (1948).
29. The earlier statutes are collected in *Ex parte* Curtis, 106 U.S. 371 (1882). See also 62 Stat. 694 (1948), 18 U.S.C. Sec. 216 (Supp. 1950); 62 Stat. 697, as amended, 18 U.S.C. Secs. 281–4 (Supp. 1950); Exec. Order No. 359 (1905).
30. The First and Second Hatch Acts [53 Stat. 1148 (1939), as amended, 5 U.S.C. Sec. 118i (1950), and 54 Stat. 767, as amended, 5 U.S.C. Sec. 118k (1950)], were upheld in United Public Workers v. Mitchell, 330 U.S. 75 (1947), and in Oklahoma v. United States Civil Service Commission, 330 U.S. 127 (1947).
31. 24 Stat. 379 (1906), 49 U.S.C. Sec. 1 (8) (1946), upheld in Delaware, L. & W. R.R. v. United States, 231 U.S. 363 (1913).
32. 56 Stat. 293 (1942), 49 U.S.C. Sec. 1011(b) (1946).
33. 48 Stat. 194 (1933), as amended, 12 U.S.C. Sec. 78 (1946), upheld in Board of Governors v. Agnew, 329 U.S. 441 (1947); 62 Stat. 694 (1948), 18 U.S.C. Sec. 217 (Supp. 1950); 62 Stat. 695 (1948), 18 U.S.C. Sec. 220–1 (Supp. 1950).
34. 54 Stat. 806 (1940), 15 U.S.C. Sec. 80a-10 (1946).
35. 38 Stat. 732 (1914), 15 U.S.C. Sec. 19 (1946).
36. 53 Stat. 1157 (1939), 15 U.S.C. Sec. 77jjj (1946).

37. In his concurring opinion in the *American Communications* case, Justice Jackson confuses the two. He says: "I have sometimes wondered why I must file papers showing I did not steal my car before I can get a license for it" (339 U.S. at 435). The licensing of cars is a privilege confined to the owners of cars; documentary proof of ownership is affirmative proof of qualification. This is very different from an act which says: "Robert H. Jackson for want of qualification is hereby forbidden to own or operate an automobile."
38.   4 *Blackstone's Commentaries* *21.
39.   259 U.S. 20, 21 A.L.R. 1432 (1922).
40.   259 U.S. at 37.
41.   2 Story, loc. cit.
42.   Chief Justice Marshall in Fletcher v. Peck, 6 Cranch 87, 136 (1810). And see Merrill v. Sherburne, 1 N.H. 199, 8 Am. Dec. 52 (1818).
43.   Hall v. Geiger-Jones Co., 242 U.S. 539, 553 (1917).
44.   260 U.S. 110 (1922).
45.   170 U.S. 189 (1898).
46.   170 U.S. at 195.
47.   Washington v. State, 75 Ala. 582 (1884); Crampton v. O'Mara, 193 Ind. 551, 139 N.E. 360 (1923), writ of error dismissed, 267 U.S. 575 (1925).
48.   N.Y. Educ. Law Secs. 6613, 6702.
49.   49 Stat. 978 (1935), 27 U.S.C. Sec. 204 (1946).
50.   54 Stat. 805 (1940), 15 U.S.C. Sec. 80a–9 (1946).
51.   48 Stat. 1086 (1934), 47 U.S.C. Sec. 311 (1946).
52.   49 Stat. 648 (1935), 7 U.S.C. Sec. 218a, upheld in Handy Bros. Co. v. Wallace, 16 F. Supp. 662 (E.D. Pa. 1936).
53.   4 Wall. at 385.
54.   *In re* Summers, 325 U.S. 561 (1945).
55.   United States v. Lovett, 328 U.S. 303, 327 (1946).
56.   133 U.S. 333 (1890). And see Murphy v. Ramsey, 114 U.S. 15 (1885).

The cases on exculpatory oaths in other jurisdictions are in conflict. In accord with the *Cummings* and *Garland* cases are *In re* Baxter, 2 Fed. Cas. 1043, No. 1118 (E.D. Tenn. 1866); Commonwealth v. Jones, 73 Ky. (10 Bush) 725 (1874); Murphy and Glover Test Oath Cases, 41 Mo. 340 (1867); State v. Heighland, 41 Mo. 388 (1867); Green v. Shumway, 39 N.Y. 418 (1868); Kyle v. Jenkins, 6 W. Va. 371 (1873). *Contra:* Cohen v. Wright, 22 Cal. 293 (1863); Shepherd v. Grimmett, 2 Idaho 1123, 31 Pac. 793 (1892); Anderson v. Baker, 23 Md. 531 (1865); State v. Neal, 42 Mo. 119 (1868); State *ex rel.* Wingate v. Woodson, 41 Mo. 227 (1867); State v. Garesche, 36 Mo. 256 (1865); *Ex parte* Quarrier and Fitzhugh, 4 W. Va. 210 (1870); Randolph v. Good, 3 W. Va. 551 (1869); *Ex parte* Hunter, 2 W. Va. 122 (1867); *Ex parte* Stratton, 1 W. Va. 304 (1866).

Of course, it is the legislative proscription and not the oath that makes the measure a bill of attainder. Agreeing with the leading cases in the absence of an oath are Baltimore v. State, 15 Md. 376 (1860); Davis v. Pierse, 7 Minn. 13, 82 Am. Dec. 65 (1862). *Contra:* Boyd v. Mills, 53 Kan. 594, 37 Pac. 16, 25 L.R.A. 486 (1894).

The same result as that in the *Cummings* and *Garland* cases may be reached under another prohibition. Communist Party v. Peek, 20 Cal. 2d 536, 127 P. 2d 889 (1942); cf. Thompson v. Wallin, 301 N.Y. 476, 95 N.E. 2d 806 (1950).
57.   339 U.S. 382 (1950).
58.   339 U.S. at 388. Congress and the Court preferred to believe the testimony of Mr. Louis Budenz that Allis-Chalmers was engaged upon defense contracts of at least $30,000,000 (5 *Hearings Before House Committee of Labor on Bills to Amend and Repeal the National Labor Relations Act,* 80th Cong., 1st Sess. 3612 [1947]), rather than that of Mr. Harold W. Story, vice president of the Allis-Chalmers Manufacturing Co., which seems to indicate that Allis-Chalmers had no government contracts:

Senator Murray: Well, I am talking about prior to the war—during the period of rearmament in this country. Didn't your company refuse to accept any contract from the United States Government for the preparation of this country; and wasn't the leadership of your organization engaged in backing America First; and weren't they making strong contributions to America First—heavy contributions to America First?
Mr. Story: Well, as far as I know, there were no contributions to America First....
Senator Murray: But it accepted no contracts for war work?
Mr. Story: It accepted all the contracts that it had an opportunity to accept, within the limit of its ability to produce, in accordance with the promised dates of shipment....
Senator Murray: Was your company at that time seeking or negotiating contracts with the Government for war production or for production of armaments for the country?
Mr. Story: We have been negotiating with the Government for contracts long before that time, Senator.
[2 *Hearings Before Senate Committee on Labor and Public Welfare, on S. 55 and S.J. Res. 22,* 80th Cong., 1st Sess. 837, 839, 841 (1947)]
59. 339 U.S. at 450. It is a matter of some interest that members of the Republican party were once proscribed by statute. In 1860 the Maryland legislature created a Board of Police for Baltimore by a statute which provided "that no Black Republican, or endorser or approver of the Helper [antislavery] Book" should be appointed to any office under the Board. The Court of Appeals said that the statute was unconstitutional "if we are to consider that class of persons as proscribed on account of their political or religious opinions. But we cannot understand, officially, who are meant to be affected by the proviso, and, therefore, cannot express a judicial opinion on the question." Baltimore v. State, 15 Md. 376, 468 (1860).
60. 339 U.S. at 391.
61. Id. at 413.
62. Id. at 414.
63. Id. at 418. This quotation provides an interesting contrast to Justice Frankfurter's attitude toward legislative decisions affecting the property of public utilities. "Foreshadowed nearly sixty years ago, ... it was decided more than fifty years ago that the final say under the Constitution lies with the judiciary and not the legislature." Federal Power Comm'n v. Hope Natural Gas Co., 320 U.S. 591, 625 (1944).
64. 339 U.S. at 422.
65. Id. at 424.
66. Id. at 424 n.2 (italics supplied).
67. Quoted in National Maritime Union v. Herzog, 78 F. Supp. 146, 181 (D.C. D.C. 1948), aff'd mem. 334 U.S. 854 (1948).
68. 339 U.S. 846 (1950).
69. Inland Steel Co. v. NLRB, 170 F.2d 247 (7th Cir. 1948).
70. 339 U.S. at 435.
71. *The Federalist,* no. 47 (James Madison).

8: THE IMPACT OF ECONOMIC LEGISLATION

1. See generally Henry W. Biklé, "Judicial Determinations of Questions of Fact Affecting the Constitutional Validity of Legislative Action," *Harvard Law Review* 38 (1924): 6; James D. Barnett, "External Evidence of the Constitutionality of Statutes," *American Law Review* 58 (1924): 88; William Denman, "Comment on Trials of Fact in Constitutional Cases," *American Bar Association Journal* 21 (1935): 805; Ralph F. Fuchs and Walter Friedman, "The Wagner Act Decisions and Factual Technique in Public Law Cases," *Washington University Law Quarterly* 22 (1937): 510; Kenneth Culp Davis, *Administrative Law* (West Publishing Co., 1951), pp.

487-97; Paul Freund, "Review of Facts in Constitutional Cases," in Edmond N. Cahn (ed.), *Supreme Court and Supreme Law* (Indiana, 1954), pp. 47-51; "The Consideration of Facts in Due Process Cases," *Columbia Law Review* 30 (1930): 360; "The Presumption of Constitutionality Reconsidered," *Columbia Law Review* 36 (1936): 283; "The Presentation of Facts Underlying the Constitutionality of Statutes," *Harvard Law Review* 49 (1936): 631; "Social and Economic Facts: Appraisal of Suggested Techniques for Presenting Them to the Courts," *Harvard Law Review* 61 (1948): 692.
2. 4 Wheat. 316 (1819).
3. Hepburn v. Griswold, 8 Wall. 603, 617 (1870).
4. E.g., Passenger Cases, 7 How. 283 (1849); Ward v. Maryland, 12 Wall. 418 (1871); Henderson v. Wickham, 92 U.S. 259 (1876); Brimmer v. Rebman, 138 U.S. 78 (1891).
5. James B. Thayer, *Legal Essays* (Harvard, 1908), p. 1.
6. Ibid., pp. 13ff.
7. Ibid., p. 21.
8. Hylton v. United States, 3 Dall. 171, 175 (1796).
9. Calder v. Bull, 3 Dall. 386, 399 (1798).
10. Cooper v. Telfair, 4 Dall. 14, 19 (1800).
11. Dartmouth College v. Woodward, 4 Wheat. 518 (1819).
12. Thayer, p. 32.
13. Westel W. Willoughby, *The Constitutional Law of the United States* (2d ed.; Baker, Voorhis, 1929) 1: 47.
14. United States v. Five Gambling Devices, 346 U.S. 441, 449 (1953).
15. Thayer, p. 30.
16. Ibid.
17. Pennsylvania Coal Co. v. Mahon, 260 U.S. 393 (1922). And see Chicago, St. P., M.O.R. Co. v. Holmberg, 282 U.S. 162 (1930).
18. Jacobson v. Massachusetts, 197 U.S. 11 (1905).
19. Price v. Illinois, 238 U.S. 446 (1915).
20. Lambert v. Yellowley, 272 U.S. 581 (1926).
21. Thayer, p. 28.
22. Ibid., p. 29.
23. Dissenting in Adkins v. Children's Hospital, 261 U.S. 525, 571 (1923).
24. Dissenting in Lochner v. New York, 198 U.S. 45, 75 (1905).
25. Laurel Hill Cemetery v. San Francisco, 216 U.S. 358 (1910).
26. Abrams v. United States, 250 U.S. 616, 624 (1919); Gitlow v. New York, 268 U.S. 652, 672 (1925).
27. E.g., Clark v. Nash, 198 U.S. 361, 369 (1905); Dominion Hotel Co. v. Arizona, 249 U.S. 265, 268 (1919).
28. E.g., Hairston v. Danville & Western R. Co., 208 U.S. 598 (1908).
29. Welch v. Swasey, 214 U.S. 91 (1909).
30. Gorieb v. Fox, 274 U.S. 603 (1927).
31. Adams v. Milwaukee, 228 U.S. 572 (1913).
32. Laurel Hill Cemetery v. San Francisco, 216 U.S. 358 (1910).
33. Patsone v. Pennsylvania, 232 U.S. 138 (1914).
34. Ohio *ex rel.* Clarke v. Deckebach, 274 U.S. 392 (1927).
35. E.g., McLean v. Arkansas, 211 U.S. 539 (1909); German Alliance Ins. Co. v. Lewis, 233 U.S. 389 (1914); Prudential Ins. Co. v. Cheek, 259 U.S. 530 (1922); Missouri Pac. R. Co. v. Norwood, 283 U.S. 249 (1931).
36. Coppage v. Kansas, 236 U.S. 1, 15 (1915).
37. Federal Power Comm'n v. Hope Natural Gas Co., 320 U.S. 591 (1944).
38. 261 U.S. 86, 102 (1923). Of course, Justice McReynolds denied the fact of mob violence, but the state admitted it by demurrer. McReynolds' whole opinion makes it clear that what he was really concerned about was federalism—i.e., deference to local authority.

250 / NOTES

39. Fort Smith Light & Traction Co. v. District No. 16, 274 U.S. 387 (1927); Missouri Pac. R. Co. v. Norwood, 283 U.S. 249 (1931).
40. Smith v. Cahoon, 283 U.S. 553 (1931). Here the statute treated a private carrier as a common carrier.
41. Cases cited n. 4 supra.
42. This requirement was stated and met in Wilson v. New, 243 U.S. 332 (1917), and Advance-Rumely Thresher Co. v. Jackson, 287 U.S. 283 (1932). And see the dissenting opinion in O'Gorman & Young v. Hartford Fire Ins. Co., 282 U.S. 251 (1931), relying on Adkins v. Children's Hospital, 261 U.S. 525 (1923), and other cases where the requirement was not met.
43. Frankfurter, J., in Kovacs v. Cooper, 336 U.S. 77, 90 (1949) (the opinion reviews the cases).
44. Interstate Transit, Inc. v. Lindsey, 283 U.S. 183, 186 (1931). Cf. McCarroll v. Dixie Greyhound Lines, 309 U.S. 176 (1940). See Sprout v. South Bend, 277 U.S. 163, 171 (1928).
45. Great Northern R. Co. v. Washington, 300 U.S. 154 (1937).
46. Near v. Minnesota, 283 U.S. 697 (1931).
47. This will not be true for what are called below adjudicative facts.
48. Adkins v. Children's Hospital, 261 U.S. 525, 560 (1923); cases cited n. 42 supra.
49. Davis, pp. 487-97.
50. Jacobson v. Massachusetts, 197 U.S. 11 (1905).
51. Price v. Illinois, 238 U.S. 446 (1915).
52. Lambert v. Yellowley, 272 U.S. 581 (1926).
53. Rast v. Van Deman & Lewis Co., 240 U.S. 342 (1916).
54. 268 U.S. 652, 669 (1925).
55. Atlantic Coast Line R. Co. v. Georgia, 234 U.S. 280 (1914); Armour & Co. v. North Dakota, 240 U.S. 510 (1916); Hebe Co. v. Shaw, 248 U.S. 297 (1919); Standard Oil Co. v. Marysville, 279 U.S. 582 (1929).
56. Jacobson v. Massachusetts, 197 U.S. 11 (1905); Price v. Illinois, 238 U.S. 446 (1915); United States v. Carolene Products Co., 304 U.S. 144 (1938).
57. United States v. Carolene Products Co., 304 U.S. 144, 154 (1938).
58. Weaver v. Palmer Brothers Co., 270 U.S. 402 (1926).
59. Jay Burns Baking Co. v. Bryan, 264 U.S. 504 (1924).
60. Louis K. Liggett Co. v. Baldridge, 278 U.S. 105 (1928).
61. This was true whether statutes were held valid: Champion v. Ames, 188 U.S. 321 (1903); Hipolite Egg Co. v. United States, 220 U.S. 45 (1911); Hoke v. United States, 227 U.S. 308 (1913); Seven Cases v. United States, 239 U.S. 510 (1916); Clark Distilling Co. v. Western Maryland R. Co., 242 U.S. 311 (1917); Wilson v. New, 243 U.S. 332 (1917); or invalid: Adair v. United States, 208 U.S. 161 (1908); Hammer v. Dagenhart, 247 U.S. 251 (1918); Schechter Poultry Corp. v. United States, 295 U.S. 495 (1935); Carter v. Carter Coal Co., 298 U.S. 238 (1936).
62. United States v. Carolene Products Co., 304 U.S. 144, 152 (1938). And see Sunshine Anthracite Coal Co. v. Adkins, 310 U.S. 381 (1940); North American Securities Co. v. SEC, 327 U.S. 686 (1946).
63. Missouri Pac. R. Co. v. Norwood, 283 U.S. 249 (1931).
64. E.g., Southern Pacific Co. v. Arizona, 325 U.S. 761 (1945).
65. Chastleton Corp. v. Sinclair, 264 U.S. 543 (1924).
66. 94 U.S. 113, 132 (1877).
67. E.g., Wampler v. Lecompte, 282 U.S. 172 (1930); Hardware Dealers Mutual Fire Ins. Co. v. Glidden Co., 284 U.S. 151 (1931); O'Gorman & Young v. Hartford Fire Ins. Co., 282 U.S. 251 (1931).
68. Lindsley v. Natural Carbonic Gas Co., 220 U.S. 61 (1911); Chicago Dock & Canal Co. v. Fraley, 228 U.S. 680 (1913); St. Louis, I.M. & S.R. Co. v. Arkansas, 240 U.S. 518 (1916).

69. 282 U.S. 251, 258 (1931). Of course, he could not refrain from offering some facts in a footnote.
70. Presumably the due process clause would prevent this. Western & Atlantic R. Co. v. Henderson, 279 U.S. 639 (1929).
71. 293 U.S. 194 (1934).
72. Ibid., p. 210.
73. Ibid.
74. Louis K. Liggett Co. v. Lee, 288 U.S. 517 (1933).
75. O'Gorman & Young v. Hartford Fire Ins. Co., 282 U.S. 251 (1931).
76. Hayes v. Missouri, 120 U.S. 68 (1887).
77. Radice v. New York, 264 U.S. 292 (1924).
78. Ozan Lumber Co. v. Union County Nat'l Bank of Liberty, 207 U.S. 251 (1907).
79. E.g., Chastleton Corp. v. Sinclair, 264 U.S. 543 (1924).
80. Railroad Retirement Board v. Alton R. Co., 295 U.S. 330, 351 (1935). This opinion is criticized in Denman, supra n.1.
81. United States v. Butler, 297 U.S. 1 (1936).
82. E.g., his opinions in Adams v. Tanner, 244 U.S. 590 (1917); Jay Burns Baking Co. v. Bryan, 264 U.S. 504 (1924); Frost v. Corporation Comm'n of Oklahoma, 278 U.S. 515 (1929).
83. 264 U.S. 543 (1924).
84. 293 U.S. 194 (1934).
85. Kenneth Culp Davis, "Judicial Notice," *Columbia Law Review* 55 (1955): 945.
86. Ohio Bell Telephone Co. v. Public Utilities Comm'n, 301 U.S. 292 (1937).
87. Barnett; "Consideration of Extrinsic Evidence to Show Unconstitutionality of Statute," 14 L.R.A. 459 (1891), 56 L.R.A. (N.S.) 458 (1915 D); "Consideration of Extrinsic Evidence on Question of Constitutionality or Unconstitutionality of Statute," 82 L. Ed. 1244 (1938).
88. Ellis v. Dixon, 349 U.S. 458 (1955); Queenside Hills Realty Co. v. Saxl, 328 U.S. 80 (1946).
89. People v. Marx, 99 N.Y. 377, 2 N.E. 29 (1885).
90. Matter of Jacobs, 98 N.Y. 98, 113 (1885).
91. Duncan v. Kahanamoku, 327 U.S. 304 (1946).
93. In Munn v. Illinois, 94 U.S. 113 (1877), the Supreme Court had held that rates fixed by the legislature were immune to judicial review. In Chicago, M. & St. P. R. Co. v. Minnesota, 134 U.S. 418 (1890), the Court held that administratively fixed rates must be subject to judicial review. In Budd v. New York, 143 U.S. 517 (1892), it attempted to maintain the immunity of legislatively fixed rates, but it abandoned this position in Reagan v. Farmers' Loan and Trust Co., 154 U.S. 362 (1894).
94. Producers Transportation Co. v. Railroad Comm'n of California, 251 U.S. 228 (1920).
95. Chastleton Corp. v. Sinclair, 264 U.S. 543 (1924).
96. Hammond v. Schappi Bus Line, Inc., 275 U.S. 164 (1927); Hammond v. Farina Bus Line & Transportation Co., 275 U.S. 173 (1927).
97. 293 U.S. 194 (1934).
98. Borden's Farm Products Co. v. Ten Eyck, 297 U.S. 251 (1936).
99. Polk Co. v. Glover, 305 U.S. 5 (1938).
100. Queenside Hills Realty Co. v. Saxl, 328 U.S. 80 (1946).
101. Ellis v. Dixon, 349 U.S. 458 (1955).
102. 94 U.S. 113 (1877).
103. Ibid., p. 130.
104. 198 U.S. 45 (1905).
105. David Ziskind, "The Use of Economic Data in Labor Cases," *University of Chicago Law Review* 6 (1939): 607, 632-33.

106. 208 U.S. 412 (1908).
107. Cases cited n. 82 supra.
108. Bunting v. Oregon, 243 U.S. 426 (1917).
109. Adkins v. Children's Hospital, 261 U.S. 525 (1923).
110. Ibid.; cases cited n. 42 supra.
111. Adkins v. Children's Hospital, 261 U.S. 525, 560 (1923).
112. Ibid., p. 571.
113. Dennis v. United States, 341 U.S. 494 (1951).
114. See Douglas, J., dissenting, ibid., at 581-2; Eugene V. Rostow, "The Democratic Character of Judicial Review," *Harvard Law Review* 66 (1952): 193; Francis D. Wormuth, "Learned Legerdemain: A Grave but Implausible Hand," chap. 7 above.
115. Hillsborough v. Cromwell, 326 U.S. 620 (1946).
116. Olsen v. Nebraska *ex rel.* Western Reference & Bonding Ass'n, 313 U.S. 236, 246-7 (1941).
117. East New York Saving Bank v. Hahn, 326 U.S. 230 (1945); Lincoln Federal Labor Union v. Northwestern Iron & Metal Co., 335 U.S. 525 (1949); Daniel v. Family Security Life Ins. Co., 336 U.S. 220 (1949); Williamson v. Lee Optical Co., 348 U.S. 483 (1955). And see Queenside Hills Realty Co. v. Saxl, 328 U.S. 80 (1946).
118. Kotch v. Board of Pilot Comm'rs, 330 U.S. 552 (1947); cf. Smith v. Texas, 233 U.S. 630 (1914).
119. Goesaert v. Cleary, 335 U.S. 464 (1948).
120. Linehan v. Waterfront Comm'n of New York, 347 U.S. 439 (1954).
121. Barsky v. Board of Regents, 347 U.S. 442 (1954).
122. American Communications Ass'n v. Douds, 339 U.S. 382 (1950).
123. United States v. Petrillo, 332 U.S. 1 (1947).
124. Lincoln Federal Labor Union v. Northwestern Iron & Metal Co., 335 U.S. 525 (1949).
125. 267 U.S. 552 (1925).
126. Breard v. Alexandria, 341 U.S. 622, 641 (1951).
127. Railway Express Agency, Inc. v. New York, 336 U.S. 106, 109 (1949).
128. Beauharnais v. Illinois, 343 U.S. 250, 262 (1952).
129. AFL v. American Sash & Door Co., 335 U.S. 538, 554 (1949).
130. Kotch v. Board of Pilot Comm'rs, 330 U.S. 552, 563 (1947).
131. Williamson v. Lee Optical Co., 348 U.S. 483 (1955).
132. Minersville School District v. Gobitis, 310 U.S. 586 (1940).
133. Feiner v. New York, 340 U.S. 315, 319 (1951).
134. American Communications Ass'n v. Douds, 339 U.S. 382 (1950).
135. Cases cited n. 88 supra.
136. 341 U.S. 651, 657 (1951).
137. 337 U.S. 1, 23-5 (1949).
138. AFL v. American Sash & Door Co., 335 U.S. 538, 550-1 (1949).
139. Dennis v. United States, 341 U.S. 494, 554 (1951).
140. Ibid., pp. 546-8.
141. Consult n. 114 supra.
142. Cited in notes 65, 79, and 95 supra.
143. East New York Savings Bank v. Hahn, 326 U.S. 230 (1945).
144. The amount of attention given varies. In Gallegos v. Nebraska, 342 U.S. 55, 61 (1951), a coerced confession case which came up on certiorari, Justice Reed held that "the state's ultimate conclusion on guilt is examined from the due process standpoint in the light of facts undisputed by the state." Perhaps if certiorari had been denied, Gallegos might have had an opportunity to prove coercion in a habeas corpus proceeding.
145. Kovacs v. Cooper, 336 U.S. 77, 90 (1949).
146. Korematsu v. United States, 324 U.S. 885 (1945); Oyama v. California, 332 U.S. 663 (1948); Takahashi v. Fish and Game Comm'n, 334 U.S. 410 (1948).

147. 339 U.S. 629, 634 (1950).
148. 339 U.S. 637 (1950).
149. Brown v. Board of Education, 347 U.S. 483 (1954); Bolling v. Sharpe, 347 U.S. 497 (1954).
150. John Dewey, *Essays in Experimental Logic* (Chicago, 1916); John Dewey, *Logic, The Theory of Inquiry* (Holt, 1938).
151. Clarence Morris, "Law and Fact," *Harvard Law Review* 55 (1942): 1303.
152. Davis, *Administrative Law*, pp. 875–910.
153. Frankfurter, J., concurring, in Trust of Bingham v. Comm'r, 325 U.S. 365, 380 (1945).
154. Dobson v. Comm'r, 320 U.S. 489 (1943).
155. Rostow, supra.

11: MATCHED-DEPENDENT BEHAVIORALISM

1. *Social Learning and Imitation* (Yale, 1941), excerpted in Melvin H. Marx (ed.), *Psychological Theory: Contemporary Readings* (Macmillan, 1951), pp. 543, 545.
2. "Scientific Models and Human Morals," in Marx, pp. 156, 157.
3. Harold D. Lasswell, *The Future of Political Science* (Atherton Press, 1963), p. 37.
4. "The Behavioral Approach in Political Science: Epitaph for a Monument to a Successful Protest," *American Political Science Review* 55 (1965): 763, 766.
5. "Toward a General Theory for the Behavioral Sciences," *American Psychologist* 10 (1955): 513, 514.
6. Ludwig von Bertalanffy, "General System Theory," in *General Systems* (1956): 1, 6.
7. Lasswell, p. 37.
8. (Wiley, 1965), p. 5.
9. Loc. cit.
10. "Toward an Inventory of Basic Trends and Patterns in Comparative and International Politics," *American Political Science Review* 54 (1960): 34, 38.
11. *Ethica Nicomachea*, 1141b–1142a.
12. See Herbert A. Hodges, *The Philosophy of Wilhelm Dilthey* (Routledge, 1952).
13. *The Theory of Social and Economic Organization* (A. M. Henderson and Talcott Parsons trans.; Free Press, n.d.), p. 88.
14. Ibid., p. 99.
15. *The Counter-Revolution of Science* (Free Press, 1952).
16. Ibid., p. 23.
17. Ibid., chap. 3.
18. *Social Causation* (Ginn, 1942), pp. 263–64.
19. Carl J. Friedrich, *Constitutional Government and Democracy* (rev. ed.; Ginn, 1946), p. 574.
20. "The New Great Debate: Traditionalism vs. Science in International Relations," *World Politics*, 19 (1966): 1.
21. When Frederick L. Schuman suggested that the *American Political Science Review* had published behavioral studies—including many of these reviewed below—in order to discredit the genre, the Editor denied this: "We publish what we publish because my referees and I think the articles make significant contributions." *American Political Science Review* 61 (1967): 149.
22. In Leonard D. White (ed.), *The State of the Social Sciences* (Chicago, 1956), p. 67.
23. *Models of Man* (Wiley, 1957), chaps. 6–8.
24. Ibid., p. 142.

25. In Joseph L. Bernd (ed.), *Mathematical Applications in Political Science* (Southern Methodist, 1966) 2: 175.
26. Ibid., p. 176.
27. Ibid., p. 184.
28. Ibid., pp. 204-5.
29. Ibid., p. 194. A similar formulation, but one which relies on graphic representation rather than explicit mathematical computation, is given in Gordon Tullock, *The Politics of Bureaucracy* (Public Affairs Press, 1965), chap. 7.
30. "The Concept of Power," *Behavioral Science* 2 (1957): 201.
31. The most impressive attempt is Lewis F. Richardson, *Arms and Insecurity* (1939; Boxwood Press, 1960).
32. *American Capitalism: The Concept of Countervailing Power* (Houghton Mifflin, 1952).
33. *The Nature of Physical Theory* (Princeton, 1936), 7.
34. Ibid., p. 10. (Italics supplied.)
35. Ibid., p. 11. See ibid., p. 24: "An essential difference between language and experience is that language separates out from the living matrix little bundles and freezes them; in doing this it produces something totally unlike experience, but nevertheless useful."
36. Percy W. Bridgman, "Some General Principles of Operational Analysis," *Psychological Review* 52 (1945): 246, 248. This essay occurs in a symposium on operationism, ibid., pp. 241-94.
37. Dahl, "The Concept of Power"; James G. March, "An Introduction to the Theory and Measurement of Influence," *American Political Science Review* 49 (1955): 431.
38. Ibid. Peter Bachrach and Morton S. Baratz, "Two Faces of Power," *American Political Science Review* 56 (1962): 947, make the point that Dahl's approach considers only events as exercises of power, whereas nonevents, or "nondecisionmaking," as they put it, which gives effect to and maintains the existing bias in affairs, may be the best evidence of power. There are two significant classes of nonevents. Friedrich, p. 589, has formulated the "rule of anticipated reactions": often the exercise of power leaves no trace, for those influenced forestall a contest by compliance. It is also the case that authority may refrain from issuing commands that are likely to meet with noncompliance or resistance.
  Duncan MacRae, Jr., and Hugh D. Price, "Scale Position and 'Power' in the Senate," *Behavioral Science* 4 (1959): 212, offer a somewhat different nominal definition. Of course, one nominal definition of power may be better than another in that it may be useful to have a name for one set of operations and of no use to have a name for another set of operations. But the utility of naming either set has not been shown. Certainly no useful purpose is served by calling any rank-ordering of senators by voting behavior a power index. MacRae and Price say: "We conclude that although the conceptualization of 'power' has been advanced[!], the operational definition of it has not yet been accomplished." Ibid., p. 218.
39. "A Method for Evaluating the Distribution of Power in a Committee System," in John C. Wahlke and Heinz Eulau (eds.), *Legislative Behavior* (Free Press, 1959), p. 358. In a study prompted by the Shapley and Shubik article, R. Duncan Luce and Arnold A. Rogow, "A Game Theoretic Analysis of Congressional Power Distributions for a Stable Two-Party System," ibid., p. 362, assume a bicameral Congress and a president, two parties, and the possibility of defection from both parties. They then tabulate eighteen situations and identify the locus or loci of power in each. The table supports familiar propositions—among others, that the president is weak when his party is in the minority, but is strong when his party is in the majority and is committed to his program.
40. Ibid., p. 359.
41. Ibid., p. 360.
42. Simon, *Models of Man*, p. 7.

43. Richard C. Snyder, "Game Theory and the Analysis of Political Behavior," in *Research Frontiers in Politics and Government* (Brookings Institution, 1955), pp. 70, 93.
44. *Behavioral Science* 4 (1959): 120.
45. Ibid., 121.
46. In Wahlke and Eulau, p. 377.
47. Ibid., p. 378.
48. "Measurement Concepts in the Theory of Influence," *Journal of Politics* 19 (1957): 202.
49. "A Scale Analysis of Ideological Factors in Congressional Voting," in Wahlke and Eulau, p. 399.
50. *Theory of Games and Economic Behavior* (Princeton, 1944).
51. F. S. C. Northrop, *The Logic of the Sciences and the Humanities* (Macmillan, 1947), chap. 13.
52. James M. Buchanan and Gordon Tullock, *The Calculus of Consent* (Michigan, 1962).
53. (Yale, 1962).
54. Ibid., p. 118.
55. Ibid., p. 23.
56. Ibid., p. 67.
57. Loc. cit.
58. Ibid., p. 24.
59. Ibid., p. 25.
60. "Idea of a Universal History on a Cosmo-Political Plan," Thomas DeQuincey (trans.), in DeQuincey, *Works* (Adam and Charles Black, 1863) 12: 133, 134.
61. See for example the series of articles in the *American Journal of Psychology*: four articles by Ward Edwards, "Probability Preferences in Gambling," 66 (1953): 349; "Probability Preferences among Bets with Differing Expected Values," 67 (1954): 56-67; "The Reliability of Probability Preferences," 67 (1954): 68-95; "Variance Preferences in Gambling," 67 (1954): 441-52; O. H. Combs and S. S. Komorita, "Measuring Utility of Money through Decisions," 71 (1958): 383; Robert F. Munson, "Decision-Making in an Actual Gambling Situation," 75 (1962): 640.
There is not agreement among game theorists themselves as to the prescriptions of rationality. See R. Duncan Luce and Howard Raiffa, *Games and Decisions* (Wiley, 1957), chap. 13; William J. Baumol, *Economic Theory and Operations Analysis* (Wiley, 1961), chap. 19.
62. Joseph I. Greene (ed.), *Clausewitz on the Art of Warfare* (McKay, 1943), p. 138.
63. *Deadly Logic: The Theory of Nuclear Deterrence* (Ohio State, 1966), chap. 2. One wishes that Secretary McNamara could read this admirable book.
64. Thomas Babington Macaulay, "Mill on Government," in G. M. Young (ed.), *Macaulay: Prose and Poetry* (Harvard, 1952), pp. 579, 609.
65. Roger Fisher, "Constructing Rules That Affect Governments," in Donald G. Brennan (ed.), *Arms Control, Disarmament, and National Security* (Braziller, 1961), pp. 56, 61, says that "the science of game theory has shown that an understanding of international relations may be acquired by comparing the rules of governmental conduct to those of a game." In an intelligent book on foreign policy, one of the authors of game theory, Oskar Morgenstern, found no occasion to make use of this tool. He commented: "Terms are frequently employed that have the appearance of authority while behind them there is exactly nothing. 'Sound military decision' and 'calculated risk' are some of these phrases. The first expression is entirely empty and the second never indicates what the risk is, how it is measured and what the alleged calculation actually consists of." *The Question of National Defense* (2d ed.; Random House, 1961), p. 4.
66. P. 99.

67. *On Thermonuclear War* (Princeton, 1960), pp. 145-49. Kahn proposed only to control the conduct of the Soviet Union, but today he would undoubtedly add China. And why not include France, Cuba, and Vietnam, and indeed all the other nations that might adopt policies inconsistent with those of Washington—that is, all the nations in the world? And why not apply the device in domestic politics, and thus eliminate riots in the ghettos, tax evasion, and Sabbath-breaking?
68. "International Politics and the Nuclear Dilemma," in John C. Bennett (ed.), *Nuclear Weapons and the Conflict of Conscience* (Scribner's, 1962), pp. 13, 31-32.
69. "Old Realities and New Myths," *World Politics* 17 (1965): 334, 355.
70. Ibid., p. 361.
71. Ibid., p. 363.
72. Ibid., p. 357.
73. "Divisions of Opinion among Justices of the United States Supreme Court," *American Political Science Review* 35 (1941): 890. See also Pritchett, *The Roosevelt Court: A Study in Judicial Politics and Values* (Macmillan, 1948), and *Civil Liberties and the Vinson Court* (Chicago, 1954).
74. Louis L. Thurstone and J. W. Degan, "A Factorial Study of the Supreme Court," reprinted in Schubert, pp. 335-40.
75. Schubert, "Prediction from a Psychometric Model," in Glendon Schubert (ed.), *Judicial Behavior* (Rand McNally, 1964), pp. 548, 554.
76. *Judicial Decision-Making* (Free Press, 1963), p. 61.
77. Loc. cit.
78. "Ideologies and Attitudes, Academic and Judicial," *Journal of Politics* 29 (1967): 3, 14.
79. 347 U.S. 483 (1954).
80. "Ideologies and Attitudes," pp. 13-14.
81. Lochner v. New York, 198 U.S. 45 (1905).
82. See Martin B. Hickman, "Mr. Justice Holmes: A Reappraisal," *Western Political Quarterly* 5 (1952): 66.
83. Clay P. Malick, "Justice Field and the Concept of the Calling," *Western Political Quarterly* 13 Supp. (Sept., 1960): 52.
84. Garner v. Los Angeles, 341 U.S. 716 (1951).
85. Schubert, "Prediction from a Psychometric Model," p. 552.
86. However, Stuart S. Nagel, "Off-the-Bench Judicial Attitudes," in Schubert (ed.), *Judicial Decision-Making*, pp. 29-53, has attempted to characterize judges by their responses to a questionnaire and to show that votes correspond to character thus established.
87. On the process of decision, see Ralph Barton Perry, *General Theory of Value* (Harvard, 1950).
88. "Conformity and Character," *American Psychologist* 10 (1955): 191, 194.
89. "The Study of Judicial Decision-Making as an Aspect of Political Behavior," *American Political Science Review* 52 (1958): 1007, 1015.
90. *Judicial Policy-Making* (Scott, Foresman, 1965), p. 120.
91. Schubert, "Prediction from a Psychometric Model," p. 569.
92. "Warren Court Attitudes toward Business," in Schubert (ed.), *Judicial Decision-Making*, pp. 79-108.
93. "Predicting Supreme Court Decisions Mathematically: A Quantitative Analysis of the 'Right to Counsel' Cases," *American Political Science Review* 51 (1957): 1. Franklin M. Fisher has argued that there was logical error in identifying the relevant facts, and that the assignment of weights was not justified. 'The Mathematical Analysis of the Supreme Court Decisions: The Use and Abuse of Quantitative Methods," ibid. 52 (1958): 321.
94. "Simultaneous Equations and Boolean Algebra in the Analysis of Judicial Decisions," in Schubert (ed.), *Judicial Behavior*, p. 477.
95. Ibid., p. 490.

96. "Using Simple Calculations to Predict Judicial Decisions," *American Behavioral Scientist* 4 (Dec., 1960): 24.
97. Reed C. Lawlor, "Stare Decisis and Electronic Computers," in Schubert (ed.), *Judicial Behavior*, pp. 492-505. See also Lawlor, "Foundations of Logical Legal Decision Making," *Modern Uses of Logic in Law* (June, 1963), p. 98.
98. *Law and the Modern Mind* (Brentano, 1930), chap. 6. It is an extraordinary thing that the judicial behavioralists should represent themselves as continuing the tradition of Jerome Frank. Frank was interested in "(1) what courts actually do, (2) what they are supposed to do, (3) whether they do what they are supposed to do, and (4) whether they should do what they are supposed to do." Jerome Frank, "A Conflict with Oblivion: Some Observations on the Founders of Legal Pragmatism," *Rutgers Law Review* 9 (1954): 425, 451n. The behavioralists address themselves only to the first question, which had no independent significance for Frank: it was preliminary to the later questions. And they do so on assumptions that were explicitly rejected by Frank.

Lawyers and judges purport to make large use of precedents; that is, they purport to rely on the conduct of judges in past cases as a means of procuring analogies for action in new cases. But since what was actually decided in the earlier cases is seldom revealed, it is impossible, in a real sense, to rely on these precedents. They could approximate a system of real precedents only if the judges, in rendering those former decisions, had reported with fidelity the precise steps by which they arrived at their decisions.

. . . .

The facts of all but the simplest controversies are complicated and unlike those of any other controversy; in the absence of a highly detailed account by the judge of how he reacted to the evidence, no other person is capable of reproducing his exact reactions.

. . . .

The uniqueness of the facts and of the judge's reaction thereto is often concealed because the judge so states the facts that they appear to call for the application of a settled rule. But that concealment does not mean that the judge's personal bent has been inoperative or that his emotive experience is simple and reproducible.

[Frank, *Law and the Modern Mind*, pp. 148-49, 150-51]
99. *Law: Its Origin, Growth and Function* (Putnam, 1907).
100. Schubert, "Introductory Note," in Schubert (ed.), *Judicial Behavior*, pp. 443, 451-53.
101. "Stare Decisis and Electronic Computers," p. 496.
102. Ibid., p. 15.
103. "Ideologies and Attitudes, Academic and Judicial," 27-28.
104. "A Psychometric Model of the Supreme Court," *American Behavioral Scientist* 4 (Nov., 1961): 14, 18.
105. *Constitutional Politics* (Holt, Rinehart and Winston, 1960), pp. 161-71.
106. Ibid., p. 161.
107. "The Analysis of Behavior Patterns on the United States Supreme Court," *Journal of Politics* 22 (1960): 629.
108. "Power and Coalition in a Nine-Man Body," in Schubert (ed.), *Judicial Behavior*, p. 461.
109. "The Power of Organized Minorities in a Small Group," ibid., p. 465.
110. "Ideologies and Attitudes, Academic and Judicial," pp. 6-10; *Judicial Policy-Making*, chap. 7.
111. "Ideologies and Attitudes, Academic and Judicial," p. 12.
112. Ibid.
113. "The policy science approach not only puts the emphasis upon basic problems and complex models but also calls forth considerable clarification of the value goals involved in policy." Harold D. Lasswell, "The Policy Orientation," in Daniel Lerner and Harold Lasswell (eds.), *The Policy Sciences* (Stanford, 1951), pp. 3, 9.

114. Any viable society must satisfy the conditions of viability, and systems theory undertakes to specify those conditions. See Talcott Parsons, *The Social System* (Free Press, 1951); Marion J. Levy, Jr., *The Structure of Society* (Princeton, 1952).
115. *Principles of the Mathematical Theory of Correlation* (William Hodge & Co., 1939), pp. 45-46.
116. "Statistical Prediction of Verdicts and Awards," *Modern Uses of Logic in Law* (Sept., 1963), p. 135.
117. "Disharmony in Federal Government," *Behavioral Science* 2 (1957): 276.
118. Iibd., 284.
119. "Scaling Legislative Behavior," in John C. Wahlke and Heinz Eulau (eds.), *Legislative Behavior*, p. 388.
120. "A Study of Consistency in Congressional Voting," in Wahlke and Eulau, pp. 384-87.
121. Ibid., p. 387.
122. Hayward R. Alker, Jr., "Casual Inference and Political Analysis," in Bernd, pp. 7-43.
123. Hayward R. Alker, Jr., "The Long Road to International Relations Theory: Problems of Statistical Nonadditivity," *World Politics* 18 (1966): 623. See also Bruce M. Russett, "The Analysis of Bloc Voting in the General Assembly: A Critique and a Proposal," *American Political Science Review* 57 (1963): 902, and the criticism by John E. Mueller, "Some Comments on Russett's 'Discovering Voting Groups in the United Nations,'" ibid. 61 (1967): 146.
124. "Discerning a Causal Pattern among Data on Voting Behavior," *American Political Science Review* 60 (1966): 913.
125. "The Long Road," p. 652.
126. "Survival Theory in Culture," in *Formal Theories of Mass Behavior* (Free Press, 1963), pp. 26-73. McPhee acknowledges the assistance of Bernard Berelson, James S. Coleman, Lee M. Wiggins, Jack Ferguson, Robert B. Smith, Harry Milholland, the Ford Foundation, the National Science Foundation, and the Center for Advanced Study in the Behavioral Sciences.
127. Obviously this is mathematically impossible. McPhee obtains his formula by using the same symbol C for an unknown constant and for a variable. The C of equations 19-21 on page 68 is not the C of equation 22.

McPhee begins with the formula $S=A+B+C$, where S is "total culture," and A, B, and C are the unknown percentages made up of A, B, and C offerings in the first year. He designates the percentage of A programs that survives the first year by a, of B programs by b, of C programs by c. For the second year he offers us the formula $S=A+B+C+aA+bB+cC$. For the nth year, assuming that the percentage values of A, B, C, a, b, and c are uniform from year to year, he gives us $S = A/1-a + B/1-b + C/1-c$. But the first equation should read $S=AS+BS+CS$; A, B, and C are percentages of S, which McPhee equates to unity. In the second year, because of the surviving programs aA, bB, cC, the input of A, B, and C programs will be less than unity, and the formula should read $S=A(S-aA-bB-cC) + B(S-aA-bB-cC) + C(S-Aa-bB-cC) + aA+bB+cC$, or, substituting one for S on the right, $S=(A+B+C)(1-aA-bB-cC) + aA+bB+cC$. a, b, and c are constant percentages of the new input, but the new input, and the magnitudes of a, b, and c, will steadily diminish each year as the number of surviving programs increases. But McPhee's formula for the nth year treats the input of A, B, and C programs in the $(n-1)$th year, and every preceding year, as equal in magnitude to those in the second year.
128. This was a revision of the nineteenth-century "steamship cult." Robert F. Dowse, "A Functionalist's Logic," *World Politics* 18 (1966): 607, 611n., has likened systems theory to the cargo cult.

12: THE WALGREEN POLITICAL SCIENCE

1. *Tax-Exempt Foundations,* Report of the Special Committee to Investigate Tax Exempt Foundations and Comparable Organizations, H. R. Rep. No. 2681, 83rd Cong., 2d Sess. 18 (1954).
2. Ibid., p. 60.
3. Ibid., p. 88.
4. Ibid., p. 31.
5. Ibid.
6. Harry V. Jaffa, *Thomism and Aristotelianism: A Study of the Commentary by Thomas Aquinas on the Nicomachean Ethics* (Chicago, 1952); Jerome Frank, "Modern and Ancient Legal Pragmatism: John Dewey & Co. vs. Aristotle," *Notre Dame Lawyer* 25 (1950): 207, 460; Francis D. Wormuth, "Aristotle on Law," in Milton Konvitz and Arthur E. Murphy (eds.), *Essays in Political Theory Presented to George H. Sabine* (Cornell, 1948), pp. 45-61.
7. John H. Hallowell, book review, *American Political Science Review,* 48 (1954): 538.
8. Eric Voegelin, *The New Science of Politics: An Introduction* (Chicago, 1952), p. 69.
9. John H. Hallowell, *The Moral Foundation of Democracy* (Chicago, 1954), pp. 95, 100.
10. Voegelin, p. 12.
11. Ibid., p. 164.
12. Hallowell, *Moral Foundation,* p. 80.
13. Ibid., p. 86.
14. Ibid., p. 101.
15. "But with regard to the essential functions of authority, there is no conflict whatsoever between authority and liberty. The more definitely a community is directed toward its common good and protected from disunity in its common action, the more perfect and the more free it is." Yves R. Simon, *Philosophy of Democratic Government* (Chicago, 1951), pp. 140-41.
16. Hallowell, *Moral Foundation,* p. 129.
17. Hallowell, however, does say that it is undemocratic to deny the right to vote on account of religious affiliation. Ibid., p. 51.
18. *Summa Theologica,* II-II, Q. xi, ad 3.
19. Simon, p. 123.
20. Hallowell, *Moral Foundation,* p. 122.
21. Ibid., p. 74.
22. Voegelin, pp. 142-44.
23. Ibid.
24. Simon, p. 123.
25. Ibid., p. 92.
26. Voegelin, p. 132.
27. Leo Strauss, *Natural Right and History* (Chicago, 1953), pp. 5, 6.
28. Hallowell, *Moral Foundation,* pp. 109-10.
29. Simon, p. 1.

13: MACROPOLITICS

1. Ruth Benedict's famous *Patterns of Culture* (Houghton Mifflin, 1934) shows by case studies that the level at which frustration is experienced and the mode of release through aggression are culturally determined.

260 / NOTES

2. The analysis here follows John Dollard et al., *Frustration and Aggression* (Yale University Press, 1939).
3. Hans Kelsen, *Society and Nature* (Chicago, 1943), attributes both causal thinking and the idea of justice—two kinds of "natural law"—to the primitive conception of retaliation, which gives rise also to magic. It is possible that behind the idea of retaliation lies the conviction that Frustration should equal Aggression.
4. *Jew-Hate as a Sociological Problem* (Philosophical Library, 1951). The importance of this book can hardly be overestimated. Lewis Coser, *The Function of Social Conflict* (Free Press, 1956) reviews other material.
5. Charles Horton Cooley, *Human Nature and the Social Order* (Scribner, 1922).
6. Cooley argued that all values were group values, that the hermit and the martyr were sustained by the opinion of an imaginary company of like-minded men.

15: THE PRESIDENCY AS AN IDEAL TYPE

1. *The Embattled Presidency* (Department of Political Science, University of Illinois, 1964), pp. 7–8.
2. James Parton, *Life of Andrew Jackson* (Houghton Mifflin, 1860) 3: 699.
3. Ibid., 695. The book was Goldsmith's *The Vicar of Wakefield*.
4. Quoted in Brooks Adams, "The Heritage of Henry Adams," in *Henry Adams: The Degradation of the Democratic Dogma* (Capricorn, 1958), p. 77.
5. Philip C. Jessup, *Elihu Root* (Dodd, Mead, 1938) 2: 180.
6. Ibid., 185.
7. Ibid., 181.
8. Loc. cit.
9. Lloyd Shearer, "Richard Nixon and Ola Florence Welch," *Parade* (June 28, 1970), p. 5. *Washington Watch* (May 1, 1973), p. 2. says: "A former Cabinet member told [Jack] Anderson of 'watching the President go through the pantomime of plunging an imaginary dagger into an opponent. "After you get your knife in," the President said gleefully, "you twist it." And he twisted his wrist to demonstrate.'"
10. Joe McGinnis, *The Selling of the President, 1968* (Trident, 1969), p. 193.
11. Quoted in Richard Harris, "Annals of Politics (The Department of Justice, 1)," *New Yorker* (Nov. 8, 1969), p. 64.
12. Machiavelli, *The Prince*, chap. xv.
13. *The Education of Henry Adams* (Modern Library, 1931), p. 365.
14. Ibid.
15. Ibid., p. 418.
16. Max Weber, *The Methodology of the Social Sciences* (Edward A. Shils and Henry A. Finch, trans.; Free Press, 1949), pp. 91–114.
17. *The Theory of Moral Sentiments* (J. Richardson and Co., 1822) 2: 107–10.
18. *Memoirs of The Peace Conference* (Yale, 1939) 1: 142.
19. George E. Reedy, *The Twilight of the Presidency* (World Publishing Co., 1970), p. 4.
20. Ibid., p. 16.
21. Ibid., p. 160.
22. Ibid., p. 98.
23. *The Prince*, chap. xviii.
24. Vilfredo Pareto, *Mind and Society* (Harcourt, Brace, 1935), Secs. 2178, 2227.
25. *Public Papers of the Presidents: Lyndon B. Johnson, 1966* (Government Printing Office, 1967) 1: 685.
26. Ibid. 693.
27. These were the words actually spoken live over television, but the printed text of the speech reads: "When you do what is best for your country, you will do what is best for me." Ibid. 2: 977.
28. *Decision-Making in the White House* (Columbia, 1963), p. 78.

29. Colin Bingham (comp.), *Men and Affairs* (Funk and Wagnalls, 1967), p. 74.
30. Ibid., p. 76.
31. Quoted in Hugh L'Etang, *The Pathology of Leadership* (Hawthorn Books, 1970), p. 9.
32. Loc. cit.
33. Ibid., p. 10.
34. Ibid., p. 43.
35. Ibid., pp. 48f.
36. Ibid., p. 51.
37. Ibid., p. 52.
38. Ibid., p. 53.
39. Ibid., p. 94.
40. Ibid., pp. 179, 181.
41. Arnold Rogow, *James Forrestal: A Study of Personality, Politics, and Policy* (Macmillan, 1963), p. 5.
42. Ibid., p. 13.
43. L'Etang, p. 71.
44. Ibid., p. 149.
45. Ibid., chap. 11.
46. Ibid., chap. 12.
47. Ibid., p. 167.
48. Ibid., pp. 187-88.
49. *Time* (Dec. 18, 1972).
50. Reedy, p. 171.
51. L'Etang, pp. 59-60.
52. Ibid., pp. 153, 155.
53. P. 168.
54. Louis Heren, *The New American Commonwealth* (Harper and Row, 1968), pp. 143-44.
55. Loc. cit.
56. "The Expert Mismanagement of the Vietnam War," *War/Peace Report* (Feb., 1970), p. 11.
57. Quoted in Heren, p. 194.

18: THE POLITICS OF BEDLAM

1. Alphonse de Lamartine, *Histoire de la révolution de 1848* (Perrotin, 1849), vol. 1, bk. 4, p. 166.
2. Bertrand Russell, *Has Man a Future?* (Simon and Schuster, 1962), p. 103. A distinguished atomic scientist, Donald N. Michael, said recently of our behavior: "The distortions and oversights are so gross that one can suspect that the individuals and institutions involved are not responding with sufficient attention to reality to be called sane by any standard." "Psychopathology of Nuclear War," *Bulletin of Atomic Scientists* 18 (May, 1962): 28. And see the lecture by the eminent psychiatrist Jerome Frank, "The Nuclear Arms Race: Sanity and Survival," distributed by the World Peace Broadcasting Foundation, 3005 High Street, Des Moines, Iowa.

Mortimer Ostrow, "War and the Unconscious," *Bulletin of the Atomic Scientists* 19 (Jan., 1963): 25, relates the irrationality of current policy to the death instinct. Dr. Lester Grinspoon told the American Academy of Arts and Scientists that the acquiescence of both decision-makers and the general public was a function of the psychological practice of denial, which excludes extreme danger from attention. *New York Times* (Western ed., Dec. 28, 1962).

3. Kennan clings to the necessity of a final act of violence like a Smith Act prosecutor or judge. But the violence which Marx thought necessary in most countries

was revolutionary class violence within a society. Kennan transfers this to the international level, converting it into a doctrine of implacable antagonism between socialist and capitalist states.

4. Atlantic, 1961.
5. Princeton, 1961.
6. Reported in Hedley Bull, *The Control of the Arms Race: Disarmament and Arms Control in the Missile Age* (Praeger, 1961), pp. 150-54. This book, prepared for the Institute for Strategic Studies in Great Britain, is the most judicious general study of the intricate problems of disarmament.
7. The terminology and the estimate are from Freeman J. Dyson, "Thoughts on Bomb Shelters," *Bulletin of Atomic Scientists* 27 (Mar., 1962): 14, 15. Dyson made the calculation of 4,000,000 megatons on the basis of uranium mined, with the assumption of 50 percent efficiency. In 1962 Ralph E. Lapp estimated that "the stockpiles of nuclear weapons have grown to a size sufficient to dispose of life on this planet in short order." *Kill and Overkill: The Strategy of Annihilation* (Basic Books, 1962).
8. *The Question of National Defense* (2d ed.; Random House, 1961), p. 4.
9. Arthur I. Waskow, *The Limits of Defense* (Doubleday, 1962).
10. Herman Kahn, "The Arms Race and Some of Its Hazards," in Donald G. Brennan (ed.), *Arms Control, Disarmament and National Security* (Braziller, 1961), pp. 89, 94.
11. Ibid., pp. 103ff.
12. Snow and Hailsham are quoted in Russell, p. 100.
13. "The Twentieth Year," *Bulletin of the Atomic Scientists* 18 (Dec., 1962): 2-3.
14. Herman Kahn, *On Thermonuclear War* (Princeton, 1960), p. 224.
15. *Arms Control*, p. 30.
16. *Defense or Retaliation* (Praeger, 1962), p. 124.
17. Joseph P. Morray, *From Yalta to Disarmament* (Monthly Review Press, 1961), has the virtue of placing the discussions in political context; Bernard G. Bechhoefer, *Postwar Negotiations for Arms Control* (Brookings Institution, 1961), is more concerned with the military context. Ambassador James J. Wadsworth, in *The Price of Peace* (Praeger, 1962), records his earnest conviction of the need for disarmament, and finds both parties at fault. See also Norman Cousins, *In Place of Folly* (Harper, 1961).

The research foundations are turning out on these topics a large literature of rather doubtful value. Robert Gilpin, *American Scientists and Nuclear Policy* (Princeton, 1962), undertakes to show that the views of scientists on supposedly technical problems are inevitably influenced by their political views. His method is to classify the scientists into schools in terms of their scientific recommendations and then attribute appropriate political views to each school. (In many cases—with both Teller and Oppenheimer—a scientific interest in testing for its own sake seems to have dictated both the scientific policy recommendations and the corresponding political formulations; but Mr. Gilpin ignores this.) The detachment Mr. Gilpin brings to his task is well shown in this passage on page 310: "The United States, *viewing massive retaliation with nuclear weapons as its principal deterrent to Communist aggression,* had, at least until the arrival of mutual deterrence, little incentive to take arms control seriously. Regrettably, even though the United States has within the past few years looked at arms control in positive terms, the Soviet Union not only continues to show little genuine interest in it but indeed now *views nuclear blackmail as a valuable instrument of national policy."* (Italics supplied.)

Probably the most honest word on this subject was spoken by William R. Frye, a veteran of the Defense and State Departments. In a reckless address at the Air Force Academy, in *Arms Control: Proceedings of the Fourth United States Air Force Assembly, April 4-7, 1962,* pp. 51-57, Mr. Frye said: "Advocacy of disarmament had served our national interest well. It had had no relation whatsover, however, to an expectation of carrying out any disarmament." Of the Baruch Plan he said: "Of course, the plan had built-in features which guaranteed that the Soviet Union would reject it"; but if the Soviets had accepted it "we could always beat it in the Senate." "The United States, at this moment, is using talk of a test ban with great skill to forward our national interest. One of our first motives in going seriously to Geneva in 1958 was to inhibit Soviet testing to preserve our lead in nuclear technology. In this, of course, we failed." "The real criterion for successful disarmament advocacy is not that a proposal should be sincere, but that it should appear to be sincere."

18. On March 6, 1958, in order to support the Teller thesis that small underground tests could not be detected, the AEC announced that a test in Nevada on September 19, 1957, had been detected only 250 miles away. Unfortunately the Coast and Geodetic Survey disclosed that it had detected the test in Alaska. *I. F. Stone's Weekly* (Mar. 17, 1958). In 1961 the AEC attempted to prove Teller's "big hole" theory by testing in the optimum substance, salt, in New Mexico, and silenced the Coast and Geodetic Survey by putting it under contract to report only to AEC; but the explosion was detected and identified as nuclear in Finland, Sweden, and Japan. Ibid., Feb. 5, Mar. 19, 1962.

On March 1, 1954, a hydrogen test in the Pacific rained fallout far outside the test area, causing illness and one death on the Japanese fishing boat *Lucky Dragon*. Chairman Strauss immediately announced that the test had raised no health hazard, and the commission published a report minimizing the effects of fallout. This was in such marked contrast to the Japanese studies that it caused loss of confidence in the AEC among American scientists. The commission's published list of tolerance levels placed these so high as not to interfere with testing; only in 1960 did it accept the international standards, which were a fraction of its own. Cousins, passim.

19. "Constructing Rules That Affect Government," in Brennan, pp. 56, 61.
20. Reported by Clausewitz, *Clausewitz on the Art of War* (Greene ed.; David McKay, 1943), p. 138.
21. *On Thermonuclear War*, p. 568.
22. "The Theory of Core Interests and U.S.-Soviet Cold War Rivalry," in *The Cold War: An Interdisciplinary Inquiry, International Studies Association Proceedings* 2 (Nov. 1961): 11, 18.
23. *On Thermonuclear War*, p. 286.
24. Ibid., pp. 375-416.
25. Walter Lippmann, *The Cold War: A Study in U. S. Foreign Policy* (Harper, 1947); Kenneth Ingram, *History of the Cold War* (Philosophical Library, 1955); John A. Lukacs, *A History of the Cold War* (Doubleday, 1961); Frederick L. Schuman, *The Cold War: Retrospect and Prospect* (Louisiana, 1962).
26. Doubleday, 1961, 2 vols.

WORKS BY FRANCIS D. WORMUTH

BOOKS

The Royal Prerogative, 1603-1649, Cornell, 1939; reprinted by Kennikat, 1972.
Class Struggle, Indiana University Studies in Social Science No. 4, 1946.
The Origins of Modern Constitutionalism, Harper, 1949.
(Coauthor) *American National Government: Law and Practice,* Harper, 1949.
(Coauthor) *Private Enterprise and Public Policy,* Macmillan, 1954.
The Vietnam War: The President versus the Constitution, Center for the Study of Democratic Institutions, 1968; reprinted in Richard A. Falk, ed., *Vietnam and International Law,* Princeton, 1962, vol. 2.
In preparation: *The War Power in History and Law,* in collaboration with Edwin B. Firmage and Francis P. Butler.

CHAPTERS OF BOOKS

"Aristotle on Law," in Milton Konvitz and Arthur E. Murphy, eds., *Essays in Political Theory Presented to George H. Sabine,* Cornell, 1948, pp. 45-61.
"Astraea and Diké: *Ius Naturale* in Roman Law," in Morris D. Forkosch, ed., *Essays in Legal History in Honor of Felix Frankfurter,* Bobbs-Merrill, 1966, pp. 585-99.

JOURNAL ARTICLES

"The Dilemma of Jurisprudence," *American Political Science Review* 35 (1941): 44-52.
"The Hatch Act Cases," *Western Political Quarterly* 1 (1948): 165-73.
"Haddock v. Civil Service Commission," *Western Political Quarterly* 1 (1948): 451-53.
"Return to the Middle Ages," *Western Political Quarterly* 2 (1949): 193-207.
"On Bills of Attainder: A Non-Communist Manifesto," *Western Political Quarterly* 3 (1950): 52-65.
"Legislative Disqualifications as Bills of Attainder," *Vanderbilt Law Review* 4 (1951): 603-19.

WORKS BY FRANCIS D. WORMUTH / 265

"Learned Legerdemain: A Grave but Implausible Hand," *Western Political Quarterly* 6 (1953): 543-58.
(Coauthor) "Politics, the Bar, and the Selection of Judges," *Utah Law Review* 3 (1953): 459-66; reprinted in Walter F. Murphy and C. Herman Pritchett, eds., *Courts, Judges, and Politics,* Random House, 1961, 1974.
"The Constitution and the Territories," *Current History* 29 (1955): 337-42.
"The Walgreen Political Science," *Indiana Law Journal* 30 (1955): 374-81.
"The Present Status of the Civil Rights Act of 1875," *Utah Law Review* 6 (1958): 153-68.
"The Impact of Economic Legislation upon the Supreme Court," *Journal of Public Law* 6 (1957): 296-318.
(Coauthor) "The International Power Elite," *Monthly Review* 11 (1959): 282-87.
"Macropolitics: Aggression in Group Theory," *Audit* 1 (Feb., 1960): 3-9.
"The Politics of George Catlin," *Western Political Quarterly* 14 (1961): 807-11.
"The Politics of Bedlam," *Bulletin of the Atomic Scientists* 19 (Dec., 1963): 28-30.
(Coauthor) "The Doctrine of the Reasonable Alternative," *Utah Law Review* 9 (1964): 254-307.
"Die Domino-Theorie," *Blaetter fuer Deutsche und Internationale Politik* 12 (1967): 212-13.
"Matched-Dependent Behavioralism: The Cargo Cult in Political Science," *Western Political Quarterly* 20 (1967): 809-40.
"Government and Science," *Center Magazine* 3 (Mar., 1970): 41-46; reprinted in Karl A. Lamb, ed., *Democracy, Liberalism, and Revolution,* James E. Freel and Associates, 1971.
"The Nixon Theory of the War Power: A Critique," *California Law Review* 60 (1972): 623-703.
"Presidential Wars: The Convenience of 'Precedent,'" *Nation* 215 (Oct. 9, 1972): 301-4; reprinted in Andrew W. Scott and Earle Wallace, eds., *Politics, U. S. A.,* 4th ed., Macmillan Co., 1974; and in Martin B. Hickman, ed., *The Problems of American Foreign Policy,* 2d ed., Glencoe Press, 1975.
"The Presidency as an Ideal Type," *Fortuna* 2 (Jan.-Feb., 1976): 18-34.
"The Political Science of Sir George Catlin," *Fortuna* 2 (May-June, 1976): 14-35.

BOOK REVIEWS

Gilchrist, Robert N. *Elements of Political Science* (6th ed.; Longmans, Green, 1939). *American Political Science Review* 33 (1939): 936.
Baumer, Franklin LeVan. *The Early Tudor Theory of Kingship* (Yale, 1940.) *American Political Science Review* 34 (1940): 395.
Brecht, Arnold. *Prelude to Silence* (Oxford, 1944). *Kenyon Review* 6 (1944): 680-82.
Rottschaefer, Henry. *Cases and Materials on Constitutional Law* (West, 1948). *Western Political Quarterly* 2 (1949): 170.
Carrow, Milton M. *The Background of Administrative Law* (Associated Lawyers, 1948). *Western Political Quarterly* 2 (1949): 275-76.
Cairns, Huntington. *Legal Philosophy from Plato to Hegel* (Johns Hopkins, 1949), and
Bentham, Jeremy. *A Fragment on Government and An Introduction to the Principles of Morals and Legislation,* edited with an introduction by Wilfrid Harrison (Oxford, Macmillan, 1938). *Western Political Quarterly* 3 (1950): 128-29.
Keeney, Barnaby C. *Judgment by Peers* (Harvard, 1949). *American Political Science Review* 44 (1950): 222-23.
Watkins, Frederick. *The Political Tradition of the West* (Harvard, 1948). *Western Political Quarterly* 3 (1950): 274-75.
Judson, Margaret Atwood. *The Crisis of the Constitution: An Essay in Constitutional*

and *Political Thought in England, 1603-1645* (Rutgers, 1949). *American Political Science Review* 44 (1950): 802.
Davis, Kenneth Culp. *Administrative Law* (West, 1951). *Western Political Quarterly* 5 (1952): 170-71.
Jaffa, Harry V. *Thomism and Aristotelianism: A Study of the Commentary by Thomas Aquinas on the Nicomachean Ethics* (Chicago, 1952). *American Political Science Review* 46 (1952): 1182-83.
Strauss, Leo. *Natural Right and History* (Chicago, 1953). *Western Political Quarterly* 7 (1954): 103-4.
Pritchett, C. Herman. *Civil Liberties and the Vinson Court* (Chicago, 1954). *Utah Law Review* 4 (1954): 289.
Lane, Robert E. *The Regulation of Businessmen* (Yale, 1954). *American Political Science Review* 48 (1954): 1170-71.
Wexley, John. *The Judgment of Julius and Ethel Rosenberg* (Cameron & Kahn, 1955). *Western Political Quarterly* 8 (1955): 632-35.
Blitzer, Charles, ed. *The Political Writings of James Harrington* (Liberal Arts, 1955). *Western Political Quarterly* 8 (1955): 637-38.
Lewis, Ewart. *Medieval Political Ideas* (Knopf, 1954). *Western Political Quarterly* 9 (1956): 1009-10.
Koestler, Arthur, with an introduction by Edmund Cahn. *Reflections on Hanging* (Macmillan, 1957), and
Sharp, Malcolm, with an introduction by Harold C. Urey. *Was Justice Done?* (Monthly Review, 1956). *Utah Law Review* 5 (1957): 569-72.
Basu, Durga Das. *Commentary on the Constitution of India* (3d ed.; Sarkar & Sons, 1955; 2 vols.). *Western Political Quarterly* 11 (1958): 156-57.
Catlin, George E. G. *Political Theory: What Is It?* (Orton, 1957). *Western Political Quarterly* 11 (1958): 894.
Friedrich, Carl Joachim. *The Philosophy of Law in Historical Perspective* (Chicago, 1958). *Social Research* 26 (1959): 245-46.
Webb, Leicester C., ed. *Legal Personality and Political Pluralism* (Melbourne University Press, 1959). *Western Political Quarterly* 12 (1959): 1145-46.
Crick, Bernard. *The American Science of Politics* (California, 1959). *Western Political Quarterly* 13 (1960): 210-11.
Runes, Dagobert D. *Pictorial History of Philosophy* (Philosophical Library, 1959). *Western Political Quarterly* 13 (1960): 833.
Kallen, Horace M. *A Study of Liberty* (Antioch, 1959). *Western Political Quarterly* 13 (1960): 1091-92.
Boyd, Julian P., ed. *The Papers of Thomas Jefferson*, vols. 7-15 (Princeton, 1953-58). *Social Research* 28 (1961): 248-50.
Kirchheimer, Otto. *Political Justice: The Use of Legal Procedure for Political Ends* (Princeton, 1961). *Social Research* 29 (1962): 117-19.
Brailsford, Henry Noel. *The Levellers and the English Revolution* (Stanford, 1961). *Western Political Quarterly* 15 (1962): 364-65.
Gatlin, George E. G. *Systematic Politics: Elementa Politica et Sociologica* (Toronto, 1962). *Political Science Quarterly* 77 (1962): 453-55.
Wiltse, Charles M. *The New Nation* (Hill and Wang, 1961). *Western Political Quarterly* 15 (1962): 581-82.
Morgenthau, Hans J. *The Purpose of American Politics* (Knopf, 1960). *Social Research* 30 (1963): 270-71.
Kallen, Horace M. *Philosophical Issues in Adult Education* (Charles C. Thomas, 1962). *Western Political Quarterly* 16 (1963): 734-35.
Fink, Zera S. *The Classical Republicans* (Northwestern, 1962). *Western Political Quarterly* 16 (1963): 989-90.
Rogger, Hans, and Eugen Weber, eds. *The European Right: A Historical Survey* (California, 1965). *Western Political Quarterly* 19 (1966): 192.

Mitchell, William C. *Sociological Analysis and Politics: The Theories of Talcott Parsons* (Prentice-Hall, 1967). *Western Political Quarterly* 21 (1968): 527.
Wheeler, Harvey. *Democracy in a Revolutionary Era* (Praeger, 1968). *Western Political Quarterly* 22 (1969): 228.
Grossman, Joel B., and Joseph Tanenhaus, eds. *Frontiers of Judicial Research* (Wiley, 1969). *Western Political Quarterly* 22 (1969): 419-20.
Midgley, Louis C. *Beyond Human Nature* (Brigham Young, 1968). *Western Political Quarterly* 22 (1969): 693-94.
White, Howard B. *Peace among the Willows* (Nijhoff, 1968). *Western Political Quarterly* 22 (1969): 699.
Graham, Howard Jay. *Everyman's Constitution: Historical Essays on the Fourteenth Amendment, the 'Conspiracy Theory,' and American Constitutionalism* (State Historical Society of Wisconsin, 1968). *Western Political Quarterly* 22 (1969): 701-2.
Kallen, Horace M. *Liberty, Laughter, and Tears* (Northern Illinois, 1968); and Kallen, Horace M. *A Study of Liberty* (Antioch, 1959). *Western Political Quarterly* 22 (1969): 972-74.
Forkosch, Morris D. *Constitutional Law* (2d ed., Foundation Press, 1969). *Western Political Quarterly* 23 (1970): 221-22.
Mitford, Jessica. *The Trial of Dr. Spock* (Knopf, 1969). *Western Political Quarterly* 23 (1970): 412.
Wheeler, Harvey. *The Politics of Revolution* (Glendessary, 1971). *Western Political Quarterly* 25 (1972): 140-41.
Franklin, Julian H. *Jean Bodin and the Rise of Absolutist Theory* (Cambridge, 1973). *Western Political Quarterly* 26 (1973): 788.
Kraines, Oscar. *The World and Ideas of Ernst Freund: The Search for General Principles of Legislation and Administrative Law* (Alabama, 1974). *Western Political Quarterly* 27 (1974): 734-35.
Kraines, Oscar. *The Impossible Dilemma: Who Is a Jew in the State of Israel?* (Bloch, 1976). *Western Political Quarterly* 30 (1977): 143-44.
Rossiter, Clinton. *The Supreme Court and the Commander in Chief* (expanded ed., Cornell, 1976). *American Political Science Review* 72 (1978): 703-04.

INDEX

Adams, Henry, 204
Adjudicative facts, 100, 102-7, 109-13, 250. See also Bills of attainder
Adkins v. *Children's Hospital,* 107
Adler, Alfred, 173, 182
Alexander the Great, 206
Alker, Hayward R., Jr., 160-61
Allied intervention in Russia (1917-20), 224-26, 233
Allport, Gordon W., 129-30
American Communications Association v. *Douds,* 82-83, 88-92, 108-9, 247-48
Anti-Semitism, 43-44, 173, 175, 181-82, 187-88, 210
Aquinas, Thomas, 45-46, 48, 131, 164-69
Aristocracy, 41-42, 186-87
Aristotle: on law, 14-26; on change, 16, 22; on character formation, 203; on circumstantial relativity of law, 16-21, 25-26, 235; on definition of law, 17; on desire, 15, 17, 22-23, 25, 237; on discretionary law, 14-18, 24-25, 235; on equity, 19, 21-24, 236; on functions of law, 16-18, 21, 24-26; on habit, 15-17, 23-25; on juries, 17-19; on justice, 15-16, 19, 21, 23-24, 171, 188; on legislation, 14-19, 24-25, 235; on moral action, 15-18, 20-26, 236; on natural law, 20-24, 238; on political man, 15, 21, 24-25; on political science, 130-32, 137; on practical wisdom, 15-19, 22, 24-25; on reason, 15-19, 22-25; on rule of law, 14-21; on universal law, 19-21, 23-25, 30; on unwritten laws, 19-24, 30; on virtue, 15-18, 21-26, 237; and Thomas Aquinas, 164
Arms race, 218-19, 224-31, 234, 261-63
Arnold, Thurman, 6, 165
Astraea, Justice of Cronus, 27-29, 33-36
AEC, 52-53, 56-60, 231, 263
Augustine, Saint, 33
Austin, John, 11-12, 47-48
Authoritarianism, 163-69, 259; decline in 16th-19th centuries, 39-40; as reaction to French Revolution, 41-43; from WWI to WWII, 43-44; from WWII, 37-40, 44-51

Bachrach, Peter, 254
Bailey v. *Drexel Furniture Co.,* 85
Baker v. *Carr,* 113, 125
Balance of power: Allied changes in 1917-20, 224-26; in nuclear era, 227-34
Baltimore v. *State,* 248
Baratz, Morton S., 254
Bay of Pigs case, 213
Behavioralism, mathematical, 129-62; translation, 134-38; nominal definition, 138-44, 254; game theory, 135, 141, 144-49, 231-32, 255-56; jurimetrics, 149-57, 256-57
Behaviorist psychologists, 129-30, 139
Belknap, George M., 159
Benedict, Ruth, 259
Bentham, Jeremy, 47, 49, 170-71

268

Bentley, E. R., 165, 168-69
Bernstein, Peretz, 173, 182, 260
Bertalanffy, Ludwin von, 130-32
Bills of attainder, 79-92, 243, 245-48
Black, Hugo, 78, 90, 92
Blackstone, Sir William, 79, 81, 85
Blanquism, 64, 179-80, 243
Bonaparte, Napoleon, 147, 179, 197-98, 207-8, 216, 231
Borden's Farm Products v. *Baldwin,* 103-6
Brandeis, Louis D., 94, 101-2, 104, 106-7, 110, 244, 251
Bratton v. *Chandler,* 86
Brennan, William J., Jr., 125
Bridgman, Percy, 138-39, 254
Brimhall, Dean R., 160
Brown v. *Board of Education,* 111, 150
Brunner, Emil, 45
Buchanan, James M., 145
Buck v. *Bell,* 115
Budenz, Louis, 65, 243, 247-48
Burke, Edmund, 39, 41, 196
Burns, James MacGregor, 200, 203
Burton, Harold H., 89, 150

Cabinets (British, U.S.), 210-13
Caesar, Julius, 206, 208
Cagots, 181-82, 197
Calvinism, 40, 45, 164
Cardozo, Benjamin, 7-8
Carlyle, A. J., 27, 34, 238
Catastrophic myth, 189, 196-99
Center for Advanced Study in the Behavioral Sciences, 131-32
Chastleton Corp. v. *Sinclair,* 104-5 110
Checks and balances, 118-26, 211-16
Chief executives. See Office
Christianity: aggression, 176, 195; anarchism, 189, 192-94, 198-99; Christian political parties, 37-38, 40, 43-45, 48-50; heritage, myths about, 37-39, 49-50; interpretation of history, 190-2, 195-97, 232; metaphysics and politics, 163-69, 206-7, 216; Stoicism, 29-30, 33, 36. See also Clericalism
Churchill, Winston, 210-11, 223, 226, 233
Cicero, 28, 31-33, 238
Civil wars, 40, 79, 179-80, 188-89, 200
Clark, J. Reuben, 120
Class struggle, 183-88, 191, 193-96
Clausewitz, Karl von, 146-47
Clemenceau, Georges, 206-7

Clericalism, 38-49, 190-95
Cohens v. *Virginia,* 125-26
Coke, Sir Edward, 33, 241, 246
Cold War, 37-38, 49-50, 216-34, 261-63
Commander-in-chief clause, 119-22, 125
Commerce clause, 93-99, 99-102, 106-9
Committee on Behavioral Sciences, 130
Communism, 37, 169, 207-8, 216-34; American, 63-78, 82-83, 88-92, 108-10, 114-15, 210, 242-45, 247-48. See also Socialism
Congress: checks and balances, 118-26, 211-16; constitutional amendment process, 10; difficulties of direct regulation, 53-54, 61-62; war-making, 118-26. See also Bills of attainder
Consent and governmental stability, 177-80, 207-8. See also Revolution
Conservatism, 167-68, 189, 196, 199
Constitutional amendment process, 10
Containment policy, in Allied foreign policy, 223-26, 232-34
Contract clause, 80-81
Cooley, Charles Horton, 173, 260
Core interests in international politics, 220-22
Corporations, and U.S. foreign policy, 215-22
Corporativism, 41-45, 49, 195
Counsel, right to, 152-53
Coup d'état, 178-79
Criminal conspiracy, theory of, 63-78, 110, 242-45
Cronus, in Greek mythology, 27-29, 33-36
Cruchfield, Richard S., 152
Cult of personality, 207-8
Cummings v. *Missouri,* 82-83, 88, 90, 246-47
Cynicism, 29, 31, 46

Dahl, Robert A., 130, 136-40, 254
Davis, David, 125
Davis, Kenneth C., 100
Davis, Otto A., 135-36
Davis v. *Beason,* 88
Declaration of Independence, 50
Defense Department, 52-61, 118-26, 131, 147-49, 210, 213-24, 227-34, 255-56
Democracy, 166-69, 183, 191, 194-95, 216; origins, 38-40, 46-47
Dennis v. *United States,* 63-78, 107, 110, 242-45
Developing nations, 219-22
Dewey, John, 111-12, 165

270 / INDEX

Diké, Justice of Zeus, 27-32, 34
Dilthey, Wilhelm, 132-33
Diogenes, 30, 32
Divine king, cult of the, 190-92
Dobson v. *Comm'r*, 112
Dodgson, Charles, 234
Doe *ex dem. Gaines* v. *Buford*, 246
Dollard, John, 129
Domino theory, 138, 220-22, 233-34
Douglas, William O., 70, 72, 78, 92, 124-25
Due process of law: adversary procedures, 54-55; privilege doctrine, 114-17; overt-act requirements, 74; subjectivity, 150-51; in character judgments, 83-86, 99, 252; in economic regulation, 94, 99, 102, 104-10, 113, 245, 248, 251; in rule making, 55; need for, against popular aggression, 99, 172, 182. See also Hearing
Dulles, John Foster, 147-48, 210, 216-22, 233-34

Easton, David, 131-32
Economic cleavage and politics, 181-88, 193-99, 207-8
Economics and game theory, 144-49
Economic system, and freedom, 39-44
Eisenhower, Dwight D., 203, 209-10, 214, 219, 234
Electoral campaigns, impact on presidents, 201-4, 208, 212-13
Eminent domain, 96-98
Empiricism, 163-69
Endo, Ex parte, 124
Environment, hazards to, 52-62
Epictetus, 31-32
Equality, 181-88, 193-99. See also French Revolution
Equal protection, 94, 103, 105, 107-8, 110-11, 113
Europe in international politics, 215-19
Euripides, 20, 22, 30, 236
Ex post facto laws, 80-82, 246
Executive-power clause, 121-22, 125
Existentialism, 165-69

Farris, Charles D., 144
Fascism, 39-45, 49-50, 167-69, 183, 188, 194-95, 240
Fearon v. *Treanor*, 116
FPC v. *Hope Natural Gas Co.*, 248
Federal Trade Commission, 56, 58
Federation, 180-81

Fichte, Johann G., 41, 43, 195
Field, David, 82-84, 120, 150, 245-46
First Amendment, 63-78, 92, 97, 99-100, 108-10, 113-17, 242-45. See also Freedom of expression
Fleming, D. F., 233-34
Fleming v. *Page*, 119
FDA, 53, 56, 60-62
Ford Foundation, 131
Foreign policy, American: aggression in group theory, 172-76; Cold War, 50, 216-34, 261-63; containment policy, 223-26, 232-34, Constitution, 118-26; "domino theory," 138, 220-22, 233-34; economic interests, 203, 215-19; game theory, 146-49, 255-56; "great presidents," 200-1; nuclear warfare, 145, 147-49, 226-34, 255-56, 261-63; presidents' personal traits, 200-1, 212-14; Senate voting, 139-40; Vietnam War, 118-26, 208, 213, 220-22, 224
Forrestal, James, 210
France, Anatole, 169, 177
Frank, Jerome, 7, 153, 257
Frankfurter, Felix, 72-74, 76-78, 82-84, 88-92, 107-10, 192, 248
Freedom of expression, 41, 47-50, 63-78, 97-100, 108-10, 113-17, 163-69, 242-45
Freedom of religion, 39-48, 109, 163-69, 259
"Free World," 216, 218-22
French Revolution, 38-43, 46-47, 49, 178-79, 181-85, 191-99, 217-18
Freud, Sigmund, 165, 168-69
Friedrich, Carl J., 134, 254
Frye, William, 262-63

Gaius, 27, 33-35, 250
Garland, Ex parte, 82-84, 87-90, 246-47
General Accounting Office, 53, 62
Gierke, Otto von, 43
Gilpin, Robert, 262
Gitlow v. *New York*, 64-65, 73-77, 100
Gnosticism, 165-69
Goldberg, Arthur S., 160-61
Golden Age, 27-30, 33-36, 190, 216
Goldwater, Barry, 120-21, 208
Green, John Raeburn, 77, 244-45
Green, Philip, 147
Green v. *Frazier*, 116
Grinspoon, Dr. Lester, 261
Griswold, Erwin N., 118-26
Grotius, Hugo, 164
Group membership: aggression, 170-76, 181-88, 193-95, 259-60; ideology, 193-99

Hallowell, John H., 163-69, 259
Hall v. *Geiger-Jones Co.,* 85-86
Hand, Learned, 66-78, 243-44
Harrington, James, 14, 137
Hawker v. *New York,* 86-87
Hayek, Frederick A., 14, 133
Haymarket case, 63, 242
Hearing, right to, 54-55, 58-62, 81, 84-92, 104, 107-13, 245-48
Hegel, Georg W. F., 41, 43, 195
Heren, Louis, 213
Herz, John H., 148
Hesiod, 24, 34, 190
Higher law, concept of, 7, 9-11, 15, 19-21, 23-24
Hinich, Melvin, 135-36
Hippias, 30
History, theories of, 190-92, 194-99
Hitler, Adolf, 207-8, 214-17, 233. See also National Socialism
Hobbes, Thomas, 36, 47, 137, 170, 173, 188-89, 241
Holmes, Oliver Wendell, Jr., 7, 9, 11, 49, 67, 96-97, 101, 104, 107-8, 115, 121, 124, 150, 241
Hughes, Charles E., 103, 123, 154-55
Hume, David, 41, 47, 177

Ideal type: concept, 205, 212; presidency, 200-14; revolution and ideology, 177-99
Ideology, 37, 144, 185-99
Individualism, 39-43, 46-49, 60, 163-69, 192, 197, 199, 204
Individual psychology and aggression, 170-76, 181-88, 193, 199, 259-60
International finance, 215-19, 221-22
International power elite, 215-19
Interposition, to protect citizens abroad, 120-21
Interstate Commerce Commission, 56, 58
Isocrates, 18
Ius civile, 32-36
Ius gentium, 27, 30, 32-36
Ius naturale, 27-36, 238. See also Natural law

Jackson, Andrew, 122-23, 201
Jackson, Robert H., 63, 76-77, 89, 91-92, 96, 110, 242, 244-45, 247
Jansenists, 164-69
Jefferson, Thomas, 47-48, 80
Jesuits, 46, 164
Johnson, Lyndon, 118, 120-26, 201, 203, 207-8, 260

Judges: civil liberties, 63-92, 114-17, 242-48; compliance with law, 5-13; impact upon, from role, 204; natural law, 47. See also Judicial review
Judicial notice, 72-74, 94-113
Judicial review: jurimetrics, 149-56, 256-57; political questions, 112, 125-26; deference to state courts, 97-99, 105, 109, 112, 249; of administrative action, 60, 98, 102, 107, 111-13, 118-26, 249-52; of legislation, 93-117, 123-26, 250-51. See also Judges
Jury, 110-11, 157; in *Dennis* v. *United States,* 63-78, 243-44
Justinian, 33, 35-36, 117

Kahn, Herman, 147-48, 229-32, 234, 256
Kant, Immanuel, 41, 146, 165, 167-69
Kaplan, Morton, 132, 134, 148-49
Kelsen, Hans, 11, 46, 113, 260
Kennan, George, 110, 223-27, 232-33, 261-62
Kennedy, John F., 208-13, 228-29
Ketteler, Bishop Wilhelm, 43
Korean War, 120-21, 220, 224
Kort, Fred, 153 54, 256

Lactantius, 29, 31
Lasswell, Harold D., 130, 132, 165, 168-69, 181, 257
Latin America, 215-17, 219
Law: definitions of, 5-13; inflexibility, 14-15; law-fact dichotomy, 93-113, 153-54; obligation, 5-13; positivism, 5-13, 47-49; Rome, 27-36, 238-39
Left-wing Protestantism, 40
Legislation: French Revolution, 41-42; generality and prospectivity, 79-92, 245-48; Rome, 27-36, 238
Legislative fact questions, 93-113, 115-17, 138, 155
Legislative power, delegation of, 53-55, 76, 118-26
Legislatures, voting, 139-44, 156-60, 254
Lenin, Nikolai, 64-77, 179-80, 216, 226, 232, 242-45
L'Etang, Dr. Hugh, 209-10
Levellers, 79
Liberalism, 190-91, 194, 197, 199
Licensing, 52-62, 81-92, 108-9, 246-47

272 / INDEX

Lincoln Federal Labor Union v. Northwestern Iron & Metal Co., 108
Lindeman, Eduard C., 38-39
Little v. Barreme, 119
Lloyd George, David, 206-7
Lochner v. New York, 106
Locke, John, 36, 47-48, 81, 166
Lower middle class in politics, 42-43, 49, 187-88, 194-95, 208
Luce, R. Duncan, 254
Lueger, Karl, 44
Luftig v. McNamara, 125-26
Luther, Martin, 40

MacIver, Robert, 133
MacRae, Duncan, Jr., 254
Machiavelli, Niccolo, 137, 181, 193, 203, 207
Madison, James, 80, 92, 122
Maistre, Joseph de, 43, 241
March, James G., 139, 143-44
Marcus Aurelius, 31, 32, 238
Maritain, Jacques, 46, 236, 241
Marshall, Thomas, 21
Marshall, John, 95, 123, 125-26
Marsiglio of Padua, 40
Marx, Karl, 42, 64-77, 137, 216, 223, 232, 242-45, 261-62
Massachusetts v. Laird, 125-26
McAuliffe v. New Bedford, 115
McCarthy, Joseph R., 203, 245
McKenna, Joseph, 85-86
McKinley, William, 122, 201, 204
McLaurin v. Oklahoma State Regents, 111
McNamara, Robert, 118, 125, 147, 229, 255
McPhee, William N., 161, 258
McReynolds, James C., 99, 249
Medina, Harold, 67, 243
Merriam, Charles E., 130, 134
Messianism, 190-91, 196-99, 211
Michael, Donald N., 261
Middle ages: Jews, 198; Justice of Cronus, 36; authoritarian aspects, 39-42, 45-46, 183-84; ending of, 39-41; literature for kings in, 213-14; return to, as political theme, 45, 50-51; social cleavage in, 180
Miller, James G., 130-32
Miller, Samuel F., 87
Miller, Neal E., 129
Milligan, Ex parte, 125
Mills, C. Wright, 216

Minersville School District v. Gobitis, 109
Minton, Sherman, 92
Monroe Doctrine, 215-17, 219
Monthly Review, 215-16, 219
Morgenstern, Oskar, 144, 228, 255
Muller v. Oregon, 106
Munn v. Illinois, 102, 106
Mussolini, Benito, 42, 44, 214

Nagel, Stuart S., 153-54, 157, 256
Nationalism, 194-95. See also Aggression
National Institutes of Health, 56, 61
NLRB, 82-83, 89-92
National Maritime Union v. Herzog, 91-92
National Procurement Authorization Act (1971), 124-25
National Socialism, 42-44, 49, 165, 169, 187-88, 195, 221. See also Hitler
NATO, 50, 216, 219, 224, 228
Natural law: aggression, 260; authoritarianism, 37-38, 43, 45-50, 167-69; Rome, 27-36, 238. See also Aristotle; Higher law
Natural reason, 27, 30-35, 235. See also Aristotle; Reason
Natural rights, 47, 115
Neal, Fred Warner, 232
Nebbia v. New York, 115
Nihilism, 168
Nixon, Richard, 118-26, 202-3, 260
Nuclear warfare, 145, 147-49, 226-34, 255-56, 261-63
Nuremberg Trials, 14, 50, 110

Office: impact on holder, 200-14; qualifications for, 81-84, 86-92, 114-17, 150, 201-4
O'Gorman & Young v. Hartford Ins., 102
Olsen v. Nebraska, 108
Osborn v. Ozlin, 117
Osman v. Douds, 92
Ostrow, Mortimer, 261
Otis, Arthur S., 160
Outcast groups, 181-82, 197
Ovid, 28-29

Palmer, Robert R., 41
Panama Refining Company v. Ryan, 55
Pentagon Papers, 118, 121-22

Peyote, religion of, 198-99
Physical science, 129-38, 156-57, 161-67
Pierce v. *Carskadon,* 82, 88
Plato: on cosmology, 190; on desire, 17; on the guardians, 116-17; on practical wisdom, 15-16, 18; on reason, 17-18, 25; on rule of law, 16-18; on tyranny, 168; on unwritten laws, 30
Police power, 96-109, 115
Political parties, 37-38, 40, 43-45, 48-50, 135-36, 141-42, 158-59, 201-4, 208, 212-13, 218, 254
Pope Leo XIII, 43
Pope Pius XI, 43-45
Positivism, 5-13, 47-49, 163-69
Postgate, Raymond, 185-86
Power analysis: mathematical behavioralism, 136-44, 154-59, 254
Power elite, domestic, 216-19
Power, institutional routinization of, 208-9
President: Congressional voting, 140-41, 143-44, 254; cult of strong presidency, 200, 212-14; drugs, 210-11; "greatness," 200-4; idiosyncracies, 212-14; strain of office, 208-12; impact of electoral process on, 201-4, 208, 212-13; impact of power and adulation on, 204-8, 212-14; in Constitution amending, 10; warmaking, 118-26, 200-1, 208-9, 122-14
Pritchett, C. Herman, 149, 151
Privilege doctrine, 114-16
Prize Cases, 119
Procopius, 117
Progressivism, 183, 189-95, 197-99
Proletariat, 42-43, 185-87
Public Safety Council (proposed), 58-62
Public Science Council (proposed), 58-62

Racial discrimination, 110-11, 181-82, 188, 198
Railroad Retirement Act, 103-4
RAND Corporation, 131, 147, 231
Rast v. *Van Deman & Lewis Co.,* 100
Reaction, 37-51, 189, 193-96, 199, 242
Reason, 163-69, 175-76
Reece Committee on Foundations, 163-65
Reedy, George, 207, 211
Reformation, 38-39

Reid v. *Covert,* 123-24
Revolution, 38-43, 46-47, 49, 63-78, 178-99, 207-8, 217-18, 242-45
Riker, William, 141-46, 155, 157-59
Roberts, Owen J., 154-55
Rogers, William P., 118-26
Rogow, Arnold A., 254
Role. See Office
Roosevelt, Franklin D., 14, 120, 201, 209, 213, 217, 233
Roosevelt, Theodore, 120, 202-4, 212
Root, Elihu, 202
Ross, Edward A., 183-84
Rousseau, J. J., 36, 47
Rule-making procedure, agency, 54-55, 58-62
Rule of law, 5-21, 49-50, 79-92, 245-48
Rusk, Dean, 209
Ryan, Msgr. John A., 48

Satire, 114-17
Schaps, Ronald, 157-59
Schechter Poultry Corp. v. *U.S.,* 123
Schenck v. *U.S.,* 64, 67
Schubert, Glendon, 149-57, 256-57
Science: need for administrative control of, 52-62
SEATO, 122, 216, 219, 224, 228
Secrecy, executive, 118, 121-22, 263
Secularism, 39-43, 46-48
Sedition, 68-78, 110, 242-45
Seneca, 29, 32
Separation of agency functions, 54-62
Shapley, L. S., 140-41, 154-55, 158-59, 254
Shubik, Martin, 140-41, 154-55, 158-59, 254
Simon, Herbert, 134-35, 141
Simon, Yves R., 163-69, 259
Smith Act (1940), 63-78, 242-45
Smith, Adam, 205-6
Smith, J. Allen, 80, 245
Snyder, Richard C., 141, 147-48
Social justice, 183, 188, 194-97
Socialism, 165-67, 183, 191, 194, 208, 223-26, 234. See also Communism
Social sciences, 129-69, 219, 253-58
Socrates, 17, 206
Sophists, Greek, 30
Sophocles, 20-21, 30, 236
Sorensen, Theodore, 209
Soviets, 179-80

Soviet Union, 37-38, 50, 148-49, 207-8, 215-34, 256; grounds for insecurity, 223-34
Specialization, administrative-agency: effects on perspective, 54-62
Speier, Hans, 187-88
Stalin, Joseph, 64, 207-8, 214, 223-26, 233
Standing to sue, 114, 117, 125
State, and aggression, 173-76, 181-82, 191-93
State, and instability, 207-8
State, Department of, 118-26, 147-48
Statism, 189-96, 199; anti-state cults, 192
Stewart, John, 21, 236
Stoecker, Adolf, 43
Stoics, 25, 27, 29-33, 36, 190
Stone, Harlan F., 100-1
Story, Joseph, 81, 84-85
Strauss, Leo, 163-69
Sutherland, George, 107, 123-24
Sweatt v. Painter, 111
Systems theory, 130-32, 137, 258

Taft-Hartley Act, 82-83, 89-92, 247-48
Taft, Robert A., 203, 218
Taft, William Howard, 85, 202
Taxing power, 99, 107-8
Teller, Edward, 231, 263
Thayer, James Bradley, 95-97
Thurstone, Louis L., 149
Tonkin Gulf Resolution, 122-24
Trade unions, 42-43, 82-83, 89-92, 109, 218, 247-48
Trotsky, Leon, 64, 72, 208
Truman, Harry, 120-21, 202, 208, 210, 217-18, 233
Tschuprow, A. A., 157
Tullock, Gordon, 145, 254
Twenty-fifth Amendment, 211-12
Tyler, Ralph W., 130-31

Ullmann, John E., 213
Ullman, Richard H., 224-26

Ulpian, 34-35
United Public Workers v. Mitchell, 114-17
U.S. ex rel. Accardi v. Shaughnessy, 55
U.S. v. Curtiss-Wright Export, 123-24
U.S. v. Lovett, 82-90
Utilitarianism, 146-49, 170-71

Value judgment, 163-69, 183-84
Verstehen (human understanding), 205; behavioralism, 129-62, 253-58
Vietnam War, 118-26, 208, 213, 220-22, 224, 233-34
Vinson, Fred M., 68-69, 74-75, 82-83, 89-91, 110, 121, 243-44
Virgil, 29, 36
Voegelin, Eric, 163-69

Wadsworth, James, 262
Waite, Morrison R., 102, 106
Walgreen Foundation, 164
War, 37, 118-26, 172-76, 215-34, 261-63
Washington, George, 119, 200-1
Weber, Max, 133, 165, 205
Webster, Daniel, 81, 245
Wheeler, Harvey, 210-11
Wilhelm II, 216-17
William of Occam, 36, 40
Willoughby, Westel W., 95-96
Wilson, Woodrow, 200-1, 206-7, 209, 218
Wolff Packing Co. v. Court of Industrial Relations, 108-9

Xenophon, 20, 30

Youngstown Sheet & Tube Co. v. Sawyer, 121

Zemel v. Rusk, 124
Zeus, in Greek mythology, 27-32, 34

LIBRARY OF DAVIDSON COLLEGE